ANCIENT ISRAEL

VOLUME TWO

ASENATH AND THE DIVINE MESSENGER

Page 114

Frontispiece, Vol. II

ANCIENT ISRAEL

VOLUME TWO

ANGELO S. RAPPOPORT

SENATE

Ancient Israel Volume Two

Previously published by
The Gresham Publishing Company, London

This edition published in 1995 by Senate, an imprint of
Studio Editions Ltd, Princess House, 50 Eastcastle Street,
London W1N 7AP, England

ISBN 1 85958 171 4
Printed and bound in Guernsey by
The Guernsey Press Co. Ltd

Contents

		Page
List of Plates	_ - - - - - - - -	vi
Preface	_ - - - - - - - - _	vii

VOLUME TWO

CHAPTER I

THE COAT OF MANY COLOURS - - - - - - 1

CHAPTER II

A FATHER'S GRIEF - - - - - - - - 17

CHAPTER III

UPON THE MOTHER'S GRAVE, OR THE JOURNEY TO EGYPT - 24

CHAPTER IV

THE PERFECT SERVANT AND THE PASSIONATE MISTRESS - 38

CHAPTER V

IN PRISON, OR THE INTERPRETER OF DREAMS - - - 63

CHAPTER VI

THE VICEROY OF EGYPT - - - - - - - 73

CHAPTER VII

THE STORY OF JOSEPH AND ZULEIKA IN ARABIC, SYRIAC, PERSIAN, SANSKRIT, AND MEDIÆVAL EUROPEAN LITERATURE - - - - - - - - - 87

iii

CONTENTS

CHAPTER VIII

Page

THE ROMANCE OF ASENATH, OR THE MARRIAGE OF THE
VICEROY - - - - - - - - - - 107

CHAPTER IX

THE VISIT OF THE BRETHREN - - - - - - 117

CHAPTER X

THE LION, THE BULL, AND THE WOLF - - - - 132

CHAPTER XI

THE LOVESICK PRINCE AND THE JEALOUS BRETHREN - - 148

CHAPTER XII

A FATHER'S BLESSING, OR THE DEATH AND BURIAL OF THE
PATRIARCH - - - - - - - - - - 156

CHAPTER XIII

JOSEPH'S MAGNANIMITY, AND THE WARS OF THE COUSINS - 169

CHAPTER XIV

THE DEATH OF THE REGENT - - - - - - 183

CHAPTER XV

THE EGYPTIAN BONDAGE - - - - - - - 189

CHAPTER XVI

THE FATE OF THE INNOCENTS - - - - - - 203

CHAPTER XVII

THE BIRTH OF THE REDEEMER - - - - - - 213

CHAPTER XVIII

THE YOUTH AND EDUCATION OF MOSES - - - - 232

CONTENTS

CHAPTER XIX

Page

THE KING OF ETHIOPIA - - - - - - - 244

CHAPTER XX

AT THE WELL OF MIDIAN, OR THE MARRIAGE OF MOSES - 250

CHAPTER XXI

THE DIVINE MISSION, OR THE HUMBLE SHEPHERD - - 270

CHAPTER XXII

THE REDEMPTION, OR THE PASSAGE THROUGH THE RED SEA 286

CHAPTER XXIII

FROM THE RED SEA TO SINAI - - - - - - 297

CHAPTER XXIV

IN THE WILDERNESS - - - - - - - 318

CHAPTER XXV

THE DEATH OF AARON, OR AARON THE PEACEMAKER - - 333

CHAPTER XXVI

THE DEATH OF MOSES - - - - - - - 343

CHAPTER XXVII

THE BIRTH AND EDUCATION OF MOSES IN HELLENISTIC, SYRIAC, AND ARABIC LITERATURE - - - - 363

CHAPTER XXVIII

THE LATER LIFE AND DEATH OF MOSES IN MOSLEM TRADITION - - - - - - - - 377

BIBLIOGRAPHY - - - - - - - - 397

Plates

VOLUME TWO

Facing
Page

ASENATH AND THE DIVINE MESSENGER   -   *Frontispiece*

THE WOLF SPEAKS TO THE SORROWING JACOB   -   -   -   22

"WHY ARE YOU MERCILESSLY FLOGGING THIS INNOCENT
MAN?"   -   -   -   -   -   -   -   -   -   60

JOSEPH AND HIS FATHER MEET AGAIN IN EGYPT -   -   -   144

THE COFFIN OF JOSEPH RISES TO THE SURFACE OF THE NILE   188

ZIPPORAH BRINGS SUCCOUR TO MOSES IN THE PIT   -   -   254

GABRIEL PROTECTS THE TRIBES DURING THEIR PASSAGE
THROUGH THE RED SEA   -   -   -   -   -   -   290

MOSES CASTS FROM HIM THE TABLES OF THE LAW   -   -   316

THE CHILDREN OF ISRAEL SEE AARON'S COUCH FLOATING IN
THE AIR   -   -   -   -   -   -   -   -   -   342

PREFACE

In the first volume of this work the reader has been made acquainted with Jewish myths dealing with the origin of the world, angels and demons, paradise and hell, the creation of Adam and Eve, and also with some of the legends related of the Patriarchs Abraham and Isaac. The present volume deals exclusively with the legends clustering round Patriarchs, Prophets, and Priests, the friends and favourites of God, the Biblical personages like Jacob, Joseph, Moses, and Aaron. The reader is again introduced to the rich and abundant storehouse of Talmudical and post-Talmudical literature, to that vast legendary lore wherein the Jewish popular imagination has given full expression to its beliefs and ideals, its yearnings and hopes. Legendary lore, it must be remembered, is a branch of national literature; it is popular poetry, the poetic creation of the people, the anonymous work of the mind and soul of the people. The pious belief and the religious yearning of a people find their expression in the many legends clustering round the founder of the national religion and round the national heroes and saints.

Legendary lore has rightly been called the " religious heroic epic ", and the " popular religious philosophy of history ". Legends wander from generation to generation, from age to age, from nation to nation, and from country to country, but they always bear the traces of their origin, namely, the mind and soul of the *people*.

Israel has no saints in its history, but just as in the Christian

legends the saints are glorified, and wonders are woven round
their lives, so in the Jewish legends, too, the pious, the faithful
servants of God, are endowed with supernatural gifts and are
represented as supermen. Such supermen were the Patriarchs,
were Joseph, Moses, and Aaron. For the sake of these pious
men, the chosen of the Lord, His faithful servants and friends,
the heavenly hosts are set in motion, the sun, the earth, and
the constellations are bidden to alter their courses, time and
space are reduced to relative values and conceptions, and the
laws of nature are changed.

From the moment of his birth, nay, even long before it,
to the day of his death, miracles innumerable are worked in
favour of the pious man, miracles which tradition records and
which the people delight in relating.

Created by the people, Jewish legends were handed down
orally until the scholars and scribes, the Rabbis and preachers
began to make use of them for the purpose of education and
instruction. They collected the legends and tales, added new
ones, and thus developed a popular and national literature
which they infused with a spirit of grandeur and sublimity.
By means of such legends and tales they managed to rivet the
attention of their audiences, of the uneducated public, and were
able to convey to them many moral lessons. The legends and
tales served to point a moral and to adorn their discourses. The
Rabbis and preachers, the scribes and scholars collected and
edited the legends, and vast compilations were handed down
to future generations. From this legendary lore the people
could henceforth draw religious edification, moral instruction,
consolation in days of oppression, and confidence in the Almighty
in the hours of distress.

As in the first volume of this work so also in the present one
comparative evidence has been provided, and the reader's
attention has constantly been drawn to similar legends and tales
related in oriental and European literature.

The comparison between Jewish and non-Jewish sources (as pointed out in the Introduction to Vol. I) makes it clear that whilst the Jewish legends bear traces of Egyptian, Indian, Persian, and Mohammedan influences, the Jews, in their turn, influenced Mohammedan tradition and Mediæval Christian legendary lore.

Although the entire work is intended for the general reader, we have everywhere indicated the original sources of the legends and tales collected. We hope that these indications will prove very useful to the more serious students.

ANGELO S. RAPPOPORT.

MYTH AND LEGEND OF ANCIENT ISRAEL

VOLUME II

CHAPTER I

The Coat of Many Colours

The birth of a son—Joseph's ravishing beauty—The history of the son a repetition of that of his father—Joseph pays attention to his personal appearance—His talebearing—The brethren amputate the limb of a sick animal—Jacob sends for his sons and gives them instructions with regard to their conduct—The hatred of the brethren—The coat of many colours—*Passim*—The meaning of the initial letters—Joseph's dreams—He begs his brethren to listen to his dreams and interpret them—The Patriarch rebukes his son, but inscribes the dream in his book of records—Joseph in search of his brethren—A father's regret—The fatal place of Shechem—The meeting with an angel—Brethren prepare to set the dogs on their brother—Reuben's pleading and advice—Reuben's real intention—Cast into the pit—The violence of a brother and the forgiving spirit of another—In the depths of the pit—The snakes and scorpions creep away and hide in the holes of the pit—A cry for mercy—Grace after a meal—Judah's speech—Ishmaelites and Midianites—Preparing for battle—The rebellious slave—The bargain—A pair of shoes—The miraculous garment—An amulet extended by the angel Gabriel—The regret of the merchant-men—The pleasant scent of the merchandise carried by the traders—Sudden darkness.

Jacob's hope to enjoy life in tranquillity and to end his days in peace in his native land was frustrated. The loss of his beloved and favourite son Joseph was a terrible blow to the old man. He loved Joseph because he reminded him of his dear and never-to-be-forgotten wife, the beautiful Rachel. For six years Rachel had remained barren, and only in the

1

seventh year after her marriage, in the month of Tishri, the Lord remembered her, and her dearest wish was at last realized. On the first day of the month of Tammuz, in the year 2199, after the creation of the world, Rachel gave birth to a son. She called him Joseph, which means the increaser. The son had inherited the ravishing beauty of the mother, but he resembled also the father more than any of the brothers. Not only in appearance, however, did Joseph resemble his father Jacob, his whole history and the course of his life were a repetition of those of Jacob.

As Jacob's mother had remained barren for a long time, giving birth afterwards to the sons, so also did the mother of Joseph. Like Rebekah, Rachel, too, suffered great pains in giving birth to her son. Both the father and the son, although not the first-born, obtained the birthright. Jacob was hated by his brother Esau, and Joseph, in his turn, was hated by his brethren. Both the father and the son travelled to a foreign country, accompanied by protecting angels, and lived and died in a strange land, among strangers. Both the father and the son served masters who were blessed and prospered exceedingly on their account. But although father and son lived in a foreign country, their remains were carried to the Holy Land where they were buried. Jacob had undergone hardship and served a master for the sake of a woman, and it was a woman who was the cause of many of Joseph's sufferings.

Joseph was only eight years old when his mother died, but he found a foster-mother in the kind-hearted and noble Bilhah, his mother's handmaid, who lavished her love upon the handsome orphan, and treated him as if he were her own son.

Until his seventeenth year Joseph frequented the schools of learning, and his father imparted to him all the knowledge he himself had received from his distinguished masters Shem and Eber.

It was a great joy for the father, when he saw how eager and anxious the boy was to study and to acquire instruction. And yet, in many ways, Joseph was boyish. He, the young scholar, paid great attention to his personal appearance, dressed his hair, endeavoured to give his eyes a beautiful expression, and always walked with a light delicate step.

Although he acknowledged and frequently paid homage to the bravery and merits of his brethren, he nevertheless thought himself superior to his brethren. He was the favourite son of his father, and he knew it, but he was also a favourite with the sons of the handmaids who loved him. He acquired the habit of bearing tales to his father concerning the conduct of his brethren. His excuse was that the tales he bore to his father were not the result of his wish to calumniate his brethren, but so as to make his father preach to them and urge them to mend their ways. Indeed, feeling himself superior to his brethren in knowledge, Joseph often offered them counsel and tried to make them abandon their ways. In his zeal, however, he went too far.

Thus he informed his father that his brethren were paying little attention to the herds and were guilty of cruelty to the flock, tearing the limbs from living animals and eating the flesh. This charge was somewhat exaggerated, for indeed Joseph's brethren always observed the rules of the ritual and always slaughtered the animals before partaking of the flesh. One day Gad, who was keeping watch over the herd, snatched a kid from the jaws of a bear, and as the animal could no longer be kept alive, he slaughtered it. Sometimes also Joseph's brethren amputated the limb of a sick animal, so as to make it sound, a remedy often employed by the Arabs. For his exaggerated zeal and the tales he bore to his father, Joseph paid dearly and was punished. It is almost an irony of fate when one remembers that the kid into the blood of which Joseph's coat was dipped had not been cruelly tortured and slain, but killed according to the ritual prevalent among the sons of Jacob.

In his exaggerated sense of justice, the lad had charged his brethren with slighting the sons of the handmaids and treating them as slaves. He was punished for this too, for he was sold as a slave to Potiphar, and was very unhappy on account of the amorous advances of his mistress.

Soon Joseph's brethren learned of their brother's tale-bearing. One day Jacob sent one of his servants to call his sons from the fields. When they appeared in his presence the Patriarch thus addressed them: " My dear sons, I am growing old, and I know not when it will please the Lord to call me unto Himself. Hearken therefore unto my words. When I am dead and gone ye will inherit all my earthly pos-sessions, my goods and chattels, my fields and vineyards, my sheep and cattle, my gold and silver. Ye will be very wealthy. Beware, however, my dear sons, of pride. Treat your step-brethren, the sons of the handmaids, Bilhah, and Zilpah, as your equals and your brothers, for you are all the sons of one father. Remember these my words, when I am no longer among you. Whenever ye eat meat, take care to slaughter the animals according to our ritual and do not let the animal suffer too much, for God hates those who are guilty of cruelty to animals. God, in His mercy, loves those who are kind and merciful to His creatures."

Thus spake Jacob, and his sons promised to take his words to heart. When they left their father's presence, however, they wondered greatly at the cause of his speech.

" Heaven grant our dear father long life," they said; " we hope that he will remain in our midst for many, many years, but it is rather surprising that he should have called us suddenly, without waiting for our return, and spoken to us as he did. Someone must have slandered us and borne tales to our father."

" Indeed, such is the case," said one of their slaves; " I have heard your brother Joseph one day charging you with cruelty to the animals and accusing you of slighting the sons of the handmaids."

When the sons of Jacob heard these words, they waxed wroth against Joseph and hated him. Their hatred increased when they noticed how Jacob constantly distinguished Joseph among his children, and saw the many tokens of their father's great love for the lad.

Among the tokens of Jacob's love for Joseph was a beautiful and costly coat of many colours, light and delicate, wonderful to behold. It was so light and of so fine a texture that it could be concealed in the palm of the hand. In Hebrew the garment was called *Passim*, and was symbolical of Joseph's subsequent fate. The four Hebrew letters constituting the word *Passim* (*P.S.I.M.*) were the initials of *Potiphar*, Joseph's master; *Socharim*, or merchantmen who bought the lad from the Ishmaelites; *Ishmaelites*, to whom he was sold, and *Medanites*, who obtained him from the Ishmaelites. *Passim* also means in Hebrew pieces and clefts, and in a prophetic vision Joseph's brethren foresaw that in days to come the Red Sea would be cleft in twain on account of Joseph's merits. The love of their father and the future glory of Joseph were cause enough to make the sons of Jacob hate their brother. Their hatred, however, was frank and open. They were fierce and cruel, these sons of Jacob, and were good haters, but there was nothing sneaky about them. They hated their brother, and he knew it, for openly they told him so. Joseph's dreams, which he never hesitated to communicate to his brothers, added fuel to their rage and increased their hatred. Joseph knew that his brothers hated him, but he nevertheless told them his dreams, so that they might interpret them, for a dream which is not interpreted is like an unread letter.

One day, when all the sons of Jacob were assembled together, Joseph thus addressed his brethren:

" As your prophets will one day beg your descendants to listen to the word of God, so do I beg you now to give ear to my words, and to interpret for me the dream sent to me by God. In my dream, behold, we were all gathering fruit; your fruit rotted, whilst mine remained sound."

The brothers knew well enough the meaning of the dream, and that Joseph was destined for great things in the future, that he would have power and dominion over them, but they pretended that they knew not the interpretation of his dream and gave it not. And yet they clearly showed what was in their minds, when, swayed by envy and jealousy, they mockingly replied: " Shalt thou really have dominion over us and reign over us?"

Thus the Lord had put the right interpretation into their mouths, and it was verified in the future in Joseph himself and in his posterity, for kings and judges were among the descendants of Joseph and ruled over Israel.

Joseph told his dream also to his father, and the latter kissed and blessed his son, for he knew that the dream would come true.

Soon Joseph had another dream. He saw the sun, the moon, and eleven stars bowing to him. He told his dream to his father, and the latter was greatly rejoiced. Jacob knew that the sun stood for himself, for when he had passed the night upon the site of the Temple, he had heard the angels exclaim: " The sun hath come." The moon stood for Joseph's mother, and the stars for the brothers.

Jacob only wondered in his mind how Joseph knew that he (Jacob) was called the Sun. He was greatly rejoiced, convinced as he was of the truth of his son's dream. In order, however, to lessen the bad impression Joseph's dream would produce upon his brethren, and in order to avert their envy and hatred, Jacob rebuked his son, when the latter repeated his dream to his brethren. In that tone of reproof in which one day the Israelites were to forbid their prophets to speak the truth, Jacob said to his son: " What is this dream that thou hast dreamed? Will the resurrection of the dead take place in our days, so that thy mother, who is dead, will rise and return to earth?" The Patriarch did not know that the moon stood for Joseph's foster-mother Bilhah, who had brought him up. But even whilst he rebuked his son, Jacob had put the right interpretation upon Joseph's dream, and the brethren knew that it would one day be realized. Their hatred of Joseph therefore increased. Jacob himself took his book of records and therein inscribed all the circumstances of his son's dream, the day, the hour, and the place, for the prophetic spirit called his attention to these things which would surely come to pass.

One day the brethren had led their flocks to the pasture grounds of Shechem, where they intended to enjoy themselves and to feed on the cattle of their father. As they were away for a long time and no news of their whereabouts had reached Jacob, he grew anxious about their fate. He feared that the Hivites might have attacked them to wreak revenge for the slaughter of Hamor and the inhabitants of Shechem.

He therefore decided to send Joseph out to find his brethren and bring him word whether all was well with them, and also to let him know about the flocks. Joseph knew that his brethren hated him, and that he was exposed to danger in visiting them, but, dutiful son that he was, he declared himself ready to do his father's bidding. In later days Jacob remembered this willingness of his son to obey his command, and his remorse greatly increased his suffering. " My poor son," he would say, " I knew that the brothers hated thee, and yet I let thee go out, and thou, too, in filial reverence never didst demur."

" Go now," said the Patriarch to his favourite son, " and find out whether all is well with thy brethren and with the herds, and send me word. Travel only by daylight, for it is right that one should enter and leave a place only by day, after the sun has risen and before it has set."

Joseph arrived safely at the fateful place of Shechem. Fateful indeed, and a place of ill omen the place of Shechem has always been to Jacob and to his descendants. It was at Shechem that Dinah was dishonoured by the son of Hamor; it was in the neighbourhood of Shechem that Joseph was cast into the pit and sold as a slave; and it was at Shechem where, in later days, the rebellion of Jeroboam took place, a great misfortune to the house of David. Not finding his brethren at the pasturing place of Shechem, Joseph continued his way, but lost himself in the wilderness. Three angels in human shape and form appeared to the lad, and one of them, the angel Gabriel, asked him what he was seeking. When Gabriel heard that Joseph was seeking his brethren, he replied: " Thy brethren have left this place, and in leaving it they have also given up the divine virtues which men should imitate: the virtues of brotherly love, kindness, and mercy. I have learned from behind the curtain " (*Pargod*) " that from to-day the Egyptian bondage of the Israelites will begin. Thy brethren have also had a prophetic vision that the Hivites would make war upon them. They have therefore left for the pasturing grounds of Dothan." And to Dothan Gabriel led Joseph.

From a distance Joseph's brethren saw him coming and prepared to set the dogs on him that would tear him to pieces.

Simeon and Levi, constant companions in deeds of violence, said: " Behold, the master of dreams cometh; let us slay him and see what becometh of his dreams."

But the Lord said: " Ye say, let us slay him, but I say, let us see what will become of his dreams, and the future will show whose word will prevail."

Reuben, however, when he learned the evil design of his brethren, did his best to dissuade them from their plan, and interceded on behalf of Joseph. He knew that, as the eldest brother, he would be held responsible by the father for Joseph's fate. He was also grateful to Joseph who, in spite of Reuben's disrespectful behaviour to his father, a conduct which made him feel unworthy of being a son of Jacob, nevertheless behaved respectfully to him. Reuben, therefore, did his best to restrain his brethren from their evil design, and attempted to save Joseph. Although Reuben's plan was frustrated, his intention was good, and his reward was that in later days Bezer—the first city of refuge, where those who were innocent of a crime they were charged with found shelter—was situated in the allotment of the tribe of Reuben. Eloquently did Reuben plead for Joseph, and thus he spoke:

" It is a heinous enterprise, my dear brethren, you are going about, and its nature is very horrid. Your action will appear wicked in the sight of God and impious before men. It is a sin to kill one even not related to us, but much more detestable is it to slay one's own brother. Have regard, my brethren, to your own consciences, and consider what mischief will betide ye upon the death of so good a child and your own brother. Fear God, who is both a witness and a spectator of the designs ye have against your brother. God will love ye if ye abstain from this act and yield to repentance and amendment, but, if ye proceed to do what ye have in mind, all sorts of punishments will overtake ye from God for this murder of your brother. Ye will be polluting God's providence which is present everywhere, and which does not overlook what is done, either in deserts or in cities, for wheresoever a man is, there ought he to suppose God is also. Your own consciences, my brethren, will be your enemies, if ye attempt to go through so wicked an enterprise. And even if the lad had injured ye, it would not be right to kill him, but rather forgive him and forget his actions even in things in which he might seem to have offended. But ye are going to kill your brother Joseph who is guilty of nothing that is really ill towards you. His young age, too, ought to move ye to mercy and pity. But, I know, that it is out of envy of Joseph's future prosperity that ye are determined to do away with him, and therefore the anger of God will be more severe upon ye. Ye will have slain one whom God has judged worthy of that prosperity, whilst by murdering the lad ye will make it impossible for God to bestow such prosperity upon him." Thus spoke Reuben, endeavouring to divert his brethren from the murder of their brother.

When Reuben, however, saw that his pleading was in vain, he begged his brethren to follow his advice in so far at least, as not to shed blood, but to cast the brother into one of the pits. He gave them this advice in the hope of being able later on to draw the lad from the pit, and restore him to his father, unbeknown to the others. The brethren agreed to Reuben's proposition.

In the meantime Joseph, rejoiced at finding his brethren, and not suspecting the fate in store for him, approached.

The brethren fell upon the lad, beat him, tore his garment, the coat of many colours, from him, stripped him bare of his other clothes, and Simeon seized and threw him into one of the pits, empty of water, but full of snakes and scorpions. Empty indeed of water was the pit, as the hearts of Joseph's brethren were empty at that moment of charity, piety, and Divine Law, which is compared to water, and severely enjoins the punishment of those who steal souls.

Simeon, who was the most violent and fierce of the brothers, bade them even throw stones at their brother.

Joseph learned afterwards of Simeon's advice, but he forgave him. For when he detained him as a hostage in Egypt, he treated him so well and provided him with such excellent food that he grew fat and looked like a leather-bottle. Such was the charitable and forgiving nature of Joseph.

When he was in the depths of the pit, surrounded by reptiles, a great terror seized the lad. But the snakes and scorpions did him no harm, for the Lord heard his cries, and the reptiles crept into the holes of the pit. In an agony of terror Joseph appealed to his brethren, and in cries of distress he begged them to have mercy upon him.

" My brethren," cried the poor and agonized lad, " what have I done unto you, and what is my transgression? Am I not flesh of your flesh and bone of your bone? Is not Jacob, your father, also my father? Are you not afraid to sin before God, in treating me so cruelly? What may be the cause of your action and how will you be able and have the courage to lift your countenances before our father Jacob?"

Thus cried Joseph and pleaded, but the brethren paid no heed to his cries.

" Judah, Reuben, Simeon, and Levi, my brothers," again cried Joseph, weeping bitterly, " have mercy upon me and deliver me from this terrible place, the pit into which ye have cast me. If I have sinned against you, you are the children of Abraham, Isaac, and Jacob, the generous men who always had compassion with orphans, fed the hungry and clothed the naked, never allowing the needy to go away empty-handed from their doors. Will you, their descendants, withhold pity and compassion from your own brother? For the sake of our father, listen to my prayers and have pity, although I may have sinned against you. If my father only knew how my brethren have spoken to me and how they are treating me!"

Thus wailed Joseph, but no heed did his brethren pay to his weeping. Afraid, however, that the lad's pitiful cries might at last move them to compassion, they left the pit and sat down at the distance of a bowshot.

They sat down to a meal, deliberating all the time whether to slay Joseph or restore him to his father. Almost unanimously they decided to fetch their brother from the pit into which they had cast him and to slay him, but before executing their design they attempted to say grace after their meal.

Judah, however, who had already on several occasions made his influence felt among the brethren, being their chief and king, arose and thus he spoke: " My brethren, we are going to commit the crime of fratricide, and yet we would bless God and are about to thank Him for what we have received. Are we not like the robber who blasphemes the Eternal even whilst he is praying?" (*Prov.* 10, 3). " What will it profit us if we slay our brother? Will not the punishment of God descend upon us? Hearken, therefore, to my words and to the good counsel I have to give you. Yonder do I see a caravan of Ishmaelites on their way to Egypt; let us follow the precedent established in the days by gone, when Canaan, the son of Ham, was cursed and made a slave, on account of his wicked deeds. Let our hand not be upon our brother, but let us sell him to the Ishmaelites who will carry him off to the end of the desert, where he will be lost among the people of the earth, and our father will never hear of him and his whereabouts." Thus spoke Judah, and the brethren agreed to sell Joseph into slavery.

But the Lord said: " At a meal ye sold your brother as a slave, and during a meal, in days to come, Haman will decree the destruction of your seed."

Before, however, the caravan of the Ishmaelites had approached, seven Midianitish merchantmen passed the pit wherein Joseph lay weeping and lamenting, and above which birds of prey were circling.

Being thirsty, looking for water, and assuming, on account of the birds they saw, that there was water in the pit, the Midianites halted in the hope of being able to refresh themselves. Suddenly they heard loud weeping and lamentations, and looking down into the pit beheld a comely youth of beautiful figure, stripped of his clothes.

"Who art thou?" asked the Midianites, "and who has cast thee into this pit?" Thereupon they dragged the lad up, took him along and continued their journey.

When they came near the brethren whom they had to pass, the latter exclaimed: "What right have ye to take along and carry off our slave whom we have thrown into the pit as a punishment for his disobedience? Return our slave immediately to us." Thus spoke the brethren of Joseph, but the Midianites only laughed at their words.

"We will pay no attention to your words," said the merchantmen, "for the lad is not your slave. His comely appearance and beautiful figure, by far excelling your own, proves the contrary, convincing us that more likely are you the slaves who have rebelled against your master. We found the lad in the pit and are going to take him along."

"If you do not immediately return to us our slave, you will feel the edge of our swords," threatened the brethren.

Their threats were of no avail, for the Midianites drew their swords and prepared for battle, uttering wild war whoops.

Thereupon Simeon jumped up, drew his sword and uttered a wild shout which resounded in the distance and caused the earth to tremble and reverberate. Terror seized the Midianites, when they heard that terrible voice, and in consternation they fell upon their countenances. And Simeon proceeded to address them: "I am Simeon, the son of Jacob the Hebrew. Alone and unaided, with my own hand, have I destroyed the town of Shechem, and together with my brethren have we annihilated the cities of the Amorites. If all your brethren, the Midianites, and all the kings of Canaan came to your assistance, you would never be able to hold out against me, for I am Simeon, the son of Jacob the Hebrew, whose name makes the inhabitants of Canaan quake. Now return our slave at once, or your flesh will soon be food for the birds of prey and the beasts of the fields."

Greatly frightened, the Midianites now spoke quite timidly: "Did ye not say that ye cast the lad into the pit on account of his disobedience and as a punishment for his conduct? What use is a rebellious slave to ye? Sell him rather to us who will pay you any price for him." The Midianites were anxious to buy Joseph on account of his comely appearance, but it was also the purpose of the Lord that they should buy him, so that the brethren might not slay him.

Having already made up their minds to sell their brother as a slave, the sons of Jacob accepted the offer of the merchantmen and sold them their brother for twenty pieces of silver.

The Midianites thus bought Joseph and carried him off, in spite of his prayers, his cries and lamentations. In vain did he implore his brethren to restore him to his father, begging them on his knees to have pity on him. The price of twenty silver pieces was very low, but the Midianites pointed out that the lad looked sickly and ill. The fear of the scorpions and snakes, and the terrible anguish the boy had endured in the pit, had driven all the blood from his face, and made him look ill and sickly indeed.

The brethren divided the twenty silver pieces among them, and each received just enough to buy himself a pair of shoes.

In days to come the Lord spoke through the mouth of his prophet, Amos. "For three transgressions and for four will I punish Israel; because they sold the righteous for silver, and the needy for a pair of shoes." (*Amos*, 2, 6.)

Now Joseph had been cast into the pit naked, for the brethren had stripped him of his clothes, and naked he would have had to travel with his masters, the Midianites. But the Lord would not suffer that such a pious and virtuous youth as Joseph should appear before men in such an unseemly condition. He therefore sent His angel Gabriel who extended an amulet suspended upon Joseph's neck, so that it became a garment covering the lad entirely. Scarcely had the brethren noticed that Joseph was clad, than they cried to the Midianites: "We sold you our slave naked and without any raiment; return therefore immediately his raiment unto us."

Joseph's new masters at first demurred and refused to comply with the request of the sons of Jacob, but they ultimately paid for the garment four pairs of shoes. Joseph was thus permitted to keep the garment made by an angelic hand, and wore it when he arrived in Egypt. He wore it as a slave, wore it in prison, appeared in it before Pharaoh, and wore it also when he ruled Egypt as Viceroy.

To Gilead the Midianites now journeyed, carrying their slave with them. On the way, however, they began to have some misgivings with regard to the statement made by the sons of Jacob. The latter's high-handed manner, the small price they had accepted, and their general conduct raised suspicions in the minds of the Midianites who feared that Joseph had been stolen. Afraid of being accused of man-theft, they were now anxious to get rid of the slave they had bought. They were pleased therefore when they suddenly beheld the company of Ishmaelites, whom the sons of Jacob had seen earlier in the day, and unanimously decided to sell the lad to the travelling company. Without losing the money they had paid for Joseph, they hoped to escape unpleasant consequences, should they be accused of man-theft. Thus Joseph quickly changed hands, the Ishmaelites buying him from the Midianites for twenty pieces of silver. Satisfied with their transaction, the Midianites continued their journey, whilst Joseph's new masters placed the lad upon one of their camels and journeyed to Egypt.

Now the merchandise the Ishmaelites were in the habit of carrying upon their camels were skins of beasts and pitch, unpleasant and ill-smelling, so that an ill smell also emanated from the merchantmen themselves. The Lord, however, had willed it that on this occasion the Ishmaelites, instead of such ill-smelling merchandise, had loaded their camels with aromatic substances and perfumery. Thus Joseph did not suffer from any unpleasant ill-smells wafted to him on his fateful journey to Egypt, but, on the contrary, inhaled the pleasant scent of perfumery and a sweet fragrance.

When the poor lad learned that his new masters were travelling to Egypt, and that he would thus be carried off so far away from his father in Canaan, he began to weep bitterly and to lament. One of Joseph's new masters, imagining that the cause of the lad's tears and lamentations was the discomfort he endured in riding upon the back of the camel, lifted him down and made him walk on foot. As the lad, however, continued to weep, unable to restrain his grief, the Ishmaelites began to beat him, and the more the lad wept the more cruelly they beat him, trying to silence him and to make him cease his wails and lamentations.

The Lord thereupon, seeing Joseph's distress, had pity upon him, and sent sudden darkness upon the men, so that they were seized with great terror, and their hands grew rigid whenever they raised them against the son of Jacob. Unaware that this was a punishment for their ill-treatment of Joseph, the men asked themselves in astonishment what this sudden darkness and terror could mean. They at last reached Ephrath, where Rachel, Joseph's mother, lay buried in her lonely grave.[1]

[1] Babylonian Talmud, *Rosh-hashana*, 11*a*; *Targum Pseudo-Jonathan*, *in loco*; *Genesis Rabba*, §§ 78, 84, 87, 91; *Midrash Tanchuma*, section *Vayesheb*; *Yalkut*, *Genesis* § 142 *Numbers Rabba*, § 14; *Midrash Lekach Tob*, *in loco*; *Book of Jubilees*, XXVIII; Josephus, *Antiquities*, II, 3; *Sepher Hajashar*; *Pirke de Rabbi Eliezer*, Ch. 38; Jellinek, *Beth-Hamidrash*, Vol. V, p. 157; Vol. VI, p. 120; Joseph Shabbethai Parhi, *Tokpo Shel Yosef*, Leghorn, 1846, see also Adolf Kurrein, *Traum und Wahrheit*, Regensburg, 1887; Lewner, *Kol-Agadoth*, Vol. I, pp. 186–194.

CHAPTER II

A Father's Grief

The remorse of the brethren—A solemn oath never to reveal the truth
—Reuben's return—His search for Joseph—His grief—Issachar's advice—
The torn coat—The blood of a lamb—A message to the father—The
Patriarch's grief—The mourning household—An unexpected visit from
Hebron—The blind Patriarch Isaac—The story of the speaking wolf—
The wolf's speech—A vague vision of the truth—The punishment of the
sons for having caused their father to rend his clothes—The torn covenant
—A faint hope—Isaac's knowledge of his grandson's whereabouts.

When the deed had been accomplished and Joseph carried
away, his brethren bitterly regretted their wicked deed. Their
hatred had abated, and they would gladly have undone the
past. It was too late, however, and they decided, binding one
another by a solemn oath, never to reveal the true state of affairs
to their father. In the meantime Reuben who had been absent,
having retired to the mountains to do penance, had returned.
According to another version he had gone home to wait upon
his father, as it was his day. He availed himself of the first
opportunity during the night to slip away to the pit with the
intention of dragging Joseph up and restoring him to his
father. He called the lad by name, but no answer came. Reuben
now feared that Joseph had died of anguish and fright or in
consequence of a snake bite. Hastily he let himself down into
the pit, but search as he might, there was no Joseph. He came
out of the pit, rent his clothes, in token of his great grief, and
hastened to rejoin his brethren whom he accused of the death
of Joseph. The brethren informed him of what had occurred;

17

how they had sold Joseph to a caravan of Midianites, and how
they now greatly regretted their heinous deed.

" We must conceal the truth from our father," they said,
" but we know not what plausible tale we could invent."

Issachar now proposed to tear Joseph's coat of many colours,
dip it in the blood of a slaughtered lamb, as the blood of a
lamb greatly resembles human blood, and send the coat to
their father. The brethren agreed to Issachar's proposal, slew
a lamb, dipped the coat of the unhappy Joseph in its blood, and
sent it by the sons of the handmaids Bilhah and Zilpah to their
father with the following message: " Pasturing our flocks, not
far from Shechem, we found in the wilderness this garment
covered with blood and dust."

It was a terrible blow to the Patriarch, when he recognized
his favourite son's coat. Like a log he fell to the ground,
remaining motionless in his great grief. Soon, however, he
rose and gave vent to his sorrow in tears and lamentations.
Jacob immediately dispatched one of his slaves to his sons,
bidding them appear in his presence without delay.

In the evening the sons returned home, their clothes torn
and ashes upon their heads in sign of mourning.

" Can ye explain the great misfortune which has befallen
me to-day?" exclaimed Jacob. " Tell me everything and conceal nothing from me."

Thereupon the brethren related unto Jacob the story which
they had made up beforehand.

" To-day," they said, " on the way leading to Shechem,
in the wilderness, we found this coat, bloodstained and dusty.
We recognized it at once as that belonging to our unhappy
brother Joseph and sent it to thee, to see whether thou wouldst
also recognize it."

" Alas," cried Jacob, " it is indeed the coat of my dear
son, who has no doubt been devoured by a wild beast. I sent
him this morning to see whether all was well with ye and also

with the flocks, and to bring me word. Willingly he went to execute my command, and whilst I believed him safe in your midst this misfortune must have happened to him."

" He did not come to us," promptly lied the sons of Jacob, " and ever since we left thee have we neither heard from Joseph nor seen him."

When Jacob heard these words he broke out into fresh lamentations. He rent his garments, put on sackcloth and strewed ashes upon his head. Desperately he bewailed the untimely and violent death of his beloved son.

" Joseph, my son! My son Joseph," he cried, amidst tears, " I am the cause of thy death. How sweet was thy life unto me, but, oh, how bitter is thy death. How I suffer on account of thy death. It were a thousand times better that I had died in thy stead. Come back, my son, come back to me. Where art thou, Joseph? Where is thy soul? Come and count my tears and be a witness of my affliction; count the tears which are flowing from thy unhappy father's eyes. Gather them and bring them before the Throne of Glory, so that the Eternal may avert His wrath from us. Why didst thou die a death which should not have befallen a son of Adam? Thou didst fall a victim to a cruel and relentless enemy. I know, alas, that it is on account of my many sins that my beloved child has been taken from me. But it was God who gave me my darling son, and it is He who has taken him from me, and whatever the Lord doeth is well done and for the best."

Thus wept and lamented the unhappy and bereaved Patriarch.

When the sons of Jacob saw the great grief of their old father, they bitterly regretted their wicked deed and wept copiously. Judah lifted the head of the venerable old man from the ground, placed it upon his knees, wiped away his tears, and tried to comfort him. But Jacob remained motion-less and rigid. Bitterly did Judah weep over the head of his father, and he was joined by his brethren, and also by the women and children and the servants of Jacob's household. They had all assembled round the old man, trying to comfort and to console him. Jacob, however, was plunged in his immeasurable grief, and would not listen to any words of consolation. Thereupon all the members of Jacob's household arranged a great mourning for Joseph and his father's affliction. The sad news soon reached the old and venerable Isaac. He and his household also wept copiously and mourned over the death of Joseph. Blind though he was, Isaac, accompanied by his servants, journeyed from Hebron to Shechem to visit his son and comfort him in his bereavement. But not even from his old father would Jacob accept consolation.

After a while Jacob arose from the floor and amidst tears he thus addressed his sons:

" Rise, my sons, take your bows and your arrows, gird your swords, and go out into the fields. Make a search for the body of my son, and if ye find it bring it to me that I may bury it. Try also to catch the first beast of prey ye meet, perchance God will have pity upon me and upon my sorrow, and let you catch the beast which has torn my Joseph, so that I can take revenge upon it." Thus spake Jacob to his sons.

Early next morning the brethren set out, and when they returned to the weeping father, they brought a wolf they had caught.

" This is the first wild beast we encountered," said the sons, " and we have brought it to thee, but we found no trace of the body of thy son."

In the agony of his soul, weeping copiously and wailing, the bereaved father seized the wolf and thus addressed him: " Cursed beast, why didst thou devour my son Joseph, and didst have no fear of God, the Lord of the Universe? Why didst thou bring down such grief upon me by depriving so suddenly my poor, innocent, and blameless son of his life,

A FATHER'S GRIEF

who was guilty of no sin or transgression? But God punisheth every unjust action." Thus spoke Jacob in his agony of soul.

And the Lord had pity upon the sorrowing father, and in order to send him some consolation, He opened the mouth of the beast which thus spoke:

" By the living God who hath created me, and by thy life, my lord, I never saw thy son, nor did I tear him in pieces. From a far and distant land did I come here, in search of mine own son who seems to have suffered a fate similar to that of thy son. For my child, too, hath disappeared, and never did return to me. I know not whether he be dead or alive. I was searching for my lost child, when thy sons met me. They seized me and thus increasing my grief brought me hither to thee. I am in thy power now, O son of man, and thou canst deal with me as it pleaseth thee, but I swear once more by the living God, my creator, that I have never seen thy son, much less killed him, and that I have never in my life tasted human flesh."

Thus spoke the wolf, to Jacob's immense astonishment.

The Patriarch let the wolf go free without molesting the beast, but he continued to mourn for his lost son. And yet, Jacob had an inkling of the truth. The very fact that he remained inconsolable made him hope that Joseph was still alive. For whilst the heart of man is accessible to consolation when he has mourned and grieved for some time over the death of a dear one, the remembrance of the living can never be eradicated from the hearts of those who love.

A prophetic vision also came over Jacob and he said:

" Only vaguely do I foresee the future, but of one thing I seem to be sure and that is that no beast hath torn Joseph in pieces, nor hath he been killed by the hand of man. I see also that a wicked woman is the cause of his distress and that Judah is also responsible for his fate."

The brethren were the cause that Jacob had rent his

clothes on account of his lost son, and, as a punishment for
this, they were to rend their own clothes later on in Egypt.
Jacob himself—although in the innermost recesses of his heart
a hope lingered that Joseph was still alive—continued to mourn
for his son, putting sackcloth upon his loins, and this sign of
mourning, namely, the rending of the clothes and the sackcloth, was adopted in later days by his descendants, especially
by the kings and princes in Israel. Thus David, Ahab, Joram,
and Mordecai at Shushan, all rent their clothes and put on
sackcloth when a great misfortune had befallen them.[1] Twenty-
two years Jacob mourned for his son, just the same number
of years during which he had been absent from home, away
from his parents, and thus had never paid his respectful homage
which a son owes to his father and mother. Jacob was also
inconsolable for another reason and that was his lost hope of
seeing the twelve tribes established.

" The covenant concerning the twelve tribes," said Jacob,
" the covenant which God made with me, is now torn. My
great aim was to establish the twelve tribes of Israel with my
twelve sons, for all the works and creations of the Lord of the
Universe correspond to the number of twelve. Twelve is the
number of the planets " (signs of the Zodiac), "twelve months
hath the year, twelve hours the day, and twelve hours the
night: and twelve stones will be set in the breastplate of the
High-Priest."

To replace Joseph his lost son by another son, in con-
tracting a new marriage, never entered Jacob's mind. He had
once made a promise to Laban, his father-in-law, never to
take any other wives besides the latter's daughters.[2] And
although both Leah and Rachel were now dead, Jacob still
considered himself bound by his promise. But because a faint
hope that Joseph was alive somewhere continued to linger in
the Patriarch's heart, he would not be consoled or comforted,

[1] *I Chronicles*, 21, 16; *I Kings*, 21, 27; *II Kings*, 6, 30; *Esther*, 4, 1.   [2] *Genesis*, 31, 50.

THE WOLF SPEAKS TO THE SORROWING JACOB

accepting consolation from no one, not even from his own
father. As for Isaac, he wept and mourned with his son, when
he was in his presence, but as soon as he left him he ceased
manifesting any grief, for Isaac, being a prophet, knew that
Joseph was still alive. He did not, however, reveal this fact to
his son.

"As the Lord," said Isaac, "hath not acquainted my son
with the fate of Joseph, I do not feel justified in doing it."

Jacob also mourned the death of Joseph for another reason.
He was now no longer certain that he would not suffer the
torments of hell in the world to come. The Lord had once
assured him that if none of his sons died during his lifetime,
he could look upon the fact as a sure sign that he would not
taste the torments of hell in the world to come. This certainty
Jacob had now lost.[1]

[1] *Genesis Rabba*, §§ 84, 85; *Yalkut*, § 142; *Midrash Tanchuma, Genesis*; section *Vayesheb*.
Targum Pseudo-Jonathan, in loco; *Pirke de Rabbi Eliezer*, Ch. 38; *Sepher Hajashar*; see also
Lewner, *Kol-Agadoth*, Vol. I, pp. 200–202, and Adolf Kurrein, *loc. cit.*

CHAPTER III

Upon the Mother's Grave, or the Journey to Egypt

The lonely grave at Ephrath—A son's distress—He implores his mother's help—The voice from the grave—The cruel masters—Sudden darkness and raging storm—The terror of the Ishmaelites—The crouching beasts —Apology and forgiveness—The journey to Egypt—The new masters— Potiphar, the captain of the royal guard—His doubts—The story of the sale of Joseph as related in his Testament—The sacrifice of a brother— He admits being a slave, so as not to put his brethren to shame—The slave and the lucky shopkeeper—The Memphian woman—Punishment for man-theft—The advice of the Memphian woman—Joseph in prison—The fear of his masters—The new mistress—The dishonest eunuch—The story of the sale of Joseph in Moslem tradition—The fond great-aunt—The precious girdle—Accused of theft—The jealousy of the brethren—The Moon of Canaan—In the well—Saved from drowning by an angel—The caravan of Arabs—Melek-ben-Dohar and Buschra—The heavy bucket—The journey to Egypt—The dazzling light—The ladies of Egypt—Adopted as a son.

When Joseph beheld his mother's grave at Ephrath, he hastened and threw himself across the sepulchre, weeping loudly. Heartrending were the cries uttered by the poor lad.

"Mother, Mother," he cried, "thou who didst bear me, arise and behold thy son sold as a slave, heartlessly and piti-lessly. Come forth, Mother dear, look at me and weep with me over my misfortune and my suffering, and see how my brethren have treated me. Arise, Mother, from thy sleep, and help me to prepare for the conflict against my brethren who have torn me away from my father. Stripped of my gar-ments, they have sold me into slavery to strangers. Awake, Mother dear, from thy sleep and plead my cause before the throne of the Eternal. Accuse my brethren of their heinous

deed and learn His judgment. Awake, O Mother, for my
father's sake, and come to comfort and to console him, for his
heart is heavy with grief and sorrow." Thus the seventeen years
old lad, who was being dragged away into slavery, wept and
lamented upon his mother's grave, the lonely grave of Rachel
on the road to Ephrath.

Exhausted by grief and sorrow, he ceased at last and remained motionless upon the cherished grave. Suddenly
Joseph lifted up his head, listening intently. Was it a dream
or a fancy of his overworked and weary brain? But no, distinctly
he heard a voice. It was the voice of his mother speaking to
him from the depth of the grave.

" My son Joseph," said the voice, " my darling son, I hear
thy complaints and I see thy suffering, thy misery and affliction.
Greatly do I suffer for thy sake, and thy terrible state increases
the burden of my affliction. But, my dear son, put thy trust
in God and wait for His help. Fear not, my darling son, for
God is with thee and will deliver thee from distress in His
own time. Go, my son, with thy present masters to Egypt,
for God is with thee, and He will never forsake thee."

Such were the words uttered by the mother's voice, a voice
choked with tears and heavy with grief.

Silently and amazed Joseph had listened to the words
coming from the depth of his mother's grave, and when it
became silent, he broke out anew, weeping more violently.

One of the Ishmaelites, seeing the lad lying upon the grave
and weeping aloud, drove him away with kicks and curses.

" The lad is mad," said the merchantman to his companions; " to-day he calls a stone mother, and to-morrow he
will address a log of wood as father."

Joseph now begged his new masters to take him back and
restore him to his father Jacob, who would certainly reward
them richly, paying them a considerable sum for his lost son.

But the Ishmaelites only laughed at him, pointing out that

he could not be the son of a rich man, for else he would not have been sold into slavery for such a paltry sum. Thereupon they beat him more mercilessly, answering all his entreaties with more kicks and blows.

But the Lord who saw Joseph's distress had pity upon him, and once more sent darkness upon the earth. Lightning and heavy thunderbolts made the earth tremble, so that the Ishmaelites knew not whither to turn, for even the beasts and camels crouched upon the ground and refused to budge. In great despair the merchantmen asked one another why such a misfortune had come over them and what transgression they had committed to have thus brought down upon themselves the wrath of God.

" Perhaps," said one of the merchantmen, " we have committed a great sin by ill-treating the slave. Let us, therefore, entreat his forgiveness, and, if the storm passes, then we shall know on whose account we have suffered and the storm has raged."

Thus spoke one of the merchantmen, and his companions agreed.

Thereupon they all begged Joseph to forgive them.

" Forgive us," they said, " for we have sinned against thee, and therefore thy God is angry with us and hath sent down this raging storm. Pray, we beg thee, to thy God that He take away this storm from us."

Joseph forgave the Ishmaelites, and consented to pray to God on their behalf. The Lord heard his prayer; the storm abated, and once more the sky became clear. The sun once more appeared in its splendour, the beasts arose from their crouching position, and the merchantmen could continue their journey to Egypt. The men now knew that it was on Joseph's account that the storm had raged, and were now afraid to treat him harshly. They also took counsel together what to do with the slave.

"Let us take him back to his father, as he wishes," said one of the men. "His father is sure not only to return the price we have paid for him, but also to reward us handsomely."

"It is too late now," replied his companions, "to retrace our steps, for we have already travelled a long distance from Canaan, and we can no longer delay our journey. The best we can do now is to proceed to Egypt and there get rid of the lad by selling him at once." And thus the Ishmaelites continued their journey to Egypt, carrying Joseph with them.

When the merchantmen reached the borders of Egypt, they met four men from the descendants of Medan, a son of Abraham, and offered them Joseph for sale.

"We have a handsome slave," they said, "whom we wish to sell, and if he pleases you, we will take nine shekels for him." The Medanites, beholding Joseph who was very comely, agreed to pay the sum demanded and bought him. Satisfied with their transaction, the Ishmaelites continued their way to Egypt, and the Medanites also soon returned. They were already aware that Potiphar, the captain of Pharaoh's guard, was seeking a good slave, comely of appearance and wise, whom he could employ as the superintendent and steward of his household, and they therefore hastened to repair to the captain and to sell him the slave they had just acquired.

When Potiphar saw Joseph, the lad pleased him greatly, and he agreed to pay for him the high price demanded by the Medanites, namely four hundred pieces of silver (twenty shekels). He was, however, struck by the noble appearance of the lad, and suspected that he was not a slave by birth, but a noble youth stolen from his parents.

"This youth," said Potiphar, "does not seem to be a slave by birth, but a free man. Many free men are now being stolen from their parents and sold into slavery. I suspect that this lad, too, has been stolen from his father who may come and claim him from me. I therefore will consent to buy him from

you and pay the price of four hundred silver pieces, on condition
that ye bring the men from whom ye bought him."

The Medanites consented, brought the Ishmaelites from
whom they had bought Joseph, and the merchantmen maintained that Joseph was indeed a slave whom they had bought
in the land of Canaan. Satisfied now with his bargain, Potiphar paid the sum of four hundred silver pieces and took
Joseph into his house. And thus Joseph, the son of Jacob the
Hebrew, a powerful and wealthy man in Canaan, was sold into
slavery by the sons of slaves and bought by Potiphar, himself a
slave of Pharaoh. But it had been ordained by Divine Providence that Joseph should be brought to Egypt and in time
become the ruler of the country.[1]

In the *Testament of Joseph* the incident of Joseph's sale, his
arrival in Egypt, and his acquisition by Potiphar is related as
follows:

When the lad came with the Ishmaelites to the Indo-
Colpitæ, the latter asked him whether he was really a slave,
to which Joseph gave answer that he was a home-born slave.
He said so because he was anxious not to put his brethren to
shame. The chief of the Indo-Colpitæ then said to him:

" Thou art not a slave, for thy appearance is manifestly
not that of a slave," and he threatened to put him to death on
account of his lie.

Joseph, however, maintained that he was a slave, a slave
of those who had sold him.

When the merchants arrived in Egypt, each of them strove
to keep Joseph for himself. As they could not agree, they at
last decided to leave him in the meantime with one of their
merchants or shopkeepers until they returned again to Egypt,
bringing new merchandise.

Thus Joseph remained for three months and five days with

---

[1] *Targum Pseudo-Jonathan, in loco*; Babylonian Talmud, *Sotah*, 13*b*; *Genesis Rabba*,
§§ 84, 86, 87; *Book of Jubilees*, Ch. 34.

the shopkeeper. He found favour in the eyes of the latter who handed over to him his keys, entrusting unto him his entire house. And the Lord blessed the shopkeeper on Joseph's account, so that he prospered exceedingly.

Now it happened that at that time the wife of Potiphar arrived at Heliopolis, returning from Memphis. She heard from the eunuchs concerning Joseph, the Hebrew slave who was abiding with the shopkeeper, and she cast her eyes upon him. Thereupon she spoke unto her husband concerning the shopkeeper (merchant) who had grown rich through a young Hebrew slave. "They say," she added, "that the lad had been stolen out of the land of Canaan. Thou shouldst, therefore, call the shopkeeper to judgment, take the youth away from him and appoint him the steward of thy house; the God of the Hebrews will then bless thee, for the grace of Heaven is upon the lad." Thus spoke the wife of Potiphar, and her husband believed her words and sent for the merchant, calling him to judgment.

"I hear evil things concerning thee," said Potiphar, "for people tell me that thou stealest souls out of the land of Canaan and dost sell them as slaves."

The merchant fell upon his face and prostrated himself before Potiphar: "My Lord," said he, "I know not what thou sayest."

"Dost thou not?" replied Potiphar. "Whence then is the Hebrew slave in thy house?"

"My Lord," replied the merchant, "the Ishmaelites to whom he belongs entrusted him to me, and he is to abide with me until they should return."

Potiphar, however, did not give any credence to the assertion of the merchant, and commanded him to be stripped naked and beaten. Wailing and lamenting, the merchant still persisted in his assertions.

Potiphar, therefore, commanded that Joseph be brought in

his presence. When the lad was brought before Potiphar, who was the third in rank of the officers of the King, he prostrated himself. Potiphar took the lad apart and asked him: " Art thou a slave or a free-born man?"

" I am a slave," promptly replied the youth, for he wished to keep his real state secret, so as not to put his brethren to shame.

" Then whose slave art thou?" Potiphar continued to question him.

" I am the slave of the Ishmaelites," replied Joseph.

" And how didst thou become their slave?" again asked Potiphar.

" They bought me in the land of Canaan," said Joseph.

In spite, however, of Joseph's assertions that he really was a slave, Potiphar refused to believe him.

" Thou liest," he said, and ordered that he be stripped naked and beaten.

Now Potiphar's wife, who saw through the open door what was happening and how the handsome youth was being punished, sent to her husband and said:

" Unjust is thy judgment, for thou dost punish the free man who hath been stolen, as if he had transgressed."

As Joseph still persisted in calling himself a slave and refused to retract his statement, Potiphar ordered him to be sent to prison, there to remain until the Ishmaelites, his masters, should return.

But Potiphar's wife again remonstrated and said: " Thou art unjust! Why dost thou detain in bonds this youth, who is a captive but manifestly noble born? Thou shouldst set him free and take him into thy house and let him wait upon thee." She was anxious to have Joseph in her house, where she could see him daily, as she had fallen in love with him.

Her husband, however, replied: " We Egyptians are not allowed to take away the property which belongs to others before the truth is proved; I cannot take away the lad from the merchant, and it is best, therefore, that he abide in prison until his owners return."

And thus Joseph was sent to prison, where he remained for twenty-four days.

Now the Ishmaelites had in the meantime learned that Joseph was really the son of Jacob the Hebrew, a mighty and powerful man in Canaan, who was mourning for the lad in sackcloth and ashes. When they returned to Egypt they came to Joseph and said:

" Why didst thou tell us a lie; saying that thou art a slave? We have now learnt that thou art the son of a mighty man in Canaan and that thy father is still mourning for thee."

When Joseph heard them speak of his father and how he was mourning for him, he could scarcely keep back his tears, but he restrained himself, not wishing to put his brethren to shame.

"I know not what ye are saying," he replied. "I am a slave whom ye have bought."

The Ishmaelites thereupon decided to sell Joseph, so that he should not be found in their hands. They were greatly afraid lest Jacob should come and wreak terrible vengeance upon them, for they had heard that he was mighty with God and with men. And as the merchant was urging them to release him from the judgment of Potiphar, who had accused him of man-theft, they came to Joseph and bade him tell Potiphar that he had been really bought and not stolen.

" Thou wilt now say thou wast bought by us with money, and Potiphar will set us free."

When Potiphar's wife heard that the Ishmaelites were selling Joseph, she informed her husband that she intended to buy the lad, "For I hear," she added, "that the Ishmaelites are selling him."

Having obtained her husband's permission she sent one

of her eunuchs to the Ishmaelites, and offered to buy the youth from them. But the eunuch returned and informed his mistress that the price the owners had asked for the lad was too high. The Memphian woman, as Potiphar's wife is called, thereupon sent another eunuch with instructions to buy the lad at any price.

" Do not spare gold," she said, " and even though they ask two *minæ*, give it to them, only buy the lad and bring him to me."

The eunuch then went and gave the Ishmaelites eighty pieces of gold, telling his mistress that he had paid one hundred. Joseph knew of the eunuch's deceit, but he never said a word, lest the eunuch be put to shame.[1]

In Moslem legend the story of how Joseph was sold and how he arrived in Egypt is told somewhat differently, although a good many incidents have been taken from Rabbinic literature both by Mohammed and the commentators of the Koran.

Joseph was the beloved son of his father Jacob, and the old man was very unhappy when he was deprived of the sight of his favourite son. The latter, after the death of his mother, had been sent to his great-aunt, a sister of Isaac, who brought him up. When Jacob claimed his son, the aunt, who loved the lad dearly, would not think of parting with him. She even went so far as to accuse Joseph of theft and to claim him as a slave, so that he would be compelled to remain in her house. The fond aunt took the family girdle—the one which Abraham, her father, had worn when he went to offer Isaac as a sacrifice, and which heirloom she had retained— strapped it round the boy's waist, brought him before the judge and accused him of theft. As a punishment for his crime, the boy was made over to the fond aunt as a slave, and had to remain in her house until her death, when he returned

---

[1] *Testaments of the Twelve Patriarchs, Joseph,* ed. by Sinker, Cambridge, 1869; Eng. trans. in Anti-Nicene Library, Edinburgh, 1890, Ch. 1–10.

to his father Jacob. Here Joseph suffered greatly, in spite of the great love his father bore him, on account of the envy and jealousy of his brethren. They were jealous of him, not only on account of their father's fond love, but also on account of Joseph's great beauty of person. He was so beautiful that he was known by the name of the " Moon of Canaan ".

Enraged, at last, by his dreams which he constantly urged his brethren to listen to, the latter decided to drive their brother out of the country or kill him. " When Joseph is no more," they said, " we will repent of our deed, and the Lord is sure to forgive us."

And thus, one day, when they had Joseph in their power, the brethren stripped him naked and cast him into a well full of water. An angel, however, had thrown a stone into the well, and upon this Joseph stood so that he was above the surface of the water, else he would have been drowned.

" My brothers," cried the poor lad, " ye have taken away my clothes and stripped me naked, wherewith shall I cover my nakedness in the well?"

" Let the moon, the sun, and stars, who have adored thee in thy dreams bring thee clothes to cover thy nakedness," mocked the brothers.

For three days Joseph remained in the well. Judah secretly let him down food, whilst the angel Gabriel lit up the darkness of the pit by hanging up in it a precious stone which shed a light. Now on the third day a caravan of Arabs, passing near the well, stopped there for the purpose of drawing water to quench their thirst. Melek-ben-Dohar, the chief of the caravan, accompanied by Buschra, a freed Indian, carrying a rope and a bucket, approached the well and let down the bucket. To their great amazement they could not raise the bucket, pull it as they might, for Joseph had put his hand upon the bucket and kept it back. Melek looked down into the well and beheld Joseph, for his face illumined the well like a lamp.

" Who art thou?" asked Melek, amazed at the beauty of
the lad in the well, " who art thou, what is thy name, and whence
dost thou come?"

" From Canaan am I," replied Joseph, " and my brethren
have cast me into this well for no guilt whatever."

Now when Melek saw Joseph he at once knew that he would
fetch a high price in Egypt in the slave market. He therefore
made up his mind not to permit the other members of the
caravan to share the price which the lad would fetch, but divide
it only with his companion Buschra.

" Hearken unto my words, Buschra," said Melek; " we
need not tell all the members of the caravan that we found the
handsome youth in a well and have drawn him out. If we tell
the truth they will, no doubt, claim a share in him; rather will
we say that we bought him from people at the well, and that
he is therefore our sole property, mine and thine. When we
arrive in Egypt we will sell him for a large sum of money,
which we will share between us."

Thus spoke Melek, and Buschra consented to the compact.
Joseph was then taken to the Arab caravan where he remained
until they decided to continue their journey. But on the
fourth day the sons of Jacob, seeing how their father was
grieving and was even suspecting them of having done away
with their brother, made up their minds to draw the lad out
of the well and restore him to his father. Finding the pit into
which they had cast him empty, they searched for him and at
last discovered him in the Arab caravan. They claimed him
as their property, a slave that had run away, and Melek offered
the brethren much money for the lad and bought him from
them.

Moslem legend also relates the incident of Joseph's out-
burst upon his mother's tomb, and Rachel's reply issuing from
the depth of the grave.

It was near sunset when the caravan entered the chief city

of Egypt, which is Heliopolis, governed at that time by Rajjan,
an Amalekite. But behold, Joseph's face, shining more radiantly
than the midday sun, cast a new and dazzling light upon the
city, so that everyone wondered, and the Egyptian ladies and
damsels rushed to the windows to contemplate the radiant
beauty of the Hebrew slave. Keen was the competition when
on the following day Joseph was put up for sale before the royal
palace, for all the noble and wealthy ladies of Heliopolis were
anxious to acquire the radiantly beautiful slave. They sent
either their husbands or their servants to bid for him, but
Aziz, the King's Treasurer, bought the lad for a high price.
As he was childless he made up his mind to adopt Joseph as
his son and heir.[1]

SOLD INTO SLAVERY

(11) They said unto Jacob, O Father, why dost thou not entrust
Joseph with us, since we are sincere well-wishers unto him? (12)
Send him with us to-morrow into the field, that he may divert
himself and sport, and we will be his guardians. (13) Jacob answered,
It grieveth me that ye take him away; and I fear lest the wolf devour
him while ye are negligent of him. (14) They said, Surely if the
wolf devour him, when there are so many of us, we shall be weak
indeed. (15) And when they had carried him with them, and agreed
to set him at the bottom of the well, they executed their design: and
we sent a revelation unto him saying, Thou shalt hereafter declare
this their action unto them; and they shall not perceive thee to be
Joseph. (16) And they came to their father at even, weeping,
(17) And said, Father, we went and ran races with one another,
and we left Joseph with our baggage, and the wolf hath devoured
him; but thou wilt not believe us, although we speak the truth.
(18) And they produced his inner garment stained with false blood.
Jacob answered, Nay, but ye yourselves have contrived the thing
for your own sakes: however, patience is most becoming, and God's
assistance is to be implored to enable me to support the misfortune
which ye relate. (19) And certain travellers came, and sent one to

[1] Koran, *Sura*, 12; Tabari, *Chronique*, I, pp. 213–214. Weil, *Biblische Legenden der Muselmänner*, 1845, pp. 100–105; cf. also Lewner, *Kol Agadoth*, Vol. I, pp. 194–197.

draw water for them; and he let down his bucket, and said, Good
news! this is a youth. And they concealed him, that they might
sell him as a piece of merchandise; but God knew that which they
did. (20) And they sold him for a mean price, for a few pence and
valued him lightly.

The Koran (Sale's translation), *Sura,* 12.

UPON HIS MOTHER'S GRAVE

And when the negro heeded not, that guarded him behind,
From off the camel Jusuf sprang, on which he rode confined,
And hastened with all speed, his mother's grave to find,
Where he knelt and pardon sought, to relieve his troubled mind.

He cried: " God's grace be with thee still, O Lady Mother dear!
O Mother, you would sorrow if you looked upon me here;
For my neck is bound with chains, and I live in grief and fear,
Like a traitor by my brethren sold, like a captive to the spear.

" They have sold me! they have sold me! though I never did them
        harm;
They have torn me from my father, from his strong and living arm,
By art and cunning they enticed me, and by falsehood's guilty
        charm,
And I go a base-bought captive, full of sorrow and alarm."

But now the negro looked about, and knew that he was gone,
For no man could be seen, and the camel came alone;
So he turned his sharpened ear, and caught the wailing tone,
Where Jusuf, by his mother's grave, lay making heavy moan.

And the negro hurried up, and gave him there a blow;
So quick and cruel was it, that it instant laid him low;
" A base-born wretch," he cried aloud, " a base-born thief art thou;
Thy masters, when we purchased thee, they told us it was so."

But Jusuf answered straight: " Nor thief nor wretch am I;
My mother's grave is this, and for pardon here I cry;

I cry to Allah's power, and send my prayer on high,
That, since I never wronged thee, his curse may on thee lie."

And then all night they travelled on, till dawned the coming day,
When the land was sore tormented with a whirlwind's furious sway;
The sun grew dark at noon, their hearts sunk in dismay,
And they knew not, with their merchandise, to seek or make their
    way.

                (*Poema de Josi, Poem of Joseph*, translated by G. Ticknor,
                    in his *History of Spanish Literature*, New York, 1849,
                    Vol. I, pp. 97–98.)

CHAPTER IV

The Perfect Servant and the Passionate Mistress

A model servant—None of the characteristic traits of a slave—Joseph throws off his sadness—The silent prayer—The suspicious master—A magic spell—The God of Joseph—Potiphar is unable to gaze at the sun—The miraculous cup of hot water—Mixed vermuth—Absinthe and wine—Spiced wine—The blessing of God—Reconciled to his fate—The wild she-bear—Joseph's opportunity to show his virtue—The love-sick Zuleika—The astrologers and the horoscope—Zuleika endeavours to attract Joseph—Changing dresses three times—Zuleika flattering Joseph—The servant rebukes his mistress—The enchantress and the virtuous lad—The image of the Patriarch warning his son—The breastplate of the High-Priest—The would-be murderess—The veiled God—The dumb idol and the living Lord—The threats of the furious mistress—Her sickly appearance—The ladies of Egypt—The story of the oranges and the blood-stained hands—Zuleika's pleading—A storm of tears—The comb-like shackle—The fasting of Joseph—Zuleika promises to abandon her idols—The dish of food upon which a magic spell had been cast—The terrible man handing Joseph a sword—Zuleika threatens to commit suicide—The festival of the Nile—Zuleika the beautiful—The image of the father—The waves of the Red Sea will recede at the approach of Joseph's coffin—The story of the speaking infant in the cradle—The scene between Joseph and Zuleika as described by Josephus.

Potiphar, or Potiphera, as he was called, became the master of the free-born Joseph, but he could not fail to notice that his first suspicion had been right. Joseph had none of the characteristic traits of the slave. Slaves are always ready to devour and waste the substance of their masters, whilst Joseph, on the contrary, constantly endeavoured to increase his master's wealth, and the Lord blessed Potiphar and he prospered exceedingly ever since Joseph came into his house. Slaves, as a rule, are guilty of robbing their masters, stealing as much as they

38

can, but Joseph, on the contrary, economized and amassed great wealth for his master whom he served faithfully. Slaves are usually leading an immoral life, but Joseph remained pure and chaste, in spite of temptation.

And as the Lord protected Joseph, he found favour in the eyes of his master who put all his trust in him and appointed him chief steward of his entire household.

And Joseph thought in his heart: " I will now throw off my sadness, and cease my weeping, but do my best to give satisfaction to my master, serving him faithfully and conscientiously. The Lord will see how earnest, hardworking, and honest I am, and He will listen to my prayers and peradventure deliver me." Joseph, therefore, put his trust in God, and whilst serving his master he constantly prayed to the Eternal, and thus he spoke: " Lord of the Universe, be Thou my shield, for I have put my trust in Thee. May it be Thy will that I find favour in Thine eyes and in the eyes of my master, Potiphar."

One day, whilst Joseph was waiting upon his master, the latter noticed how Joseph's lips were moving silently, and he suspected his servant of being a magician and preparing to cast a spell upon his master.

" What is the meaning of this whispering," cried Potiphar, " dost thou intend to make use of occult arts against me, and to bring magic into Egypt, the land of magic and magicians?"

" Far be it from me," replied Joseph, " to do such a thing."

" Then why are thy lips moving silently?" asked Potiphar, still suspicious.

" I am praying to my God," said Joseph, " imploring Him to make me find favour in thine eyes."

" And where is thy God?" asked Potiphar. " Show Him to me that I may see Him."

" Lift up thine eyes to the heavens above and look at my God," replied Joseph.

Potiphar lifted up his eyes to the heavens above him, but soon had to turn away his gaze on account of the brilliance of the sun.

" My master," said Joseph, " only looked at one of the creations and servants of my God, and he has been dazzled by its splendour. How could he expect to behold the Creator of the Universe, and the Sovereign of all the worlds?"

Potiphar was convinced, especially when he saw that Joseph was always successful in his work and in whatever he undertook, that God was indeed with him. It happened that Potiphar once asked his perfect servant to bring him a cup of hot water, and Joseph hastened to comply with his master's request. Potiphar took the cup and said:

" I have made a mistake, for it is a cup of tepid water I really wanted."

And Joseph replied: " The water is tepid, as my master desires."

Potiphar dipped his finger in the water, and behold it was tepid indeed. Potiphar wondered greatly and made up his mind to test Joseph's powers even further.

" It is not water at all I wanted, but a glass of mixed vermuth."

" If my master will drink from the cup in his hand he will find that it contains mixed vermuth," said Joseph.

Potiphar drank, and to his amazement found that the cup really contained a delicious wine. Continuing to test Joseph he said again:

" I would rather have absinthe mixed with wine."

And Joseph replied: " My master has only to drink from the cup to find that it contains absinthe mixed with wine."

And indeed Potiphar convinced himself that the cup Joseph had brought him contained absinthe mixed with wine.

Continuing his test, Potiphar again said:

" It is spiced wine I would rather drink," and once more

he discovered that his cup contained spiced wine. And when he saw that God was clearly on Joseph's side, and fulfilled all his desires, he honoured him greatly, taught him all the liberal arts, and placed before him better fare than the food offered to the other slaves. He also placed the keys of all his possessions and treasures in Joseph's hand, appointing him his chief steward.

Joseph now ruled over Potiphar's household, and all received the necessary orders from him, for Potiphar " knew not aught that was with him ". The blessing of God was the result of Potiphar's action and of his treatment of Joseph, and he often had occasion to say: " Blessed be the day on which I bought Joseph." And when Joseph saw that his master was satisfied with him and treated him no longer as a slave, but as a trusted friend and companion, he was happy indeed, and thanked the Lord for His protection. Feeling quite happy in his present state, the lad reconciled himself to his fate.

Once more Joseph began to pay attention to his appearance. He dressed his hair and walked elegantly, and in every respect once more became the very image of his radiantly beautiful mother, Rachel. With keen satisfaction he now remembered the envy and hatred of his brethren and how they had made him suffer, whenever he had received a token of love from his father.

" I thank Thee, God Almighty," he said, " for the freedom and happiness Thou hast bestowed upon me."

Thus spoke Joseph who was not only quite happy to have been removed from his brethren, but was also forgetting his old father who was mourning for him in distant Canaan. For this indifference he was soon to be punished, for the Lord spoke:

" Thou art an egotist! In sackcloth and ashes thy old father is mourning, bewailing thy loss, whilst thou art thinking of thine own welfare, feeling happy in thy present state, and paying careful attention to thy personal appearance. Thy mistress, who is like a wild she-bear in her passion, will rise up against thee and bring affliction over thee."

Joseph, however, was glad when the trouble in store for him came. He had always wished for an opportunity to prove his piety, even as his fathers had proved their piety whenever it was tested. The Lord, therefore, whilst punishing the lad for his indifference with regard to his father, also wished to give Joseph his longed-for opportunity to show his virtue and his moral strength in the moment of temptation.

Joseph was exceedingly handsome, the very image of his mother Rachel who had been a ravishing beauty. No wonder, therefore, that the passionate Zuleika, the wife of his master Potiphar, cast her eyes upon Joseph. The more she had occasion to see the youth, the more violent became her love for him. Not venturing as yet to declare her love to her slave, Zuleika tried to attract his attention to her person. As it was customary in those days, especially in Egypt, she asked astrologers to cast her horoscope, and was informed that she was destined to have descendants through Joseph. This astrologic forecast was true in a certain sense, for Joseph later on married Potiphar's daughter Asenath who bore him children.

Zuleika, however, did not understand the prophecy and now hoped that her heart's desire would speedily be fulfilled. She did her best to seduce Joseph by feminine artifice and to enrapture the lad by her beauty. She omitted no occasion to enter into conversation with him, hoping thus to attract his attention. Several times during the day did she change her attire, arraying herself in beautiful and costly garments in the morning, at midday, and in the evening. But all her efforts and all her feminine artifices proved of no avail and had no effect upon the virtuous and chaste son of Jacob.

Under the pretence of visiting Joseph, Zuleika often came to him at night, pretending to regard him as her own son, for she had no male child. Joseph, thereupon, prayed to the Lord, and Zuleika gave birth to a son. But still she continued to visit him and to kiss and embrace him as if he were her own son.

In his innocence, Joseph did not recognize her deceit, and her evil and wanton thoughts. At last, however, his eyes were opened and he became aware of the Egyptian woman's criminal passion for him. When Joseph perceived what was in Zuleika's mind, he was very sad and grieved and lamented for her. He constantly persuaded her to turn away from her evil design and to eradicate from her heart her wanton passion for him.

When Zuleika saw that all her wanton efforts remained ineffectual, and that Joseph never, by either word or look, expressed his love for her, and steadfastly refused to look into her eyes shining with love, she decided to declare to him her love in undisguised terms. Joseph, she thought, is only timid and durst not raise his eyes to his beautiful mistress, but if I declare my love to him, he will be happy to reciprocate my passion. Thus thought Zuleika, reared in an Eastern harem and unable to understand the steadfastness and moral strength of her handsome slave. She now began to pursue him openly with her love and with her constant flattery.

" Fair is thy appearance," she said, " and comely is thy form, thou handsomest of all men. Never did I behold a slave who equalled thee in beauty."

But Joseph replied modestly:

" I am only the work of God who hath created and fashioned me, as He hath fashioned and created all men and women."

" Glorious and beautiful are thine eyes," continued Zuleika, " and no wonder that thou didst charm and stir up love in the hearts of all the ladies in Egypt."

" My eyes may be beautiful whilst I am alive," replied the son of Rachel, " but thou wilt recoil in horror when thou wilt behold their ghastly expression once I am dead and lying in the grave."

" Sweet and charming is thy voice," declared the woman

reared in the atmosphere of an Egyptian harem; "sweet is thy voice, and pleasant is thy speech, thou favoured of the Gods. Take up the harp which is lying idle in the house, play and sing to me, that I may hear thy voice and enjoy thy song."

"Pleasant and lovely are my words only when I proclaim the glory of the Eternal," replied Joseph.

But Zuleika would not be rebuked. Caressing the fair head of the beautiful Joseph, she exclaimed:

"Dost thou know that thy hair is exceedingly beautiful? I will comb it with my golden comb."

The amorous talk of the harem beauty made Joseph at last lose his patience. Disgusted with her wanton talk and her enticements, he exclaimed:

"How long, O woman, wilt thou thus speak to me, trying to seduce me? It would be better for thee to think of thy husband and to remember thy household duties."

"My household duties," laughed Zuleika. "There is nothing in the house I care for. Since I have seen thee," she added passionately, "there is nothing I can think of but thee and my love for thee."

The virtuous lad, unaccustomed to such amorous declarations and such wanton enticements, was shocked by the conduct of his mistress, and silently looked to the ground, never raising his eyes to his passionate mistress's face. The woman, however, did not consider herself beaten, but, on the contrary, continued her pursuit of the lad, practising her artifices in the hope of winning his love with her enticements and her harem tricks.

The more steadfast Joseph proved, the more deaf he seemed to be to her words of love, the more ineffectual Zuleika's blandishments seemed to be, the more violent became her passion. She forgot all womanly shame and decency, and in passionate words begged her handsome slave to yield to her desire.

The enchantress was beautiful, and the temptation was great, fraught with danger for a lad unequal to the fight against the enticements of an Egyptian passionate beauty, well versed in all feminine artifices and harem tricks. There were moments when his steadfastness threatened to forsake Joseph, and there was danger that he would not be able to resist the temptation. At such a moment of weakness, the image of his beloved father suddenly appeared before his mind's eye, and Joseph seemed to hear the voice of the latter warning him.

" A day will come," Jacob said, " when upon the breast-plate of the High-Priest the names of thy brethren will be engraven. Dost thou wish to forfeit this honour through thy sin of immoral conduct?" Thus spoke Jacob, and Joseph, on the point of yielding to the passion of the Egyptian woman, silenced the voice of temptation. In calm and sensible tones he tried to cure his mistress of her violent passion and to bring her back to her senses.

" The Lord," he said, " the Creator of the Universe, is in the habit of choosing among the favourite members of our house one whom He destines to be a sacrifice unto Himself. Should He desire to choose me as a sacrifice, I would make myself unfit for such an honour were I to commit the sin thou temptest me with. In visions of the night the Lord hath also frequently appeared to my worthy ancestors. Would He appear to me, if I were to defile myself with the sin of adultery? For a small transgression only Adam, our first parent, was expelled from the Garden of Eden and was heavily punished. How much greater will be my punishment, if I commit the grievous sin of adultery, and transgress the most sacred law of marriage? I also fear the wrath and punishment of my old father in Canaan. On account of a similar sin he deprived my eldest brother Reuben of his birthright and gave it to me. If I do thy desire, he would, with equal right, deprive me, too, of the gift of birthright. I also fear my master, thy husband, in whose eyes I have found grace and favour, and to the sin of adultery I would also add that of ingratitude, were I to fulfil thy wanton desire."

" My husband," stormed Zuleika, carried away by violent passion, " my husband, the hateful Egyptian, I will kill him, so that he will no longer be in the land of the living and stand in the way of our love."

" Murderess," cried Joseph in indignation, " wilt thou add the crime of murder to that of adultery? In thy violent wanton passion thou hast lost all womanly decency and shame, but dost thou not fear God who knows all and sees all?"

" God?" said the Egyptian woman, " come with me and I will show thee how I can hide our love from God." Thereupon she seized the reluctant lad by the hand, and dragged him from chamber to chamber until she reached her own quiet and secluded room. Above her bed an idol hung. Zuleika seized a cloth, and covering the idol thus spoke:

" See, I have covered the image of my god, and he will no longer be a witness to our sin, if sin it is, as thou sayest. He is a severe and revengeful god, but now our love will be hidden from him."

" Foolish woman," replied Joseph, " thou dost fear thy idol, whose face thou coverest, shall I not fear my God too? His face, however, thou canst not cover, for He is everywhere, and His eyes run through the whole earth. Now, I swear to thee, as the Lord, whom I worship, liveth, that I will never so far forget myself as to commit the sin thou biddest me do."

Joseph's constant refusal increased the more the woman's passion, especially since she hoped that he could not escape her. And thus she continued to pursue him with her amorous declarations, begging him daily to give her his love, or at least a friendly look. But still Joseph remained unshaken, refusing to give way. Unable to prevail upon the steadfast lad, Zuleika tried to threaten him.

"If thou refusest to do my will, I will have thee thrown into prison and have thee chastised," she said.

But Joseph only shrugged his shoulders and replied:

"The Lord who created man looseth the prisoners and He will also protect me and deliver me from thy punishment."

Zuleika's desire and her passion increased to such an extent, that Joseph's refusal to listen to her amorous talk and to accept her advances threw her into a sickness and she began to look very ill. Her husband had already noticed this before, but when he inquired after the cause of her illness, she only evasively replied that she had a pain in her heart. Now, her friends, the women of Egypt, came to visit her, and surprised at her wasted looks and sallow and sickly appearance, wondered greatly and asked:

"Whence cometh thy sickly appearance and wasted looks? It is impossible that the wife of such a great and esteemed prince of the realm as Potiphar is could lack anything that her heart desired. Tell us," they urged, "the cause of thy sickness and what it is that thy heart desireth?"

"To-day," replied Zuleika, "ye shall learn the cause of my secret grief."

She thereupon commanded her maidservants to prepare a festive meal for her friends, and a rich banquet was accordingly spread out before the ladies. Zuleika then bade Joseph appear before her, arrayed in his most beautiful and costly garments, and wait upon the noble ladies of Egypt. Zuleika had placed upon the table oranges and knives to peel them. She called Joseph in just at the very moment when the noble ladies were busy peeling the fragrant oranges with the knives in their hands. And so profound was the impression the startling and almost supernatural beauty of the son of Rachel had produced upon the Eastern ladies, that they could not turn their eyes away from him. Mechanically they continued to peel their oranges, but so enchanted were they with the lad's beauty, that they never noticed how they were cutting their hands with their knives, dyeing the red oranges redder still. With a start the enraptured ladies awoke from their enchantment, when in triumphant tones Zuleika suddenly exclaimed:

"What are ye doing? Ye are all cutting your own hands instead of peeling the oranges!"

"It is the fault of thy handsome slave," replied the ladies, "for his beauty is so great that we could not turn our eyes from him."

"Alas," sighed Zuleika, "well do I know to my misfortune the magic power of his supernatural beauty. Ye have only looked at him for one fleeting moment, and so enchanted were ye that ye could not resist the temptation of feasting your eyes upon his countenance. Now ye can understand my agony. Day after day and hour after hour I see him in the house and behold his countenance, and my heart yearneth for him. How can I refrain myself and not waste away and be sick to death?"

Thus spoke Zuleika, and her friends assured her with all the outward signs of pity that they were greatly sorry for her.

"We understand thy sickness now," said the noble ladies of Egypt. "No woman could control herself in the presence of such a man, and few indeed would remember either virtue or decency in such a case. And yet, we fail to understand the cause of thy suffering. He is thy slave, and it would be better for thee to tell him what thou desireth rather than waste away thy life."

"Ye know not Joseph," replied Zuleika. "I have already told him in unmistakable language what my heart desireth, I have begged and entreated, I have implored his love, but all in vain. All my enticements and all my promises remain without effect."

The woman's sickness increased daily, but neither her household nor her husband knew or even suspected the cause of her wasted appearance. Whenever her husband inquired after the cause of her fallen countenance and her wasted looks, Zuleika answered only evasively. But her lady friends now frequently came to visit her, and, as she had told them that her love for Joseph was the cause of her sickness, they advised her to try and entice the youth once more in secret, and persuade him to return her love so that she might not die of a broken heart. Zuleika, in her passionate unrequitted love for the handsome son of Rachel, was wasting away to a shadow, and her countenance looked sad and woebegone. She felt so ill that she could hardly stand.

Now it happened one day that Joseph came into the house to do his master's work. Zuleika suddenly appeared, threw her arms round him and in passionate language begged for his love. With all his strength Joseph warded her off. Thereupon Zuleika, woman-like, broke out into a storm of tears. She begged and entreated, pleaded and reproached the handsome youth who, in her harem imagination, ought to have been only too happy to accept the love of his mistress.

" Look at me," she cried in an agony of soul, and in a tone of wounded pride, " look at me! Hast thou ever seen or heard of another woman my equal in beauty, and much less of one whose beauty exceeds mine? Look at me," she cried passionately, " am I not beautiful and attractive? And yet daily do I try to persuade thee, to beg for thy love which thou dost refuse. My love for thee is wasting away my health, and I am grievously sick. Is it not an honour that I, one of the most beautiful and attractive women in Egypt, am conferring upon thee, and yet thou dost refuse to listen unto me. It is impossible that thou dost not love me, and only the fear of thy master refrains thee from hearkening unto my voice. But, as the king liveth, I swear unto thee that no harm will come to thee and

not a hair of thy head will be harmed on account of thy love
for me, for thy master will never know anything. Oh, my love,
hearken unto me at least for the sake of the honour I am conferring upon thee, or out of pity for my suffering. Take away
the certain death from me, for I shall surely die if thou dost
persist in thy refusal, and why should I die on account of thee?"

Thus begged and wailed Zuleika in a paroxysm of passion.
Her tears and supplications, her peerless beauty, her passionate
love for him made the lad waver for a moment. But once
more the image of his father appeared before his mind's eye,
and he triumphed over his momentary weakness. In spite
of her failures, the Egyptian was not discouraged, but constantly and unremittingly pursued her handsome slave with
her solicitations. She could not understand the lad's steadfastness, and it nearly drove her mad when she noticed that
he would not even look at her, for whenever she fell upon him,
he modestly cast his eyes upon the ground.

" I will compel thee," she cried, " to look into my beautiful
face, into my eyes shining with love." And she placed a comb-
like iron shackle under Joseph's chin, so that he was forced
to hold up his head and look into her countenance and read
her immeasurable love in her eyes. All her efforts, however,
remained ineffectual, and her amorous attacks recoiled from
the mail-coat of Joseph's moral strength and chastity.

On another occasion when Joseph, in a moment of weakness,
was almost on the point of giving way to Zuleika's attacks,
he was saved from sin by Divine interference. It seemed to
him that the Lord appeared to him, holding the stone of foundation in His hand and threatening him, if he committed the
sin, to cast away the stone of foundation and reduce the Universe to ruins.

Zuleika, as an Egyptian, bred and brought up in the atmosphere of a harem, was still convinced that Joseph's refusal
was due only to his fear of being discovered and punished

by his master. She therefore endeavoured to convince him that their love and relations would never be discovered.[1]

" I am a married woman," she would say, " and our relations will never be discovered."

" Foolish woman," replied Joseph, " a son of Jacob would defile himself even by his love for an unmarried daughter of the heathen, and much more so if he were to give his love to a married woman. I refuse to enjoy thy love in this world and to share thy punishment in the next."

When Zuleika saw that her enticements were of no avail, she frequently resorted to threats. She used to summon Joseph into her presence, and give him over to punishments, so as to make him comply with her request. Regretting, however, her harshness a moment later, she would call him back and once more supplicate him to fulfil her desire.

" My love," she would cry, " I am thine, and all that I possess is thine. Thou shalt be my lord and rule over me and over my house; thou shalt be my master, only give me thy love."

Joseph, however, remembered the words of his father, and retiring to his chamber wept and prayed to the Lord to save him from the shameless woman who was urging him to transgress and commit the sin of adultery.

He fasted for many days, although the Egyptians believed that he lived in plenty and even in luxury, so well did he look, for those who fast for the sake of God are made beautiful of face. He drank no wine, and for three days abstained from food, giving it away to the poor and to the sick. He prayed to the Lord to deliver him from the Egyptian woman who constantly pursued him.

[1] *Genesis Rabba*, §§ 86, 87; *Midrash Tanchuma*, section *Vayesheb*; *Yalkut*, §§ 145–146, *Midrash Abkhir* quoted in *Yalkut*, *Genesis*, § 146; *Midrash Lekach Tob*, in loco; *Targum Pseudo-Jonathan*, in loco; Josephus, *Antiquities*, II, 4; *Sepher Hajashar*; *Pirke de Rabbi Eliezer* Ch. 39; Babylonian Talmud, *Yoma*, 39; *Sotah*, 36b; *Gittin*, 7a; see also *Midrash Agadah*, ed. Buber, Vol. I, pp. 93–94; *Midrash Haggadol*, col. 579–594; Gaster, *The Chronicles of Jerahmeel*, pp. lxxxv and 94; A. Kurrein, *loc. cit.*

" Thou needst not fear the wrath of my husband, the hateful Egyptian," she cried. " He thinks that thou art a holy man and very chaste, for often have I spoken of thee to him, praising thy conduct and lauding thy chastity. He is so persuaded of thy chastity that he would never believe any tale concerning thee. Thou art, therefore, safe, my friend, and having nothing to fear, thou canst enjoy thy happiness."

Thus spoke the Egyptian, but Joseph brought up upon the moral teaching of his father Jacob, put on sackcloth, slept on the ground, and prayed to the Lord to deliver him from the snares of the woman.

Zuleika never neglected any means by which she thought she could endear herself to Joseph and win his love. One day she came to him and thus addressed him: " If thou wilt only give me thy love, I will abandon my idols. Instruct me in the law of thy God, and we will walk in His ways. I will also persuade the Egyptian " (meaning her husband) " to abandon his idols. I am ready to do anything for thy sake, only hearken unto my voice and give me thy love."

But Joseph only sadly shook his head and replied:

" The Lord hath no use in the reverence of those who live in impurity, and He taketh no pleasure in those who commit adultery." And again Joseph prayed to the Lord to deliver him from the woman. Often Zuleika suggested to Joseph that she would do away with her husband.

" I will kill the Egyptian," she cried, " and marry thee lawfully." When Joseph heard these words and learned that the woman was even ready to commit murder, he rent his garments, and thus addressed her:

" Woman, if thou dost commit such a crime, I will proclaim it to all men and accuse thee of the deed. Fear the Lord, therefore, for if thou dost commit such an evil deed thou wilt be destroyed."

Zuleika, afraid lest Joseph would declare her device to her

husband, begged him never to breathe a word of what she had said in a moment of aberration. She went away and sent him many gifts, hoping thus to soothe him. Thereupon she sent Joseph a dish of food upon which she had cast a magic spell, hoping thus to beguile him and make him yield to her desire.

When the eunuch brought Joseph the dish, the boy suddenly beheld a terrible man who was handing him a sword together with the dish. Joseph knew that Zuleika's evil design was to seduce him and to lead his soul to perdition. When the eunuch had left, he wept and left the dish untasted. On the following day Zuleika came to visit him, and noticing the untasted food she asked:

" Why didst thou not partake of the food I sent thee?"

" Because," replied Joseph, " thou hast filled it with death. Didst thou not say thyself that I come not near to idols, but the Lord alone? Know then, that the God of my father hath sent unto me His angel and revealed unto me thy great wickedness. I have kept the dish so as to convict thee, so that thou mayest see it and repent. Think not, however, that I was afraid to partake of the food thou didst send me on account of thy magic spells, for they can have no power over me. Over them that fear God in chastity the wickedness of the ungodly hath no power."

Thus spoke Joseph, and praying to the God of his fathers and the angel of Abraham to be with him, he took up the dish and partook of the food in Zuleika's presence.

When the woman saw this, she fell upon her face at his feet and burst out in tears. He raised her up and gently admonished her, and she promised him not to commit this sin again.

Her love, however, for Joseph she could not eradicate from her heart. Again and again she would rush unto Joseph and plead and beg for his love. One day she appealed to his pity for her and to his kindness of heart.

" If thou wilt not love me," she cried, " I will take away my own life. I will hang myself, drown myself in the well, or jump from the top of the cliff." But Joseph prayed to the Lord to calm the storm that was raging in the woman's breast, and he himself gently addressed her and thus he spoke:

" Why art thou so excited and blinded by thy passion, that thou canst think of nought but thy sinful love? Remember that if thou dost kill thyself, Sethon, thy husband's concubine, and thy rival, will ill-treat and beat thy children and destroy thy very memory from off the earth." Thus spoke Joseph. But his words had a different effect upon Zuleika than he had expected.

" Then thou dost love me a little," she cried. " Thou dost love me a little, and it suffices me, for thou dost think and care for me and for my children. It proves to me that I am not indifferent to thee, and I now hope that thou wilt share the passion which is raging in my breast for thee."

Zuleika could not understand that Joseph had spoken thus only for the sake of the Lord. But the woman was so engrossed in her wanton desire and her wicked passion, and so enslaved by it that whatever kind word she heard and whatever good thing she noticed, she at once interpreted it as a sign that her heart's desire would soon be fulfilled. The passionate Egyptian, however, in whose breast the unholy fire of her criminal love was burning, never gave up hope.[1]

" I will wait for a favourable opportunity," she thought, " when I will resort to constraint and use force, should all my enticements and entreaties prove futile and ineffectual."

Such a longed-for opportunity at last came. On the day when the Nile overflowed its banks, Egypt celebrated an annual festival and a public holiday. On this festive occasion, accompanied by musicians who played on various instruments, Egypt's inhabitants, from the King and his princes to the

---

[1] *Testaments of the Twelve Patriarchs, Joseph*, Ch. 1-10.

lowest peasant, all repaired to the banks of the Nile. Men, women, and children thronged the river's banks.

Potiphar and his entire household went out to take part in the festival.

Joseph did not go, because as a Hebrew he did not share the Egyptian adoration of the River Nile.

As for Zuleika, she remained at home under the pretext of sickness. She hoped to make most of the absence of her husband and of the entire household, and that alone now with Joseph in the vast palace she would compel the reluctant slave to yield to her desire.

When she was alone, she arrayed herself in her most beautiful and costly garments, placed gold and silver ornaments and precious stones in her raven dark hair, employed the thousand and one means to which the ladies of the harem resort to beautify their faces and bodies, and perfumed the house with various perfumes calculated to excite the senses. Thereupon she sat down in the vestibule of the house where she knew Joseph had to pass.

She had not long to wait, for soon Joseph returned from the field to do his work which consisted in examining his master's books of account. Startled at the dazzling appearance of his mistress and divining her purpose, fearing also that his steadfastness might forsake him, the lad tried to slip away into another part of the house, where he would not behold the tempting beauty of his mistress. Zuleika noticed this quickly enough, and smilingly exclaimed:

" Why, Joseph, what prevents thee from passing to thy accustomed place to do thy master's work? See, I will make room for thee, so that thou mayest pass to thy place."

Pulling himself together, Joseph passed to his accustomed place in the house. But suddenly Zuleika, resplendent in her beauty, enhanced by her magnificent raiment, exhaling all the perfumes of Arabia which excite the senses, stood before

Joseph. The temptation was great indeed, and his senses entranced, the lad felt that his steadfastness was leaving him and that he no longer was able to resist the attractiveness of the Egyptian, versed in all the artifices of the harem. With triumph in her heart and her eyes shining with love, Zuleika threw her arms round Joseph. But suddenly he pushed her back, disengaging himself from her embrace. At this critical moment the images of his beloved father and of his never-to-be-forgotten mother appeared before Joseph's mind's eye. His rising passion cooled down, and he once more felt himself strong enough to resist the temptation.

"What aileth thee?" cried Zuleika, "Why dost thou suddenly hesitate and dost refuse to take thy happiness?"

"The vision of my father refrains me from committing a sin," replied Joseph, now completely sobered.

"Thy father?" asked the woman in astonishment. "This is idle talk, there is no one in the house besides ourselves!"

"And yet it is so;" persisted Joseph, "thy criminal desire and wild passion make thee blind so that thou dost perceive nothing, but I am one of the descendants of Abraham who are endowed with spiritual vision."

Mad with passion, wild at the thought that she was again being baulked in her desire, when she had thought herself so near happiness, Zuleika was beside herself. Seizing Joseph by his garment and swiftly drawing a sword which she had hidden under her dress, she pressed the weapon against his throat and cried vehemently:

"I will not be baulked in my desire. As the king liveth, fulfil my desire or thou diest."

With all the strength at his disposal, Joseph disengaged himself, pushed the woman back, and ran out of the room. In so doing, however, he left a piece of his garment in Zuleika's hands. The virtue of his ancestors, which Joseph constantly endeavoured to imitate, had saved him from sin, and it was on account of Joseph's virtue that the nation of Israel passed later on unharmed through the waves of the Red Sea.

"As thou didst fly from temptation," said the Lord, "so the waves of the Red Sea will recede at the approach of thy coffin."

As for Zuleika, in her mad passion for Joseph, she caressed and kissed the fragment of cloth which her beloved had left in her hand. Quickly, however, she perceived the danger of her position, and began to fear her husband's severe punishment, should he learn from Joseph of her sinful conduct.

In the meantime her friends, the noble ladies of Egypt, had returned from the festival, and, hearing of her sickness which they shrewdly suspected to have been only a pretext, came to visit her. Ostentatiously they came to inquire after her health, but secretly they hoped to hear the details and the result of Zuleika's efforts. To her intimate friends Zuleika confessed the truth, telling them all that had occurred, how she had failed and how she now feared the wrath of her husband and his punishment for her wanton conduct.

"Our advice," said the noble ladies of Egypt, "is to accuse thy slave of immorality before thy husband. He will give credence to thy words rather than to those of the slave, and will throw him into prison."

Zuleika promised to follow their advice, and implored her friends to support her.

"Ye, too, my friends, complain to your husbands against the Hebrew slave, and accuse him of having pursued you with his amorous proposals."

Her friends promised their help and departed. In the meantime Zuleika decided to resort to a ruse in her accusations of Joseph. Laying aside her magnificent garments and taking off all the ornaments with which she had beautified her person, she put on her ordinary clothes, and placed by

her side the fragment torn from Joseph's garment which
she still secretly covered with passionate kisses. Thereupon
she called a little boy, one of her attendants, into the sick-
room where she now remained, and ordered him to summon
her household. When the men of her house appeared in her
presence, she thus addressed them:

"See how the Hebrew slave, whom your master hath
brought into the house, hath behaved towards me, his mistress.
Scarcely had ye left the house, and gone away to the festival
of the Nile, when he came into my room, and, knowing that
I was alone in the house, he tried to force me and make me
yield to his desire. I seized him by his garment, tore it and
raised my voice. When he saw my indignation and heard me
cry aloud, he became frightened and fled."

Thus spoke Zuleika, trying to save herself, should Joseph
accuse her to her husband, and also because she wanted to
wreak vengeance upon Joseph for having rejected her passionate amorous advances. The men of her household listened in
silence to her story, and full of indignation went to their master,
who had in the meantime returned, and informed him of what
had occurred.

Potiphar, on hearing the report of his servant's immoral
conduct from the lips of his men, hastened to the room of his
wife, whom he found seemingly full of moral indignation
against the daring slave who had made such a cowardly attempt
against her honour. Bursting into tears, and pretending that
she had been outraged in her feminine honour, she urged her
husband, whom she received with many expressions of her
unbounded love for him, to punish the wicked slave for his
immoral conduct. Zuleika's friends kept their promise, and
Potiphar heard from their husbands of Joseph's alleged behaviour, and how he had pursued and annoyed them. He
therefore believed his wife's story, and ordered his men to flog
Joseph mercilessly. In his agony, when the blows fell upon

him, the chaste and innocent son of Rachel prayed to the Lord, and thus he spoke:

" Sovereign of all the worlds, Thou knowest that I am innocent of the crime I am charged with, and why should I die to-day by the hands of these impious and unjust heathens, on account of lies and calumnies?" The more mercilessly the servants of Potiphar flogged him, the more heartrending became Joseph's cries which ascended to Heaven. And the Lord had mercy upon Joseph, the innocent victim of a wanton woman, furious because she had not succeeded in her criminal desire. God opened the mouth of an infant of eleven months which was lying in its cradle, and it thus addressed Potiphar's servants:

" Why are you punishing and mercilessly flogging this innocent man, for innocent is he of the guilt he is charged with by my mother? Lies did she tell you, and what did really happen differs greatly from the tale she told you." In detail the infant described the scene between Joseph and Zuleika, who had made desperate efforts to win Joseph's love. Potiphar himself and his men listened in great astonishment to the report of the child, which, its tale finished, spoke no word again. Ashamed of his injustice, the perplexed husband bade his men leave off flogging the innocent victim, and decided to make an inquiry and bring the matter before the priests and the judges of the land.

Joseph now appeared in court before the priests who asked him to tell his tale. He related to the judges what had really happened, and how he had rejected the lady's proposal. He swore that he was innocent, and that only in her fury, because she had been unsuccessful in her attempt, did his mistress now accuse him falsely.

The judges listened to his words, and ordered that this torn garment be brought for a minute examination. If the garment is torn on the front part, thought the judges, it will prove that it was the woman who had tried to hold him and that the man was innocent of the crime he is charged with. The garment was brought into court and examined by the judges who, from the nature of the tear, decided that the man was innocent. Joseph was freed from the penalty of death with which he had been threatened, but he was nevertheless condemned to prison, so as to silence the rumour which had spread concerning Zuleika's immoral conduct.

Potiphar himself was now convinced that Joseph was innocent and that his wanton wife had lied shamelessly. He had sufficient sense of justice to tell Joseph so, and to excuse himself for casting him into prison.

"I am convinced," spoke Potiphar, "of thy absolute innocence, and know too well, alas, that my wife's accusation against thee is only a ruse on her part, to save her own reputation. But I must cast thee into prison, lest my honour and my good name suffer, and my children bear the consequences of the stain upon their mother's honour."

Joseph was thus cast into prison, although innocent. It was his punishment to suffer, though innocent, the consequences of a trumped-up charge, and of calumny and slander, for having once calumniated his brethren and accused them before their father. As he had, however, refused to violate the laws of morality even in secret, and had thus sanctified the name of the Lord, he was rewarded for his chastity. One of the letters of the name of God, the letter " He " was added to his name, and henceforth the son of Rachel was called *Je-ho-seph*, and is always considered as the head of all the truly pious men.

Now Potiphar had grown so used to Joseph's services, that he could not spare them. Convinced of the lad's innocence, he obtained from the keeper of the prison permission for Joseph to spend some time in his master's house, where he could minister to the latter's needs. He cleaned the silver, dressed

"WHY ARE YOU MERCILESSLY FLOGGING THIS INNOCENT MAN?"

the table, and made his master's bed, and executed other tasks.
As for Zuleika, she still persisted in her pursuit of Joseph,
and availed herself of the opportunity his presence in the
house offered her to renew her proposals, and to make him
yield to her wishes. She promised him release from prison,
if he only gave her his love. But Joseph replied that he preferred to remain all his life in prison rather than to commit
a crime against God. When her promises and enticements
proved ineffectual, the wanton woman once more resorted to
threats: " I will increase thy suffering and punishment," she
cried in her fury. " I will use other means to make thee feel
my power."

" God sends justice to the oppressed," replied Joseph.

" I will deprive thee of food," she threatened.

" God feedeth the hungry," Joseph replied.

" I will have thee cast into irons."

" God looseth the prisoners," replied Joseph.

" I will blind thine eyes," cried the woman in a rage.

" The Lord openeth the eyes of the blind," replied the
steadfast youth.

" I will crush thy spirit and cause thy tall stature to be
bent down."

" The Lord raiseth up them that are bowed," said Joseph.

" I will sell thee as a slave into a strange land," she cried.

" The Lord protects the strangers," replied Joseph.

When the lad was cast into prison, Zuleika suffered greatly,
but Joseph praised the Lord in the house of darkness and
joyfully, with glad voice, thanked Him Who had delivered
him from the Egyptian woman. But even whilst Joseph was
in prison, Zuleika did not give up hope. She would often send
to him saying:

" If thou wilt consent to my wish, I will at once release
thee from thy bonds, and set thee free from the darkness."

Often, although sick and oppressed with grief, she would

visit him at night, at unlooked for times, to persuade him or at
least to listen to his voice. And when she heard him praying to
the Lord, and glorifying the Creator, she went away groaning
loudly. When Zuleika saw at last that all her efforts, her enticements, and her threats were of no avail, she gave up hope
and let the youth alone.

Josephus describes the scene between Zuleika and Joseph
as follows: When she had the opportunity for solitude and
leisure, that she might entreat the lad again, the woman used
more kind words to him than before.

" It was good of thee," she said, " to have yielded to my
first solicitation, and to have given me no repulse, both because
thou didst bear reverence to my dignity who am thy mistress,
and also because of the vehemence of my passion. Although
I am thy mistress, I am compelled on account of my vehement
passion to condescend beneath my dignity." She assured
him that it was only on his account that she had pretended
sickness, so as to have an opportunity of declaring her love
once more.

" If thou wilt comply with my request," she added, " thou
mayest be sure of enjoying all the advantages thou already
hast, but if thou dost reject me, I will make thee feel the consequences of my revenge and hatred."

But neither her tears nor her threats had any effect upon
the chaste son of Rachel.[1]

---

[1] *Sepher Hajashar*; Adolf Kurrein, *loc. cit.*; see also note 1, p. 51; and Lewner, *Kol Agadoth*, Vol. I, pp. 202–208.

CHAPTER V

In Prison, or the Interpreter of Dreams

The favoured prisoner—Public attention diverted from Joseph—A new court scandal—The two court officers—The plot to poison the King—Joseph waits upon the chief butler and the chief baker—The strange dream—The story of Kimtom, the famous physician—Thirst for knowledge—The tramp and the physician—The dying boy and the incredulous father—Men are judged by their outward appearance—The skill of Kimtom—The bitter regret of a bereaved father—The dream of the chief butler—A prophecy concerning Israel's redemption—The meaning of the vine and the three branches—Joseph is punished for having put his trust in man—An unfavourable prophecy concerning Israel—The meaning of the three baskets—The three nations to whom Israel will once be made subject—The butler's plans to remember Joseph are frustrated by an angel—The Lord alone remembers Joseph.

The master of the prison soon noticed Joseph's zeal and his conscientiousness in executing all the tasks he set him. Charmed also by the youth's extraordinary beauty of person, the master of the prison conceived a great liking for Joseph, and did his best to make life easy for his prisoner. He took off his chains and ordered for him better food than the ordinary prison fare. And as he could find no wrong in the lad, for God was with Joseph in his misfortune, he found it unnecessary to keep a close watch over him as over the other prisoners. He even went so far as to place all his fellow-prisoners under the youth's command, bidding all obey Joseph's instructions.

Now, as people were constantly talking of Joseph's alleged misconduct, and of the accusation raised against him by a wanton and passionate woman, the Lord wanted to divert public attention from the innocent youth and make people think and talk of something else, and thus prepare the way for Joseph's future greatness.

Soon indeed the Egyptians found another *chronique scandaleuse* to talk about, for two high officers of state, the chief butler and the chief baker, accused of high treason and other crimes, were put in ward. The two officers were accused of having secretly conspired to poison Pharaoh, and thus remove him, so that one of the officers could marry the King's daughter. A fly had been discovered in the cup of wine which the chief butler had handed to the King of Egypt, whilst the bread served upon the royal table contained a pebble or a small piece of clay.

And thus, Divine Providence, by raising the wrath of the Pharaoh against the two officers, was paving the way for Joseph's future greatness and high honour.

The chief butler and the court baker were liable to the penalty of death, but God ordained that they should be first detained in prison for some time, before suffering the extreme punishment. They were put in ward in the house of the captain of the guard, but, in consideration of the exalted position they had occupied at court, Joseph was appointed to wait upon them. All this God had ordained for the sake of Joseph, so that the chief butler and the chief baker might in time be the cause of his deliverance.

For twelve months or, according to others, for ten years, the two distinguished court officials had been detained in prison and daily waited upon by the handsome son of Rachel, when they both dreamed a dream. Curiously enough, each of them dreamed a dream and at the same time saw the interpretation of his colleague's dream.

When Joseph, as was his custom, brought them in the morning their water for washing, he found them in low spirits, sad and dejected. Politely and in a wise manner the youth inquired after the cause of their depression and why they looked quite different on that day from other days. " We have both dreamed a dream this night," replied the prisoners, " and in spite of the difference between the dreams and certain details the two dreams seem to us to be one dream." " We are greatly troubled," they concluded, " because there is no one here who could interpret to us our dreams."

" Tell me your dreams," said Joseph, " and let me interpret them. It is God who granteth understanding to man to interpret dreams, but anyhow, my interpretation, if not useful to you, can do you no harm." Thus spoke Joseph, ascribing beforehand all merit and credit to God. And because he had done this, and on account of his modesty, he was raised to an exalted position.[1]

" We are sad and in low spirits," said the two court officials, " because we have dreamed a strange dream, and there is none here to interpret it to us. Go thou now and ask the master of the prison to send to us one of the magicians that he may interpret our dreams to us."

" What use is a magician to ye?" said Joseph. " Relate your dreams unto me, and the Lord may put wisdom in my heart so that I will be able to interpret your dreams."

When the chief butler heard these words from Joseph, he waxed very wroth and exclaimed: " Art thou not the slave of Potiphar? Then how durst thou pretend to be an interpreter of dreams? Is an ass able to read in the stars its future destiny?"

Joseph only smiled at the angry reply of the chief butler and calmly said:

" My lord, hast thou ever heard of the famous physician Kimtom?"

" I have heard of him," replied the chief butler, " and know that he was a very great physician indeed."

[1] *Genesis Rabba*, §§ 88, 89, 90; *Midrash Tanchuma*, sections *Vayesheb* and *Mikkez*; *Targum Pseudo-Jonathan, in loco*; *Midrash Lekach Tob, in loco*; Josephus, *Antiquities*, II, 5; *Sepher Hajashar*; *Book of Jubilees*, 46; *Seder Olam*, Neubauer, *Mediaeval Jewish Chronicles*, II, 28.

" Then may I tell my lord what once happened to the great Kimtom?"

" Thou mayest tell us the story," said the chief butler " and we will listen."

Then Joseph related to the two prisoners the following story: "Kimtom was a great physician, and his fame had travelled far and wide. In spite of his greatness and his vast knowledge, Kimtom, as befits a really learned man, was very modest, and his thirst for more knowledge was great. One day, therefore, he thought unto himself: ' I will travel into foreign countries, where I may perchance find physicians whose knowledge excelleth mine, and I may learn from them new remedies by which to heal the diseases of men.' Thus thought Kimtom, and having filled his knapsack with all sorts of drugs and medicines, he saddled his ass and set out upon his journey. He visited many foreign towns and countries and everywhere he healed the sick and cured them of their diseases, without asking any remuneration for his labours, for Kimtom was a benefactor of men and practised his art neither for fame nor for money. One day he halted outside a big city so as to give his ass a little rest and also to repose himself from the fatigues of a long and wearisome journey. Being very tired, he stretched himself out upon the ground and soon fell asleep. A tramp, unkempt, ragged and torn, happened to pass by and saw the sleeping stranger. Swiftly he took off his own rags, took Kimtom's dress from the sleeping physician, and stole away, riding upon Kimtom's ass. When the physician at last awoke, he was not a little amazed to see himself stripped naked and his ass gone. ' I have been robbed,' said the physician greatly vexed.

" There was nothing left for the great physician to do but to cover his nakedness with the miserable and dirty rags the tramp had left behind, and thus arrayed continue his journey on foot. Taking up his knapsack which the tramp had disdained to take with him, Kimtom walked along until he reached the town. Now it happened that when he was passing through one of the streets he heard a loud wailing and weeping. Entering the house, the great physician, clad in dirty rags, perceived three doctors bending over a couch on which lay a young man on the point of death. The parents of the lad, sobbing bitterly, entreated the men of science to save the life of their only child, promising them high reward. Kimtom looked at the face of the youth and knew that he could bring him back to life and health. Forgetting that he had the appearance of a low tramp, he boldly stepped forward and addressed the weeping parents:

" 'Entrust the patient to me, and I promise you to make him well again with the medicines I carry in my knapsack.' The three doctors shrugged their shoulders and scornfully said: ' This tramp is mad, imagining himself to be a doctor.' The father of the boy, judging from Kimtom's miserable appearance that he was a low thief, exclaimed: ' Get out of the house, thou miserable wretch; hast thou come here to mock me in my misery?' And seizing Kimtom by the collar of his ragged coat he threw him out of the house. But when the three doctors, declaring their patient to be past human help, had left the house, the mother of the boy said to her husband:

" ' Thou hast acted too hastily in sending away so unceremoniously the poor beggar, for who knows, he might perhaps have been able to cure our child.'

" ' Why dost thou indulge in idle talk?' retorted her husband, ' didst thou not notice the miserable rags the man had on his back? His knapsack, too, contained no medicines, but, no doubt, a piece of dry bread and a pair of old torn shoes. No, be sure that the man was only a madman who had taken it into his muddled head that he was a skilled physician."

'Whilst the parents of the boy were thus talking among themselves, their son died, and they wept and lamented over him until they had no strength left to cry any more. In the meantime, Kimtom said unto himself: 'They did not know that I am Kimtom, the great physician, whose fame has travelled far and wide, and they would have had faith in me had I told them my name.' Kimtom, as it appears, was still ignorant of the fact that people are mostly judged by their clothes. He therefore walked through the streets of the town calling aloud: 'Let all those afflicted with any disease come to me and I will heal them, for I am Kimtom, the famous physician!' But the people only laughed at him, thinking that he was not right in his mind. When Kimtom saw that no one was inclined to believe him, he sat down in the market place, putting his various medicines in front of him. Attracted by the delightful smell of his pharmaceutic products, the people, somewhat astonished, gathered round the ragged physician, curiously examining his phials and bottles.

" 'If thou art indeed Kimtom,' asked one of the crowd, noticing that the tramp was anyhow talking quite sensibly, 'if thou art indeed Kimtom, why didst thou come among us clothed in rags?' Kimtom then told them his story, how he had been robbed and stripped naked.

"Thereupon one man, afflicted with a sore disease, decided to try the skill of him who pretended to be Kimtom. Great was the astonishment of the people when they saw that the beggar was indeed a great physician. They now believed his story, and crowds of patients gathered round him imploring his medical assistance. When the father of the youth who had died the day before heard what had occurred, he rent his clothes and wept bitterly. 'I alone am guilty of my son's death,' he cried; 'had I not scorned and despised the beggar because of his rags, my son would have been cured, and alive now. I now see that a man must never be judged by his clothes, but by his countenance, his deeds, his intelligence, and his merits.'

"This is the story of Kimtom, the great physician," concluded Joseph, "and to this I will add only a few words. Thou, my lord, dost look upon me as a slave, and as such thou dost despise me, not believing that a slave has knowledge and wisdom enough to interpret dreams, even like the magicians and interpreters of dreams in Egypt. My lord is mistaken, for I am not a slave by birth, but the son of a noble, powerful, just, pious, and wise man, who has taught me wisdom and imparted unto me much knowledge. I was stolen from my native country and sold into slavery, and even here I am guilty of no transgression, but have been cast into dungeon for no crime whatever." [1]

And when the chief butler and the chief baker heard Joseph's words, they believed him and told him their dreams.

When Joseph heard the details of the two dreams, he at once noticed that, apart from their importance and significance for the two dreamers, they contained a prophecy concerning the future of Israel. Clearly did he see the recondite meaning of the three branches of which the chief butler had dreamed. He interpreted them as the three influential men who would arise in Israel and bring about the redemption of the nations, both in Palestine and in Babylon. He also saw hope and consolation in the fact that, although in exile, three princes of the nations would offer protection and a refuge to Israel. Joseph furthermore saw in the dream of the chief butler an image of the world. The vine represented the world, the three branches were the three Patriarchs, Abraham, Isaac, and Jacob, and the three mothers of Israel, whilst the ripe berries stood for the tribes of the nation. Joseph further interpreted the vine as the Holy Law, and the three branches as the three leaders and teachers of Israel, Moses, Aaron, and their sister Miriam.

[1] Joseph Shabbethai Farhi, *Tokpo shel Yosef*; see also Lewner, *loc. cit.*, pp. 209–213.

Rejoiced at the prophecy and the glad tidings announced to him in the dream of the chief butler, happy at the prophecy concerning the deliverance of Israel, Joseph exclaimed:

" Thy dream is full of great prophecies, and the interpretation I will give thee is a very favourable one. Be thou of good cheer, for in three days thou wilt be delivered from prison."

Josephus relates the incident as follows:

Having given a favourable interpretation to the dream of the chief butler, Joseph begged his fellow prisoner to remember him in his days of prosperity, and to liberate him from the dungeon into which he had been cast through the intrigues of a wanton woman.

Joseph had thus put his confidence in a man, in a mortal being, and had entirely forgotten his usual faith and confidence in God alone. He had entirely forgotten for the moment the words of the Lord: " Cursed is the man who trusteth in man, and maketh flesh his arm, and whose heart departeth from the Lord " (*Jeremiah*, 17, 5). And also the words: " Blessed is the man that trusteth in the Lord, and whose hope is God ".

Twice did Joseph ask the chief butler to remember him in his days of prosperity, twice calling his attention to the fact that he had been stolen from the land of the Hebrews and had committed no crime in Egypt. And because Joseph had twice put his confidence in mortal man, the Lord ordained that the chief butler should forget his promise to Joseph and the latter remain in prison another two years.

When the court baker heard Joseph's favourable interpretation of the butler's dream, he at once knew that the interpretation the youth had given was correct, for in his own dream he had also seen the interpretation of his friend's dream. He now related his own dream to Joseph who at once knew that the baker's dream, too, conveyed a prophecy with regard to Israel's future.

The prophecy was not a favourable one, for it announced the suffering of the nation. The three baskets which the chief baker had seen in his dream, Joseph interpreted as the three kingdoms to whom Israel would be made subject, whilst the uppermost basket stood for the fourth kingdom, destined to extend its sway over the nations of the earth, who would threaten Israel with annihilation. (The bird was the Messiah who would appear to redeem Israel.) The three baskets Joseph also interpreted as the three heavy tasks which the Pharaoh of Egypt would one day lay upon Israel. And as the dream of the chief baker contained nothing pleasant with regard to Israel, but, on the contrary, conveyed to Joseph the prophecy of Israel's suffering, he gave the baker an unfavourable interpretation of his dream, telling him that in three days he would be hanged.

And on the third day it really came to pass even as Joseph had foretold. A minute inquiry into the case of the two court officials who were languishing in prison had finally proved that the chief butler had taken no part in the alleged conspiracy against the life of the King. It was further discovered by the King's counsellors that through no fault of the butler had a fly dropped into the cup of wine he had presented to the Pharaoh. The butler was therefore declared free of guilt and restored to his former position. On the other hand, it was discovered that the chief baker had been really guilty of conspiring against the King's life, and it was therefore assumed that he had intentionally put the small pebble in the bread served upon the royal table. The chief baker was consequently condemned to death and promptly hanged, even as Joseph had foretold.

The butler had not forgotten Joseph and was constantly thinking of ways and means how, without causing any harm to himself, he could save the youth and deliver him from dungeon. But God had ordained that all the butler's plans should be frustrated, and an angel of the Lord always made him either forget his promise or miss the longed-for opportunity. In vain, therefore, had Joseph hoped for human interference, and in vain did he expect to be delivered from prison soon after the release of the butler. The Lord, however, had not forgotten Joseph in his distress, and in His own time He saved him. On account of his dreams Joseph had been sold into slavery, and through a dream, a dream dreamed by the Pharaoh of Egypt, he was liberated and raised to high honour and to the position of ruler of Egypt.[1]

[1] See note 1, p. 65; see also Lewner, *loc. cit.*, pp. 210–214.

CHAPTER VI

The Viceroy of Egypt

The royal dreams—The meaning of Pharaoh's dreams—The interpretations of the magicians and wise men of Egypt—The seven daughters—Seven rulers of Egypt—The conquest of seven fortified cities—The seven royal wives and their fourteen sons—The war of the brothers—The rebellion of seven princes of the realm—The King's anger—The decree to put to death all the wise men of Egypt—The speech of the chief butler—The Hebrew slave—The throne with seventy steps—An audience with the King—The knowledge of languages—Pharaoh puts Joseph to the test—The token of truth—The birth of a prince and the death of another—The King and his counsellors—The objection of the princes of Egypt—The angel Gabriel teaches Joseph all the seventy languages in one night—The additional letter " H "—Joseph ascends all the seventy steps of Pharaoh's throne—The King's secret—Joseph's promise—The new Viceroy—Virtue rewarded—The golden chain and the royal signet ring—Young in years but old in wisdom—Zaphnath Paaneah—The meaning of the letters—The revealer of secret things—The story of Asenath, the daughter of Dinah—The gifts of the ladies of Egypt—The mysterious amulet—Setirah, the hidden one—The great procession—The disappointed damsels—Joseph renders thanks to the Lord—The royal gifts—The sumptuous palace and the magnificent throne—The Viceroy's army—The war between the people of Tarshish and the Ishmaelites—The Viceroy's victory.

Pharaoh had dreamed a royal dream, the dream of a king in whose hands lies the destiny of nations. A worshipper of idols, he saw himself above the Nile, the river he worshipped as a god and from which, as he imagined, both abundant harvests and famines depended. In days of prosperity and of plenty, in days of happiness and abundant harvests, love and harmony reign supreme, and men live in peace and in unity, entertaining friendly relations among themselves. Such was the meaning of the seven fat kine who came up out of the river, keeping together. But in days of adversity, of famine and war and suffering, brotherly love and harmony among men are destroyed. Men turn away from each other and grow selfish and grasping, and such was the meaning of the seven ill-favoured, lean kine, who came up out of the Nile, each turning its back upon the others and finally swallowing the fat kine, but remaining lean for all that. Pharaoh awoke for a brief space of time, but soon fell asleep again. He dreamed another dream, and then finally awoke. In his dream, the king had also seen its interpretation, but this he forgot in the morning, and he was greatly distressed and sad.

Immediately, Pharaoh summoned all the wise men of Egypt, the magicians, with which Egypt abounded, and the interpreters of dreams. All endeavoured to find a plausible interpretation of their royal master's dreams, but none of them satisfied the perturbed King. Some of the wise men of Egypt interpreted the royal dreams as follows: " The seven fat kine," they said, " mean seven daughters to be born unto thee, O King, whilst the seven lean kine stand for seven daughters thou wilt bury. The seven rank and good ears of corn mean that thou wilt conquer seven provinces, whilst the seven blasted ears of corn stand for seven provinces which thou wilt lose."

Other interpreters explained the royal dreams differently. " Seven kings," they said, " will issue from thy house and will rule over Egypt, but in days to come seven other princes will rise up against them and destroy them." The interpreters also said that the seven fat kine stood for seven fortified cities which Pharaoh would build and which would ultimately be conquered by seven nations of Canaan who would wage war against Egypt. The seven ears of corn meant that the descendants of Pharaoh would in days to come reconquer the seven fortified cities and also capture seven fortified places in Canaan and subdue seven nations there, thus regaining sovereign authority.

Other interpreters again maintained that the royal dreams referred to his wives and male issue. " Seven wives will the King marry, but they will all die in his life-time, after having given birth to fourteen sons. Seven of these sons will wage war against their seven brethren and kill them in battle." Thus the strong sons would be destroyed by the weak sons, just as the rank ears of corn had been swallowed up by the withered ears of corn. Another interpretation of the royal dreams was as follows: " The seven fat kine betokened seven sons to be born unto Pharaoh. They will be killed by seven princes who will rise up against them, but seven other princes will then come and wage war against the usurpers. They will avenge the death of the sons of Pharaoh, and the sovereignty will ultimately remain in the house of Pharaoh."

None of these interpretations did satisfy the King, for God had ordained that the efforts of all the wise men of Egypt should meet with no success, but excite the wrath of their royal master. God had also ordained that the King should first narrate his dreams to the wise men of Egypt, so that they could not say afterwards: " Had the King narrated his dreams to us, we too, like Joseph, would have found the right interpretation." God had deprived Egypt's wise men of their wisdom and intelligence, so as to prepare the way for Joseph's greatness.

And so it came to pass that the King, little pleased with the numerous interpretations of his dreams, vexed and greatly distressed, was sick to the point of death. In his anger he decreed that all the magicians, wise men of Egypt and inter-preters of dreams, be put to death and none of them be left alive, since their much vaunted wisdom had left them. Already the princes of the royal guard began their preparations for the execution and the wholesale massacre, when the chief butler appeared before the King and asked permission to speak. He was greatly alarmed at the turn events had taken, and feared that the death of the King, who seemed to take matters so much to heart, would result in his own misfortune and loss of his influential post. A change of Government is always fatal to the safety of court dignitaries.

Prostrating himself before his royal master, the chief butler thus spoke: " Long live the King, great is his power upon earth. Loaded with the burden of two transgressions do I this day appear before my master. I saw thy distress, O King, on account of the wrong interpretation of thy dreams, and yet I did not remember the man who is able rightly to interpret dreams. I did not let thee know of the existence of this man. I am also guilty of the sin of ingratitude, for I have omitted to fulfil the promise I once gave this man to speak to my master on his behalf. Two years ago it pleased the Lord God that Pharaoh should be wroth with me and with his chief baker and cast us into prison. Now in the dungeon, where we were confined, there was also a young slave of the captain of the guard. He was a simple youth, this slave, and one of the despised race of the Hebrews, but he knew how to interpret our dreams, mine own and that of the chief baker, for his interpretation came to pass, and it so happened as he had foretold us. Let the King, therefore, not kill the wise men of Egypt, but summon the Hebrew slave to appear in his presence. He is still confined in dungeon, and will interpret the King's dreams rightly."

Thus spoke the butler who, although he now remembered Joseph, described him in contemptuous terms, calling the King's attention to the fact that Joseph was a slave and one of the despised race of the Hebrews. In his own interest the butler was urging the King to summon Joseph, but he was anxious to make it impossible for the son of Jacob, of whom he was already jealous, to attain a high post at court. A slave and a Hebrew, thought the chief butler, could never be raised to high dignities by the ruler of Egypt. In spite, however, of

his chief butler's contemptuous description of Joseph, the
King at once ordered that Joseph be summoned into his presence, and he revoked the decree of death issued against the
wise men of Egypt. The King also ordered that Joseph be
not excited and hustled, lest, in his confusion, he failed to
interpret the royal dreams correctly.

The servants of the King hastened to execute their master's
command, and brought Joseph out of prison. But before
Joseph appeared in the presence of the ruler of Egypt, he
insisted upon being allowed to cut his hair, and out of respect
for majesty he put on fresh raiment, so that he could appear at
court in fitting attire. It is said that an angel brought him his
raiment from Paradise, whilst, according to others, Joseph
wore the garment into which the amulet suspended upon his
neck had once been extended by an angelic hand.

When Joseph was brought into Pharaoh's presence, the
King was sitting upon his royal throne, arrayed in royal garments, and clad in a gold-worked robe. The crown upon
Pharaoh's head sparkled and flashed with many precious
stones and gems, so that Joseph stood amazed at the appearance
of the King.[1]

It was customary in Egypt that when a prince or some
other distinguished person came to have an audience with the
King, the latter descended thirty-nine steps of the throne,
after the person seeking an audience had mounted thirty-one
steps. If, however, a man of the people came to seek an audience
with the King, he was only allowed to mount three steps, and
the King came down four steps, all in accordance with the
ceremonial of Egypt. It was also the custom at the court of
Egypt that those who knew all the seventy languages of the
world were permitted to ascend all the steps of the royal throne

[1] *Genesis Rabba*, §§ 89, 90, 91; *Midrash Agadah*, ed. Buber, pp. 96–97; *Midrash Tanchuma*,
section *Mikkez*; *Targum Pseudo-Jonathan, in loco*, Babylonian Talmud, *Sotah*, 36b; *Midrash
Lekach Tob, in loco*; *Pirke de Rabbi Eliezer*, Ch. 39; *Sepher Hajashar*; *Zeenah Urenah, Genesis*.
See also Adolf Kurrein, *loc. cit.*; Lewner, *loc. cit.*, pp. 219–221.

to the very top and there have speech with the King. Those who could speak only a few languages were allowed to ascend as many steps as they knew languages. The ruler of Egypt, however, seated upon the throne of the country, had to know all the seventy languages of the world. When Joseph appeared at court, he bowed to the King and mounted three steps, whereupon the King descended four steps and spoke to Joseph:

" O young man! my servant spoke unto me concerning thyself, declaring thee to be an excellent man and very discerning. Vouchsafe therefore unto me the same favourable action as thou didst bestow on him, and tell me what events my dreams are foreshadowing. Do not conceal the truth from me, nor shalt thou, out of fear or a wish to please me, flatter me with lying words, should the truth be sad. No one has been able to interpret my dream, and thou alone, an adept at interpreting dreams, mayest now endeavour to do so." Thus spoke the ruler of Egypt, and Joseph modestly replied:

" To God alone all merit should be ascribed. Neither I nor any other man are really adepts at interpreting dreams, but through my mouth God will announce pleasant tidings unto Pharaoh."

And a voice from Heaven exclaimed:

" Thou hast spoken well, Joseph, and as thou never didst manifest pride at thy knowledge, thou shalt be rewarded with greatness and the sovereignty over Egypt."

Pharaoh now began to narrate his dream to Joseph, but in order to test the youth's intelligence and his powers, he told only parts of his dream and not in such detail as he had really seen them. Inspired by the Divine Spirit, Joseph corrected the King's tale, supplementing the points omitted by the King, or adding the correct details of the dreams exactly as the King had seen them, so that the King was greatly amazed. Joseph then gave the King the true interpretation of the dreams that had visited him. Although greatly satisfied with Joseph's interpretation of his dreams, Pharaoh still had some doubts, and asked for a token which would finally convince him of Joseph's prophetic powers. This Joseph did, saying: " This, O King, will be a token of the truth and of the correctness of my words and of my interpretation: The Queen, thy wife, will this day give birth to a son, and thou wilt greatly rejoice, but soon after the birth of this thy youngest son, thy eldest son, born unto thee two years ago, will suddenly die, and thou wilt find consolation in the newly-born prince." Thus spoke Joseph, bowed to the King, and withdrew from his presence.

Scarcely had Joseph withdrawn from the royal presence, when the events he had foretold really occurred, so that Pharaoh was now completely convinced of the truth of the interpretation Joseph had given him. He was now quite sure that his dream indicated seven years of plenty, and seven years of famine, and exclaimed: " As Joseph has been present at my dreams, he shall be set over my house." He thereupon summoned into his presence all his servants, the princes of Egypt, the governors of provinces, and the grandees of his realm, and thus addressed them:

" Ye have all heard the words of the Hebrew. The signs he has given have been accomplished, and ye will now admit that his interpretation of my dreams is the correct one. Advise me now whether a man of wisdom and understanding such as the Hebrew can be found in the entire land. Ye have heard the advice of the Hebrew, and his plan by which the land of Egypt can be saved from the consequences of the famine which threatens us, and I myself feel convinced that his is the only true and correct one." Thus spoke the King, and his princes and grandees unanimously replied:

" Excellent indeed is the advice of the young Hebrew, and thou, O King, hast the power to act in the country as thou pleasest."

" If we traversed the whole earth from one end to the other," said the King, " we could never find a man who, like Joseph, has received from God the spirit of prophecy. If ye are not opposed to my decision, I will set Joseph over the land of Egypt, that he may save us from destruction by his wisdom."

But the astrologers and princes of Egypt raised an objection to the King's proposition: " Dost thou intend, O King," they said, " to set over us as our master one who is a slave, and who was bought for twenty pieces of silver?"

" He is not a slave," maintained the Pharaoh, " for I perceived in him the bearing and manner of a king."

To this the princes again replied that, even were it so, Joseph could not be set to rule over Egypt: " It is a law of our country that none can be king or even viceroy if he does not know all the seventy languages of men. How could this Hebrew serve as viceroy and rule over us, considering that he does not even speak the language of our land, knowing none but his own tongue which is Hebrew? Let the King therefore have the young Hebrew fetched to court and examined in all things, and then he may decide as it seemeth right to him."

The King agreed to the advice of his grandees, and, promising to give his decision on the following day, after examining Joseph, dismissed them.

Joseph had in the meantime returned to prison, for his master, fearing his wife and no longer trusting her, would not allow his servant to stay overnight in his house. During the night, Joseph was roused from his sleep by the angel Gabriel who had been sent by God to teach Joseph all the seventy languages of the world. At first the youth had some difficulty in learning all the languages so quickly, but when the angel Gabriel had added one of the letters of the *Tetragrammaton*, or the Divine name, namely, the letter *HE*, to Joseph's own name, calling him *Jehoseph*, the youth acquired the knowledge very quickly. Amazed at and overawed by the appearance of the divine messenger, Joseph went again to sleep until the morning, when he was once more awakened by the servants of the King who came to fetch him.

The next morning Joseph was brought into the presence of Pharaoh, surrounded by the princes of Egypt and the grandees of the realm. As Joseph knew all the seventy languages of the world, he ascended all the seventy steps of the throne until he reached the top, where he took his seat by the side of the King. Pharaoh and his nobles were greatly rejoiced to find that Joseph was really fit to occupy the high position of viceroy. Joseph's knowledge of Hebrew, however, caused the King some temporary embarrassment, for when the son of Jacob addressed the Pharaoh in the sacred tongue, the latter did not understand him.

" What is this language thou art speaking?" asked the ruler of Egypt."

" It is Hebrew, the sacred tongue," replied Joseph.

The King had to admit that he did not know Hebrew. He therefore said to Joseph: " If the princes of the realm and the people find out that I am ignorant of one language out of the seventy, and thus do not fulfil all the requirements needed by a King of Egypt, they may depose me. Swear therefore to me that thou wilt never reveal this secret to my people."

Joseph took a solemn oath never to betray the King and make known to the people that he only knew sixty-nine languages.

Thereupon the King thus addressed Joseph: " Thou didst advise me to set a wise man over the land of Egypt that he may by his wisdom save the country from the ravages of the famine which is threatening us. As I have found none wiser than thou, thou shalt henceforth be the viceroy of Egypt, and none but thou shall give me the kiss of homage. According to thy word only the princes will occupy their high positions at court, and according to thy commands my people shall go in and out, only in the throne will I be greater than thee."

The King then bestowed upon Joseph high distinctions, which were the rewards granted to him by the Lord for his virtue. The mouth that had refused the kiss of adultery received the kiss of homage from the people of Egypt; the body that would not participate in sin was clothed in garments of byssus; the neck that steadfastly refused to bow unto the unlawful was adorned with a golden chain; the hand that did not stretch out to touch sin received the royal signet ring which Pharaoh had taken off from his own finger; the feet that refused to hurry towards an alluring woman ascended the steps of the royal chariot; and the mind of Joseph which had not been defiled by sin was publicly proclaimed as wisdom. " Young in years, but old in wisdom", Pharaoh said of Joseph.[1]

" I am Pharaoh," said the King, " but thou art my second, and without thee none shall raise his hand to take up arms; without thee none shall put his foot in the stirrup of a horse in the whole land of Egypt."

Pharaoh called Joseph *Zaphnath Paaneah*, or the revealer of secret things, he who can bring to light secret things with ease and understanding and thus pacify the minds and hearts of men. The title Zaphnath Paaneah has also a symbolical meaning, for, as in the case of *Passim*, each letter has a separate meaning being the initial of a word. The letter " Z " stands for *Zopheh*, or seer; the letter " P " stands for *Podeh*, or redeemer; the letter " N " for *Nabi*, or prophet; the letter " T " for *Tomekh*, or supporter; the letter " P " for *Poter*, or interpreter of dreams; the letter " A " for *Arum*, or clever; the letter " N " for *Nabon*, or discerning, wise; and the letter " H " for *Haham*, or wise.

Joseph was also called the revealer of secret things, be-

[1] *Sepher Hajashar.*

cause he had discovered the secret of Asenath's history and of her parentage, and had taken her to wife. Asenath, the daughter of Dinah, and Shechem, the son of Hamor, whom an angel had brought to the borders of Egypt, was the adopted daughter of Potiphar, Joseph's master. Joseph discovered her identity in the following manner: When the newly appointed viceroy, riding in the royal chariot, was being conducted in a brilliant procession through the streets of the metropolis, all the noble women and maidens of Egypt, who had heard of Joseph's supernatural beauty, rushed to their windows and balconies to gaze upon the handsome son of Rachel. Enchanted by his great beauty, and anxious to attract his attention, they threw into his carriage their valuables, golden chains, jewels, and rings. Asenath alone, as it happened, had nothing upon her person which she could offer to the viceroy in token of her admiration. Quickly therefore she took off the amulet suspended upon her neck, the amulet upon which the story of her parentage was engraved, and which her grandfather Jacob had once fastened round her neck, and threw it at the viceroy's feet. The efforts of the noble ladies remained ineffectual, for Joseph never raised his eyes to gaze upon the alluring beauties of Egypt. But the amulet which fell at his feet attracted his attention, and upon reading the words engraved upon the gold plate, he discovered the identity of the damsel. And thus he discovered her who was also called *Setirah*, or the hidden one, for on account of her extraordinary beauty Asenath was kept concealed by her parents. It is also related that it was Asenath who had saved Joseph from the penalty of death which Potiphar was about to inflict upon his slave for his alleged outrage of his mistress. When Joseph was being flogged by Potiphar's servants, the child hurried to her foster-father and informed him that the lad was being accused wrongly, for he was innocent of any guilt.

At the command of the King, Joseph was conducted

through the streets of the city in solemn procession. He rode in the royal chariot accompanied by two thousand musicians, striking cymbals and blowing flutes. Five thousand men with drawn swords preceded the procession, whilst twenty thousand men of the King's grandees with gold-embroidered belts marched at the right, and so many at the left of Joseph. Women and maidens mounted the roofs and the city walls, and thronged the thoroughfares, all anxious to feast their eyes upon the supernatural beauty of the Viceroy and his handsome and noble appearance. Never did the Viceroy look at them, and as reward God ordained that no evil eye could ever hurt either Joseph or any of his descendants. All the royal servants, marching in front or behind the chariot wherein sat Joseph, burnt incense and cassia and all sorts of spices, and strewed the path with myrrh and aloes.

Twenty heralds proclaimed: " See, this is the man whom the King hath appointed to be his second, and all affairs of state shall be administered by him. Whoever acts against his commands and whoever refuseth to bow to and prostrate himself before the Viceroy shall be condemned to death as a rebel against the King and his representative."

When the people of Egypt heard this proclamation, they prostrated themselves before Joseph and called:

" Long live the King, and long live his Viceroy."

From his seat in the royal chariot, the son of Jacob raised his eyes to Heaven and prayed to the Lord of the Universe. " Lord of Hosts," he said, " blessed is the man who placeth his trust in Thee, for Thou dost raise up the poor out of the dust, and dost lift up the needy from the dunghill."

Thus Joseph journeyed through the whole country of Egypt, accompanied by Pharaoh's servants and the princes of his realm, viewing the whole land and all the King's treasures, and on his return once more appeared before the King.

Then the King gave his Viceroy royal presents: fields and

vineyards, and also 3000 *kikars* of silver and gold, and precious stones, and many other costly presents. The King also commanded that every Egyptian, under penalty of death, give Joseph a gift. A platform was therefore erected in the open street, and costly cloths were spread out wherein everyone deposited his gift. The Egyptians, anxious to obey the command of the King, and also to show their own admiration for Joseph, vied with one another in generosity. They deposited golden rings, brooches, armlets, coins, gold and silver vessels, and also precious stones. The princes, too, and all the servants of the King offered Joseph many gifts and honoured him greatly, when they saw that the King had appointed him to be his deputy. Pharaoh was anxious that the Viceroy should live in accordance with his new dignity. He therefore made him a present of one hundred slaves to serve him, and Joseph himself acquired many more.

Near the royal residence a sumptuous palace was built for Joseph which contained a vast hall of state. In this hall of state a magnificent throne was erected, fashioned of gold and silver, inlaid with precious stones and with a representation of the whole land of Egypt and of the River Nile watering the country. Thus Joseph, whom his brethren had sold into slavery, sat upon a throne and ruled over Egypt, and God increased his wisdom, so that the people of Egypt, the royal servants, and the princes of the realm loved and honoured him. The blessing of the Lord accompanied Joseph everywhere, and the fame of his greatness spread in the land of Egypt and travelled far and wide.

Joseph also equipped an army consisting of 4600 men, well armed and ready to do his bidding. He provided his soldiers with shields, spears, bucklers, helmets, and slings, so that they were well prepared to fight the King's battles against hostile nations. This army was increased by the princes of the realm, the royal servants and many of the inhabitants of the country, who were all ready to render a service unto their king, and to fight for him and for the country. Soon Joseph had an opportunity to make use of the army he had equipped in a war against the people of Tarshish.

In those days it came to pass that the people of Tarshish made war upon the Ishmaelites whom they conquered, taking possession of their territory. The Ishmaelites, few in number in those days, were unable to resist the invasion of the enemy, valiantly though they fought, and in their need sent a deputation to the King of Egypt, entreating him to come to their assistance: " Great King," the deputation said, " send thy servants and army led by the princes, and help us to repel the men of Tarshish who are invading our country and are threatening us with destruction."

The King thereupon sent out Joseph at the head of his army and a host of heroes, who marched into the land of Havilah to help the Ishmaelites against their enemies, the men of Tarshish. Joining forces with the Ishmaelites, Joseph won a splendid victory over the men of Tarshish, conquered their land, and settled it with the Ishmaelites who henceforth inhabited it.

As for the routed and defeated men of Tarshish, whose land had thus been conquered, they fled and took refuge in the territory of their brethren, the Greeks. Covered with glory, Joseph and his host of heroes returned to Egypt, and not a man had they lost in the fight.[1]

[1] See note 1, p. 77; see also Lewner, *loc. cit.*. pp. 219–227.

CHAPTER VII

The Story of Joseph and Zuleika in Arabic, Syriac, Persian, Sanscrit, and Mediæval European Literature

The story of Joseph and Zuleika in Moslem tradition—The story of the camel from Canaan—Joseph in love with his mistress—The faithful nurse—Zuleika's confession—The nurse's advice—The festival of the Nile—Zuleika's sickness—The enchantress—The sudden flight of the lover—The neighbour's gossip—The story of the ladies who cut their hands—The story of the Greek ambassador—A plot to assassinate Rajjan—The old Greek woman—Kamra, the chief butler, comes to fetch Joseph from prison—Joseph refuses to leave his dungeon before his innocence had been proved—The ladies of Egypt confess their guilt—Zuleika's excuse—The Viceroy and the beggar-woman—Joseph marries Zuleika—Firdusi's poem—Food from Paradise—The speaking wolf—Yusuf and Zuleika by Jami—Adam marvels at the beauty of Joseph—*Kathakautukam* by Crivara—Ephrem Syrus—The story of Joseph and Zuleika described by Christian authors—Potiphar's complaint—Joseph's magnanimity—The *Poema de Jose el Patriarca*—The *Leyendas*—The story of the ladies and the oranges in mediæval European literature—The story of Joseph in mediæval drama—Purim plays.

The story of Joseph, and more particularly the incident between the son of Rachel and the wife of Potiphar, is a favourite subject of many Oriental and European authors. Mohammed devotes one of the most beautiful suras in the Koran to the history of Joseph. The Arabic commentators have borrowed many incidents from Jewish sources, although Jewish authors have also copied many details in their description of Joseph and Zuleika from Arabic works. In Moslem tradition the love affair of Joseph and Zuleika is described as follows:

Zuleika, the wife of Potiphar, or Aziz, conceived a violent

love for the handsome Hebrew slave. She gave him new clothes, a separate garden house, where he could live, and appointed him to tend the fruit and the flowers.

One day an Ishmaelite leading a camel passed Potiphar's gate. Joseph happened to be standing at the gate and behold, when the camel approached, it crouched at his feet, and shed tears over his feet. Pull and drag the beast as he might, the owner failed to make it budge. Amazed at the strange conduct of the camel, Joseph examined the beast and recognized it as one of the camels belonging to his father, a camel to which he had often given bread. Upon inquiry, he learned from the Ishmaelite that he had bought the beast from Jacob in Canaan.

Moslem legend continues to relate that Joseph, the seventeen years old lad, had also fallen in love with his beautiful mistress, but durst not hope that his love would be reciprocated. Now, although Zuleika had loved Joseph from the very first moment she had set eyes on him, she kept her passion a secret and was quite contented to look at Joseph from her window, whilst he was busy in Potiphar's garden. Gradually, however, her love for the handsome slave became so violent that Zuleika grew ill and began to waste away. Pale and haggard looking, she walked about the house, and no one knew or even guessed the cause of the suffering which was undermining her health and the secret yearning which consumed her whole being. Many physicians did Potiphar consult, but none of them seemed to be able to cure the love-sick lady. One day, however, Zuleika's faithful nurse thus addressed her pale and sickly-looking mistress:

" Well do I know, my dear, that it is not thy body, but thy soul that is in great pain. Confess the truth to thy faithful nurse, O Zuleika, and tell her the cause of thy secret grief which is gnawing at thy heart, undermining thy health and driving away the bloom of youth from thy cheeks. Confess, my dear, to thy nurse who has nurtured thee with her milk and taken the place of a mother since thy infancy."

Thus spoke the shrewd old nurse, and Zuleika was glad of being at last able to confide in a loving human being, and find some consolation in her suffering. Weeping bitterly, she threw herself into the arms of her faithful old nurse and told her the cause of her secret passion and suffering.

" For six long weary years," she sobbed, " have I loved the handsome Joseph, and for six years have I endeavoured and made vain efforts to conquer this love and eradicate from my heart the passion which is consuming me."

" Be of good cheer, my dear," said the old nurse. " Thou hast done thy best and fought valiantly against this passion, but considering that thy husband is old and feeble thou shouldst be excused for loving the handsome Hebrew. None of thy sex would have waited so long or tried so valiantly to conquer her passion. Now take care of thyself, try to regain thy health and beauty; eat and drink, and dress with care, as thou didst before. Joseph cannot but love thee when he sees thee in all thy alluring beauty. Besides," shrewdly added the old Egyptian, " he is thy slave and used to obey thy commands."

Zuleika felt her courage and hope revive. She followed the advice of her nurse, and soon she once more looked healthy and well, having regained all her former beauty and charm of person. She now only waited for an opportunity when she would find herself alone with Joseph who could surely not remain blind to her charms.

Now, one day, Zuleika's nurse came in and thus spoke to the wife of Potiphar: " To-morrow, my child, is the great festival of the Nile, on which all Egyptians, without distinction of sex, age, or rank, are visiting the temple. Pretend to-night that thou art sick, so that thou mayest remain at home to-morrow. Thou wilt thus be alone in the house with thy beloved

Joseph who, as a Hebrew, will take no part in our festival. Thou wilt then have the longed-for opportunity to reveal unto Joseph that thy heart is full of love for him. Beautiful and alluring as thou art, he will not resist thee."

Zuleika acted as her nurse had advised her, and the next day, when the house was empty, she invited her handsome slave into her private room. Now Joseph loved Zuleika as much as she loved him, for she was exceedingly beautiful, but in his modesty, and remembering his position, that of a slave to a noble and wealthy lady, he never dared to raise his eyes to Zuleika. When, therefore, on the day of the great festival, Potiphar and the entire household had gone to the banks of the Nile, and Zuleika invited Joseph to her private room, he joyfully obeyed his mistress's command.

Zuleika served wine and fruit, and invited the handsome youth to partake of the refreshments. Seated upon a soft couch, covered with silken cushions, sipping sweet wine, the Egyptian lady hinted at last to her slave that he had only to stretch out his arms for her to fall into them. The eyes of his mistress were shining with love and passion, and Joseph was rejoiced when he saw that his love was being reciprocated. Forgetting the fact that his lady-love was a married woman, and that it was a sin for the son of Jacob and of Rachel to love her, he was about to take her into his arms and to press her to his breast. Suddenly, however, Joseph drew back, to the astonishment and annoyance of the lady. He was brought to his senses by the sudden appearance of the image of his father. The love-sick youth saw his father standing in the door and warningly and reproachfully shaking his finger at him. Hastily, Joseph arose and rushed towards the door. Amazed at his sudden flight, Zuleika tried to detain him.

"Why this sudden haste, beloved of my heart," she cried, "why art thou growing so deathly pale? There is no one in the house and we are safe from detection."

" Never," replied Joseph, " will I commit a sin against my God and against my master."

Zuleika, her passion aroused, would not let Joseph go and tried to detain him by force. She subsequently brought false accusations against Joseph. He was mercilessly flogged by the outraged husband's servants, but was saved by the miraculous interference of an infant in its cradle which had witnessed the scene. One of Zuleika's neighbours, however, who, on account of sickness, had stayed at home instead of attending the festival of the Nile, had also seen all that had taken place, and naturally gossiped. Zuleika's conduct soon became common talk, and all the ladies of Egypt, in their virtuous indignation, blamed their beautiful and passionate friend. They blamed her guilty love, but more perhaps her subsequent hatred of the youth who had virtuously opposed her. It was only when Zuleika became aware of the town talk and of friends' gossip and criticism that she invited the ladies to a feast with a view to giving them a lesson. She would show them that no noble lady of Egypt could remain indifferent to the supernatural beauty of the son of Rachel. It was at that banquet that she placed the oranges before the beauties of Egypt who, absorbed in the contemplation of the handsome slave, cut their hands and deluged the table and their own dresses with blood.

" This is the handsome and steadfast youth," said Zuleika, " on whose account I have become the talk of the town and am criticized so severely by you. You see now that none of you, my friends, could help being amazed at and enchanted by his extraordinary and superhuman beauty. But, though I had loved him passionately before, he has hurt my woman's pride, and my love has turned to hate." And thus Joseph, although innocent, was cast into prison. The Lord, however, was with him, and his cell was illumined with a celestial light, whilst a fountain did spring up

in the midst of it, and a fruit-bearing tree grew before the
door.

Joseph had not been long in prison, when he was already
well known and highly esteemed for his cleverness, his wisdom
and his great ability in interpreting dreams.

And now it came to pass that in those days the King of
Greece, who was waging war against the King of Egypt, sent
a deputation to Rajjan, then Pharaoh of Egypt, with peace
proposals. Officially, the Greek ambassador was supposed to
have come for the purpose of concluding an honourable peace,
but secretly he hoped to be able to find an opportunity how
to assassinate the heroic King of Egypt. The Greek ambassador
addressed himself to an old Greek woman who had lived for
many years in Egypt, and asked her advice.

" I know of no other way," said the woman, " of carrying
out thy plan, and of realizing the purpose thou hast come
for, than that of bribing the chief butler or the cook of
the King, paying them a large sum so that they poison the
King."

The Greek ambassador was well pleased with the advice of
the old woman, and acted accordingly. He made the acquaintance of both the royal butler and the royal baker, and bribed
them with much money. At last he persuaded the baker to put
poison in Pharaoh's bread. The ambassador then went to
inform the old Greek woman that he had succeeded in his plan.
But when he came to see her before his departure she was not
alone, and he therefore could not tell her openly what he had
accomplished. He simply said that he was well satisfied with
his work in Egypt, as he had been very successful and had
obtained the object he had come for.

These words were soon reported to Pharaoh, and, as they
could not refer to the ambassador's peace negotiations which
had been broken off, Pharaoh suspected that the Greek ambassador must have had some secret business in Egypt. The

old Greek woman was sent for and questioned, and at last, under torture, she confessed the truth.

" Either the royal butler or the royal baker," she said, " has been bribed to poison the King."

Both officials were therefore cast into prison, pending a minute inquiry. In dungeon, the chief butler and chief baker made the acquaintance of Joseph who interpreted their dreams. Seven years after his liberation, the butler came to fetch Joseph to Pharaoh who had dreamed a strange dream and was greatly troubled. But Joseph, who had remained in prison another seven years, because Zuleika's friends had also lodged complaints against him, and, in order to support their friend, had pretended that the Hebrew had been annoying them, refused to leave his dungeon before his innocence had been proved. He informed the butler, whose name was Kamra, of what had occurred and how, though innocent of guilt, he had been cast into prison.

" The wife of my master," he said, " had confessed her wanton passion to her friends, making no secret of it. At a banquet to which she had invited all the noble ladies, whose names I can mention, she had confessed that she loved me. These ladies the King may call as witnesses, if he wishes to prove me innocent before I appear in his presence."

Thus spoke Joseph, and Kamra, the chief butler, hastened to the King and informed him of Joseph's reply. At the command of Pharaoh, Zuleika and all the ladies of Egypt who had attended her banquet were brought to court, and they confessed that they had indeed slandered Joseph. Zuleika herself fell upon her knees and confessed to the King that in her annoyance and vexation, because Joseph had rejected her love and taken no heed of her great passion, she had calumniated him and caused him to be cast into prison.

" My great love for him," she concluded, " is my only excuse."

The King thereupon sent a royal messenger to Joseph, informing him that his sentence was quashed and that he was free. Pharaoh moreover gave Joseph a document bearing the royal seal, wherein it was declared that the youth had been falsely accused and wrongly detained in dungeon.

Joseph now arrayed himself in the garments King Rajjan had sent him and betook himself to the royal palace, where the King, surrounded by his magnates and the princes of his realm, sat upon his throne. Well pleased with Joseph's interpretation of his dream, the King appointed Joseph to be his chief treasurer and manager of all his estates in the place of Potiphar, Joseph's former master. It was now Joseph's business to travel all over the country and to purchase all the corn which, on account of the superabundant harvest, could be had at a very low price, and to store it away in storehouses especially built for the purpose.

Now one day, when Joseph was riding out to view one of his magazines situated at some distance from the city, he noticed a beggar woman whose whole appearance was very miserable. The chief treasurer, moved to compassion, approached the beggar woman, and soon noticed that in spite of her present position, she still bore traces of former greatness and must have seen better days. He held out a handful of golden coins, and was surprised to notice the woman's hesitation to accept his gift.

Sobbing loudly, the woman said: " Great prophet of God! I am not worthy to receive thy gift! And yet, it was my fault and transgression which served thee as the ladder upon which thou didst ascend to thy present happy position." Amazed, Joseph looked more closely at the beggar and recognized in her his former mistress, Zuleika, the wife of Potiphar, who had loved him passionately and in her fury at being rejected had caused him to be cast into prison. Joseph inquired after Potiphar, and learned from Zuleika that after his loss of office her husband had suffered greatly and died in poverty and distress. She further told him that Potiphar had never been anything to her but a husband in name, and that she had been his wife only in so far that she had borne his name. When Joseph heard these words, he raised Zuleika and brought her to the house of a relative of the King, where she was treated well and taken care of as if she were his sister. Joseph had always loved Zuleika and only rejected her love because she was a married woman and he would not commit a sin.

Soon Zuleika regained her former beauty, and Joseph, with the permission of the King, took her to wife.[1]

In his religious-romantic poem *Yusuf and Zulaikha*, the Persian poet Firdusi, who is better known as the author of the *Shahnameh*, describes the love of Joseph and Zuleika and the entire history of Joseph. The poem begins with the acquisition of the birth-right by Jacob, his demand for the hand of Rachel, and ends with the death of Joseph in Egypt. The poet describes the scene of the sale of Joseph, how he is cast into the well, where he is received by the angel Gabriel, so that he is not hurt in his fall. The angel provided the lad with food from Paradise, and clothed him in a celestial garment. The poet further describes Jacob's lament and the legend concerning the speaking wolf. Jacob, who had examined the garment and noticed that it had not been torn, had expressed his doubts as to the truth of the story his sons had told him. They, therefore, pretended that they had caught the wolf who had devoured Joseph.

During his journey to Egypt, Joseph passes Ephrath where Rachel lies buried, and slipping away from his masters, he throws himself upon the grave of his mother, weeping and lamenting.

[1] Weil, *Biblische Legenden der Muselmänner*, 1845, pp. 115–126; Geiger, *Was hat Mohammed aus dem Judentum genommen*, 1833; Grünbaum, in *Z.D.M.G.*, Vol. XLIII, p. 1 *et seq.*; see also T. Schapiro, *Die haggadischen Elemente im erzählenden Teil des Korans*, Leipzig, 1907, pp. 33–53.

The love affair of Joseph and Zuleika is described with many details, mostly following Moslem tradition. The story of the ladies of Egypt who cut their hands whilst peeling the oranges is not omitted. Many elements from the Haggada are also interwoven in Firdusi's poem, although these incidents in Jewish legendary lore may have been borrowed by Jewish writers themselves from Arabic sources.[1]

Another Persian poem dealing with the history of Joseph is that of Jami, entitled *Yusuf and Zulaikha*. Jami relates how Adam saw in a dream all his posterity pass before him. In the long procession he noticed Joseph, at the side of whom beauty faded and the stars grew dim. Marvelling greatly at the glorious beauty of this his descendant, he asked the Lord who this radiant apparition might be, so perfect in beauty. A voice from Heaven informed Adam that this was Joseph, the son of Jacob, whose loveliness will excite the envy of everyone. Our first parent was then ordered to bestow upon this beautiful " fair gazelle " all the natural and supernatural gifts which the Lord had granted him. Adam thereupon bestowed upon Joseph beauty and charm and also strength to keep him pure in the face of temptation.[2]

A Sanscrit poem by Crivara, entitled *Kathakautukam*, based upon the work of Jami, also relates the history of Joseph and Zuleika.[3]

With regard to Joseph's treatment of his master, Ephrem Syrus relates the following incident: When Potiphar, Joseph's former master, heard and saw to what high dignity his slave had been raised by the King, and what honour he was enjoying, he came home and thus addressed his wife: " Joseph who was once our slave is now our ruler and master; he to whom we gave his raiment is now dressed in purple by Pharaoh; he

[1] Firdusi, *Yusuf and Zulaikha*, translated into German by Schlechta Wssehrd; see also *Z.D.M.G.*, Vol. XLI, p. 578.
[2] Translated into English by Ralph T. H. Griffith (Trübner's Oriental Series) 1882.
[3] Translated into German by Richard Schmidt, 1898.

whom we had driven out of our house is now riding in the royal chariot, wearing a crown upon his head instead of iron chains."

Thus spoke Potiphar, but his wife replied: " It is true that I loved Joseph, dazzled and enchanted as I was by his extraordinary beauty, and out of love for him I treated him unjustly. And yet, he owes his present greatness to us, for without us he would never have attained such high honours." When Potiphar subsequently appeared before Joseph, the latter forgave his former master his harsh treatment, for he knew that such had been the will of the Lord.[1]

Some of the Christian authors tell the story of Joseph and Zuleika as follows: Zuleika had fallen in love with the son of Rachel, and offered to poison her husband so that she could be married legally to Joseph. " As a rule," she said, " men make love to women, but thou, being my slave, durst not open thy lips to speak to me. And so I have condescended to reveal unto thee the secret of my heart." When Joseph rejected her love, she exclaimed: " Great is thy beauty, but small thy understanding, for whilst everyone is anxious to be free, thou art content to remain a slave. If thou wilt hearken unto my words, thou wilt be free and happy. Thou wilt be the master, and I thy maidservant. If thou art afraid to commit a sin lest thy God punish thee, then take gold and silver and distribute it among the poor as an atonement for thy sin." Joseph refused, and was cast into prison. When Potiphar heard what high post his former slave was occupying at the court of Egypt, he was greatly afraid. Bitterly did he reproach his wife for her conduct, for he was now convinced that it was Zuleika who had conceived a wanton passion for Joseph and accused him falsely.

" Thou hast put me to shame before the King and before his magnates," he said. " Joseph, who was our slave and whom

[1] See Grünbaum in *Z.D.M.G.*, Vol. XLIII.

in consequence of thy wanton passion I had cast into prison, is now father and ruler at the court of Pharaoh. How shall I now dare stand before him and look up to him. I knew from the very first that he was no slave, but a free-born man and therefore I appointed him steward over my house. Joseph had never committed any sin, but thou, in thy wanton mind, didst cast an eye upon him, desiring his beauty."

But Potiphar's fears were unfounded, for in his magnanimity Joseph harboured no illfeeling towards his former master and his wife. He sent them presents and splendid raiment, and invited them to court. Arrayed in the costly garments Joseph had sent them, Potiphar and his wife hastened to court to Joseph, who received them very graciously.[1]

In a poem which Ticknor discovered in the National Library at Madrid, written in Arabic characters, but composed in Spanish, the history of Joseph is told with many legendary additions. The poem, called *Poema de Jose el Patriarca*, begins with a description of the jealousy of the brothers of Joseph at his dreams, and describes in full the love of the fair Zuleika, " who fills a space more ample than usual in the fancies of the present poem ". The scene of Joseph's lamentation at his mother's grave is also described, varying from the description given in Jewish and Arabic sources, and so is the incident of the speaking wolf brought by the brethren as the animal that had killed Joseph. In the description of Zuleika's passion for Joseph, the story of the ladies of Memphis, who were so enraptured with the lad's beauty that they cut their fingers whilst peeling their oranges, is not omitted.[2]

Yusuf and Zuleika, the Moslem Song of Songs of Love, is also the subject of a Spanish Arabic work called *Leyendas*, written in Arabic characters and in the language of the Mori-

[1] M. Weinberg, *Die Geschichte Joseph's von Basilius dem Grossen aus Cäsarea*, Halle, 1893, pp. 34–35.
[2] Ticknor, *History of Spanish Literature*, New York, 1849, Vol. III, pp. 433–458, and Vol. I, pp. 95–99; R. Kœhler, *Kleinere Schriften*, Berlin, 1900, Vol. II, p. 82; Grünbaum, *Z.D.M.G.*, Vol. XLIII, pp. 27–28.

scoes.[1] The contents resemble greatly those of the Moslem tradition and the poem of Firdusi.

The incident of the ladies of Memphis cutting their hands whilst peeling their oranges has passed not only into oriental but also into mediæval European literature. We have referred to the poem of Firdusi, *Yusuf and Zulaikha*, to Jami's *Yusuf and Zulaikha*, and to Crivara's *Kathakautukam*.

With regard to mediæval European literature, the incident is borrowed in *Olivier de Castille et Arthus d'Algarbe*, and in the *Romance of Blonde of Oxford and Jehan of Dammartin*, by Philippe de Reimes, a trouvère of the thirteenth century. It is also found in the German poem, *Spruch von aim Konig mit Namen Ezel*, and also in a Russian song about Eupraxia, wife of Vladimir.

The difference between Orient and Occident is interesting. Whilst in the Hebrew works, in the *Midrash Tanchuma*, the *Midrash Haggadol*, and the *Sepher Hajashar*, in the Persian poems and in the Koran, it is the ladies who are so absorbed in the contemplation of the beauty of the Hebrew slave that they cut their fingers, unaware that their blood is soiling their garments, in the mediæval poems it is the man who cuts his finger, absorbed as he is in the contemplation of his beloved. The Russian song, on the other hand, is oriental in its conception, and here, too, it is the lady who is casting glances of love upon the handsome hero.

In the romance of Olivier the story runs as follows: Olivier of Castille was in the service of Princess Helen of England, occupying the post of *premier écuyer tranchant*. He fell violently in love with the princess, and one day, whilst serving at table, he was so absorbed in the contemplation of the lady's beauty that he cut his thumb: " Elle n'avoit rien devant soi de tranché pour manger, pour ce lui dit-elle: Olivier, mon loyal ami, si mangerois-je bien si vous me donniez de quoi; et lui, tout honteux, commença à la servir: mais comme celui-ci n'avoit pas son entendement bien présent, il se coupa le pouce presque tout jusqu'à l'os ".[1]

A similar story is told of Jehan of Dammartin who was in the service of the Count of Oxford, and fell violently in love with the earl's daughter Blonde. One day, whilst waiting at table, he is so absorbed in the contemplation of Blonde's beauty that he cuts his finger.[2]

In German literature the incident is related of King Ezel. At the palace of King Ezel a beautiful maid once appeared, whilst the King and his heroes were at table. All were so enchanted by the extraordinary beauty of the maid that they cut their fingers instead of their meat.[3]

In the Russian song, on the contrary, it is Eupraxia, wife of Vladimir, who is so struck by the handsome appearance of Tshurillo that she can hardly take her eyes off him. Absorbed in the contemplation of the hero's beauty, the lady cuts her hand, like the ladies of Memphis. Turning to her women, she then said: " Wonder not that I have cut my hand, I am losing my head, and my senses are disturbed as soon as I perceive the handsome Tshurillo." [4] At his sight, " her reason grew dark and dim, and madness possessed her for the love of him ".

The history of Joseph is also the subject of numerous dramatic works. During the Middle Ages, religious subjects were dramatized in Spain, France, and England, and one of the most favourable themes was the history of Joseph, wherein many elements from the Haggada were interwoven.

In the *Mistère du Viel Testament* [5] which appeared towards the end of the fifteenth century, the history of Joseph is treated fully, and many incidents directly remind us of the legendary

[1] See Kœhler, *loc. cit.*, p. 80.
[2] Edited by Leroux Lincy, and printed for the Camden Society in 1858; see also Kœhler, *loc. cit.*, p. 84.
[3] *Erzählungen aus altdeutschen Handschriften*, Gesammelt durch Adelbert von Keller.
[4] A. Rambaud, *La Russie Epique*, Paris, 1876, p. 97.
[5] Edited by J. de Rothschild, Paris, 1881.

history of Joseph as related in Talmud and Midrash. As in the Jewish legend, Potiphar's wife excuses herself from attending the public festival to which the entire household went. She thus has the longed-for opportunity of remaining alone in the house with Joseph. Whilst, however, according to the Haggada, it was the annual festival of the Nile, in the *Mistère du Viel Testament*, the occasion is a public festival in honour of the King, on the occasion of his miraculous escape, for the chief baker and the chief butler had planned to poison him. In the majority of mediæval passion-plays a parallel is drawn between Joseph, the just and pious, and the person of the Saviour. Besides the passion-plays,[1] there are also independent dramatic productions, some of them even written in the dialect called Yiddish (Jewish jargon). One of these plays, which were produced at the *Purim* festival, is reproduced by Schudt,[2] and another by Ave Lallemant, in his great work *Das deutsche Gaunertum* (Vol. III, p. 491). These plays were acted by strolling players, going from house to house, on the festival called *Purim*, the day on which, according to the *Book of Esther*, the Jews were saved from the plot of Haman.[3]

In the majority of cases, the play, enacted on that day, was a dramatic production containing the history of Esther, but the drama of the sale and greatness of Joseph was also frequently played. It may be remarked, *en passant*, that Goethe wrote a Joseph drama in his youth.[4] In the majority of the dramas composed on the history of Joseph during the sixteenth century, the lady endeavouring to win the love of Joseph is called Zenobia,[5] Berenica, Moscha, or Seraphim, but never Zuleika. There also exists a Hebrew drama entitled *Joseph and Asenath*, by Susskind Raschkow (1817), and Joseph is the subject of a novel by Grimelshausen.

[1] Weilen, *Der aegyptische Joseph im Drama des 16ten Jahrhunderts*, Wien, 1887.
[2] *Jüdische Merkwürdigkeiten*.
[3] See also Landau, *Hebrew-German Romances and Tales*, in *Teutonia*, Heft 21, Leipzig, 1912, p. xxx.
[4] Weilen, *loc. cit.*, p. 189.   [5] Cassel, *Mischle Sindbad*, pp. 23–24.

THE LADIES OF EGYPT

(30) And certain women said publicly in the city, The noble-
man's wife asked her servant to lie with her; he hath inflamed her
breast with his love; and we perceive her to be in manifest error.
(31) And when she heard of their subtle behaviour, she sent unto
them and prepared a banquet for them, and she gave to each of them
a knife; and she said unto Joseph, Come forth unto them. And when
they saw him they praised him greatly, and they cut their own hands,
and said, O God! this is not a mortal; he is no other than an angel,
deserving the highest respect.

The Koran (Sale's translation), *Sura*, 12.

THE WOMEN OF MEMPHIS AND THE ORANGES

Like a bed of roses in perfect bloom
That secret treasure appeared in the room.
The women of Memphis beheld him, and took,
From that garden of glory, the rose of a look.

One glance at his beauty o'erpowered each soul,
And drew from their fingers the reins of control.
Each lady would cut through the orange she held,
As she gazed on that beauty unparalleled.
But she wounded her finger, so moved in her heart,
That she knew not her hand and the orange part.

One made a pen of her finger to write
On her soul his name who had ravished her sight.
A reed which, struck with the point of the knife,
Poured out a red flood from each joint in the strife.

One scored a calendar's line in red,
On the silver sheet of her palm outspread,
And each column, marked with the blood drops, showed,
Like a brook when the stream o'er the bank has flowed.

When they saw youth in his beauty's pride,
" No mortal is he," in amazement they cried,

" No clay and water composed his frame,
But, a holy angel, from heaven he came."

Yusuf and Zulaikha, a poem by Jami, translated by Ralph
  T. H. Griffith (Trübner's Oriental Series), London, 1882
  (p. 229).

THE SERVANT AND HIS MISTRESS

LA DAME

Or ne sçay je par quelle voye
De son amour Joseph tempter,
De peur que esconduite ne soye;
C'est cella qui me faict doubter
S'il me veult de luy debouter,
Et, on le sçait, je suis infame.
D'autre part, c'est honte que femme
Prie l'homme de villenie,
Principallement une dame
Comme moy; je suis esbahye,
Je considère ma follye,
Mais, bref, amour me contrainct tant
Qu'il sera force que je prie
Joseph pour estre mon amant,
Et le prieray que en ce dormant
Avecques moy seulement couche.

PUTIPHAR

Veez cy jour solemnel et hault
Que tout s'esbat et se delicte
Selon la manière d'Egipte;
Mesmement ad ce jour les dames
Viennent avecques autres femmes
Pour la feste solemnizer,
Et pour tant je vueil adviser
Ma femme de ce mettre a point,
Affin qu'elle n'y faille point
Plus que les autres de la terre.

LA DAME

Amour, tant tu me fais de guerre,
Amour, tant tu me maine grief,
Amour, tant tu me tiens en serre,
Se je ne jouys de Joseph!
J'é le cueur aussi froid que nef,
Aucunes fois, et, l'autre, ardant
Comme feu en le regardant,
Tant suis de son amour esprise.

PUTIPHAR

M'amye, ma femme, je advise
Que au jour d'huy la solemnité
Se faict en la communité;
Preparez vous honnestement
Pour venir a l'esbatement
Et y veoir les choses nouvelles,
Comme les autres damoyselles
Qui y prendront plaisir et joye.

LA DAME

Mon amy, voulentiers je iroye;
Mais, je vous pry, ne vous desplaise
Reposer vueil, mais qu'il vous plaise
Tant que les esbas on fera.

PUTIPHAR

Faictes ainsi qu'il vous plaira,
Car ce n'est pas ma voulenté
Que ne gardez vostre santé
Plus que autre femme naturelle.

LA DAME

Il m'est pris une douleur telle
Que je ne le puis exposer.

PUTIPHAR

Je vous lesse donc reposer,
Et vois a la solemnité.

Le Mistère du Viel Testament, Ed. by J. de Rothschild, Paris,
1881, Tome III, pp. 67–69, v. 18732–18789.

JOSEPH'S PRAYER

Vray Dieu puissant, souverain roy des roys,
De qui je vueil garder les sainctes loix
Sans fraction, et le commandement,
La mauvaistié de ceste femme vois;
Preserve moy et garde en touz endroiz
De luy donner aucun consentement.
Je congnois bien son faulx entendement,
Son fol desir, son villain pensement,
Ou, se Dieu plaist, je ne m'accorderay.
S'elle me veult donner empeschement,
Elle ne peult, sinon tant seulement
De mon manteau qui luy est demouré.
  S'on me faict mal, j'endureray;
  S'on me tance, je me tairay;
  S'on me impose vice ne blasme,
  Tant doulcement m'excuseray,
  Et a tesmoing appelleray
  Dieu qui gard mon corps et mon ame.

Ibid., pp. 73–74, v. 18897–18914.

BLONDE OF OXFORD

Blonde, qui si le voit penser,
De cel penser le veut tenser;
Si li dist que il pense tost,
Mais il ne l'entent pas si tost.
Puis li redist: " Jehan, trenchiés!
Dormés-vous chi, ou vous songiés?

S'il vous plaist, donés m'à mengier;
Ne ne welliés or plus songier."
A cel mot Jehans l'entendi;
S'est tressalis tout autressi
Com cil qui en soursaut s'esveille.
De s'aventure s'esmerveille.
Tous abaubis tint son contel,
Et qui da trenchier bien et bel;
Mais de penser est si destrois
Que il s'est trenciés en ij dois;
Si sans en saut et il se liève.

Blonde of Oxford and Jehan of Dammartin, by Philippe de Reimes (see Kœhler, *loc. cit.*, pp. 84-85).

CHAPTER VIII

The Romance of Asenath, or the Marriage of the Viceroy

Asenath supposed to have been the daughter of Dinah and Hamor—
Joseph and Asenath, a novel of the Middle Ages—The journey of the Viceroy—The proud beauty—Fit to be queen of Egypt—The son of a Canaanitish herdsman—The damsel at the window of her palace—Asenath's
regret—The proud virgin who never looked at men—The humble salute—
A kiss refused—The blessing of a brother—The disappointment of the
maid—Asenath's conversion—Sackcloth and ashes—The visit of the angel
—The city of refuge—Honey from Paradise—The seven virgins—Eleven
columns of the city of refuge—The fiery chariot—The arrival of the Viceroy
—The kiss of betrothal—" Let me wash thy feet, my lord "—The overjoyed parents—Marriage postponed—The royal gift—A seven days feast.

Joseph is said in *Genesis* to have married Asenath, daughter
of Potiphera, priest of On. Legend was busy inventing incidents which would whitewash the son of Rachel from the sin
of having married a heathen. Asenath, therefore, is represented
as the daughter of Dinah, and consequently Joseph's niece,
whose identity he had discovered.

Legend relates that Asenath, the daughter of Dinah and
Shechem, was deposited at the frontier of Egypt by the angel
Gabriel (or Michael), carried there by a flood, or brought to
the borders of the country by a travelling caravan. Here she
was adopted by Potiphera, and subsequently married Joseph.[1]
This legend is also repeated by certain Syriac authors, whilst
it is criticized by Samaritan and Caraite writers.[2]

---

[1] *Midrash Abkhir*, quoted in *Yalkut, Genesis*, § 146; *Pirke de Rabbi Eliezer*, Ch. 38; Trac-
tate *Soferim*, 21, 8; see also *Revue des Etudes Juives*, Vol. XXI, pp. 87–92.
[2] See Payne Smith, *Thesaurus, s.v. Dinah*.

According to Moslem tradition, Joseph married, by command of the King, Zuleika, the wife of his former master, who was now a widow. (See D'Herbelot, *Bibliothèque Orientale*, *s.v. Yussuf*.)

Another version of the story of the viceroy's marriage to Asenath is contained in an apocryphal work called *Joseph and Asenath*, a novel well known during the Middle Ages.[1] The romantic story of Joseph's love and marriage runs as follows:

In the course of the second year of Joseph's rule in Egypt, his prophecies were confirmed, for the seven years of plenty, even as the new Viceroy had foretold, began. God had ordained that the famine which was to visit Egypt should last fourteen years, but Joseph had prayed to the Lord and his prayer was heard, so that the fourteen years were reduced to seven. During the years of plenty, the Viceroy gathered up all the grain in the country, laying up the produce of each district in the city situated in the middle of the district. He ordered that ashes and earth from the very soil on which the corn had grown be strewn on the collected grain to be preserved. These precautions were taken in order to preserve the food from rot. For the purpose of garnering food, collecting the produce and preserving it against the need of the years of famine, Joseph frequently journeyed through the land of Egypt, visiting many cities. It was during one of these journeys that he met and married his wife Asenath.

Asenath was the proud daughter of Potiphera, the mighty prince and priest of Heliopolis and a counsellor of Pharaoh. She excelled in beauty all the comely maidens of Egypt whom she did not resemble. She was more like Sarah, Rebekah, and Rachel, being tall like Sarah, comely like Rebekah, and

---

[1] *Life and Confession*, or *Prayer of Asenath*, published (Greek and Latin) by P. Batiffol, in *Studia Patristica*, Paris, 1889–1890; see also Oppenheim, *Fabula Josephi et Asenathae Apocrypha*, Berlin, 1886—Fragments of this novel appeared in Fabricius, *Codex Pseudo-epigraphicus Vet. Test.*, II, 85–102, and an abridged Latin translation was published by Vincent de Beauvais in his *Speculum Historiale*, Ch. 118–124. See also the article in *Jewish Encyclopedia*, *s.v. Asenath*.

beautiful like Rachel. The fame of her beauty spread far and wide, and many were her admirers and suitors for her hand. But Asenath disdained them all. A proud beauty, reared in luxury, she inhabited a magnificent castle where she was waited upon by seven virgins. Brought up in the religion of Egypt, she worshipped innumerable idols, whose golden and silver images filled her rooms, and whose names were engraven upon the gems of her necklace.

The offers of all the suitors for her hand she disdainfully refused, for only the son of Pharaoh would she marry. The King, however, forbade this union. Potiphera, too, was rather in favour of his daughter marrying Joseph, the Viceroy of Egypt, the mighty man of God. When Potiphera expressed his wish that his daughter should marry the mighty man of God, as he called Joseph, who would soon honour him with a visit, Asenath scornfully replied:

" I am fit to be the wife of the son of Pharaoh and sit on the throne of Egypt. How canst thou expect me to marry a former slave, the son of a shepherd in Canaan?"

Thus spoke Asenath in her indignation. But she knew not Joseph and had never contemplated his divine beauty, which made all the ladies of Egypt fall in love with him.

Now it happened that in the first year of plenty Joseph was journeying through Egypt to collect corn. He was expected to visit also Heliopolis, and he sent word to Potiphera that he would put up at his house. Potiphera was very glad at this, for he now hoped to be able to arrange a marriage between Joseph and his daughter Asenath.

But when he informed his daughter of the visit of the Viceroy, telling her that it would be his dearest wish to see her become Joseph's wife, the girl once more scornfully refused to entertain such a proposal, as it was only the King's son she would marry.

The next day Joseph arrived, seated in the royal chariot, all of gold, and drawn by four snow-white horses. He was radiantly beautiful, dressed in a magnificent tunic with gold embroidery, and from his shoulders hung a crimson robe woven with gold. A circlet of gold was round his temples, and he carried an olive branch in his hand. No lady of Egypt could see Joseph and remain indifferent, for no woman had ever given birth to a son who could be compared to the son of Rachel, the radiantly beautiful, or, as the Egyptian ladies called him, the son of God. Joseph was received by Potiphera and his wife in the hall of state, and they paid him due homage.

Although Asenath had spoken angry words of Joseph, and scornfully refused to listen to her father's proposal, her feminine curiosity nevertheless made her look out of her window when the Viceroy arrived. When she beheld the ruler of Egypt, she bitterly regretted her harsh words.

" He is not a slave," she said, " nor is he the son of a shepherd, but the son of God, for only the son of God could be so radiantly beautiful."

Bitterly did Asenath now regret her scorn of Joseph. Ah, how gladly would she now consent to marry him whom she had so disdainfully called a slave, if he would only consent to take her to wife. Not his wife, but his slave and handmaiden would she be only to be near his enchanting personality. Thus mused Asenath, looking out of the window of her apartments, unable to turn her eyes away from the glorious and radiant son of Rachel.

Joseph, in the meantime, had noticed the proud beauty looking out of the window, and he requested Potiphera that she be ordered away, for he did not permit women to look at him so insistently. The Viceroy was indeed weary of the advances of the Egyptian ladies who constantly pursued him and gave him no respite.

" My lord," said Potiphera, the priest of On, " this is my daughter, a proud virgin who never looks at men and keeps aloof from them. She is very modest and retiring, and until this day she hath seen no man save myself, for she dwells in her own apartment, waited upon by seven virgins. If it please thee, my lord," added Potiphera, " she shall come down and salute thee."

When Joseph heard that Asenath hated the sight of men, he asked Potiphera to have her brought down, so that he might treat her as his sister. Quickly did the proud Asenath now obey her father's request, and hurried down into the hall of state to salute him whom she had only recently called a contemptible slave. She came down and greeted the son of Jacob with the words:

" Hail, my lord, blessed of the most High God."

And Joseph replied:

" May the Lord who vivifies all bless thee." Thereupon Potiphera bade his daughter kiss Joseph.

" Go, my daughter," he said, " and kiss thy brother."

Asenath advanced to do the bidding of her father, but Joseph warded her off.

" It is not meet," said he, " for one who blesses with his mouth the living God, who eats of the blessed bread of life, who drinks out of the blessed cup of incorruptibility, to kiss a strange woman who blesses dumb idols, eats bread from their table, and anoints herself with the oil of corruption."

Joseph's speech and action produced a deep impression upon Asenath who grew very sad, her eyes filling with tears. When Joseph saw her tears, he had compassion on the poor maiden. Laying his hand upon her head he thus spoke:

" Lord of my father Israel, Thou who didst create light out of darkness, truth out of error, and life out of death, bless this maiden, quicken her and renew her with Thy spirit, that she may eat of the bread of life and drink out of the cup of blessing. Number her days with the days of Thy people

whom Thou hast chosen in the days before the world ever
was, so that she may enter Thy rest which Thou hast prepared for Thy elect, and dwell in Thy eternal life until eternity."

Thus Joseph blessed the weeping Asenath.   Thereupon
he departed, announcing, however, that he would soon return.

Asenath, glad and happy at the blessing Joseph had bestowed
upon her, but sad and grieved at her former scornful words,
retired to her apartments. Divesting herself of her resplendent
raiment, she put on dress of mourning, cast the idols she had
worshipped out of the window and began to do penance,
sitting in sackcloth and ashes, praying and weeping for seven
days and seven nights.   Thus she remained alone, shut up in
her apartment, for even the seven virgins, her constant companions, were not allowed to come near her.   And Asenath
prayed to the living God, the God of Joseph, to forgive her
her sins and to pardon her former idolatrous life.

" Lord of the Universe," she prayed, " I have now done
with the dead and profitless idols of Egypt. I no longer honour
them, but have flung them away from me.   Here am I now,
an orphan, repulsed by my people, I the daughter of a great
and powerful lord of Heliopolis.   Only a short time ago, in
my arrogance and pride, I rejected the offers of my many
suitors, but now I come before Thee, O Lord, humbled and
penitent, and, like a frightened child, I seek Thy protection.
Forgive me, O Lord, for having spoken scornfully of my
lord Joseph, whom I have treated as the son of a Canaanitish
herdsman.   I did not know, unfortunate sinner that I am,
who he was, but now I love him with all my heart and all my
soul, and am ready to be his handmaiden and slave all the
days of my life."

Thus Asenath wept and prayed and did penance for seven
days.   At dawn of the eighth day she arose, for she knew that
God had hearkened to her prayers.   And indeed, she saw the
morning star arise and the sky rent with a great light; and a

man, a divine messenger, radiant with light, appeared before the girl.

"Arise, Asenath," he called.

"Who calleth me?" queried the maiden.

"I am a prince of the house of God," replied the voice, "and a prince of the army of the Lord."

Asenath arose and beheld before her a man who greatly resembled Joseph. He was radiantly beautiful, and his eyes sparkled and shone like the rays of the sun. Upon his head he wore a crown and in his hand he held a royal staff. Overawed and frightened, Asenath began to tremble, but the man before her said:

"Be not afraid, Asenath, but cast off thy garments of mourning, thy black robe and thy sackcloth; remove the ashes from thy head and rejoice. Thy name is now written in the book of the living, and never will it be blotted out. Thou hast been newly born and quickened, and now thou shalt eat of the bread of life and of blessing, drink out of the cup of incorruptibility and be anointed with the holy unctions. This day I have given thee as a spouse to Joseph, and thy name shall no longer be Asenath, but the 'pillar of refuge', for Penitence, which is the daughter of the Most High and is a virgin modest and mirthful, has prayed for thee before the Eternal Throne."

And Asenath said:

"If I have found grace in thine eyes, my lord, sit down upon my couch, upon which no man has ever sat down, and I will dress the table, bring bread and wine that thou mayest refresh thyself before departing."

The divine messenger accepted the invitation of the hospitable maid, but when she had brought bread and wine and placed the refreshments upon the table, the angel produced a honeycomb.

"This honeycomb," said he, "hath been made by the bees in Paradise and from the dew of the roses there. Of this heavenly food the angels partake, and those who approach the Lord in repentance shall also eat of it." And the angel placed a portion of the honeycomb upon Asenath's lips, bidding her eat it.

Asenath ate, and the divine messenger thereupon said:

" Now thou hast eaten of the bread of life, drunk out of the cup of immortality, and hast been anointed with the holy unction of incorruptibility."

Thereupon Asenath said to the angel:

" My Lord, I have seven companions, virgins born with me on the same day; and if I have found favour in thine eyes, I would fain call them so that thou mayest bestow thy blessing upon these seven maidens who are unto me like sisters."

Having obtained the divine messenger's permission, Asenath called the seven virgins, her companions, and the angel bestowed upon them the blessing of eternal life, calling them the seven columns of the city of refuge. Thereupon her visitor departed, and Asenath saw him rise heavenwards in a fiery chariot, drawn by four horses who were like lightning.

Asenath now understood that she had been conversing not with mortal man, but with an angel from Heaven, and she thanked the Lord who had vouchsafed unto her such grace. Whilst she was thus uttering her prayers and thanking the Lord, one of Potiphera's maid-servants came to announce to her young mistress the arrival of Joseph. Quickly Asenath washed her face to prepare for the reception of her beloved. The reflection of her face in the water filled her with amazement, so changed was she, and so great was now her beauty. And indeed, so dazzling was the maiden's beauty that when Joseph, whom she hastened to greet, beheld her face, he failed to recognize her.

" Who art thou?" asked the Viceroy in great astonishment.

" I am Asenath, thy slave," replied the maid; " Asenath who hath cast away her dumb and useless idols. This day an angel from Heaven came to visit me and gave me heavenly food to eat. He also said unto me: ' This day I have given thee as a spouse unto Joseph, thy bridegroom, and he will be thy rightful husband into all eternity '. The angel further said that no longer will my name be Asenath, but the city of refuge, for through me many nations will find refuge under the protection of the Most High. The angel informed me, my lord, that he had thus spoken to thee this day concerning thy humble servant, and now thou knowest whether the angel did visit thee."

Thus spoke Asenath, her eyes shining with profound love for Joseph, and Joseph replied:

" Blessed be thou by the Most High, and blessed be thy name in all eternity, for the Lord God hath indeed sent unto me His angel and he hath spoken to me concerning thee. And now approach, my beautiful and beloved maid, why dost thou stand at such a distance from me?"

Bashfully Asenath approached, and they kissed each other. Thereupon Asenath said:

" My Lord, come into the house and let me wash thy feet."

Joseph at first objected to this service being performed by his bride-elect.

" Is there no other maid in the house," asked the Viceroy, " who could perform this service?"

But Asenath insisted upon being permitted to perform this act of love.

" No, my lord," she replied, " it is for me to perform this act of love and hospitality, for thou art my master and I am thy loving maid. And why should, as thou sayest, another maid wash thy feet? Thy feet are mine, and thy hands are mine, and thy soul is mine."

Thereupon the parents of Asenath arrived and were greatly amazed at their daughter's beauty. When they heard what had occurred they rejoiced exceedingly. A banquet was spread, and the parents and relatives of Asenath partook of the meal and blessed the Lord. Thereupon Potiphera, the priest of On, said unto Joseph:

"I will now invite all the high officials and courtiers of Pharaoh and also the princes of Egypt to a sumptuous wedding feast, at which thou wilt take to wife my daughter Asenath."

But Joseph declined this offer.

"No," said the Viceroy, "I could not accept this offer of thine, of giving the wedding feast here in thy house. I must first proceed to Pharaoh, the King of Egypt, who is my father here; I will inform him of my choice and ask him to give me to wife thy daughter Asenath."

Thus spoke Joseph, and Potiphera agreed that he had spoken wisely.

"Go in peace," said he, "and do as thou thinkest right."

When Pharaoh was informed of Joseph's choice and heard his Viceroy's request, he immediately sent for Potiphera, the priest of Heliopolis, and for his daughter Asenath. The King greatly admired the maiden's beauty and placed upon their heads golden crowns, the most beautiful that were in the house of the Pharaohs. Laying his hands upon their heads, he blessed them, saying:

"May the Most High bless you and glorify you for ever." Thereupon he made Joseph and Asenath kiss each other. The King then ordered a seven days feast to be held to which all the princes of Egypt were invited. The feast was also proclaimed a public and national holiday, for under penalty of death, by order of Pharaoh, no one was allowed to do any work during the nuptial festivities of Joseph and Asenath.[1]

[1] See Batiffol, *loc. cit.*

CHAPTER IX

The Visit of the Brethren

The greedy king and the generous Viceroy—The famine in the land of Canaan—Jacob's stores—An opportunity to search for the lost brother—" Ye are spies "—The hero of Shechem—The valiant men who broke their teeth—" A blow worthy of one of my family "—Joseph's uncanny knowledge—The grandchildren cry for bread—A touching scene—The powerful ruler of Egypt—Judah's pleading—The Patriarch's letter to the ruler of Egypt—Prayers and veiled threats—The magic cup—The astrolabe —Benjamin's astonishment—The long-lost brother—The sons of Jacob are put to the test—Benjamin insulted by his brethren—Thief and son of a thief—The reward of the meek—The punishment of Manasseh for having caused the sons of Jacob to rend their clothes—A private audience—The anger of the Viceroy—" The rope followed the bucket ".

When the famine, even as Joseph had foretold, broke in upon the inhabitants of Egypt, they were at once compelled to apply to Joseph. They had put aside some grain saved from the superabundant harvest, but when they opened their stores, they found that the grain had rotted. The Egyptians went to Pharaoh and cried: " Give us bread, so that we may live, for all our grain is unfit for food, because Joseph willed it so."

When Pharaoh heard that his people had no food whatever, he was greatly troubled in his mind. " If I command Joseph," he thought, " to feed all the inhabitants of the land, little will remain for myself and my family." Pharaoh therefore sent word to Joseph to conceal in a safe place all the grain he had gathered in the royal granaries, and let the Egyptians manage as well as they could.

Joseph, however, took no notice of the King's command, but fed all the hungry inhabitants of Egypt who blessed him

for it. The Viceroy had been secretly hoping that the famine
would soon bring his brethren to Egypt to buy corn. And
indeed, his hope was realized, for the famine soon spread to
Arabia, Phœnicia, and Palestine. " It is quite possible, however," thought Joseph, " that my father will send some of
his slaves to Egypt to buy corn, and I will miss the opportunity
of seeing my brethren." He therefore issued a decree enacting
that anyone who desired to buy grain in Egypt could not entrust
his slaves with the business, but would have either to come
himself or send his sons. Joseph also placed guards at the gates
of the city, commanding them not to permit anyone to enter
the city unless he had given his name, and the name of his
father and of his grandfather. " When you will have taken
down the names of the visitors," said Joseph, " you will submit
the lists to my son Manasseh."

Jacob was not yet exactly in want, and he still had grain
in his stores, for he had known long ago that a famine would
break out, but he advised his sons to go down to Egypt for
the purpose of buying corn. " Go down to Egypt, my sons,
and buy corn, for otherwise we will arouse the envy of the
sons of Esau and of Ishmael and of the other inhabitants of
Canaan who will say: ' Jacob is in a comfortable state and his
stores are full of corn.' They will fall upon us, kill us, and
seize all we possess."

Thus spoke the Patriarch, and his sons were ready to go
down to Egypt, because having long repented their unbrotherly
treatment of Joseph, they hoped to find him on the banks of
the Nile.

The sons of Jacob were therefore glad of the opportunity
to search for their brother and redeem him from slavery.

" If we find Joseph," they said, " we will ransom him,
however high a price his master should demand. Should
Joseph's master refuse to sell him, we will use force."

Thus the brethren of Joseph came to Egypt, and, obeying

the instruction of their father, they entered the city through different gates so as not to attract the attention of the people by their heroic stature and their handsome appearance. They searched the town for three days, hoping to find Joseph.

The latter, who had in the meantime been informed of the arrival of his brethren, had them seized and brought into his presence. He accused them of being spies, and ultimately permitted them to depart only if they left Simeon as hostage. Joseph said unto himself that if he detained both Simeon and Levi the two of them might destroy the whole city, as they had once destroyed the city of Shechem. Besides, Levi was a great favourite with the brothers, whilst Simeon was not. The brethren, Joseph feared, would sooner wage war against the whole city rather than depart without Levi. It was not an easy matter though to seize Simeon and put him in dungeon.

When Joseph ordered his men to seize the hero of Shechem, the brethren gathered round him, ready to defend him, but Simeon waved them back.

" Stand aside," he exclaimed, " I do not need your assistance, for I can fight these slaves single-handed."

Joseph thereupon sent a messenger to Pharaoh and asked him for seventy valiant men to help him arrest robbers who had been caught, and to cast them into prison.

When the valiant men appeared, Joseph commanded them to seize Simeon and cast him into prison. Scarcely, however, had the Egyptians approached the hero of Shechem and made an attempt to lay hands on him, when he uttered such a loud cry that they fell to the floor and broke their teeth. All the other servants who stood around fled in a great fright, so that only Joseph and his son Manasseh remained.

Joseph thereupon bade his son seize Simeon and cast him into prison. Manasseh then dealt Simeon such a mighty blow on the back of his neck that it nearly stunned him. Simeon

was amazed to find such strength in a mere youth, whom he
took to be an Egyptian. " It is strange," said he to his brethren,
" that this Egyptian youth should be endowed with such
heroic strength. His blow, I assure you, was one which any
member of our family might be proud of. In fact, I could
have taken my oath on it that the blow was dealt by one of
our family."

Simeon was bound and cast into prison, but as soon as the
brethren had left Joseph gave orders that he should be treated
kindly. He sent one of his servants to minister to all his wants,
and to set before him the best meat and drink.

When Joseph's brethren returned to Canaan and told the
Patriarch all that had occurred, and that the ruler of Egypt
had commanded them to bring their youngest brother with
them when they came again, the old man was greatly grieved.
He suspected his sons of being guilty, not only of Joseph's
disappearance, but also of Simeon's detention. As for Benjamin's going to Egypt, the Patriarch would not hear of it.
" Wherefore," he reproached his sons, " did ye tell the man in
Egypt that ye had another brother?"

" Your reproach, Father, is undeserved," replied one of
the brothers; " we were not such fools as to acquaint the ruler
of Egypt with our family history, but his knowledge is something uncanny. He seemed to know all our family relations to
the smallest detail, down to our babies and the very wood out
of which their cradles are fashioned." For the moment, however, Jacob remained adamant, firmly resolved not to let
Benjamin out of his sight.[1]

A day, however, arrived when the supplies of corn came to
an end, and the family began to suffer hunger. When the

---

[1] *Genesis Rabba*, §§ 91, 92, 93; *Midrash Tanchuma*, section *Mikkez* and *Vayigash*; *Yalkut*,
§ 150; *Midrash Abkhir*, quoted in *Yalkut Shimeoni*, section *Mikkez*; *Midrash Agadah*, ed.
Buber, pp. 98–100; *Targum Pseudo-Jonathan, in loco*; *Midrash Lekach Tob, in loco*; *Midrash
Haggadol*, col. 637; Babylonian Talmud, *Baba Mezia*, 39; *Taanit*, 9a, 10b; *Pirke de Rabbi
Eliezer*, Ch. 39; *Sepher Hajashar*; see also *Tokpo shel Yosef*; Kurrein, *loc. cit.*; Lewner,
loc. cit.; Schapiro, *loc. cit.*, pp. 54–56.

provisions bought in Egypt were exhausted, the sons of Jacob sent their children to the old man to ask him for bread.

One morning, therefore, the sons of Reuben, Judah, and Issachar appeared before the Patriarch and cried: "Grandfather, give us bread, for we are dying of hunger, and our fathers say they have no bread to give us."

"What can I do," replied Jacob; "I am old and feeble, and am compelled to remain at home. Go and ask your fathers to journey to Egypt and buy us corn."

And whilst he was thus talking to his grandchildren, there arrived the sons of Levi dressed for a long journey, their knapsacks upon their backs and their staffs in their hands. "We have come to say good-bye, Grandfather, for we are going on a long journey. Pray for us to the Eternal to protect us on our way."

"And whither are you going, my children?" asked the Patriarch.

"We are going to Egypt," replied the youngsters. "We asked our father for bread, but he had none to give us and advised us to go to Egypt. 'Go to Egypt,' he said, 'where you will join my brother Simeon, who has been cast into prison. You, too, will no doubt be arrested and detained in dungeon, but, at least, you will be fed there and not lack bread.' Thus spoke our father Levi, and we are taking his advice, for it is better to be a prisoner than die of hunger."

Thereupon Yemuel, Yemin, and Chad, the sons of Simeon, arrived, their sticks in their hands. They fell upon Jacob's servants and slaves and drove them out of the house.

"What is the meaning of your action?" asked the Patriarch; "wherefore did ye ill-treat these faithful servants and drive them out of the house?"

"Because," replied the boys, "we are anxious to take their place. As thy servants thou art feeding them, and so we thought of offering ourselves to thee as slaves, and take the place of the strangers so that thou wilt feed us. Our father who provided for us is no longer here, being a prisoner in a distant land, and we shall soon be compelled to sell ourselves to some master. It is better, therefore, that thou shouldst buy us as thy slaves rather than some strange master."[1]

These scenes moved the old man greatly. He summoned his sons and bade them go down to Egypt and buy some provisions.

But Judah replied that they could not go unless Benjamin accompanied them. "Thou shouldst know, Father," he said, "that there is none equal to this King of Egypt, either in power or in wisdom. We, who have beheld many kings of the earth, know of none who could be compared to this King of Egypt. Thou hast seen, O Father, that the greatest and most powerful among the kings of Canaan is Abimelech, but know that even Abimelech cannot be compared to one of the ministers of the King of Egypt. We have been surprised, O Father, by the magnificence of his palace and of his throne, and by his many servants. We have beheld him amidst all the royal pomp and splendour, and our eyes have been dazzled by the grace and wisdom with which the Lord hath favoured his person. Thou shouldst have heard, O Father, the words of wisdom, prudence, and sagacity which the Lord hath placed in his mouth when he did converse with us. He knows all that has happened unto us from the very beginning, and he asked us with great concern: 'Your aged father, is he well?' No one addresses himself unto Pharaoh, because all orders are given by the Viceroy. When he did accuse us of being spies we waxed wroth indeed, and were on the point of dealing with Egypt as we have dealt with the city of the Amorites. But the ruler of Egypt inspired us with such awe and respect that we dared not give vent to our anger. I therefore pray thee, O Father, to confide the lad to me, and I promise thee faithfully to bring

[1] *Tokpo shel Yosef.*

him back to thee. Have pity upon the little ones who are crying for bread, and have also faith in the Lord."

Thus pleaded Judah, and the Patriarch finally consented. With tears in his eyes, he now bade them travel to Egypt.

"Take Benjamin with ye," he said, "as ye cannot appear without him before the ruler of Egypt." He handed over Benjamin to Judah who promised on his happiness in the next world, which he offered as surety, to bring the lad back.

"Now," said the old man, "take some presents with ye for the ruler of Egypt, and here is money; do ye require anything else?"

"Yes," said his sons, "we require thy blessing and a prayer to the Lord on our behalf."

Jacob was well pleased with their reply, and thus prayed to the Lord on behalf of his sons:

"Sovereign of all the worlds! Thou who at the moment of creation didst call ' Enough ' to Heaven and to Earth, when they were stretching themselves out into infinity, say ' Enough ' also to my sufferings. And may it be Thy will that my sons find mercy before the ruler of Egypt that he may release unto them my missing sons."

Jacob also wrote a long letter to the ruler of Egypt and put it into the hands of Judah. And thus the Patriarch wrote in his letter:

"To the Royal Majesty and wisdom of Zaphnath Paaneah, the King of Egypt, from thy servant Jacob, the son of Isaac, the son of Abraham the Hebrew, peace. My lord, the King of Egypt, is no doubt well aware that the famine is very heavy in the land of Canaan. I am compelled therefore to send my sons to thee to buy food for our sustenance. I have already once sent my sons to Egypt in order to obtain some provisions from thee, and to buy food for our sustenance. Numerous are my descendants in whose midst I dwell, and I am surrounded by seventy children and grandchildren. But I am old myself

and cannot see with mine eyes, which have grown dim, both
on account of my advanced age as on account of my constant
tears shed for my lost son Joseph. It was I who commanded
my sons not to enter the city all together through one gate, so
as not to attract the attention of the people of Egypt. It was I
also who charged them to go about in the city and to look
round, as perchance they might find their lost brother Joseph.
Thou didst, however, accuse them of being spies, although
thy wisdom, the report of which has spread abroad, ought
to have made thee know from their looks that they were not
spies. Thou art famous, in consequence of thy interpretation
of Pharaoh's dreams, for telling the coming of the famine, and
it is strange that a man possessing great wisdom should have
made such a mistake regarding the appearance and character
of my sons and take them for spies. My Lord and King!
as thou didst command, I am sending unto thee my son
Benjamin, and I implore thee to have an eye on him until
thou dost send him back to me with his brethren. As a reward
for thy action, the Lord will take care of thee and have His
eye on thee and on thy kingdom. Thou hast no doubt heard
what our God once did unto a Pharaoh when, against all right,
he wanted to take to wife my grandmother Sarah, and also
what happened unto Abimelech on her account. Hast thou
not heard that our father Abraham, followed by a few men,
conquered and killed the seven kings of Elam, and that two of
my own sons, Simeon and Levi, destroyed eight towns of the
Amorites to avenge the wrong done to their sister? Now the
presence of Benjamin has somewhat consoled them for the
loss of Joseph, and thou canst easily imagine to what excesses
they will go if one of thy people so much as raised his hand
against their brother or tried to snatch him away from them.
Thou shouldst also know, O King of Egypt, that the mighty
help of our God is always with us, and that the Lord always
hearkens unto our prayers and never abandons us. When my

sons told me how thou didst treat them, accusing them of being spies, I had only to call upon my God, and long before the arrival of Benjamin thou and all thy people would have been destroyed. But I refrained from calling upon God to punish thee, because at this moment my son Simeon is in thy house and perhaps thou art being kind unto him, treating him well. Now my son Benjamin cometh to thee, together with his brethren, and I appeal to thee to treat the lad well, and direct thine eye upon him. Thou wilt be rewarded for this, for the Lord will also direct His eye upon thee and upon thy kingdom. All that is in my heart I have now said, and I ask thee once more to grant entire liberty to my sons, whilst they are abiding with thee, and to permit them to depart in peace."

This letter the Patriarch handed over to Judah for delivery to the ruler of Egypt.

When the sons of Jacob arrived in Egypt and presented themselves at the palace of the Viceroy, they were invited by Manasseh, the steward of Joseph's house, to dinner. It was a Sabbath meal, for Joseph observed the Sabbath even before the Israelites were bidden in the law to observe the seventh day. The steward also brought out Simeon unto them, and the brethren were not a little astonished to notice how well the prisoner looked.

Simeon told his brethren how well he had been treated during their absence. " Scarcely had you left the city," said the hero of Shechem, " when I was released from prison and treated like a distinguished guest in the Viceroy's house."

Joseph now appeared, and Judah, leading Benjamin by the hand, presented the lad to the ruler of Egypt, to whom he also handed his father's letter. When he beheld the handwriting of his aged father in distant Canaan, the Viceroy was deeply moved. Unable to restrain his tears, he withdrew into an inner apartment to weep freely.

He soon returned, and was overjoyed to see how closely

Benjamin resembled his father, being the very image and counterpart of the Patriarch. He summoned his brother to approach and entered into conversation with him. During the meal Joseph made Benjamin take his place at his own table, pretending to consult his magic cup for all the seating arrangements. Taking up his famous magic cup, whence he drew his knowledge, the Viceroy thus addressed his brethren: " My cup tells me that Judah is king among you, and he will therefore sit at the head of your table, whilst Reuben, who is the first-born, will sit next to him. Simeon, Levi, Issachar, and Zebulun, being the sons of one mother, will sit together on one side; and Gad and Asher, Dan and Naphtali on the other. Now my cup further tells me that Benjamin lost both his mother and brother, and he is like me who have neither mother nor brother. He may therefore take his seat at my own table, by the side of my wife and sons."

For twenty-two years neither Joseph nor his brethren had tasted any wine, having led the life of Nazarites, but at this meal of reunion, although only Joseph was aware of the fact, they all partook of wine. During the meal Joseph continued to converse with Benjamin, asking him many questions, and afterwards led him into his private apartment. Thereupon he bade one of his servants bring his magic astrolabe, whereby he was enabled to read future events.

" I have heard," he said to Benjamin, " that the Hebrews are well versed in all wisdom, and I wonder whether thou dost know anything about the signs of astrology."

Benjamin smiled.

" My father," he replied, " has imparted much knowledge to me and taught me many things; thy servant is therefore quite at home in many sciences, including that of astrology."

" Then take up this astrolabe," said Joseph, " read in it and find out whether thy brother Joseph, who as you all pretend was taken to Egypt, is to be found in this country."

Benjamin took up the astrolabe and examined it carefully. Thereupon he divided the sky of Egypt into four astrological regions, and suddenly stood up amazed. He had read in the astrolabe that he who was sitting upon a throne before him was none other than his lost brother Joseph.

Joseph, noticing Benjamin's astonishment, asked him: " What hast thou read in the astrolabe that thou seemest so moved and excited?"

Pointing to the instrument, Benjamin replied: " I have read here that my lost brother Joseph is facing me, seated upon a throne."

" This is quite true," replied Joseph, " for I am thy brother. It is true," continued Joseph, " I am thy brother Joseph, the son of Rachel who died on the way to Ephrath." Thereupon he embraced his younger brother and kissed him, and both shed tears of joy at the happy reunion.

" And now, my dear brother," said the Viceroy, " I will ask thee to keep our secret for some time, for I wish to put my brethren to the test and find out whether they have repented of their sin against me."

Thereupon he told Benjamin how he had been sold into slavery, and what suffering he had endured until the Lord had released him and raised him to such a high position. " But tell me, brother mine, what tale did my brothers bring to my father and how did they account for my disappearance?"

" They dipped thy coat in blood," replied the lad, " and said that a wild beast had torn thee. Our old father rent his clothes and has mourned ever since."

" It was a cruel deed," said the Viceroy, " although God had willed it so. Now I am going to put my brethren to the test to see if they have repented of their sin. I will send you all away to Canaan, but I will give instructions that before you have travelled a long distance, you all be stopped and accused of having stolen my magic cup. It will be found in thy sack, and you will all be arrested and brought back. I will claim thee as my bondman, and then I will see how our brethren behave and what attitude they take up. If they are ready to fight for thee and take thee away by force, risking their lives in thy defence, then I will know that they have repented of their cruelty to me, and that thou art dear to them. I will then make known to them my identity, and they will rejoice. Should they, however, consent to thy becoming my bondman and be ready to leave thee behind, then I will fight them and take my revenge, but thou wilt abide with me for ever. And now," he concluded, " return to our brethren, but never breathe a word concerning our secret."

In blithe spirits Benjamin joined his brethren who wondered at his evident happiness and smiling countenance. " The Viceroy," explained the lad, " has promised me to find out the whereabouts of our brother Joseph."

The brethren only shrugged their shoulders, for they had now given up all hope of ever discovering among the living the brother whom they had sold into slavery.

With the break of dawn the brethren left the city on their homeward journey, because Joseph had so arranged that they should travel by day. " By day only," he thought, " these fierce, powerful and courageous men can be compelled by my servants to return to Egypt. In the night, however, an encounter with them is dangerous, for when roused they are like wild beasts which no one can resist in the darkness. Rightly has Judah been called a lion, Dan a serpent on the road, and Naphtali swift as a running hare." The brethren, on the other hand, also remembered the instructions of their father to leave a city after sunrise and to enter it before sunset.

The sons of Jacob had scarcely left the city, when they were followed by Joseph's messengers who accused them of having stolen the Viceroy's magic cup. Their sacks were searched, and, to the amazement and vexation of the brethren, the cup was discovered in Benjamin's sack. The fury of the brethren was great, and turning to their youngest brother they thus addressed him: " Now we understand the reason of thy contentment and happiness last night. Thou art a thief and the son of a thief, for thy mother once stole the Teraphim of our grandfather Laban. Thou shameless thief, thou hast brought shame upon us, even as thy mother, the thief, once brought the blush of shame to the cheek of our father, when the Teraphim were discovered in her possession."

Thus they hurled abuse and even blows upon Benjamin who bore it all in patience and humility. He was rewarded for his conduct in later days, for the Holy Temple was situated in the allotment of the tribe of Benjamin, and the Glory of God dwelt between his shoulders (*Deuteron.*, 33, 12).

The brethren then rent their clothes in sign of grief, and because they had been compelled to do so on account of Benjamin, one of his descendants, Mordecai, was destined to rend his clothes on account of the children of Israel. On the other hand, if the sons of Jacob now rent their clothes it was a Divine punishment for the crime they had committed in causing their old father to rend his clothes at the loss of his son.

Manasseh, too, who, at the head of Joseph's servants, had searched the sacks of his kinsmen and inflicted upon them such humiliation, did not escape Divine retribution. In later days the allotment of the tribe of Manasseh was " torn " into two parts, situated on the two banks of the River Jordan. As for Joseph, who had caused his brethren to rend their clothes, one of his descendants, Joshua, rent his clothes after the defeat of Ai (*Joshua*, 7, 6). Thus, sooner or later, Divine Providence metes out retribution for every reprehensible act.

Without raising any protest, the brethren followed Manasseh and his men back to the city, and were brought into the presence of Joseph.

The Viceroy received them in his private apartments, for, in order to spare his brethren shame in public, he had announced that he would hold no court on that day. Outwardly calm, but inwardly boiling with rage, Judah and his brethren were already contemplating the eventuality of using force, should Joseph insist upon detaining Benjamin in bondage.

The capital of Egypt was a big city, but to the heroic sons of Jacob it appeared only like a small hamlet with ten inhabitants which they could easily destroy, if driven to extremes. Judah, however, who was king among Jacob's sons, and their spokesman, decided to plead at first, before resorting to force. Brought into the presence of the apparently furious ruler of Egypt, the eleven brethren fell to the earth and prostrated themselves before Joseph, thus realizing and making true the dream of the latter. In apparent rage, Joseph thus addressed them:

" Why did ye steal my magic cup? No doubt, ye were anxious to practise magic, and with the help of the cup discover the whereabouts of your lost brother."

" My Lord," replied Judah, " we are not guilty of the crime we are charged with, and cannot acknowledge ourselves as thieves, because we are innocent. Appearances, however, are against us, for the cup hath been found in the sack of our brother. God hath found out our iniquity, and it is His will to punish us. Now although the cup was found in the sack of our youngest brother, we, who were in the company of the supposed thief, are all equally responsible."

Shaking his purple mantle in royal dignity, Joseph replied: " It is not worthy of a king to punish the innocent. I am not accusing ye all of the theft committed, but only your youngest brother, who will be punished accordingly. Ye may, therefore, return to your old father in peace, whilst this young man will remain as my bondman." And mockingly Joseph added: " If ye are worried concerning the report ye will have to give to your old father, to whom ye must account for the disappearance of this your brother, ye can easily invent some plausible story. When this lad's brother, who was no thief, had disappeared years ago, ye did not hesitate to inform your father that a wild beast had torn him. It will be easy for ye now to separate yourselves from a brother who is a thief and tell your father that 'The rope has followed after the bucket.' Benjamin, therefore, remains here, and ye all may return to Canaan in peace!"

"Thou mayest call it peace," replied Judah, "but we call it war, for the foundations of peace will have been destroyed if Benjamin is separated from us."

Without deigning to reply, Joseph waved his hand, indicating that the audience was at an end, carried Benjamin off, and locked him up in a chamber. Losing all hope of rescuing Benjamin, the brethren were on the point of giving in and of abandoning their youngest brother, who, they thought, had really stolen the cup. Judah, however, who had stood surety for the lad, was determined to liberate the lad at all costs. Should further arguments, pleadings, and entreaties fail, I will use force, thought the heroic son of Jacob.[1]

---

[1] See note 1, p. 120; see also *Midrash Haggadol*, col. 661–663; Schapiro, *loc. cit.*, pp. 56–74.

CHAPTER X

The Lion, the Bull, and the Wolf

The dispute of two kings—The roaring lion—The penalty for theft—Benjamin's grandmother—The strength of Manasseh—Judah's argument—His responsibility—His towering rage—Tears of blood—Hushim the deaf jumps from Canaan to Egypt—The terrific noise—The rage of Jacob's son—The broken marble pillar—Naphtali counts the streets of the city—A stone crushed to dust—The fire of Shechem and the fire kindled to burn Tamar—The expert dyers—A brother's tears and his forgiveness—Why Joseph wept upon the neck of Benjamin—The destruction of the two temples—The happy return to Canaan—Serah the beautiful maid and clever musician—The glad tidings—" Uncle Joseph liveth "—Jacob blesses Serah and bestows upon her eternal life—The joy of the Patriarch—A banquet offered to the kings of Canaan—The cedars once planted by Abraham—Pharaoh lends his royal crown to Joseph—The Viceroy makes ready his chariot——The meeting of father and son—The Patriarch would not interrupt his prayers—The joy of Egypt—The low door—The miracle of a raised door—Og the giant's astonishment—Joseph's treasures—Their hiding places.

Judah is called a lion, Joseph a bull, and Benjamin a wolf, and a mighty contest now ensued between the bull and the lion concerning the wolf. Joseph knew him to be innocent of guilt, but accused him of theft, whilst Judah thought him guilty, but did his best to liberate him. Two kings stood facing one another, and the brethren listened in silence, not venturing to interfere. It was a mighty contest, a fight at which even the angels in Heaven did not disdain to be spectators.

" Let us descend," said the angels, " and witness the fight of the bull against the lion. As a rule the bull fears the lion whom he recognizes as his master, but here the two combatants are equal in strength. Their present combat is only the beginning of a long and mighty contest which will continue for ages between the descendants of these two, until the day when the Messiah arrives."

Roaring like a lion, Judah had approached the locked door, broken it, and in a threatening attitude was now standing before the ruler of Egypt. Outwardly calm, but inwardly boiling with suppressed fury, he decided to plead at first and to resort to argument, and he thus addressed Joseph:

" My Lord, according to our laws, a thief is sold into slavery only when he has no money to make restitution. Benjamin, however, can make restitution and pay, according to our laws, double the value of the object he has stolen. Therefore, I request that Benjamin be set free. Besides, if it is a slave thou dost require, take me as thy bondman in the place of the lad, for I am stronger than he and will be more useful to thee both for military service and for manual tasks. Let also the words I am about to address unto thee find entrance into thine ear. Know that years ago the Pharaoh of Egypt and his entire household were stricken with plagues because the King had detained in his palace the grandmother of Benjamin for one night against her will. Know further that two of us once destroyed the town of Shechem, to avenge the honour of our sister, and we will do more to set free our brother in whose allotment the Holy Temple will once be situated. I warn thee, my lord, that I can destroy the whole of Egypt, for I have only to utter a word in this thy palace, and pestilence will be the result outside, carrying destruction as far as the city of No. Thou didst say that thou dost fear God, but methinks thou art like Pharaoh who maketh promises but doth not keep them. In thy country Pharaoh is the first and thou art the second, but in *our* country of Canaan my father is the first and I am his representative. If I but draw my sword, I will kill thee first and then Pharaoh."

When Joseph heard these threats uttered by his brother,

and knowing full well that he was quite capable of carrying them out, he made a sign to his son Manasseh, and the latter stamped his foot on the ground with such force that the whole palace shook and trembled.

" This young Egyptian," muttered Judah, " seems to be endowed with extraordinary strength which, strange enough, equals that of our own family." He wondered greatly at the strength and stamping of Manasseh, whom he took to be a young Egyptian of the race of Ham.

Mitigating his tone, Judah spoke again: " Why, my lord, did thy reception of us differ so greatly from the reception accorded to all the men who came to Egypt from different countries for the purpose of buying corn? Why didst thou single us out from among all the other visitors, inquiring into all the details of our family affairs, as if we had come here not to buy corn but to ask the hand of thy daughter in marriage? Or was it, perhaps, because thou didst have the intention of taking our sister to wife, and wast, therefore, anxious to learn all about our family? From the very beginning thou didst try to find quarrel with us, accusing us first of being spies, and now charging us with theft."

" Thou art a clever and impressive talker," said Joseph, " but I really have very little time to stand here, listening to thy eloquence. Tell me, though, why art thou alone among all thy brethren pouring out this eloquence, whilst some of them are older than thou?"

" Because," replied Judah, " I alone am responsible for the lad, having stood surety for him to my father."

" And wherein did thy surety consist?" queried Joseph; " if it was gold and silver, I will pay it for thee."

" There is no question of gold and silver," replied Judah, contemptuously. " I promised my father to bring Benjamin back, otherwise I lose my happiness and my portion in the world to come. It is for this reason that I so insist upon setting

Benjamin free, and upon remaining here in his stead as thy bondman. Besides, I could never return to my father without the lad, for I could not witness the old man's grief over his youngest son."

" Thou wast not so much concerned for thy father's grief on another occasion, and didst not venture to be surety for the other brother whom ye sold into slavery for twenty pieces of silver. Then thou *couldst* witness the grief of thy old father, telling him that a wild beast had devoured his favourite son. And that brother of yours had done thee no wrong, whilst Benjamin hath brought shame upon thee, because he hath committed theft. It will be easy for thee to tell thy father that the rope has followed the bucket."

Thus spoke Joseph, still resolved to put his brethren to the test, and to see whether they would really fight for Benjamin, and risk their lives in an attempt to set him free.

Breaking out into sobs, Judah cried: " What shall I say to my father when I return without the lad?"

" I have already told thee to say the rope has followed the bucket."

When Judah saw that his entreaties and arguments remained without effect, his towering rage once more broke out. He seized a piece of brass, bit it with his teeth and spat it out as fine powder. He roared like a lion, and his voice carried four hundred parasangs; it was heard by Hushim, the son of Dan, in distant Canaan. With one bound Hushim jumped from distant Canaan to Egypt and stood beside his uncle, joining his voice with that of the heroic son of Jacob.

Egypt trembled from their joint noise; two cities, Pithom and Ramses, which the Jews were afterwards forced to rebuild, collapsed and fell into ruins. Joseph's valiant men were hurled to the ground by the terrific noise and lost their teeth. Judah's brethren, too, fell into a rage, assumed a threatening attitude, and stamped upon the ground with such force that the dust rose high, and the ground looked as if deep furrows had been made in it by a ploughshare. The towering rage of Judah rose higher and higher. His right eye shed tears of blood, and the hairs upon his chest bristled and grew stiff, piercing the five garments he wore.

Joseph knew well enough these signs of his brother's rage, foreboding mischief, and he began to fear for his life and for the safety of the country. In order to impress his brethren, and to show that he, too, was a powerfully strong man, he pushed with his foot against the marble pillar he was seated upon so that it broke into splinters.

Judah was amazed to notice that the ruler of Egypt was his equal in strength. He made an attempt to draw his sword, but it would not move from the scabbard, and he concluded that the man facing him was not only a hero like himself, but a God-fearing man, too. He dispatched his brother Naphtali, who was as swift as a hart, to run out and count the streets of the city. Simeon, however, exclaimed: " I will go up to the mountain, seize a huge stone, hurl it over the city and kill all its inhabitants." Naphtali soon returned and reported that the city was divided into twelve quarters.

" Now," said Judah to his brethren, " I have done with argument, and it is war. We are going to destroy the city. I myself will undertake to destroy three quarters, whilst each of you will deal with one of the remaining quarters."

" Egypt though," remarked the brethren, " is not like Shechem; if Egypt were now to be destroyed, the whole world would suffer, for it is this country that is providing food for the whole world."

Joseph, who understood their talk, was well pleased with these sentiments they had expressed.

Judah once more turned to Joseph and cried: " I swear to thee that I alone, even without the help of my brethren, am capable of destroying the whole country. I have only to draw my sword, and rase the country to the ground."

" I will break thy sword upon thine own head, and crush thy arm," replied Joseph.

" I will raise my voice, and Egypt will fall into ruins," cried Judah.

" I will shut thy mouth with a stone," replied Joseph.

Judah at once seized a huge stone with one hand, hurled it into the air, caught it up again and sitting down upon it crushed it to dust.

Joseph was little impressed by this feat of strength, for at a sign from him his son Manasseh did the same with another stone. Joseph remained inexorable.

" Thy judgment is wrong and unjust," cried Judah.

" Not so unjust as the sale of a brother who had done no wrong," replied the Viceroy.

" Verily," thundered Judah, in a paroxysm of rage, " the fire of Shechem is burning in my heart."

" I may be able to cool thy fire," replied Joseph. " Perhaps the remembrance of the fire which threatened to burn Tamar, thy daughter-in-law, may cool and even extinguish the fire in thy heart."

" I will dye Egypt red," thundered Judah.

" I am not surprised," mocked Joseph, " ye were always expert dyers, for did ye not dye your brother's coat red, dipping it in the blood of a kid, and telling your father that a wild beast had devoured his son."

The shaft went home and increased Judah's wrath. He made now serious preparations to destroy the city of Egypt. He would risk his life in the struggle sooner than return to his father without Benjamin.

Joseph now realized that things had gone far enough. He was satisfied with his test, convinced that Judah would lay down his life in his attempt to set Benjamin free, ready

to atone for his sin against Joseph. There was no necessity to
see Egypt laid in ruins. The Viceroy, therefore, made up his
mind to make himself known to his brethren. This scene,
however, during which his brethren would be put to shame,
should not be witnessed by strangers, and the Viceroy accordingly bade all his servants and valiant men leave him.

Addressing his brethren in more gentle tones, he said:
" Ye told me that the brother of Benjamin is dead, but this
is a lie, for he was sold into slavery and I bought him. I will
bid him come hither and appear in the presence of his brethren."
Raising his voice, he then called aloud: " Joseph! Joseph,
son of Jacob, come hither and speak to thy brethren who
once sold thee into slavery."

Abashed, the sons of Jacob looked round, turning their
eyes to the four corners of the room, but they saw no Joseph
coming forward.

" Why do ye look hither and thither?" cried Joseph.
" Your brother is here, he is standing before ye, for I, the
ruler of Egypt, am Joseph whom ye did sell into slavery!"

At these words, the brethren were so abashed that their
souls fled from them and they remained lifeless. But God
wrought a miracle and sent them new life. They would not
believe Joseph at first, for he had changed so greatly. The
bearded, handsome ruler of Egypt, arrayed in royal robes,
clad in purple and wearing a crown upon his head, could
not possibly be the smooth-faced, beardless youth they had
once cast into the pit and afterwards sold into slavery. They
were, however, convinced at last that the ruler of Egypt
was their lost brother, and then the sons of Jacob were both
ashamed and afraid. They were ashamed of their sins and of
their former heartless cruelty towards a brother, and afraid
lest this brother, now a powerful ruler, wreak now his revenge.
Judah raised such an outcry, that the walls of the city of Egypt
tumbled down, pregnant women miscarried, and both Pharaoh

and Joseph rolled from their seats. Three hundred of Joseph's heroes fell to the ground, knocking out their teeth. Others who had turned their heads to look round and find out the cause of the tumult, became immobile and their heads thus remained forever facing backwards.

Joseph, seeing his brethren's shame and fear, calmed them and gently called them to come nearer and kiss him. They yielded at last, timidly approached the ruler of Egypt who fell upon their necks and wept. He wept for joy, but he also wept in sorrow, for in a prophetic vision he foresaw that their descendants would be enslaved by the nations of the earth. He wept upon Benjamin's neck even more, because the two holy temples, situated in the allotment of the tribe of Benjamin, would be destroyed. Benjamin, too, wept upon Joseph's neck, because he foresaw that the sanctuary of Shiloh, situated in Joseph's allotment of territory, would also be destroyed. Tears were shed at Joseph's reconciliation with his brethren, and tears will be shed when Israel is once more redeemed by the Lord. (*Jerem.*, 31, 9.)

Pharaoh, who had wondered at the noise and tumult going on in the Viceroy's palace, was informed of the quarrel between Joseph and the Hebrews. He was well pleased when he heard the news of the reconciliation, for he had feared for the safety of the country. He now sent his servants to Joseph to rejoice with him, and all the magnates of the realm too came to take part in their Viceroy's joy. An invitation was extended to the brethren of Joseph to come now with their families to Egypt and to dwell in the country of Goshen, where they could take up their abode. The country of Goshen belonged to them by right, for it had once been made a present of to Sarah by the Pharaoh of the time.

Richly laden with presents for themselves and their families, such as embroidered clothes, gold and silver apparel, costly raiment, jewels and precious stones, the brethren left Egypt.

They travelled in wagons placed at their disposal by Joseph, who also sent the chariot wherein he had ridden on his appointment as Viceroy for his father's use. Joseph himself accompanied his brethren to the frontier of Egypt, and insisted upon their speedy return.

"Tell my father," he said, "should he hesitate to believe your words, that when I took leave of him he had been teaching me the section dealing with the law of the heifer whose neck had been broken in the valley."

The return of the sons of Jacob to Canaan was a happy one, and in high spirits they travelled home. But when they approached the boundary of Canaan they said to each other: "If we come to our father and suddenly inform him of what has happened, the glad tidings may frighten him and he may also refuse to give credence to our words." Not far from Hebron, however, they caught sight of Serah, the daughter of Asher, who had come out to meet them. The sight of the little maiden, who was as beautiful as she was clever, gave them an idea. Serah was a clever musician and could sing sweetly, accompanying herself upon the harp. When she came up and kissed her father and her uncles, they told her the great news. Thereupon they gave her a harp and instructed her to go and play to her grandfather.

"Go now, little one," they said, "into thy grandfather's tent and sing and play to him, and in thy song tell him the glad tidings, how his son Joseph liveth and is ruler of Egypt."

The little maiden took the harp and hurried into her grandfather's tent. She was a great favourite with the Patriarch, who loved to listen to her singing and playing. Serah sat down beside the old man and began to sing the following song:

> "My Uncle Joseph is not dead,
>   For he liveth all the while;
> A crown he weareth on his head,
>   As King of Egypt by the Nile."

Her melodious sweet voice, her soft music, soothed the old man, and he was pleasantly thrilled.

"Play again, child," he said, "for thy singing has put new life into me."

Serah repeated her words again and again, and peace entered Jacob's heart. A wave of joy swept over his whole being, and in that moment the spirit of prophecy came over him, and he knew that the words of his granddaughter were true.

Approaching the child, Jacob laid his hand upon the comely head and blessed the little maid: "My dear," said the Patriarch who had mourned for his beloved son twenty-two years, "may death in all eternity never have power over thee, because thou hast brought joy to my afflicted heart. Repeat this song often to me, for it is balm to my wounds and brings joy to me."

And whilst Jacob was still blessing his granddaughter his sons arrived, happy and radiant. The Patriarch lifted up his eyes and was amazed at beholding his sons arrayed in costly and magnificent garments, riding in royal chariots, and servants running before them. He would not believe them at first, when they communicated to him the glad tidings, for he dared not give credence to their words that Joseph was not only alive, but also ruler of Egypt. The presents, however, the chariots, the servants, the jewels and raiment, were real and not a dream, and he was soon convinced of the truth. Great was his joy when he heard from his sons that honours, power, and wealth had not made his son swerve from the path of virtue, and that he was constant in his piety.

"Joseph," said the brethren, "as ruler of Egypt, is beloved and blessed by all, for he feeds the hungry and metes out justice to the oppressed. There is none so generous and magnanimous like Joseph." These words brought great joy to the heart of the old man. He was even more happy to hear of his son's piety and noble deeds than of his power, wealth, and honours. Rising from his seat and lifting up his eyes to Heaven, he gave thanks to the Lord:

" Blessed art Thou, the God of my fathers, who hast given strength to my son to withstand all the sufferings, and hast enabled him to remain steadfast in his piety. My son," continued Jacob, " is even more constant in his piety than I, for did I not say ' My sufferings seem to be hidden from the Lord ', and yet, the Lord has bestowed many gifts and blessings upon me. He saved me from Esau and from Laban, and from the Canaanites who did pursue me. I have hoped to receive more benefits, but never did I hope for this joy. Now I am convinced that the Lord will bestow even greater blessings upon me."

Thereupon Jacob and the members of his household put on the costly garments Joseph had sent them, and rejoiced exceedingly. All the kings and magnates of Canaan came to visit Jacob and rejoiced with him. The Patriarch prepared a banquet for his noble guests and thus addressed them:

" Ye know that I had lost my favourite and beloved son Joseph, and mourned for him these twenty-two years, but now my sorrow hath been turned into joy, for my son liveth and is ruler of Egypt. What gladdens my heart most is the fact that, although ruler of a great country before whom nations bow down, Joseph is still steadfast in his piety, is charitable and generous, feeds the hungry, clothes the naked, and comforts the afflicted. Let this be a proof to ye, my noble guests, that the living God whom I worship, even as did before me my grandfather Abraham, and my father Isaac, never abandons those who put their trust in Him. A day cometh when He comforteth the afflicted, rewardeth the pious, and punisheth the wicked and the hypocrites."

The Patriarch had now decided to travel to Egypt and see

his son, but then to return to Canaan, as he would not dwell in a country like Egypt where there was no fear of God, and where idols were worshipped. But a divine vision came to him, and the Lord bade him go down to Egypt and remain there:

"Go down to Egypt," said the Lord, "and do not fear, for I shall be with thee and with thy descendants who will become a great nation."

But before leaving Canaan, his native land, Jacob first went to Beer-Sheba. A prophetic vision had descended upon the Patriarch and he knew that his descendants would one day build the Tabernacle. He therefore went to Beer-Sheba to hew down the cedars once planted by Abraham. "These cedars," he said, "my sons will plant in Egypt, and hew them down afterwards to carry them into the desert and build the Tabernacle."

Judah was sent ahead to inform Joseph of his father's arrival. "Our father is coming," said Judah, "and he bade thee erect dwellings for him and for his household, but, first of all, construct a house of learning and a school where he can continue to impart to his children the knowledge of the Lord, and teach them the laws of justice and of loving-kindness." Thus spoke Judah, and Joseph rejoiced exceedingly, and gave orders that his father's request be carried out. The Viceroy now made all necessary preparations to meet his father, and all the nobles and magnates of Egypt decided to accompany their Viceroy.

"Let us go out," they said, "to meet the pious man from Canaan, and pay homage to the father of such a generous and just man as is our present ruler."

Pharaoh sent unto Joseph his royal crown and bade him wear it for this occasion.

"Wear this crown," said the King, "in honour of thy father."

Crowds of nobles and magnates, all the valiant men and heroes of Egypt, musicians and players upon all sorts of instruments, gathered round Joseph, ready to follow the procession and greet the grand old man from Canaan.

Joseph himself, arrayed in purple, went down to make ready his chariot with his own hands. Amazed were the nobles and magnates of the land, when they saw their Viceroy dragging out the chariot and harnessing the horses with his own hands, although numerous slaves were standing about, ready to do their master's bidding.

" I am going out to meet my father, whom I have not seen for twenty years," said Joseph, " and I cannot permit anyone to perform this loving action in making ready my chariot." The Egyptians wondered at his words and praised their Viceroy who thus honoured his father. To the sound of music, of cymbals and timbrels, the great procession, headed by nobles, arrayed in byssus and purple, by valiant men and heroes in warlike attire, marched on. Flowers, myrrh, and aloes were strewn on the way, and the women and maidens of Egypt ascended the roofs and walls of the city to greet Jacob upon his arrival. At a distance of about 50 ells from his father, Joseph descended from his chariot, walking on foot the rest of the way, and all the nobles of Egypt, riding in chariots or on horseback, followed the example of the Viceroy. When the Patriarch beheld the splendid procession which had come out to meet him, and saw among them a man arrayed in purple and wearing a crown upon his head, he bowed down, thinking it was the King.

" Who is this man," he asked his son Judah, " the Egyptian in royal attire, wearing purple upon his shoulders and a crown upon his head? He has just left his chariot and is coming towards us on foot?"

" It is thy son, Joseph," replied Judah.

And because Joseph had allowed his father to bow to him,

JOSEPH AND HIS FATHER MEET AGAIN IN EGYPT

he was punished afterwards, for he died before his other brothers.

In the meantime Joseph had approached, bowed low to his old father and then fell upon his neck, kissed him and wept. Jacob, too, wept for great joy and happiness, but he did not yet kiss his son. At that moment, the Patriarch was praying to the Lord, rendering thanks to God for the benefits bestowed upon him, and the pious old man would not be interrupted in his prayer. He was just reciting the words: " And thou shalt love the Lord, thy God, with all thy heart and all thy might." When he had finished his prayers, Jacob said: " Were I to die now, I would be comforted, for my death will only be in this world and not in the world to come."

The procession now returned to Egypt, and the whole country reverberated from the shouts of joy and from the sounds of music. Joseph thereupon took his father and set him before Pharaoh.

Now the door through which one entered into the royal palace of the Pharaohs of Egypt was very low, so that all the visitors were compelled to bow and bend their heads before the idol standing in the entrance. When Jacob came to visit Pharaoh, an angel appeared and raised the door so that the Patriarch could pass without stooping.

Pharaoh marvelled greatly at this wonder, and thought that it was Abraham who was standing before him.

" Years ago," said Pharaoh, " such a miracle occurred at this very door, when Abraham the Hebrew came to visit one of my predecessors. Is it possible that the famous Patriarch Abraham is still alive?"

It is also related that at that moment Og happened to be with Pharaoh, and the giant, who had known Abraham well, was so struck by the resemblance of Jacob with his grandfather that he actually believed it was Abraham who was standing there. Therefore Pharaoh asked Jacob: " How old art thou?"

to which the Patriarch replied: " Few and evil have been the days of my life."

Thereupon Jacob blessed Pharaoh, saying: " May the waters of the Nile rise at thy approach, overflow their banks and water and fructify the land of Egypt." And the Lord blessed the country on account of the pious Patriarch, for the famine soon came to an end.

The Egyptians now came to Joseph and said: " Give us seed, O our ruler, that we may cultivate the land and sow." Joseph granted their request, but he did not permit them to remain in their native districts. He gave them fields and seed and settled them in other cities, thus making them aliens everywhere. " The Egyptians," said Joseph, " will now no longer be able to speak of my brethren as aliens and exiles in the country, for they, too, having changed their dwelling places, are aliens and exiles."

Jacob and his family were now settled in the country of Goshen, and Joseph provided for them very generously, giving them food, drink, and even clothing, whilst the Patriarch and his sons took their meals daily at the Viceroy's table. Joseph also gathered much treasure, gold, silver, and precious stones which the Egyptians gave in exchange for the grain he sold them, whilst Pharaoh was keeping his stores for his own use and would not part with them. His possessions and treasures Joseph divided into four parts, burying them in the desert, near the Red Sea, on the banks of the River Euphrates, and in the desert near Persia and Media. The remainder he gave partly to his brethren and partly to Pharaoh who put it into his treasury. But Joseph also gathered the treasures of other nations besides the treasures of Egypt, for money from various parts of the world flowed into the country. These treasures the Jews took along with them in the time of the exodus. As for the treasures which Joseph had hidden in different spots, one part was discovered by Korah, the other by the Emperor

Antonine, the son of Severus, whilst the remaining two hiding places are still unknown, the treasures being reserved for the pious, among whom they will be distributed in the days of the Messiah.[1]

[1] *Genesis Rabba*, §§ 93, 94; *Targum Pseudo-Jonathan, in loco*; *Midrash Tanchuma*, section *Vayigash*; *Midrash Agadah*, ed. Buber, pp. 102–105; *Yalkut*, §§ 151, 152; *Midrash Haggadol*, col. 661–663; *Babylonian Talmud*, *Pesachim*, 119a; *Pirke de Rabbi Eliezer*, Ch. 39; *Sepher Hajashar*; see also Schapiro, *loc. cit.*, pp. 56–74.

CHAPTER XI

The Lovesick Prince and the Jealous Brethren

Asenath visits the Patriarch at Goshen—The wonderful old man—
The affection of the sons of Leah and the jealousy of the sons of the handmaids—The lovesick prince—A plot to assassinate Joseph—The loyal
brothers—The heroes of Shechem draw their swords—The frightened
prince—The heir to the throne and the sons of the handmaids—A false
accusation—The treachery of the stepbrothers—The jealousy of Dan and
the hatred of Gad—Naphtali's visions—The ship of Jacob—In ambush
in the ravine—The king passes a sleepless night—The disappointment of
the son who would assassinate his father—The attack—Benjamin jumps
from the chariot and wounds the prince with a pebble—Simeon and Levi
appear upon the scene—The fight for Asenath—Her forgiving nature—
The death of the prince.

Immediately upon Jacob's arrival in Egypt, Asenath came to
see him.[1] " I will go to Goshen and pay a visit to thy father,"
said Asenath unto Joseph, " because thy Father Israel is like
a God unto me."

And Joseph replied: " Come with me and thou wilt see
my father."

When Asenath arrived at Goshen and beheld the Patriarch,
she was greatly impressed by his beauty and nobility of appearance. Although a very old man, Jacob nevertheless resembled
a vigorous youth. His hair was snow white, and his long
white beard covered his chest, his eyes were shining brightly,
and had lost none of their powerful youthful expression,
whilst his arms and shoulders were powerful, and his legs and

---

[1] For the entire episode see *The Life and Confession*, or *Prayer of Asenath* (Part II),
published (Greek and Latin) by P. Batiffol, *Studia Patristica*, Paris, 1889–1890.

feet were those of a giant. Greatly impressed by the appearance of the Patriarch, Asenath bowed low and bade him
greeting.

"Is this thy spouse?" asked Jacob, addressing Joseph.

"She is," replied Joseph. Thereupon Jacob blessed her,
and bidding her come near kissed her. "May the Eternal
bless thee," said the Patriarch, "for thus is welcomed the
warrior who hath escaped the dangers of the battle-field and
returneth home." [1]

The sons of Leah took a great liking for their sister-in-law,
but not the sons of Zilpah and Bilhah, the handmaids, who
seemed to have been jealous of Joseph's greatness and happiness, and also of the favour Asenath had found in the eyes of
their father and of the blessing the latter had bestowed upon
his daughter-in-law.

Joseph and Asenath left Goshen and returned home, accompanied by Levi, so that Joseph was on the left of his wife
and Levi on her right. Asenath had conceived a great respect
and liking for Levi, for he was a very intelligent man. But
Levi was more than an intelligent man. He was a saint and a
prophet, could read the heavenly writings, and instructed
Asenath in them. Levi also, during his ascension to Heaven,
had seen in the highest Heaven the place destined for Asenath
in the next world.

Now, on their journey home, Joseph and Asenath had to
pass the royal residence, and the eldest son of Pharaoh, beholding the beautiful wife of the Viceroy, fell in love with
her. He made up his mind to kill Joseph, and to take his
widow to wife, but he knew that unaided he could never get
his rival out of the way. The Prince therefore sent for Simeon
and Levi, and thus addressed them:

"I know that you two are powerful and brave men, and

---

[1] In his Introduction Batiffol points out that in these words Jacob probably refers to
Asenath as his granddaughter who had joined the family.

that by your hands the town of Shechem was destroyed and the inhabitants exterminated. I know that your swords send terror into the hearts of brave and warlike men. Now if you are willing to stand by me and help me in what I am about to carry out, great will be your reward. I will give you great treasure, much gold and silver, man servants and maid servants, asses and camels. I hate your brother Joseph, because he took Asenath to wife, the maiden who ought to have been betrothed to me. If you will help me to kill Joseph by the sword, so that I can marry Asenath, you will always be unto me like my brothers and trusted friends. Should you, however, refuse to fulfil my request, you will certainly regret it."

" We are God-fearing men," replied the brothers, " and our father is a servant of the Lord, and our brother, too, is a God-fearing man. We will commit a great sin before the Lord, if we consent to accomplish such a wicked deed. Shouldst thou, however, persist in thy design, know that we will fight for our brother and if needs be die fighting." Saying this, the brothers drew their swords from their scabbards, saying: " These are the swords with which we destroyed the city of Shechem, when we came to avenge our sister's dishonour. The same swords will serve us to defend our brother's life, and to avenge his death, should some coward attempt to take it. Now, thou art warned," concluded the two heroes of Shechem.

When the son of Pharaoh heard these words and saw the drawn swords of the brothers, he was greatly frightened and nearly fainted.

Although afraid of Joseph and of his brethren, the heir to the throne nevertheless persisted in his desire to kill Joseph, so as to marry his widow. He was torn between his deep passion and his abject fear.

Thereupon his faithful servants, when they saw their master in such affliction and so perturbed in spirit, said unto him:

" The sons of the handmaids will no doubt be persuaded to listen to thy words and do thy bidding, for they are hostile to and jealous of the sons of Leah and Rachel."

The son of Pharaoh listened to the advice of his servants, sent for the sons of Bilhah and Zilpah, and thus addressed them: " Either blessing or death await ye soon, O sons of Bilhah and Zilpah, and I advise ye to choose blessing rather than death. I have heard your brother Joseph speak to my father Pharaoh concerning ye, and thus he said: ' They are only sons of the handmaids, and not my real brothers. I will wait for the death of my father and then I will destroy them and all their seed, so that they may not inherit with us. I also have a grudge against these sons of slaves, because they were guilty of my having been sold into slavery to the Ishmaelites. I will, therefore, punish them for their treatment of me, and repay hatred with hatred.'

" My father, Pharaoh," continued the heir to the throne, " applauded your brother's words and promised to help him in the execution of his deed." Thus spoke the son of Pharaoh, inventing a falsehood, so as to excite the hatred against and fear of Joseph in the hearts of the sons of Bilhah and Zilpah.[1]

Now the sons of the handmaids knew in their hearts that they had been guilty of deep hatred against Joseph, and had resolved on his death on that fatal day when the future ruler of Egypt was thrown into the pit.

Dan had been very jealous of Joseph, and more than once the evil spirit had stirred him up to take his sword and slay Joseph, crush him as a leopard crusheth a kid. He regretted it deeply afterwards, and, on his death-bed, he exhorted his children to keep away from anger and wrath, and never be moved to anger, even if any one spoke evil against them.

Gad, too, confessed on his death-bed that he had hated

[1] See note 1, p. 148.

Joseph in his early youth, on account of the latter's talebearing.
Very valiant in keeping the flocks, it was Gad's duty to guard
them at night. When a lion, wolf, or any other wild beast came,
he used to pursue the beast, and seizing its foot with one hand
hurl it about until he killed it. One day, he succeeded in delivering a lamb, snatched and carried away by a bear. The
lamb, however, had been grievously hurt and could no longer
live, and the brethren, therefore, slew it and ate its flesh.
Now Joseph had been with the flock for thirty days until he
had fallen sick on account of the heat. On his return home to
his father, he told the latter that the sons of Bilhah and Zilpah
were slaying the best of the flock and eating them without
asking the permission of either Reuben or Judah. Gad, therefore, hated Joseph from his heart, and often wished to kill
him, to " lick him out of the land of the living, even as an ox
licketh up the grass of the field ". No wonder, therefore, that
Dan and Gad, who felt guilty of their former treatment of
Joseph, were afraid of the powerful ruler's revenge and gave
credence to the story told them by the son of Pharaoh.[1]

" And what shall we do, my lord?" asked Gad and Dan.

" My plan," replied the Prince of Egypt, " is as follows:
This night I will kill my father, the King of Egypt, for he is
unto Joseph like a father and loves him greatly, whilst ye will
kill your brother Joseph, the Viceroy. Thereupon I will take
me to wife Asenath and ye will be to me like my brethren, and
inherit everything with me."

Thus spake the son of Pharaoh, and Dan and Gad agreed
to his plan, whilst Naphtali and Asher demurred.

Naphtali had been greatly loved by Joseph's mother,
Rachel, who constantly used to kiss him and to wish for a son
from her own womb like Naphtali. And when Joseph was
born he was like Naphtali in all things. Naphtali, too, saw

---

[1] R. H. Charles, *The Testaments of the Twelve Patriarchs*, London, 1917 (*Testament of Gad*, pp. 82–83).

visions, and also used to dream dreams which he told to his father who replied that the things he saw would be fulfilled in due season.

Naphtali had once seen a vision or dreamed a dream, wherein he beheld his father standing by the shore of the sea of Jamnia. Thereupon a ship, without either sailors or pilot, came sailing by, and upon the ship was written: "The ship of Jacob". The Patriarch then said to his sons: " Come, let us embark on our ship." This they did, and Jacob took the helm. But, lo, a mighty storm arose, and a terrible tempest raged, the ship being tossed about by the angry waters. It was ultimately broken up. Jacob departed from his sons, Joseph fled away upon a little boat, whilst the other brethren held fast to nine planks, until they were scattered to all the corners of the earth. But Levi prayed for them all to the Lord, the storm ceased, and the ship reached the shore. Thereupon Jacob returned, and they were all re-united.

Naphtali and Asher, therefore, tried to dissuade their brothers from committing the wicked deed, but in the end they followed them.[1]

" We know," said Dan and Gad, " that to-morrow Asenath is going down to the country and will be accompanied by an escort of six hundred valiant men, whilst Joseph will go to town to sell corn. Now, if my lord will send with us a greater number of warriors, we will start this night, lie in ambush in the ravine, and hide in the thicket, whilst thou wilt precede us with a vanguard of fifty spearmen. When our sister-in-law approacheth our hiding-place, we will fall upon her escort, kill all the men, and let Asenath escape, so that in her flight she will fall into thy hands for thee to do unto her as thou pleasest."

Thus spoke Dan and Gad, and the son of Pharaoh, on hearing their words, was greatly pleased, and put 2000 men

[1] Charles, loc. cit., p. 80.

at the disposal of the brothers who started at once on their errand.

During the night the prince made an attempt to penetrate into the royal apartments, but the guards on duty would not allow him to pass.

" Thy father," they said, " having suffered from an acute headache, passed a sleepless night, and is now resting awhile. He has, therefore, given orders that no one be allowed to pass and enter his room, not even his eldest son."

Greatly disappointed, the prince, unsuccessful in his parricidal design, went out to capture Asenath, taking with him five hundred spearmen. He stationed himself not far from the place where Dan and Gad were lying in ambush.

Early the next morning Asenath left town for the country. " I am going," she said, " but it grieves me greatly to leave thee, my beloved."

" Have no fear, my dear," replied Joseph, " and put thy trust in God who will guard thee and protect thee. I cannot accompany thee, as I am bound to go to the storehouse, there to distribute corn to the hungry."

They separated, and Asenath, accompanied by a body-guard of six hundred valiant men, proceeded on her journey. Scarcely had they reached the place where the prince's forces led by the sons of Bilhah and Zilpah were lying in ambush, when the latter came forth from their hiding-place and attacked Asenath's bodyguard. When Asenath perceived Pharaoh's son, she called upon the Lord to help her and fled from her chariot. Benjamin, too, who was accompanying his sister-in-law, leaped from the chariot and prepared to face the enemy.

Gathering small pebbles from the ravine, he hurled them at the son of Pharaoh, hitting him in the forehead and inflicting a severe wound, so that the prince fell down from his horse, like one dead. Supplied with pebbles by the charioteer,

Benjamin, who resembled a lion in power, continued to cast his stones against the prince's spearmen, killing fifty of them.

In the meantime one of Asenath's bodyguard had escaped, carrying the news of the attack to the other brethren of Joseph, although Levi already knew what was happening, thanks to his prophetic gifts. Simeon and Levi soon appeared upon the scene and set the spearmen in flight.

The sons of the handmaids meanwhile made an attempt to fall with drawn swords upon their sister-in-law, but she prayed to the Lord and the swords of her assailants turned to ashes. They now regretted their crime, and falling upon their knees implored Asenath's forgiveness and her protection against the wrath of Simeon and Levi. She readily forgave them their murderous attempt, advising them to hide behind the thicket until she had succeeded in appeasing the anger of Simeon and of Levi.

When the latter returned from their pursuit of the prince's spearmen, they looked round for the sons of the handmaids, having decided to punish them as they deserved. To their surprise they found in Asenath an advocate of the criminals.

" Do not kill them, O sons of Jacob," she pleaded, " for they are your brethren, the sons of your father. If ye kill your brethren ye will commit a heinous deed, cause deep sorrow to your old father, and be shunned by men."

The brethren forgave the sons of the handmaids, and Levi even washed the wounds of the prince. The heir to the throne died, however, soon afterwards, and Pharaoh grieved greatly.[1]

[1] See note 1, p. 148.

CHAPTER XII

A Father's Blessing, or the Death and Burial of the Patriarch

The Patriarch's last request—His reasons for wishing to be buried in Canaan—The dead who will roll through the hollowed earth—Jacob's humiliation before his death—Ephraim brings the sad tidings—The prophetic spirit forsakes the Patriarch—Joseph's prayer—The Patriarch adopts the sons of Joseph—The discontent of the sons of Jacob—He who hath to him it is given—Blessings enough for all of ye—Reuben deprived of birthright, kingship, and priesthood—Simeon and Levi rebuked—It is not the destiny of Israel to draw the sword and commit deeds of violence—The offspring of Judah—Merchant princes will issue from Zebulun and scholars from Issachar—The fair daughters of Asher—The Patriarch's last instructions—The order in which his sons are commanded to carry his bier—The couch upon which reposed the body of the Patriarch—The guard of honour —The Queen intercedes on behalf of Joseph—The royal secret—Pharaoh is compelled to grant Joseph leave of absence—The golden bier of the Patriarch—He has the appearance of a living king—The funeral procession —The perfumed carpet—The kings and magnates of Canaan join the procession—Disarmament in honour of Jacob, the man of peace—The thirty-six crowns suspended from Jacob's bier—The arrival of Esau—The lord of Seïr claims his portion of the family tomb—The deed of sale—The disputed document—Naphtali runs to Egypt—The anger of Hushim the deaf—He knocks his great uncle's head off—The head of Esau is buried in the cave of Machpelah—The fight for the headless body of Esau—The capture of Zepho, son of Eliphaz—The return to Egypt.

For seventeen years Jacob had dwelt in Goshen, when he felt his end approach. Seventeen years of peace were granted to the Patriarch as a reward for the seventeen years which he had devoted to the bringing up and education of Joseph. When Jacob knew that his end was near, he summoned his favourite son, the ruler of Egypt, and thus addressed him:

" If I have found grace in thine eyes, O my son, do not bury me in the land of Egypt, but carry my remains to the land of Canaan, the land which the Lord did promise to give to my descendants. A day will come, my son, when the dead will awaken and come to life again, but those buried in the Holy Land will rise first to new life, whilst the dead buried in other places of the world will roll through the hollowed earth until they reach Canaan. Besides, the Egyptians, who look upon me as a saint, might turn my grave, if I were to be interred in this country, into an object of idolatrous worship. A day will also come when the country will be visited by ten plagues, one of them vermin with which the soil of Egypt will swarm. My grave will thus be desecrated, and my corpse exposed to uncleanness. I am also anxious, even as my fathers were before me, to lie in the Holy Land, for the Lord once promised me to give it to my descendants. ' The land whereon thou liest,' He said, ' I will give it to thee and to thy seed.' If I have, therefore, found grace in thine eyes, carry my remains to the Holy Land for burial, but take with thee some of the earth of Egypt upon which my corpse will have lain to strew it over my dead body. Swear to me, my son, that thou wilt carry out my request."

When Joseph promised to do his father's bidding and to carry out his request, the Patriarch bowed low before his own son, who was the ruler of Egypt, so as to let come true Joseph's dream wherein he had seen the sun (his father) bowing low before him. But Jacob also bowed low to the Majesty of God (which had appeared at the head of his bed), thanking the Lord for the blessing He had vouchsafed unto him in giving him such a son. Jacob had nevertheless humiliated himself before his own son, both in repeating his request three times and asking a favour and a service of Joseph, and in bowing low to him. Just as death in itself is a humiliation for man, just as Moses and David had to experience this humiliation

(*Numbers*, 25, 7; *Kings*, 2, 1) so Jacob also humiliated himself before his death.

" And where shall I bury thee in Canaan?" asked Joseph.

" Bury me in the double cave which I bought from my brother Esau," replied Jacob.

Some time afterwards, Ephraim, the son of Joseph, who was constantly with his grandfather who instructed him in the knowledge of God, came over from Goshen and informed his father that the Patriarch was grievously sick. The Viceroy at once hastened to his father's bedside, taking with him, at the urgent request of his wife Asenath, his two sons, so that the pious Patriarch might bless them.

When Jacob raised his hands to bless his grandsons, he suddenly saw in a prophetic vision that Jeroboam, the son of Nebat, and Ahab, the son of Omri, their descendants, would introduce idolatry in Israel. He saw crowds worshipping idols, and the Holy Spirit forsaking him, he could not bestow his blessing upon Ephraim and Manasseh.

" I cannot bless thy sons," he said unto Joseph, " for they seem to be unworthy of it. Who are they? Whose sons are they? Are they the offspring of a worthy mother whom thou didst marry according to the law?"

" Whoever they are," replied Joseph, " they are my sons, and I did marry their mother Asenath according to the law, and here is the marriage contract."

Joseph also prayed unto the Lord to have mercy on him and his sons and permit his father to bless them. " Do not put me to shame to-day," he prayed, " O Lord of the Universe, and may Thy Holy Spirit once more descend upon my father so that he may bless my sons who are innocent of the sin to be committed one day by their descendants."

Thus prayed Joseph in the agony of his soul, and the Lord hearkened unto the prayer of Joseph the Just. The Holy Spirit once more descended upon Jacob, and he blessed his grand-

sons, giving the birth-right to Ephraim from whom would issue
Joshua, the son of Nun, who was to lead Israel into the land
of Canaan. Joshua, Jacob saw, would work wonders in the
presence of Israel, for he would one day bid the sun and the
moon stand still and wait until he had brought to a successful
issue the war he was waging.

"May the Lord protect ye," said the Patriarch, "against
all evil, and may ye grow and multiply like the fishes in the
sea, and may the evil eye have no power over ye for the sake
of the merits of your father Joseph."

Happy and in blithe spirits, Joseph left his father who had
bestowed his last blessing upon his sons. When the brethren
beheld Joseph's radiant countenance, they murmured: "Such
is the way of the world: he who hath, to him it is given, and
a favourite of fortune is favoured and loved by all. Joseph is
king and ruler of Egypt, and therefore our father, too, hath
bestowed his blessing upon him and his sons, and left none
for us."

When Jacob heard these words, he said to his sons: "It
is not so. I have blessed Joseph and his sons not because
your brother is more powerful than ye, but because he is just,
pious, and generous. As for ye, fear the Lord, practise justice,
and be pious and generous, and ye will never want anything,
for those who honour the Lord are blessed. I will bless ye
too, my sons, for I have blessings enough for all my sons."
Thereupon the Patriarch summoned all his sons and bestowed
his last blessing upon each of them separately.

He rebuked Reuben for the sin he had once committed
with regard to Bilhah, pointing out that one sin committed
makes a man lose many privileges and benefits. "Thou art
my first-born, the beginning of my strength, and the crowns of
birth-right, priesthood, and kingship ought therefore to have
been thy share. But the birth-right is given to Joseph, the
priesthood to Levi, and the kingship to Judah. I bless thee,

however, my son, and from thee will issue priests to the
Lord, heroes and kings."

Jacob also rebuked Simeon and Levi, because they had
been the first to draw their swords, and had thus imitated the
example of their uncle, Esau, who lived by his sword. " Know,
my sons, he said, that it is not the destiny of Israel to draw
the sword and to commit deeds of violence. It is not seemly
for the sons of Jacob to shed blood and for Israel to wage wars.
Our prayers are our weapons, and our supplications are our
arrows."

When Judah heard these rebukes, he was greatly alarmed
and feared his father's reproaches, which he knew he well
deserved. " I will slip away and not be put to shame by my
father's reproaches," thought Judah. But the Patriarch called
him back and spoke gently to him:

" Thou, my son, didst once confess thy sin publicly in
the case of thy daughter-in-law Tamar; thou also didst save
the life of thy brother Joseph. Thy brethren, therefore, will
praise thee, and the nation will be called after thee and known
as Judæans (Jews) from Judah, and not as Reubenites, Simeon-
ites, or Levites. From thee will issue kings, rulers and teachers
of the law, judges and prophets."

The Patriarch thereupon blessed Zebulun and Issachar,
Dan, Naphtali, Gad, and Asher. The descendants of Zebulun
will be distinguished by their commercial careers, for merchant
princes and business magnates will issue from him, and they
will grow prosperous. They will inherit the sea-coasts, and their
merchant ships will ply the high seas. With their abundant
wealth they will support the sons of Issachar, whose descendants
are destined to devote themselves to the study of the law, giving
issue to great scholars and members of legal assemblies.

In blessing Dan, the Patriarch saw in a prophetic vision the
hero Samson who would issue from him, Samson who would
redeem Israel from their oppressors the Philistines. But he

saw Samson standing between the two pillars in the temple of the Philistines, blind and defeated, and he knew that although he would bring victory to Israel, Samson was not the redeemer of Israel.

To Naphtali he said: " Thou wast always as swift as a hart to do my bidding; in thy domain will be the plain of Gennesaret, famous for its gardens and its delicious fruit, which will ripen quickly and be served upon royal tables.

" From Gad famous heroes and warriors will issue, and the descendants of Asher will be famous for the beauty of their women, and kings and high-priests will seek their wives among the daughters of Asher."

When Joseph's turn came the Patriarch thus addressed him: " Thou art mighty and powerful, my son, and thou hast been strong in life; thou art like the vine planted at the edge of the water, its roots being in the depth of the earth and its branches surpassing and excelling all the other trees. Thy wisdom excelleth the wisdom of the magicians of Egypt, and thy pious deeds conquered them all. When Pharaoh placed thee in his chariot and men called out before thee: ' Long live the ruler of Egypt, old in wisdom but young in years!' the daughters of kings and princes rushed to their windows, casting their eyes upon thee. They threw down gold and silver ornaments, trying to draw thy attention to them, but thou didst not look at them nor wast thou enticed by their beauty. The instruction thou didst receive from thy father has rendered thee worthy of being the feeder of men. May the blessing thy father now bestoweth upon thee and the blessing which his fathers, Abraham and Isaac, gave him—and which the great ones of the earth, Ishmael, Esau, and the sons of Keturah envied—rest upon thee and be a crown upon thy head. Mayest thou enjoy their fruits in this world and in the next."

To Benjamin Jacob foretold that the first King of Israel

would issue from his tribe and that the Holy Temple would
be built in his allotment.

The Patriarch was on the point of revealing the future to
his sons, but the Holy Spirit left him, and he was unable to
communicate to his sons the mysteries of the future of the
nation.

" Be united, my sons," said the Patriarch, " for union will
be your strength, and will bring about the redemption of Israel,
who will be driven into exile twice." Thereupon the Patriarch
commanded all his sons to abstain from idolatry and to love
truth, peace, and justice. His sons faithfully promised to obey
his commands. He then gave them instructions how to bear
his body and transport his bier from Egypt to Canaan.

" No stranger shall help to bear my body, and not even
your sons, for some among you did marry heathen wives.
The order ye will observe shall be as follows: Judah, Issachar,
and Zebulun shall march to the east, in front; Reuben, Simeon,
and Gad to the right of the bier, or the south; Dan, Asher,
Naphtali to the left, or the north; and Ephraim, Manasseh,
and Benjamin behind, or to the west."

It was the same order in which the tribes were afterwards
to march through the desert, bearing their standards.

Joseph and Levi were rather astonished at the instructions
their father had given them with regard to the order in which
they were to transport his bier.

" Why, Father," they complained, " didst thou exclude us
from the last honour to be paid unto thee?"

" Thou, my son Joseph," replied the Patriarch, " art the
ruler of Egypt, and it is not seemly that thou shouldst help
bear my bier, whilst Levi is destined one day to carry the ark
of the Lord. Therefore, he too shall not carry the bier containing my dead body.

" Know, my sons," concluded the Patriarch, " that great
suffering will be your lot in this land of Egypt, but if you serve

the Lord and teach your children to walk in His ways, He will send you a redeemer who will deliver you from bondage and lead you into the Holy Land which the Lord promised to your fathers. A day will come when this redeemer will bless the tribes of Israel, but his blessing will only be bestowed upon you when you will observe the commands written in his law."

When the Patriarch had finished blessing his sons and giving them his last instructions, he breathed his last, dying gently as if sent to sleep by Divinity, his soul lured from his body by a Divine kiss.

The brethren rent their garments, girded their loins with sackcloth and strewed dust upon their heads in sign of mourning. They wept and lamented the death of their pious father.

When the news of Jacob's death became known in the land, the great ones of the realm and the women of Egypt came to weep over the Patriarch.

The sons immediately began to make preparations for the burial. Joseph gave orders to his physicians to embalm the corpse of his father, an operation to which they devoted forty days. But Joseph's command displeased the Lord, who alone preserves the corpses of the pious from corruption.

Jacob's body was placed upon a couch made of cedar wood, covered with gold and set with gems and precious stones. A drapery of purple was hung over the couch, fragrant wine was poured out at the side, and aromatic spices and perfumes were burnt. A guard of honour stood round the bier of Jacob, among them being heroes of the house of Esau, and heroes of the house of Ishmael, and also Judah, the bravest hero among the sons of Jacob.

For seventy days the Egyptians mourned over the death of the Patriarch. "Come," they said, "let us mourn the pious man on account of whose merits the famine in our land has been reduced from forty-two to two years."

Joseph now made the necessary preparations to transport

the body of his father from Egypt to Canaan. First, however, he had to obtain Pharaoh's permission to absent himself from the country. As he did not wish to appear at court during the time of mourning, he decided to address himself to the queen, asking her to put his petition before Pharaoh and to intercede on his behalf. He sent for the governess of the royal children and asked her to put his petition before the queen, so that she might speak favourably to the King and influence him to grant the required permission.

" I have given a solemn oath to my father," said Joseph, " to carry his body up to Canaan, and I must, therefore, absent myself from the country for some time."

Pharaoh was at first not inclined to grant the permission Joseph craved, and advised the Viceroy to obtain an absolution from his oath from the wise men of Egypt.

Joseph thereupon sent to Pharaoh the following reply:

" If I seek absolution from the oath I have given my father, I will also seek absolution from the oath I once swore unto thee, never to reveal thy secret. I will now be free to inform the princes of thy realm and thy people that thou art ignorant of Hebrew, and dost not fulfil the condition under which only a man who was supposed to know all the seventy languages could be appointed ruler of Egypt."

When Pharaoh heard these words, he trembled greatly, for if the secret were to be betrayed, the people might depose him and raise Joseph to the vacant throne. Pharaoh, therefore, speedily granted Joseph his request, permitting him to carry the body of his father from Egypt to Canaan. The funeral procession consequently started for Canaan.

In a bier, made of pure gold, inlaid with onyx and bdellium, reposed the body of the Patriarch. An artistically woven cover of gold, fastened to the bier with hooks of onyx and bdellium, covered it. Upon the head of the Patriarch, Joseph placed a golden crown, and in his hand he put a golden sceptre, so that even in his death the Patriarch had the appearance of a living king. The bier was borne by Jacob's sons, but first came the valiant men of Pharaoh and the valiant men of Joseph, in warlike attire and brilliantly arrayed. The rest of the inhabitants, all in coats of mail and girt with swords, walked behind, at some distance from the bier, accompanied by weepers and mourners. Close behind the bier walked Joseph and his household, with bare feet and weeping, accompanied by servants in splendid warlike attire. Fifty of Joseph's servants walked in front of the bier, strewing, as they passed along, myrrh and aloes and aromatic spices, so that the sons of Jacob carrying the bier walked upon a perfumed carpet. Thus the procession moved on until it reached the boundary of Canaan and halted at *Goren Heatad*, the threshing floor of Atad, beyond the Jordan, where " they lamented with a very great and sore lamentation ".

When the kings of Canaan heard the tidings of Jacob's death, they ordered their servants to saddle their horses, mules, and asses, spreading black cloth over them, and came out to join the procession, and to show their respect to Jacob the Hebrew. Before approaching the bier, the kings loosed the girdles of their garments and bared their shoulders in sign of grief and mourning. They also took off their weapons and laid them down upon the ground, not daring to approach the bier of Jacob, the man of peace, in their accoutrements and with their weapons of war which he had abhorred. When they saw Joseph's golden crown suspended from the bier of the Patriarch, the kings of Canaan also took off their crowns and placed them round the bier, so that thirty-six crowns were attached to it.

The news of Jacob's death had also reached his brother Esau at Seïr, who, accompanied by his sons and numerous followers, hastened to the threshing floor of Atad to meet and join the procession.

Joseph and his brethren now proceeded to Hebron, there to bury the Patriarch in the Double Cave, or the Cave of

Machpelah. But scarcely had they reached the burial place, when Esau came forward and made an effort to prevent the burial of his brother in the cave.

" I will not permit you," said Esau, " to bury my brother Jacob in this cave, for the only place available in it belongs to me by right."

" How so?" queried Joseph, angry at his uncle's aggressive attitude.

" Thou knowest," replied Esau, " that there is room in this cave for eight people only. Now, Adam and Eve, Abraham and Sarah, Isaac and Rebekah, lie buried here, and thus only two places remained, one for Jacob and one for me, the sons of Isaac. Thy father Jacob, however, buried his wife Leah in his place, and the remaining vacant place therefore is my portion."

Thus spoke Esau, but Joseph waxed wroth and replied:

" This is idle talk, for thou hast forfeited thy portion in the family tomb. Twenty-five years ago, when my grandfather Isaac died, my father offered thee to choose between a heap of gold and silver and thy portion in the family tomb. Thou didst choose the gold, resigning thy portion in the family tomb. My father acquired it from thee in a legal way, and a bill of sale was made out. I know all this, although I was not in Canaan at that time, for the bill of sale, duly signed, is in Egypt."

Esau, however, denied that any such document existed. " Produce the document," he replied, " and I will comply with thy request to permit thy father to be buried here in this cave."

Joseph, therefore, speedily dispatched his brother Naphtali, the swift runner, to Egypt, bidding him hurry and fetch the disputed document. Swift as a hart, Naphtali hurried away, running up-hill and down-hill, over dales and mounts, on his way from Canaan to Egypt.

When Esau saw that Naphtali had been dispatched to fetch the bill of sale which he well knew did exist, he summoned his sons and all his followers to prepare for battle against Joseph and his brethren.

In the meantime Hushim, the son of Dan, who was deaf, wondered at the tumult and the evident dispute which he did not understand. He endeavoured to find out the cause of the altercation, and the reason why they did not proceed with the burial of Jacob. By signs it was made clear to Hushim that the hairy man yonder was the cause of all the trouble. He would not permit the Patriarch to be buried in the cave, and they would have to await Naphtali's return from Egypt. When Hushim grasped the facts his indignation knew no bounds.

" What?" cried he, " shall my grandfather lie here dishonoured awaiting burial?" Seizing a club, he rushed into the midst of Esau's men and with one vigorous blow knocked the hairy one's head off. Esau died, and his eyes fell upon Jacob's knees.

Esau being dead, his sons and followers no longer dared interfere with the sons of Jacob who buried their father in the cave of Machpelah. The head of Esau, however, rolled into the cave and dropped into the lap of his father Isaac where it remained.

Joseph and his brethren mourned for seven days and then prepared to return to Egypt. But as soon as the period of seven days had elapsed, a war broke out between the sons of Esau and the sons of Jacob for the body of the lord of Seïr, which still lay unburied on the field of Machpelah. The sons of Esau were defeated, loosing eighty men, and Joseph captured Zepho, the son of Eliphaz, the son of Esau, and fifty of their men whom he sent down as prisoners to Egypt. The remaining men of the house of Esau took to flight, carrying with them the body of their chief, which they buried on Mount Seïr. The sons of Jacob pursued the enemy, but slew none of them out

of respect for the headless corpse of their Uncle Esau. They
returned to Hebron, but on the third day were once more
attacked by the enemy. The sons of Esau had gathered all the
inhabitants of Seïr and the children of the East and led a
mighty army against Joseph and his brethren, marching right
down into Egypt. Joseph, however, at the head of the heroes
of Egypt, met the enemy on the way and a fierce battle was
waged. The sons of Seïr and the children of the East suffered
a great defeat, their entire army being destroyed. Joseph and
his brethren pursued them as far as Succoth, and then returned
to Egypt.[1]

[1] *Genesis Rabba*, §§ 96–100; *Targum Pseudo-Jonathan, in loco*; *Midrash Tanchuma*, section
Vaichi; *Midrash Agadah*, ed. Buber, pp. 105–117; *Midrash Lekach Tob, in loco*; *Yalkut
Shimeoni, in loco*; *Numbers Rabba*, section *Nassoh*; Babylonian Talmud, *Sotah*, 13a, 36b; *Pirke
de Rabbi Eliezer*, Ch. 39; *Sepher Hajashar*; see also Gaster, *The Chronicles of Jerahmeel*,
p. 95 (XL, 3); Adolf Kurrein, *loc. cit.*; Lewner, *Kol Agadoth*, pp. 254–270.

CHAPTER XIII

Joseph's Magnanimity, and the Wars of the Cousins

Joseph no longer invites his brethren to have their meals at his table—His reasons for doing so—The fear of the brethren—Bilhah's message—Joseph's reply—His love and affection for his brethren—His gratitude to the sons of Jacob—He cannot act against the decrees of Providence—The death of Pharaoh—King Magron—Joseph the actual ruler of the country—The quarrel of the sons of Esau and the sons of Seïr—King Agnias of Africa—The war between the sons of Esau and the sons of Seïr—The victory of the sons of Esau—The election of a king—Bela, the son of Beor—The sons of Esau make war upon Egypt—Joseph's victory—Jobab, King of Edom—The escape of Zepho—At the court of Agnias, King of Africa—'Uzi of Pozimana—The fair Yaniah—The people of Kittim—The suitors for the hand of Yaniah—Turnus, King of Benevento—The reply of the men of Kittim—Lucus, King of Sardinia—The war between Agnias and Turnus—In the plain of Campania—The death of Neblus, son of Lucus—The golden statue and the two graves—Zepho's plan of revenge—The campaign against Egypt—Balaam, the magician—The wax figures—Zepho's flight to Kittim—The monster in the cave—The festival of Zepho—The sickness of Yaniah—The waters of Africa and Kittim—The waters of Forma for Queen Yaniah—Zepho is elected King of Kittim.

Since their return to Egypt, Joseph had ceased to invite his brethren to take their meals at his table and to entertain them, as he had been in the habit of doing for seventeen years whilst the Patriarch was still alive. Joseph's attitude, however, was not the result of any altered feeling on his part, but was dictated by a sentiment of justice. " So long as my father was alive," thought the Viceroy, " I used to sit at the head of the table, obeying therein my father's command. Now, however, it is not seemly, and I have no right to do so, for Reuben is after all the first-born, whilst kings will issue from Judah.

And yet, being the ruler of Egypt, I cannot allow anyone to sit at the head of the table."

For this reason Joseph hesitated to invite again his brethren to take their daily meals at his table. The brethren, however, unaware of Joseph's motives and of his fine scruples, attributed his changed attitude to a change of feelings. They now feared greatly that Joseph hated them and would avail himself of the first opportunity to wreak his vengeance. What he had not dared to do whilst the Patriarch was still alive he would not hesitate now to accomplish. Thus thought the brethren, and decided to ascertain what was in the Viceroy's mind and whether he intended to do harm unto them.[1]

They sent Bilhah as their deputy to Joseph with an invented message, and informed the Viceroy of their father's last wish, conjuring him in the name of Jacob to condone the brethren's former aim.

When Joseph heard Bilhah's words and knew that his brethren still suspected him of harbouring hostile feelings towards them, he wept copiously and was greatly grieved. He hastened to assure his brethren of his love and affection, and consoled them as well as he could.

" If I did no longer invite you to sit at my table, the Lord knoweth my reason and that my action was dictated by my respect for you. Fear not," said the Viceroy, " for why should I repay you evil for good? You have rendered me a great service when you came to Egypt. Before your arrival in the country the Egyptians looked upon me as a slave, the son of an obscure shepherd, who was released from prison and became their ruler. They never would believe that I was really of noble birth and the scion of a great house. By your advent here you have proved to all Egypt that I am a man of noble birth. I am therefore grateful to you, and will not forget what

---

[1] *Midrash Tanchuma; Genesis Rabba,* § 100; *Targum Pseudo-Jonathan; Midrash Agadah; Yalkut Shimeoni.*

I owe unto you. Besides, it is in my own interest to treat you well and to show you every mark of love and affection. Were I to act otherwise, were I to kill you, then my proofs of being the scion of a noble house would at once no longer hold good. The Egyptians would say: ' Either this man is devoid of all brotherly feelings, and doth not keep faith with his own kith and kin and is not to be trusted, or he is a deceiver. He induced a gang of young men to come down to Egypt and give themselves out as his brothers, but now that they have served his purpose and have become rather troublesome he quickly found a pretext to get rid of them.' I beg you, therefore, my brethren, to banish all suspicion from your hearts, for I harbour no evil thoughts against you, and be convinced of my brotherly love and affection. Besides, are ye not like the dust of the earth, the sand on the seashore, and the beasts of the field? Could they all be exterminated, leaving no trace? Have ye not seen that ten stars were unable to do ought against one? Then how could one star destroy ten? I could not act against the decrees of Providence and the laws of nature. The day hath twelve hours, and twelve hours hath the night. Twelve months hath the year, twelve is the number of the constellations, and twelve tribes are we. I am the head, whilst ye represent the body, but the head cannot continue to live without the body. Go therefore home in peace, my brethren, and remember our father's last words and his instructions. The Lord will then be with ye, and ye need fear no man." Thus spoke Joseph, and the brethren were greatly relieved and consoled.[1]

Now when Joseph was seventy-one years of age—it was thirty-two years after the arrival of his brethren in Egypt—Pharaoh died, and his son Magron ruled in his place.

Before departing this life Pharaoh called Joseph and thus he spoke to him: " I beg thee to guide my son Magron with thy counsel and be a father unto him."

[1] *Ibid.*

The Egyptians, who loved their Viceroy greatly, for he had found favour in their eyes, were well pleased with Pharaoh's last injunctions, and they made Joseph the actual ruler and regent of the land, whilst Magron bore the royal title and was called Pharaoh, as is the custom in Egypt to call the kings. Magron, however, left all the affairs of the state to be administered by Joseph's hand, who was thus the real ruler of the country.[1]

As regent and actual ruler of Egypt, the son of Jacob was just and generous as before. He was also as modest and humble on the throne as he had been years ago, when a slave in the house of Potiphar. The Lord was therefore with Joseph, and he was successful in all his undertakings. He was well beloved by all his subjects, and his fame travelled far and wide. He also extended his rule over the land of the Philistines, of Canaan and Sidon, and the land east of the Jordan, and the inhabitants of these countries sent rich presents to the ruler of Egypt and brought him a yearly tribute. The sons of Jacob dwelt in Goshen, happy and peaceful, and served the Lord as they had been commanded by the Patriarch before he died. They did not mix with the Egyptians, who worshipped idols, and cherished their own tongue, the Hebrew language.

Now when the sons of Esau and the sons of Seïr had returned to their own country after their campaign, they began to quarrel among themselves: " It is because of you," said the sons of Seïr, " that we were forced to wage a war against the sons of Jacob. And now you have brought misfortune upon us, for we have suffered a great defeat and have lost all our valiant men, none having remained who know the art of war. Leave, therefore, our territory and go to Canaan, the home of your ancestors. Why should your children possess this country together with our own descendants?"

Thus spoke the sons of Seïr, wishing to get rid of the sons

[1] *Sepher Hajashar*; *Exodus Rabba*, § 1; *Pirke de Rabbi Eliezer*, Ch. 48.

of Esau. As the latter refused to leave the country, the sons
of Seïr decided to expel by force those whom they called *aliens*
in their midst. The sons of Esau, however, secretly sent a
deputation to Agnias, King of Denaba, in Africa, asking him
for help.

" The children of Seïr," they informed Agnias, " have
decided to expel us from their country, and we therefore
urgently beseech thee to send us armed assistance that we may
be able to resist our enemy."

Agnias, who at that time was favourably disposed towards
the sons of Esau, immediately sent 500 foot soldiers and
800 mounted men.

The sons of Seïr had in the meantime addressed themselves
to the children of the East and to the Madianites for help.

" You have seen," they wrote, " what misfortune the sons
of Esau have brought down upon us. Against our will they
involved us in a war with the sons of Jacob in which all our
valiant men have perished. Now, we want to get rid of the
sons of Esau who are dwelling in our midst. Come therefore
to our aid and help us expel them from our land and to revenge
the death of our brethren of which the sons of Esau are the
cause."

The sons of the East granted the request of the sons of
Seïr, and immediately sent them 800 men well versed in the
art of war.

The two hostile armies met in the desert of Paran, where
a fierce battle was waged. The battle ended with a complete
defeat of the sons of Esau, who lost 200 men. On the following
day they once more gathered their forces and returned to the
charge. This time, too, the God of battles was against them,
and they lost heavily. Twenty-eight men of the army of Agnias
had also been killed, and many of the sons of Esau deserted
their brethren, joining the ranks of the enemy. On the third
day, the sons of Esau thus spoke to each other:

" What shall we do unto our brethren who have forsaken us in our hour of need?"

Thereupon they once more sent a messenger to Agnias, requesting him to send them fresh support.

" Twice," they wrote, " have we suffered a defeat at the hands of the sons of Seïr, who are superior to us in number."

Agnias once more put at their disposal an army of 600 valiant men to help the sons of Esau in their need. Ten days later, the latter again attacked the enemy in the desert of Paran and this time gained a decisive victory. The hostile forces were routed, all the valiant men, 2000 in number, fell in the combat.

The children of the East and the Madianites were put to flight, and were pursued by the sons of Esau who slew another 250 men. The sons of Esau themselves had only lost thirty men slain by their own brethren, who had joined the hostile army.

On their return to Seïr, the sons of Esau slew all the women and children who had remained behind, sparing only fifty boys whom they made slaves, and fifty maidens whom they took to wives. They thereupon divided among themselves all the possessions of the sons of Seïr, all the land and the cattle. They also divided the whole land into five districts, according to the number of the sons of Esau.

Some time afterwards the sons of Esau determined to elect a king who would rule the country and command the army in times of war. They swore, however, that never would a son of their own people rule over them, for ever since the treachery of their brethren during the wars with the sons of Seïr they had no faith in their own people, and every one suspected his brother, his son, or his friend.

There was among the officers sent to them by King Agnias, King of Denaba, a warrior named Bela, son of Beor. He was a gallant soldier, handsome and well made, comely of person, well versed in all the sciences, and of good counsel. There was none like him among the officers of King Agnias. The choice of the sons of Esau fell upon Bela, whom they chose as their ruler. They proclaimed him King, prostrated themselves before him, and cried aloud: " Long live the King!" Thereupon they spread out a carpet whereupon all deposited their gifts, consisting of precious ornaments and gold and silver pieces, so that the King became very rich, possessing much gold, silver, and precious stones, and lived in opulence. The sons of Esau also constructed a throne for their King, set a golden crown upon his head, and built for him a sumptuous palace as his royal residence. Bela reigned over the sons of Esau for thirty years. The valiant men of Agnias thereupon returned to their own country, after having been well paid for their services by the sons of Esau.[1]

Many years had passed, when the sons of Esau, who had grown mighty during the reign of their King Bela, and had recovered from the defeat they had once suffered, again decided to wage war against the sons of Jacob and the Egyptians. Their purpose was to take their revenge for the defeat they had once suffered and also to deliver Zepho, the son of Eliphaz, and the other prisoners who were still being detained in Egypt.

Thereupon the sons of Esau concluded an alliance with all the sons of the East, and also with the sons of Ishmael, and a mighty army numbering 800,000 men, infantry and cavalry, gathered before the town of Raamses.

At the head of a company of 600 men, Joseph marched against the mighty host of the enemy, and, aided by his brethren, the heroic sons of Jacob, won a splendid victory. Over 200,000 slain of the enemy's army covered the battle-field, among them being King Bela. The remainder of the army took to flight, and were pursued by Joseph and his valiant soldiers. Joseph only lost twelve men, all Egyptians.

[1] *Sepher Hajashar.*

On his return, the Regent of Egypt put Zepho and the other
prisoners in fetters, and made their captivity even more bitter
than it had been before.

After the death of Bela, the sons of Esau appointed a new
king to rule over them in his place. They elected Jobab, son
of Zara of Bozrah, who reigned for ten years, but desisted
from making any war upon the sons of Jacob. As for the sons
of Esau, they were now convinced that it would be futile to
fight against any of the heroic sons of the Patriarch. They
therefore abstained from waging any new wars against Joseph
and his brethren, but their hatred of their cousins increased
and grew fiercer from generation to generation.

Jobab, King of Edom, was succeeded by Husham of
Theman, who ruled over the sons of Esau for twenty years.
It was during his reign, seventy-two years after the arrival of
the children of Israel in Egypt, that Zepho, who had been
a prisoner in Egypt for many years, managed to escape with
his fellow prisoners. They sought refuge at the court of Agnias,
King of Africa, who received them very kindly, and appointed
Zepho Commander-in-Chief of his armies.

Zepho, having found favour in the eyes of King Agnias
and of his people, availed himself of his influence and endeavoured to persuade his sovereign to declare a war on Egypt
and the sons of Jacob. He was anxious to induce the King
and his nobles to gather an army and invade Egypt, so that
he could revenge the death of his brethren. But King Agnias
and his nobles, in spite of Zepho's constant arguments, refused
to listen to him.

King Agnias was only too well acquainted with the strength
of the sons of Jacob, and he still remembered how they had
dealt with his army on a former occasion.

In these days it happened that a man named 'Uzi, who
lived in the city of Pozimana, in the land of Kittim, and whom
his countrymen venerated as a god, died. He left a daughter

named Yaniah, and Agnias, who had heard from his men of
the wisdom and beauty of the damsel, sent messengers to
Kittim to sue for her hand. His request was readily granted
by the people of Kittim, but scarcely had the messengers of
King Agnias left the country taking with them the promise
that Yaniah should become the wife of Agnias, when a new
deputation arrived. Turnus, King of Benevento, had also
heard of the fair and wise Yaniah, and was anxious to take
her to wife, but his request was rejected.

" We have already promised the hand of Yaniah," said
the men of Kittim, " to Agnias, King of Africa, and we cannot
break our promise, for we fear Agnias who will come down
with an army and exterminate us. Your King Turnus," they
continued, " will not be able to protect us against the mighty
King Agnias."

Thus spoke the men of Kittim, and the ambassadors of
Turnus returned to their King who, on hearing their words,
swore to take his revenge. Thereupon the men of Kittim sent
a message to Agnias, King of Africa, wherein they informed
him of what had occurred.

" We have refused the hand of Yaniah to Turnus," wrote
the men of Kittim, " but we now learn that he has gathered
a mighty army and is determined to invade thy country. His
design is first to invade Sardinia, and make war upon thy
brother Lucus, and after having defeated him, to march
against thee."

When Agnias read the message from the men of Kittim,
he waxed very wroth, gathered a great army and hastened
to Sardinia to the assistance of his brother Lucus. Neblus,
son of Lucus, hearing of the arrival of his uncle, came out
with a numerous suite to meet him, welcoming him very
warmly. He begged his uncle to intercede on his behalf with
his father that the latter might appoint him commander
of his armies. The request of Neblus was granted, for his

father appointed him Commander-in-Chief of the Sardinian troops.

The two armies of Agnias and Lucus crossed the sea and arrived in the region of the Asthores. They met Turnus and his army in the plain of Campania, where a fierce battle was fought. The encounter was at first fatal to Lucus and to his army, for he lost nearly all his men, and his own son Neblus was among the slain. But Agnias once more engaged in battle, and came out victorious. He slew Turnus with his own hand, and the latter's entire army was routed. Those who had not been slain fled, closely pursued by Agnias and Lucus, as far as the cross road between Rome and Albano. Thus Agnias revenged the death of his nephew Neblus, and the destruction of his brother's army.

The King thereupon commanded his men to construct a golden statue, and to put the body of Neblus inside of it. The statue was put in a bronze coffin and buried on the cross road between Rome and Albano, and over the grave of the slain General Neblus a high tower was erected. The body of Turnus, the slain King of Benevento, was also buried here, and the two graves are opposite each other, on the cross road between Rome and Albano, and a marble pavement runs between them.

After the burial of Neblus and Turnus, King Lucus, with the remainder of his army, returned to Sardinia, whilst King Agnias proceeded to Benevento, the capital of Turnus.

When the inhabitants of the city heard of the approach of the victorious king, they came out to meet him, and amidst tears and supplications, begged him to have mercy upon them and not to put them to death, and also to spare their city. Agnias granted the request of the inhabitants of Benevento, for the city was considered at that time as belonging to the federation of the children of Kittim. But thenceforth frequent incursions were made into the land of Kittim by soldiers from the army of the King of Africa, sometimes led by General Zepho, and sometimes by the King himself. Now and again the bands came to pillage these provinces, carrying off rich booty.

From Benevento Agnias proceeded to Pozimana where he married Yaniah the daughter of 'Uzi, taking her to his capital in Africa.[1]

Zepho, the Commander-in-Chief of the African armies, had never given up his plans of revenge. Continually he urged King Agnias to invade Egypt and to attack the sons of Jacob, but he always met with a refusal on the part of the King who, knowing the strength and the courage of the sons of Jacob, feared to meet them in the open field. At last, however, a day came when Agnias was persuaded by his general and granted the latter's request. A vast army, as numerous as the sand on the seashore, was equipped, ready to march and invade Egypt, and attack the sons of Jacob.

Now it happened that among the servants (shield-bearers) of Agnias, there was a youth called Balaam, the fifteen years old son of Beor. He was a very clever lad and well versed in the science of magic. Agnias, knowing that Balaam, the son of Beor, was an adept in magic, said to the lad:

"Try to ascertain by virtue of thy magic what will be the issue of the battle and who will be victorious in the war we are about to wage, we or the sons of Jacob." Thus spoke King Agnias, and Balaam, the young son of Beor, had wax brought to him out of which he moulded and fashioned the figures of men on horseback, and war chariots, and he so disposed the wax figures as to represent two hostile armies facing each other. He thereupon plunged the wax figures into magic water, and, holding a palm branch in hand, he practised incantations. He saw the figures representing the army of Agnias subdued by those representing the sons of

---

[1] *Sepher Hajashar; Josippon*, ed. Venice, p. 1*a*; Gaster, *The Chronicles of Jerahmeel*, p. 96.

Jacob. This vision he communicated to the King who grew frightened, lost his courage, and dared not proceed with the war.

Zepho, thereupon, seeing that Agnias had definitely given up the Egyptian campaign, and being now quite convinced that he would never succeed in persuading the King to invade Egypt, gave up his post, fled the country and went to the land of Kittim.

He was received with open arms by the men of Kittim who offered him rich presents and invited him to stay with them and conduct their wars.

The troops of Agnias were still continuing to make incursions into the land of Kittim, and the inhabitants were compelled to take refuge on the mountain of Koptizah (or Kophitra).

One day Zepho went out in search of an ox he had lost, and he discovered at the foot of the mountain a spacious cave, the entrance to which was barred by a huge stone. He broke the stone to pieces, and entering the cave perceived a strange animal devouring his ox. The upper part of the monster was that of a man whilst the lower part was formed like a quadruped. Zepho killed the monster with his sword.

When the men of Kittim learned of Zepho's deed, they rejoiced greatly and said:

"What honours shall we show unto this man who has killed the monster which had for a long time been devouring our cattle?"

They unanimously decided to set aside one day of the year and call it the festival of Zepho. And every year, out of gratitude to their deliverer, they offered sacrifices in honour of Zepho, and brought him many presents.

Now it came to pass in these days that Yaniah, the daughter of 'Uzi and wife of Agnias, fell into a sickness, and the King and his courtiers were greatly grieved. Agnias consulted the physicians, asking them to find a remedy for his wife's sickness and to make her recover her health.

"Great King," replied the physicians, "the climate and the water of our land are not suitable for the Queen and not so good as the climate and waters of her native land of Kittim. Both the climate and the water of Africa are the cause of her sickness, for even in her native land the Queen was accustomed to drink the water of Forma (Firmium) which her parents had caused to be drawn to the house by means of an aqueduct."

When Agnias heard these words, he commanded his servants to fetch water from Forma (Firmium) in a vessel, and the water being weighed was found to be lighter than the water of Africa. Agnias thereupon commanded his officers to gather stone-cutters by thousands and myriads and employed them to hew a vast number of stones for building. He then gathered a great number of stone-masons and ordered them to build a huge aqueduct by means of which the waters of Forma were drawn to Africa. The water was for the sole use of Queen Yaniah who employed it for drinking and cooking, for her baths and even for the washing of her linen. She even made use of it to water her plants and fruit trees. The King also had earth and stones brought in ships from Kittim to Africa, and the architects built a palace for the Queen, who soon regained her former health.[1]

In the course of the next year the African troops once more invaded the land of Kittim for the purpose of pillage as in the past. Zepho, now in command of the army of Kittim, marched against the enemy and won a decisive victory. The hostile armies were put to flight, and the country was saved from their depredations. Out of gratitude for their heroic commander and admiration for his valour, the men of Kittim chose Zepho as their king. His first act as ruler of the country was to undertake a campaign against the sons of Tubal, to subdue

[1] *Sepher Hajashar*; Gaster, *The Chronicles of Jerahmeel*, pp. 97-98; *Josippon*, p. 2a-b.

them and to take possession of the neighbouring islands. He
was very successful, and on his return the men of Kittim
once more confirmed Zepho in his kingship and built for him
a great palace. The King also built a throne for himself, and
reigned over the land of Kittim and the whole country of Italy
for fifty years.[1]

[1] *Sepher Hajashar*; Gaster, *The Chronicles of Jerahmeel*, pp. 97–98; *Josippon*, p. 2a–b.

CHAPTER XIV

The Death of the Regent

Joseph's early death—His punishment—The oath of the sons of Jacob —Joseph exhorts his sons—Love and forgiveness—The death of Joseph— The advice of the magicians—The royal tomb and the magic dogs—The iron coffin in the Nile—The redemption of Israel—The search for the bones of Joseph—Moses on the banks of the Nile—His perplexity—Serah, the daughter of Asher—The swimming iron coffin—The wanderings of Israel— The two shrines—Joseph's reward—The shrine of the living God, and the shrine of the dead—The burial of Joseph.

Joseph had lived in Egypt ninety-three years, and for eighty years had ruled the country, when he felt his end approach. He was 110 years of age, and his end came ten years sooner than it ought to have come. This was a punishment for his having permitted his brethren to repeat ten times the words: " Our father, thy servant," and because he had also given orders to have the dead body of his father embalmed by the physicians of Egypt. He had not had faith enough in the Lord who preserves the bodies of the just, as it is promised by the prophets. When he felt his end near, Joseph sent for his brethren and his entire household and thus addressed them:

" I am soon going to die, but the Lord will remember ye and redeem ye from bondage in this country and lead ye into the land He has promised as an inheritance to our fore-fathers. He will never forsake ye, either here, or in the midst of the waves of the sea, on the banks of the rivers of Arnon, or in the desert, in this world or in the next. Now promise me that when the Lord will send the Redeemer to lead ye into the promised land, ye and your descendants will carry my body with ye to bury it in the Holy Land. Swear also unto me that neither yourselves nor your descendants will ever try to force the hand of Providence and make an attempt to shake off the yoke of the Egyptians who will put heavy tasks upon ye. Swear unto me that ye will patiently await the moment when the Lord Himself will send unto ye His Redeemer to lead ye out of bondage, as He hath promised. My father of his free will came out to Egypt, but I carried his body to Canaan for burial. Me, however, ye have stolen from the land of the Hebrews, therefore, swear unto me that ye will return my body to the land whence I had been dragged away against my will." [1]

Joseph made only his brethren take an oath, but not his own sons, for fear that the Egyptians might not grant to them the permission to carry the body of their father to Canaan. Joseph also reminded his children and all his household of the great things he had endured, because he had refused to put his brethren to shame. He exhorted them to love one another and to hide one another's faults, for the Lord delighteth in the unity of brethren and in the hearts that take pleasure in love. He thereupon exhorted them to walk in the ways of the Lord and to obey His commandments, and if they did so the Lord would exalt them and bless them with good things for ever, and ever.

And Joseph further said unto his sons:

" After my death, the Egyptians will change their love for ye into hatred and will afflict ye and your seed. But in His own time the Lord will send you a Redeemer and lead ye out of bondage into the land which He promised unto your fathers. Carry therefore my bones with ye, for when my bones will be taken up to the Holy Land the Lord shall be with ye in light, whilst the Egyptians shall be in darkness with Beliar."

[1] *Sepher Hajashar*; *Mekhilta*, 13, 9; *Targum Pseudo-Jonathan*; Babylonian Talmud, *Sotah*, 13b.

He also enjoined them to carry up their mother Asenath and to bury her near Rachel.[1]

Soon afterwards Joseph died, and his body was embalmed by the physicians of Egypt. Thereupon the counsellors of Pharaoh came and thus spoke to the King:

" We have heard that the brethren of Joseph and all their descendants are bound by a solemn oath never to leave this country without taking with them the body of the Viceroy. Now we advise thee, O King, to order that the bones of Joseph be placed in a heavy iron coffin and sunk into the Nile, so that no one will ever be able to find his burial place. The sons of Israel will then be compelled to remain in Egypt for ever and serve us. The King may also order that the body of Joseph be buried in the royal tomb, and we will place golden dogs in front of it. By virtue of our magic art, we will so contrive that these dogs will raise a terrible howling whenever a stranger will attempt to approach the royal tomb." Thus spoke the wise men of Egypt, but Pharaoh replied:

" Ye had better make an iron coffin and sink the body of Joseph into the Nile. Thus, on the one hand, the waters of the river will be blessed on account of the merits of Joseph, will water the land and fructify it, whilst, on the other, the burial place of the son of Jacob will never be discovered. The Israelites, this industrious and wise people, will therefore remain our slaves for ever."

Thus spoke Pharaoh, and the coffin wherein the body of Joseph had been placed was consequently sunk into the Nile.[2] Joseph's wish to have his body carried to the Holy Land was fulfilled after many years, at the moment when the nation of Israel was redeemed from bondage and led by Moses out of Egypt. It was Moses himself, the great leader, who thought of the oath once taken by the sons of Jacob. And whilst the

[1] R. C. Charles, *The Testaments of the Twelve Patriarchs, Testament of Joseph*, XX, p. 101.
[2] *Exodus Rabba*, § 20; Babylonian Talmud, *Sotah*, 13*b*.

Israelites were busy amassing wealth and carrying with them out of Egypt as much booty as they could as a reward and compensation for the many years of slavery and for the heavy labour they had accomplished, Moses himself was thinking of the oath once taken by the sons of Jacob, and made every effort to discover the coffin wherein reposed the body of Joseph.

" Verily," said the Lord unto Moses, " in thee are fulfilled the words: ' The labour of the righteous tendeth to life '." (*Proverbs*, 10, 16.)

" As a son of Jacob, it was once Joseph's duty to bury his father, but thou art a stranger to him, and it is not incumbent upon thee to render him this service. As a reward for thy service, when thy own time arrives to die, I myself will bury thy body and render thee a similar service."

But Moses was greatly perplexed, for he knew not the place where the coffin of Joseph could be discovered. He was not even quite sure whether it had really been sunk into the Nile or placed in the royal tomb.

Plunged in meditation, Moses stood on the banks of the River Nile when Serah, the aged daughter of Asher, who, in consequence of the blessing bestowed upon her by Jacob, was never to taste death, approached him.

" Man of God," she spoke, " the coffin of Joseph was sunk into the Nile, so that its waters may be blessed on his account, and also in order to make impossible the exodus of the Israelites."

Moses thereupon wrote the words " Arise, O *Shor*" (bull) upon a piece of clay and thrust it into the Nile. He then called aloud: " Joseph, the time hath come when the Lord is at last redeeming his children from bondage. For thy sake, and on account of the oath once taken, the majesty of the Lord is detained in Egypt, and the redemption of Israel is being delayed. Reveal unto us thy resting-place, so that we may carry out our duty and fulfil thy last wish."

Thus spoke Moses, and lo, the waters of the Nile suddenly stirred and to the surface rose up the coffin of Joseph.

For forty years during the wanderings of the Israelites in the desert, the coffin of Joseph was carried in their midst. It was Joseph's reward for his promise to his brethren to nourish them and to take care of them. And the Lord said: " For forty years the Israelites will take care of thy bones and carry thy coffin in their midst." Thus two shrines were carried by Israel in the desert: one contained the Ark of the Covenant, and the other the bones of Joseph. It was Joseph's reward for his virtues, and a great distinction vouchsafed unto him. For whilst the coffin containing the remains of Jacob had been accompanied by Joseph, the servants of Pharaoh, the nobles of the land, and all the inhabitants of Egypt, Joseph's coffin was surrounded by the Divine Majesty and the pillars of cloud and accompanied by priests and by Levites.

And the nations, when meeting the two shrines, wondered and asked: " What is the meaning of these two shrines, one containing the dead and the other the Law of the living God?"

And the answer was given unto them:

" The dead whose body reposes in one shrine fulfilled the commandments written in the Law enshrined in the Ark. In the Law it is written, ' I am the Lord, thy God ', and he said: ' Am I in the place of God?' In the Law it is written, ' Thou shalt have no other gods before My face ', and he said: ' I fear the Lord '. In the Law it is written: ' Thou shalt not take the name of the Lord in vain ', and he, therefore, said: ' By the name of Pharaoh ', abstaining from swearing by God. In the Law it is written: ' Remember the Sabbath ', and he commanded his overseer to ' make ready everything ' on the day before the Sabbath. In the Law it is written: ' Honour thy father and thy mother ', and he honoured his father and obeyed his commands even when the latter sent him on a perilous mission. In the Law it is written: ' Thou shalt not

commit adultery ', and he refused to sin and commit adultery
with the wife of Potiphar. In the Law it is written: ' Thou
shalt not steal ', and he never stole any of Pharaoh's treasures.
In the Law it is written: ' Thou shalt not bear false witness ',
and he never informed his father of the cruel treatment he
had met at the hands of his brethren. In the Law it is
written: ' Thou shalt not covet thy neighbour's wife ', and
he never did covet the wife of his master Potiphar. In the
Law it is written: ' Thou shalt not hate ', and he never hated
his brethren, but comforted them. In the Law it is written:
' Thou shalt not take revenge ', and he never revenged himself upon his brethren, but nourished them and took care of
them."

The work which Moses had begun, namely that of carrying the bones of Joseph to Canaan, he was unable to complete,
for he died on Mount Nebo. But on their arrival in the Holy
Land the Israelites buried the bones of Joseph at Shechem,
for from Shechem Joseph had once been stolen, and unto
Shechem he was returned and buried there.[1]

---

[1] *Mekhilta*, 13, 9; *Yalkut*, § 227; see also A. Kurrein, *Traum und Wahrheit*, pp. 178–182;
cf. also Grünbaum, *Neue Beiträge*, pp. 149–152.

THE COFFIN OF JOSEPH RISES TO THE SURFACE OF THE NILE

Facing page 188, Vol. II

CHAPTER XV

The Egyptian Bondage

Joseph and King Magron—The rule of the foreigner—The Hebrews in Egypt are deprived of their former privileges—Anti-Semitism in Egypt—The death of Levi—The oppression of the aliens—The effeminate Egyptians and the industrious Hebrews—The fear of the Egyptians—King Melol—The heavy tasks—The invasion of Egypt and the war of liberation—The war between Zepho, King of Kittim, and Agnias, King of Africa—Zepho's message to Hadad, King of Edom—The reply of the sons of Esau—Their refusal to help Zepho—The prayer of Zepho to the God of his fathers—The command of King Agnias to the inhabitants of Africa—The victory of Zepho—The arrival of Balaam at Kittim—The royal banquet—Zepho's plan of revenge—The Egyptian campaign—Zepho's message to the sons of Esau—The Egyptian volunteers—The Hebrew regiment—The natives mistrust the aliens—The failure of Balaam's magic—The defeat of the Egyptians—The assistance and victory of the Hebrews—The ingratitude of the Egyptians—The counsellors of Pharaoh—The fear of the aliens—The advice of Pharaoh—The fortresses of Pithom and Raamses—National work—The decree of Melol—The royal proclamation—Patriotic Hebrews—The example set by the King—Basket and trowel—The production of bricks—The toil of the Hebrews—Their enormous tasks—The labour of the women—The bitter life—Pharaoh *Meror*—The sons of Levi are exempted from doing national work—Semla of Masreca, King of Edom—The threat of a new war—The Egyptian taskmasters, and the voice from Heaven—The noble women of Israel—Words of comfort.

With soft and hypocritical words the descendants of Jacob were drawn into servitude soon after the death of the Patriarch. During the life of Joseph, however, the position of the Israelites in Egypt was a favourable one, for the Viceroy had found favour in the eyes of Magron, the successor of the Pharaoh who had once raised the son of Rachel to high dignities. Joseph was not only the first counsellor of the King, but the actual ruler of the country, Magron having left to him the administration of all affairs of state, retaining only the royal title. The majority of the inhabitants of Egypt all loved Joseph, and only a few raised their voices and murmured against the ruler, dissatisfied that a foreigner should exercise such extensive powers in the country. Things, however, changed soon after the death of Joseph, and half a century later the Hebrews were gradually deprived of their former privileges, and the apparent love of the Egyptians for Israel disappeared. The hostility towards the aliens and foreigners became open, and the hatred implacable. The more the descendants of Jacob were endeavouring to assimilate themselves with the inhabitants of the land— learning their ways, imitating their manners and customs, speaking their language, and even abandoning the sacred rite of circumcision—the more the Egyptians repulsed them and looked askance at them as intruders and aliens. What is called in modern times Anti-Semitism was prevalent in Egypt. God had so ordained that the love of the Egyptians for the children of Israel should be changed into hatred, so that they should turn to the Lord. Oppression of the Israelites now began. Heavy taxes were laid upon them, from which they had been hitherto exempt as free-born strangers in the country. Soon the King issued a decree commanding his people to build him a sumptuous palace. The Hebrews, too, were compelled to give their labour without receiving any pay, and even to erect the castle at their own cost.[1]

Levi was the son of Jacob who had outlived all his brethren, and he died twenty-two years after Joseph. And now all consideration for the descendants of Jacob disappeared completely. The strangers and aliens were oppressed and enslaved. Their property was confiscated, the fields, vineyards, and houses which Joseph had given his brethren soon after the death of his father were claimed and appropriated by native Egyptians. The latter hated work, were effeminate and fond of pleasure,

---

[1] *Midrash Tanchuma*, section *Shemot*; *Midrash Agadah*, section *Shemot*; *Sepher Hajashar*; see also Beer, *Das Leben Mosis*, in *Jahrbuch für die Geschichte der Juden*, 1863, Vol. III, p. 11.

and formed a contrast to the industrious and clean-living Hebrews, whose prosperity they envied. Leading a moral and virtuous life, the Hebrews were thriving exceedingly in Goshen, and their numbers increased daily, for the Hebrews' wives bore sometimes six, twelve, and even sixty infants at a birth. All the children were strong and healthy, and by virtue of industry, thrift, and energy, the Israelites acquired wealth and position in the land. The native Egyptians began to fear lest the Hebrews should increase and become a danger to the native population. They might seize the power in the land and enslave all Egyptians. In vain, however, did the Egyptians urge their King to enslave the Hebrews completely.

" Ye fools," said the Pharaoh, " hitherto the Hebrews have nourished us and ye want me to enslave them! Had it not been for Joseph, we would not have been alive to-day, but died during the years of famine."

But his words were of no avail. The King was deposed from his throne and imprisoned, and only when he had given way to the demands of his people was he reinstalled in his dignity.

Nine years afterwards the King of Egypt died, and a new ruler, named Melol, was proclaimed. The heroes and magnates of Egypt of the generation of Joseph and his brethren had all died, and the new generation no longer remembered the sons of Jacob nor the services they had rendered to the country on many occasions. The Egyptians now laid heavy tasks upon the Israelites and oppressed them, ignoring or forgetting the fact that Joseph and his family had saved Egypt in her hour of need. Melol was twenty-six years of age when he ascended to the throne, and he reigned ninety-four years. He took the title of Pharaoh, as it was the long established custom of the country. In those days Egypt was once more invaded by a hostile army. A fierce war ensued, and although the Israelites had done their best to assist the Egyptians in the war of liberation, sparing neither blood nor money, their help was soon forgotten. On the contrary, their position became worse, as soon as the war had been terminated. The new enemy who had threatened the country was none other than Zepho, King of the land of Kittim. For many years the grandson of Esau had been ruling over his country, undisturbed by the incursions of the African troops, but now it came to pass that the peace of Kittim was once more disturbed by a new invasion of the soldiers of Agnias. Zepho, who had ruled for thirteen years over the country, at once marched to their encounter and mowed them down so that none was left to carry the sad tidings to King Agnias. When the latter at last heard of the annihilation of his troops to the last man, he was greatly alarmed, and assembled all the men of Africa, a mighty host as numerous as the sand on the seashore. He also sent a message to his brother Lucus, asking him to hasten to his assistance with all the men at his disposal.

"Come at once," he wrote, "and help me to defeat Zepho and the men of the land of Kittim who have exterminated my entire army."

Lucus immediately hastened to join his brother with a great host.

When Zepho and the men of Kittim heard of these preparations, they were greatly alarmed and their hearts were agitated by fear and despair. The King wrote therefore to Hadad, son of Badad, King of Edom, and to all the sons of Esau, his brethren, and thus he said: " I am informed that Agnias, King of Africa, and his brother Lucus are marching against me at the head of a mighty army, and we are greatly afraid. Now, my brethren, if you would not have us perish altogether and be exterminated by the enemy, come to our assistance and help us repulse the soldiers of Agnias."

The children of Esau, however, replied to Zepho as follows:

" We cannot take up arms against Agnias and his people,

for already in the days of King Bela, the son of Beor, we concluded an alliance with the ruler of Africa. There is also friendship between us and this King since the days of Joseph, son of Jacob, the ruler of Egypt, against whom we fought beyond the Jordan, when he came to bury his father. We are therefore compelled to refuse thy request."

Thus wrote the sons of Seïr, and Zepho, abandoned by his brethren, the sons of Esau, who refused to come to his aid, was in great despair, but he determined to face the enemy alone and unaided.

In the meantime, Agnias and his brother Lucus, having organized their vast army which consisted of 800,000 men, reached the territory of Kittim. Zepho, mustering only a small company of 3000 men, all that he could gather, went out to face the mighty host. Then the people of Kittim spoke to their King, and thus they said:

" Pray for us unto the Lord and invoke the help of the God of thy ancestors. Perchance He will protect us against Agnias and his people, for we have heard that He is a mighty God and protects those who put their trust in Him."

Thereupon Zepho prayed unto the Lord and thus he said: " O Lord, God of Abraham and Isaac, my fathers, may it be known to-day that Thou art the true God, and that the gods of the nations are all vain and false. I pray Thee to remember this day unto me Thy covenant with Abraham, our father, which our ancestors have transmitted unto us. For the sake of Abraham and of Isaac, our fathers, be gracious unto me this day and save me and the sons of Kittim from the hands of the King of Africa."

And the Lord hearkened unto the prayer of Zepho for the sake of Abraham and Isaac, his ancestors.

Zepho now engaged in battle, and the Lord delivered into his hand the army of Agnias and of Lucus, so that by the end of the first day 400,000 men were slain.

Agnias, having lost his entire army, sent a decree to his people and commanded that all males of the land who had attained their tenth year were to join immediately the army. Whoever would disobey and not hasten to fight for King and country would be punished by death and his property confiscated.

Frightened by the threat of the King, all the males of Africa, men and boys to the number of 3,000,000, hastened to join their King and to swell the ranks of the soldiers he still commanded. After ten days the King engaged in a new battle against Zepho and the men of Kittim, but in spite of his new accessions he was beaten and lost a great number of men, among the slain being his general Sosipater. The remainder of the soldiers, at their head Agnias, his son Asdrubal, and his brother Lucus, saved themselves by flight, pursued by Zepho and his men. Discouraged, they arrived in Africa, and henceforth never dared to invade the land of Kittim or to wage any new wars against Zepho.

Balaam, the son of Beor, the great adept of magic, had accompanied Agnias on his expedition. But when the young magician saw his King defeated, he forsook him and betook himself to the land of Kittim. He was received with great honours by Zepho and his people, who had heard of Balaam's great ability as a magician and of his deep wisdom. Balaam fixed his abode at the court of Zepho who gave him rich presents and attached him to his service.

Now, on his return from the war, Zepho summoned all the sons of Kittim whom he had led, and he found that not one was missing. Great was his joy, for such a splendid victory strengthened his kingship and his power, and he offered a great banquet unto all those who had served him and helped him to win the war. But he never remembered the Lord who had protected him and helped him in his hour of need, saving him and his people from the hand of the King of Africa.

Zepho continued to walk in the wicked ways of the people of Kittim and of the sons of Esau, serving idols and strange gods as he had been taught by his brethren, the sons of Esau. As the proverb rightly saith: " Out of the wicked cometh forth wickedness ".

Having won such a splendid victory, Zepho now took counsel with the sons of Kittim and determined to march upon Egypt and to make war against the posterity of Jacob and against Pharaoh. He knew that not only all the valiant men of Egypt and all the heroes of Pharaoh, but also Joseph and his brethren had long ago been gathered to their fathers and were sleeping their last sleep. Now was the time, thought Zepho, to revenge his brethren, the sons of Esau, whom Joseph, with the help of the Egyptians, had slain, when he came to Hebron to bury his father Jacob.

Thereupon Zepho dispatched a message to Hadad, son of Badad, King of Edom, and to all the sons of Esau, his brethren, and thus he wrote:

" You said that having concluded an alliance with Agnias, King of Africa, you could not take up arms against him. I was therefore compelled to face his mighty host with a small band and I won a splendid victory. Now I have determined to invade the land of Egypt and to make war against the posterity of Jacob who dwell in the land. Thus will I revenge the death of mine and your brethren, the sons of Esau, and repay the sons of Jacob for the harm their fathers had done unto us, the sons of Esau, when they came to Hebron to bury the Patriarch Jacob. Come, therefore, to my assistance and together let us revenge the death of our brethren."

This time the sons of Esau granted the request of Zepho, their kinsman, and joined him in great numbers. Zepho also sent messengers to the sons of the East and to the sons of Ishmael, and they all answered to his call, so that a mighty army was gathered and covered the space of a three-days' journey. They marched against Egypt and camped in the valley of Pathros, near Daphé.

When the news of the approaching host reached the Egyptians, there came from all parts of the country men ready for battle to the number of 3,000,000. At the request of the Egyptians, some of the posterity of Jacob came from Goshen, to the number of 150, and joined the ranks of the natives. The Egyptian army marched to the encounter of the enemy, but the natives mistrusted the Hebrews, and would not allow them to proceed beyond a certain spot. The Israelites were to remain in the rear, and only to take part in the fight when the need arose and the Egyptians were losing.

" The sons of Esau and the sons of Ishmael," said the Egyptians, " are of the same blood as the Hebrews, and a defection is greatly to be feared on the part of our allies, who might deliver us into the hands of their kinsmen." They therefore bade the Israelites remain in the rear and only come forward when they were urgently needed.

" Should the enemy be getting the upper hand and prove stronger than we, then you will hasten to our assistance." Thus spoke the Egyptians, and went out to meet the enemy without having a single Hebrew in their ranks.

Now Balaam, the son of Beor, had accompanied Zepho on his expedition, and the King asked him to find out by means of his magic art who would be victorious in the battle that was to take place. Balaam at once prepared to learn the outcome of the combat and made magic exercises and incantations, but his repeated attempts to divine the future failed, and it remained closed to him. In despair Balaam gave up his attempts, for the Lord had chained up all the impure spirits and withheld all knowledge from the magician, so that Zepho's army would fall into the hands of the Israelites who were praying to the God of their fathers and putting their trust in Him.

Thus the Egyptians marched against Zepho and his mighty host, without taking any of the Israelites with them. But the issue of the battle was fatal to the Egyptians. They lost 180 men, whilst of the troops of the enemy only thirty were slain. Put to flight, the Egyptians, who had been driven back upon the camp of the Hebrews, appealed to the latter for help. Although they were only a small company, the Hebrews hastened to the assistance of the nation in whose midst they were dwelling. Courageously they fought and defeated the mighty army of Zepho and his allies.

The Lord was with the Israelites, and the hostile army, thrown into confusion, was routed. The Hebrews pursued the fugitives to the confines of Ethiopia, slaying many thousands of the enemy, whilst they themselves had not lost one man. Great, however, was their astonishment when they discovered that their allies, the Egyptians, to whose assistance they had rushed, had fled and deserted them, hiding like cowards and leaving the Israelites to fight the battle alone. Full of wrath and cursing the Egyptians for their ingratitude, they returned to Goshen.[1]

Thereupon the counsellors of Pharaoh and the elders of Egypt appeared before the King, and prostrating themselves thus they spoke: " Verily the children of Israel constitute a nation within a nation, they are stronger and mightier than we, and thou knowest well, O King, how courageously they have fought during the last war. Only a handful of them defeated a mighty army, and had there been more of them they would have entirely exterminated the armies of our enemy. They are a danger to us, the natives, for if they are permitted to increase in numbers, they will soon be a constant menace unto us, and may one day resolve upon seizing the power in this land. During the next war they may join the enemy and fight against us. They may then either exterminate us or drive

---

[1] *Sepher Hajashar*; Beer, *loc. cit.*, pp. 12-15.

us out of the country.   Give us therefore an advice, O
King, and tell us how we can best exterminate the Hebrews
slowly."

Thus spoke the counsellors of the King, and Pharaoh
replied: " Hearken ye to my advice and act upon it.   The
cities of Pithom and of Raamses are not strong enough to
withstand a foe for any length of time, and must therefore be
strengthened.   It is therefore incumbent upon all the inhabitants of the land to strengthen these places by ramparts and
make them impregnable fortresses which could withstand the
attacks of our foes.   Now I will issue a decree commanding all
the inhabitants of Egypt and of Goshen, both Hebrews and
Egyptians without distinction, to come forward and help to
build the new fortresses.   At first ye, too, will work, so as to set
the Hebrews an example, frequently repeating my proclamation
so as to stimulate their ardour and their patriotism.   Ye will
also pay them their daily wages.   After a time ye will gradually
cease work, leaving the Hebrews to the task, and after a time
ye Egyptians will be appointed as overseers, officers, and commissaries, and as such ye will use force and compel the Israelites
to work hard, and finally pay them no wages.   We shall thus
gain two advantages; the cities of Pithom and of Raamses will
be strengthened, and the Israelites will be weakened."

Thus spoke Melol, the Pharaoh of Egypt, and the Egyptians
were well pleased with his advice.   A royal decree was accordingly issued, and it went forth over all the land of Egypt and
Goshen.   " O men, inhabitants of Egypt, of Goshen, and of
Pathros," it said, " ye know that the children of Esau and the
children of Ishmael have made an incursion into this country
and have tried to invade our territory.   In order to protect
ourselves against new incursions of hostile powers and to be
able to withstand our foes, the King commands all the inhabitants to come forward, build ramparts and walls, and strengthen
the places of Pithom and of Raamses.   All of ye, Egyptians

or Hebrews, who will enlist and help to build will receive their daily wages."

The decree was proclaimed throughout the land, in Egypt and in Goshen, and in all neighbouring towns. The King thereupon called the Israelites and appealed to their sense of honour and their patriotism, and invited them to participate in the great national work of strengthening the fortresses of Pithom and of Raamses. The King himself set an example, put a brick mould on his neck, took basket and trowel in hand, and started to work. No one, of course, could be a slacker if the King himself worked so hard, and everybody hastened to imitate the noble activity of Pharaoh. Numerous Egyptians, and all the children of Israel, joined the ranks of the labourers. The nobles of Egypt and the high officers of Pharaoh also pretended to be working with the Israelites, who were paid their wages regularly. Energetically the Israelites went to work, and at the close of the first day, working conscientiously and assiduously, they had produced a respectable number of bricks. This number was at once fixed as their normal amount, and subsequently exacted as their daily task. A month had scarcely passed when the Egyptians were gradually withdrawn from the work and the Hebrews alone left to toil on, though they were still being paid their wages. But when a year and four months had elapsed, all the Egyptians who had been making bricks had been withdrawn, whilst the Hebrews were kept to their tasks. The harshest and most cruel Egyptians were appointed as overseers, officers, and commissaries, who relentlessly compelled the Hebrews to toil on, finally stopping their wages. Other Egyptians were appointed as tax collectors, and they exacted from the Israelites heavy sums, taking from them in dues the wages which they had previously earned by their hard work. Whenever one of the Hebrews dared to claim his wages or refused to work unless he was paid, or maintained that he could not work on account of weakness or sickness,

he was cruelly punished, beaten, or laid in fetters. Gradually
the Hebrews were compelled to strengthen the whole land of
Egypt. They were forced to build storehouses and pyramids,
to construct canals for the Nile, and to surround the cities with
dykes, so that the water should not overflow and form swamps.
This work had to be done over and over again, as the con-
structions frequently tumbled down or were carried away by
the inrushing waters.

The Israelites were thus compelled to undertake tasks
beyond their strength, and had not only to make bricks and
build, but also to do all sorts of work in the field, to plough,
dig, and prune the trees. They were also forced to learn various
arts and crafts and trades, so as to become used to hard work
of any kind. Neither were the Hebrew women spared. They,
too, were employed to do all sorts of work, and forced to
accomplish tasks which are only fit for men. They carried
water, hewed down trees, gardened and pruned the fruit
trees. As for the men, after the completion of their day's work,
they were not permitted to take any rest, but were employed
in housework, such as kneading, baking, and so on. Neither
rest nor proper sleep were they allowed to take, but were
forced to sleep in the open air upon the bare ground. The
Egyptian taskmasters and overseers pretended that the Hebrews would lose too much time if they were to go backwards
and forwards from their work to their houses. Thus the Egyptians hoped to separate the Hebrews from their wives. The
Israelites were also forced to put aside all signs in their outward appearance that could remind them of their origin. Bitter
indeed became the life of the Hebrews in Egypt during the
reign of the Pharaoh Melol, and they consequently called
him *Meror*, or the bitter one, instead of Melol, because he
had embittered their life.

It was not enough, however, and soon matters grew worse.
The only people who were exempt from the forced labour

and the hard tasks were the sons of Levi. They had kept
aloof when the royal invitation was issued to come forward
and to help in building the fortresses. They refrained from
enlisting in the labour battalions, for they suspected that there
was guile in the hearts of the King and of his counsellors.
And as they had kept away from the labour which was represented as of national importance, the Egyptians left them in
peace for the future.[1]

In the meantime Hadad, son of Badad, King of Edom,
had died, and was succeeded by Semla of Masreca who
reigned for eighteen years. The new king gathered a mighty
army and decided to make war upon Zepho and the men of
Kittim, because they had attacked Agnias, King of Africa
and Edom's ally, and exterminated his armies. But the sons
of Esau said to their King: " We cannot make war upon Zepho,
son of Eliphaz, because he is our kinsman." And the King of
Edom renounced his plan to make war upon Kittim. There
was danger now that the King of Edom, who had raised
a considerable army, would make use of it elsewhere and
probably invade Egypt.[2] When the Egyptians heard of the
danger threatening them, they availed themselves of the
opportunity to lay still heavier tasks upon the Hebrews, appealing, however, all the time, to their patriotism and duty:

" Hurry and complete the fortresses you are building,"
they urged, " for the sons of Esau may surprise us and fall
upon us unawares. It behoves you to do the work diligently,
for if the sons of Esau invade the country, it will be solely on
your account."

Thus spoke the Egyptians, anxious to let no opportunity
pass which gave them a chance to weaken the Hebrews and
to diminish their numbers. And whilst their Egyptian taskmasters were constantly endeavouring to exterminate the

[1] *Sepher Hajashar*; *Exodus Rabba*, § 1; *Midrash Agadah*, section *Shemot*; *Midrash Tan-chuma*, section *Shemot*; Babylonian Talmud, *Sotah*, 12b; see also Beer, *loc. cit.*, pp. 15–18.
[2] *Sepher Hajashar*.

Hebrew race, diminish its numbers and crush its spirit, a voice was heard from Heaven, saying: " In spite of your oppression this race will increase and multiply."

This heavenly voice gave hope and courage to the long-suffering Hebrews. They were also comforted by their wives who proved noble and faithful companions in hours of need and misfortune. These faithful women were ever ready to labour for their husbands, to relieve and strengthen them, whenever the latter felt exhausted after their unspeakable sufferings, and their daily tasks. Whenever the women saw their husbands tired out, bodily and mentally, losing courage and falling into gloomy brooding, they sustained them with words of comfort and hope. Daily they hastened to the springs, there to draw pure water for their husbands to drink. And the Lord in His mercy ordained that the pitchers of the women of Israel contained each time half water and half fish. The noble, gentle, and faithful women dressed the fish, and prepared it with loving hands, bringing the food and other tastefully prepared meats to their hard-working husbands. They looked after the men, took care of them and were not only anxious for their bodily welfare, but also cheered up the minds of the oppressed with gentle words of encouragement.

" Be of good cheer," they said, " for these sufferings cannot be for ever, and the day will soon come when the Lord will have mercy upon us and redeem us from bondage." Thus spoke the faithful women of Israel, and the loving care of their wives and their constant gentle attention moved the men, soothed their hearts, and gave them fresh hope and courage to live and to suffer. In vain was the calculation of the Egyptians to diminish the number of the Israelites, for their posterity increased and multiplied.[1]

[1] See note 1, p. 201.

CHAPTER XVI

The Fate of the Innocents

The wise men of Egypt and the King—The advice of Job of Uz—
The command to the midwives to kill the babes—Jochebed and Miriam—
The heroic midwives—Shifrah and Puah—The indignation of Miriam—
Persuasion and threats—Pharaoh's dream—The old man and his balance—
The sucking lamb and the inhabitants of Egypt—The interpretation of
Balaam—The Hebrew child that will destroy Egypt—The national calamity
—The three members of the Privy Council—Jethro the Midianite—His
advice and plea for Israel—Jethro's disgrace and his flight to Midian—The
silence of Job—The advice of Balaam—Destroy Israel by water—Fire and
sword will not prevail against them—The God of Israel protected Abraham,
Isaac, and Jacob—Heavy tasks will not crush the spirit of Israel—The
drowning of the Innocents—The Egyptian spies—The heroic women of
Israel — Angels attend mothers and new-born babes — The miraculous
preservation of the babes—The polished pebbles full of milk and honey—
The earth hides the babies and vomits them out—The drowned children
rejected alive upon the river's banks—The prediction of the soothsayers—
The child whose death will be caused by water—The new decree of Pharaoh.

It now came to pass that when 125 years since the arrival
of Jacob in Egypt, and fifty-four years after the death of Joseph,
had elapsed, the elders and wise men of Egypt presented
themselves before Pharaoh, and thus they spoke:

"Long live the King! Thou didst give us an advice the
result of which has had consequences contrary to our expecta-
tions, for the children of Israel are increasing and multiplying,
and the land is full of them. Now give us a new advice, O
King, in thy wisdom."

"Well," said the King, turning to his counsellors, "find
ye now some means by which we could gain our purpose."

Thereupon one of the King's counsellors, a young officer

named Job of Uz, in Mesopotamia, rose up and thus he spoke:

" Long live the King! and may it please his Majesty to listen to my words. Excellent and to the purpose was the advice given by the King to lay heavy tasks upon the shoulders of the Hebrews, but something more should now be done, for this device is not sufficient. Whilst it is necessary to continue enslaving the Hebrews by laying heavier and heavier tasks upon them, new means ought to be devised how to diminish their numbers more effectively. I therefore make so bold as to suggest to his Majesty the following plan. May the King issue a decree to all midwives and nurses and command them to kill every Hebrew male child as soon as it is born. If his Majesty will issue such a decree and have it recorded in the Statute Book and incorporated in the Code of Laws of Egypt, so that it becomes obligatory and has force of law, the number of the Israelites will surely diminish, and they will no longer constitute a danger to us in case of war."

Thus spoke Job of Uz, in Mesopotamia, who was one of the counsellors of Pharaoh, and his counsel pleased well the King and also the other counsellors and wise men of Egypt. Pharaoh thereupon summoned into his presence the two Hebrew midwives and commanded them to kill all Hebrew male children at their birth. The two midwives were mother and daughter, and their names were Jochebed and Miriam, the mother and sister of Moses. According to others, they were mother-in-law and daughter-in-law, and their names were Jochebed and Elisheba, whilst another version makes them two pious Egyptian proselytes. Miriam was only five years old, but already she was of considerable assistance to her mother, to whom she lent a helping hand in her difficult calling. Both mother and daughter showed great kindness to and gently nursed the new-born babes. They washed and dressed the little ones, soothed them with cheerful sounds, strengthened the mothers with cordials and draughts, and in every possible way furthered the growth and development of the children. Thanks to the loving care of these two kind and energetic midwives, Israel could boast of a vigorous, flourishing and speedily increasing posterity. The people, out of gratitude, called the two midwives *Shifrah* (or the beautifier and the soother) and *Puah* (or the caller and the sprinkler). To these two noble, gentle, kind-hearted but energetic ladies Pharaoh issued his command to kill the new-born babes of Israel. The mother, more experienced in the ways of the world, remained silent for a while, but a wave of moral indignation swept over young Miriam's frame. With flashing eye and flushed face, she raised her hand, and pointing to the tyrant on the throne called out:

" Woe unto this man when the day of retribution comes and God punishes him for his evil deed." They were daring words uttered by the future prophetess, and Pharaoh was on the point of ordering his executioner to put to death the precocious and troublesome maid for her audacity. Her mother hastened to implore the King's pardon and to soothe his anger.

" Forgive her, O King," she begged, " and pay no attention to her words, for she is still a foolish child who talks idly and without understanding."

Pharaoh consented to forgive the audacious child, and assuming a more gentle tone he explained to the evidently more reasonable elder lady that all the newly born *daughters* of Israel were to be saved, and that it was only the *male* children that he wanted put to death. " This deed," he added, " you can accomplish quietly without letting the mother know anything or guess the cause of her baby's death." The King at first tried to gain the consent of the midwives by gentle words and promises, making even amorous proposals to the younger one, which, however, she indignantly rejected. Pharaoh finally threatened them with death, if they refused to obey his commands. " I will have you and your houses consumed by fire if you refuse to do my bidding." [1]

Five years had elapsed, and it was the year 130 since the arrival of Jacob in Egypt, when Pharaoh dreamed a dream. In his dream he saw himself seated on his throne and before him stood an old man, holding a balance in his hand and in the act of hanging it up. Thereupon the old man seized all the princes and nobles and elders of Egypt, and all the inhabitants of the land, men, women, and children, bound them together and put them into one scale. He then took a sucking lamb and put it into the other scale, and lo, the scale containing the sucking lamb outweighed all that the other scale contained. Pharaoh marvelled greatly and failed to understand the reason of this strange phenomenon, a sucking lamb weighing more than all the inhabitants of Egypt. When he awoke, he at once summoned all the wise men, magicians, and soothsayers of Egypt, related his dream in their ears and asked them to interpret it. Thereupon Balaam, the son of Beor, who, together with his sons Jannes and Jambres, was now dwelling at the court of Egypt, rose up and thus he spoke.

" Long live the King! this dream, O King, signifies a great misfortune which will break upon this land of Egypt. A male child shall be born among the Hebrews who, when he grows up, shall lay waste our land, weaken the power of the Egyptians, but raise up the Hebrews, and with a strong hand bring them out of the land. The virtues of this male child will excel those of all men, and its name will for ever be gloriously remembered. And now, O King, our master, we must devise means how to destroy all the children of Israel and crush their hope. It is only thus that we shall be able to avert a great misfortune from Egypt."

Thus spoke Balaam, the son of Beor, and the King, greatly

---

[1] *Exodus Rabba*, section *Shemot* (I, 17); *Sepher Hajashar, Sotah,* 11*b*; see also Beer, *loc. cit.*, pp. 19–21.

dismayed, asked: " What shall we do? All that we have done hitherto and all that we have devised has failed, and this people is, on the contrary, increasing and multiplying. Give thou now an advice, Balaam, and tell us what means we should devise in order to diminish the number of the children of Israel.

And Balaam replied: " May the King first hear the advice of his other two principal counsellors, then will I speak and give my opinion."

The other two counsellors of Pharaoh, besides Balaam, the son of Beor, were Job of Uz, and Reuel, called also Jethro, the Midianite. Invited by the King to give his opinion, Reuel, the Midianite, thus spoke:

" May the King live for ever! If it pleases the King to hearken unto my words, this is the advice I give. Give up thy plan of persecution. Leave the people of Israel in peace and do them no harm. They are the chosen of the Lord, and His possession, and He has preferred them to all other nations and to all the Kings of the earth. Whoever oppresses them is punished. Is there anyone who resisted them and was not brought to destruction? Whoever has raised his hand against them was speedily destroyed by the Lord. Hast thou not heard how one of thine ancestors, the Pharaoh of Egypt, was visited by plagues, because he had dared to usurp Sarah, the wife of Abraham, who had come to Egypt to seek hospitality? Abimelech, King of Gerar, met with a similar fate, for the God of Abraham appeared to the King in a dream, and the King speedily returned his wife to the Patriarch and gave him many presents. Another of their ancestors, Jacob, was saved from the hands of his brother, and the Aramæan Laban could not prevail against him. Thou knowest also, O King," continued Reuel, " that the King of this land, thy grandfather, the Pharaoh of former days, found it necessary to raise Joseph the Hebrew to high dignities, because he had discerned the wisdom of the son of Jacob, and the inhabitants of Egypt were thus saved from famine. And as Egypt was indebted to the Hebrews for its salvation, the latter were invited to dwell in the land of Goshen in peace and tranquillity, Goshen being apportioned unto them as their *legally assured home*. My advice, therefore, O King, is to leave off oppressing the Hebrews and let them live in peace and security. If their presence in this country doth not please thee and it is not thy will that they dwell here, then permit them to go forth from here in peace and to return to Canaan, the home of their ancestors, where they sojourned."

Thus spoke Reuel, or Jethro of Midian, but his advice pleased not the King who grew exceedingly wroth when he heard these words of his counsellor. Dismissed from the Privy Council, Reuel left the royal presence in disgrace and on the very day left Egypt for the land of Midian.

The King thereupon turned to Job of Uz, in Mesopotamia, and said: " Job, give us thy opinion now and tell us what we shall do with the Hebrews."

But Job never said a word, neither did he open his lips.

According to another version, Job's reply was very brief and non-committal. " Great King," said he, " are not all the inhabitants of Egypt in thy power? Do, therefore, with the Hebrews as it seemeth good in thine eyes."

It was now the turn of Balaam, the son of Beor, the third member of the Egyptian Privy Council, to speak. The great magician then rose and said:

" All the attempts made hitherto to destroy the Israelites have failed, and they will all fail if the King doth not follow my advice. It will be useless to try and diminish the number of the Israelites by fire, for their God will deliver them from the fire. Thou wilt never prevail against them, for their God once saved their father Abraham from the furnace into which he had been thrown by Nimrod at Ur, in Chaldæa. Neither wilt thou, O King, prevail against the Hebrews, if thou thinkest to try the sword against them and destroy them. Knowest thou not that their ancestor Isaac was saved from death by the sword at the very moment when he was about to be slaughtered? When the knife was raised, Isaac was delivered by an angel from Heaven, and a ram was sacrificed in his place. No, iron and steel will never destroy Israel, nor diminish the numbers of this people. Think not, O King, of crushing their spirit and exterminating them by hard work, forced labour and heavy tasks, for the hardest labour will not break the resistance of this people. It hath already been tried without effect by Laban against their father Jacob. He was forced to accomplish heavy tasks and do all manner of hard work, and yet he prospered exceedingly. One way only remains of proving the Israelites, a way which hath not yet been tried against them or any of their ancestors. None of the Israelites hath been saved from water, and by water thou mayest hope to exterminate the Hebrews and wipe them out from the face of the earth. If, therefore, it please the King, let him hearken unto my advice and decree that all the male children born unto the Hebrews be cast into the river. Do not fear to incur any harm thyself and to be punished for this deed, for God always pays measure for measure, and He hath sworn once, as tradition tells us, never to bring a flood again upon men, nor to destroy the human race by water. Thou art, therefore, perfectly safe from the wrath of the God of Israel, and canst destroy the Israelites by water."

Thus spoke Balaam, the son of Beor, the great magician and counsellor of the King of Egypt, and his advice was accepted by Melol, the Pharaoh of Egypt, and by all the Egyptians, for it pleased them well. The King did not hesitate to issue a decree commanding that all the new-born sons of Israel be cast into the river. In order to secure the faithful execution of his decree, the King also decreed that only Egyptian midwives should assist the wives of the Israelites at a birth. They were instructed to watch carefully and find out the exact time when the women of Israel expected to be delivered, and to report whenever a male child was born. Egyptian children were also sent to the baths frequented by the women of Israel, so as to observe the Hebrew women and give precise information as to the probable time of their delivery. Whoever dared to evade the law and to hide a newborn male child, and thus save it from drowning, would be put to death with his whole posterity.[1]

Terrible was the effect the new decree produced upon the Hebrews, who were thus threatened with complete extermination. Many of the Israelites at once separated themselves from their wives and kept away from them; but others put their trust in God, hoping that He would not permit their race to be destroyed and wiped off from the face of the earth.

The women of Israel behaved heroically in those days of oppression. When the time of their delivery arrived, they used to go out into the fields and there, in distant solitude, in secluded spots, under the shadow of the fruit trees, they went to sleep, putting their trust in God. They were delivered during their sleep, and the Lord, who had made a covenant with Abraham, and sworn to multiply his seed, looked upon the mothers and remembered His covenant. He sent down his ministering angels from the heavenly heights to attend the mothers and new-born infants of Israel. The angels washed and dressed and anointed the babes and swathed them in pretty garments. They also placed in the hands of the babes two polished pebbles, out of which the little ones sucked milk and honey, or they smeared their hands with butter and honey so that they could lick them.

The Lord also caused another miracle to happen. The hair of the babes grew at once until it reached their knees, and thus kept them covered and well protected.

And when the mothers awoke and beheld the wonders

---

[1] *Sepher Hajashar*; *Exodus Rabba*, section *Shemot*; Jellinek, *Beth-Hamidrash*, Vol. II, pp. 1–11; see also Beer, *loc. cit.*, pp. 22–24.

of the Almighty, they exclaimed: " Blessed be Thy name, O God of the Universe, who art omnipresent, and dost not forsake the seed of Abraham. Into Thy hands do we commit our offspring, and may Thy will be done, O Lord."

But the servants of Pharaoh and his emissaries, who were constantly spying upon the women of the Hebrews, used to follow them about everywhere. It was almost impossible to escape the vigilance of these emissaries, who came to seize the newly-born infants and drown them.

But once more the Lord did not forsake those who had put their trust in Him. Obeying the will of the Almighty, the earth suddenly opened her mouth and swallowed up the babes, receiving them in subterranean caves and hiding them there until they had grown up.

The Egyptians, who witnessed the miracle, and saw how the little infants vanished, hastened home and brought out their yokes of oxen. They then ploughed up the earth at the spot where the babes had disappeared, thus hoping to destroy them. But their efforts were in vain, and they could not harm those whom God protected.

When the babies, fed all the while by angels' hands, were grown up, the earth once more opened her mouth and vomited them out, returning them to the light of day. Like the herbs of the fields and the grass of the forests, one could see these young, vigorous, and healthy Hebrew boys sprouting from the soil, and unhesitatingly walking away to their homes.

Thus Balaam's advice and all Pharaoh's attempts to diminish the numbers of the Hebrews and gradually exterminate the entire seed of Abraham proved futile, for the Hebrews in Egypt increased and multiplied exceedingly.

In the meantime Pharaoh's emissaries were constantly visiting Goshen, where the children of Israel dwelt, and whenever they discovered a male infant at its mother's breast, they tore it away by force from the weeping mother's arms, and cast it into the river. Some say that about 10,000 were thrust into the Nile, whilst according to others, their number reached 600,000. But even those who were cast into the Nile, the Lord did not forsake, for alive they were rejected upon the river's banks. And here milk and honey flowed from the rocks to feed the babes, and oil to anoint them until they had grown up. Thus the persecution of the Israelites continued for three years and four months, and the decree of Pharaoh to kill the innocents by drowning still persisted, when one morning, on the seventh day of the month of Adar, the soothsayers and astrologers presented themselves before Pharaoh and informed him of an important event.

" This day," spoke the astrologers, " this day, O King, will be born the boy foretold by thy dreams, the boy who will deliver Israel from bondage. Not only this have we read in the stars, but also the fact that the death of this child will be caused by water. We do not know, however, whether this child to be born be of the race of the Hebrews or of the Egyptians, for the stars are silent respecting this." Thus spoke the soothsayers and astrologers of Egypt, and Pharaoh immediately decreed that henceforth *all* male children, whether of Egyptian or Hebrew origin shall be cast into the river until the day when the fate of the future redeemer of Israel will have been settled.[1]

[1] *Sepher Hajashar*; *Exodus Rabba*; *Midrash Agadah*; Babylonian Talmud, *Sotah*; 11b; Jellinek, *loc. cit.*; see also Beer, *loc. cit.*, pp. 25–26.

CHAPTER XVII

The Birth of the Redeemer

Adina, the graceful—The saintly Amram—Jochebed, the daughter of Levi—The birth of Miriam and Aaron—Amram divorces his wife—Miriam's prophecy—She rebukes her father—Amram takes back his wife—Miriam and Aaron dance at the wedding—Amram's prayer—His vision—The birth of Moses—Miracles accompany his birth—The cries of the Egyptian and Hebrew babies—The ark of bulrushes—The wonder of the angels—The voice from the Throne of Glory—Melol, the King of Egypt and his daughter Thermutis—The scorching heat and the baths in the Nile—The princess and her maids—The angel Gabriel punishes the Egyptian servants—The lengthened arm of Thermutis—The radiantly beautiful baby—The angel Gabriel gives Moses a blow and causes him to cry—The baby refuses to take the milk of the Egyptian women—The prediction of the astrologers—The waters of Meribah—The new-born babes of Israel are saved from drowning—The merits of Moses—Shemaiah ben Nethanel—The baby at the royal palace—Bithia, the daughter of God—The pretence of Bithia—The education of Moses—The wonder-child—His loveliness and understanding—Bithia's confession—Pharaoh] kisses the wonder-child—Moses tramples the royal crown under his feet—The advice of Balaam—The Hebrews always endeavour to rule over kings and nations—The conduct of the Patriarchs—The angel Gabriel appears among the royal counsellors—The advice of the disguised angel—The live coals and the precious stones—Moses burns his fingers—He becomes slow of lips and slow of tongue—The masters of Moses—He is looked upon as the future sovereign.

Now it came to pass that Amram, who belonged to the tribe of Levi and enjoyed the high esteem of his brethren, decided to divorce his wife. He loved her dearly, but as soon as Pharaoh's decree to drown all the male children born unto the Hebrews became known, he thought it best to separate from his wife. Amram was the son of Kohath, the son of Levi, the son of Jacob. Levi's wife Adina (the graceful), a daughter of Jobab, the son of Joktan, the son of Eber, had borne unto him in

Canaan three sons, Gerson, Kohath, and Merari, and on their way to Egypt she gave birth to a daughter, who was named Jochebed. Amram excelled all his ancestors in piety and saintliness. So saintly indeed was he that on his account and for his merits the Glory of Divine Majesty, which after the fall of our first parents had ascended to Heaven and refused to dwell among men, came down again. Amram had no equal in knowledge, gentleness, and modesty, and he was free from sin and so saintly that, had it not been for the Divine decree that all the children of Adam are doomed to die, death could not have touched him. He married Jochebed, and she bore him a daughter called Miriam (or bitterness), because it was at the time of the maiden's birth that the Egyptians began to embitter the life of the Hebrews. Four years later Jochebed bore a son whose name the parents called Aaron, from *hara*, to conceive, because Pharaoh's command to the midwives to kill all the Israelitish children was issued during the months before Aaron's birth.

Amram enjoyed the high esteem of his brethren and was appointed head of the Hebrew Council. When he learned of Pharaoh's intention to slay all the Hebrew male children he suggested to his brethren that under such circumstances it would be better for the Hebrews to live separated from their wives. He was the first to set an example and to thrust away his wife, and his example was naturally followed by many other Hebrews.[1]

Three years had elapsed when the spirit of prophecy came over Miriam, the daughter of Amram and Jochebed, and she said:

"Another son shall be born unto my parents; he shall redeem Israel from bondage and deliver them out of the hands of the Egyptians." Turning to her father she thus spoke to him:

[1] *Sepher Hajashar.*

" Woe, my father, what hast thou done? Thy decision is
even more cruel than the decree of Pharaoh, for he hath only
in mind the destruction of the male children, whilst the result
of *thy* decision will be to deprive the Hebrew nation of all
posterity. By his decree, Pharaoh is anxious to kill the new-
born sons of Israel and to deprive them of life, but he can only
deprive them of life in this world and not in the next, whilst
thou and the other Israelites will deprive them even of future
life by not allowing them to be born. It is doubtful whether
the wicked and cruel decree of Pharaoh will prevail against
Israel, but *thy* decree, Father, will be upheld, for thou art a
pious and just man, and thy enactments will be executed." [1]
Thus spoke the youthful Miriam, reproving her father for
having sent away his wife, because he would spare her the
sorrow of seeing her male child drowned.

Amram listened to his daughter's reproof and unhesitatingly decided to take back his banished wife. Once more he
led his wife Jochebed under the wedding canopy, accompanied by the Angel Gabriel and encouraged by a voice from
Heaven.

Miriam and Aaron danced about it, whilst the angels in
Heaven sang joyfully: " Thus rejoiceth the mother of the
children " (*Psalms*, 113, 9).

Amram's example was soon followed by other men in Israel,
who now took back their divorced wives.[2]

Jochebed was 130 years of age, but once more she became
resplendent in her beauty as in the days of her youth, when
she was still unmarried and known simply as the daughter of
Levi.

Soon Jochebed became pregnant, and Amram, remembering the royal decree, was greatly concerned about his wife's
state. He prayed to the Lord and thus he said:

[1] *Sotah*, 11b; 12a; *Megillah*, 14a; *Exodus Rabba*, section *Shemot*; *Sepher Hajashar*;
Josephus, *Antiquities*, II, 9, 3; Beer, *loc. cit.*, p. 29.
[2] *Sotah*, 12a; Jellinek, *Beth-Hamidrash*, Vol. II, pp. 1-11.

" Lord of the Universe! Have compassion upon thy people of Israel, upon those who are worshipping Thy name, and deliver them at last from their misery. Frustrate the hope of the Egyptians, their enemies, to destroy the nation of Israel."

The Lord hearkened unto the pious Amram's prayer, and in a dream He appeared to him, exhorting him not to despair of the future.

" I will remember thy piety," said the Lord, " and reward ye for it, even as I have vouchsafed my favour unto your fore-fathers. I granted my favours unto Abraham who came to Canaan from Mesopotamia. His wife bore him a son in her old age, and I have also blessed his son Ishmael to whom I have given the land of Arabia, while the sons of Ketura received the land of the Troglodytes. To Isaac, however, I have given Canaan which will be the inheritance of his seed. With 70 souls Jacob came to Egypt, and now ye number more than 600,000. With loving care I shall prepare the welfare of Israel, and thy own fame, O Amram, son of Kohath, will be great. For thy wife, Jochebed, will bear unto thee that child whom the Egyptians so greatly dread, and for whose sake they have doomed to death all the children of Israel. Concealed he will remain and be brought up in a miraculous way. He shall then redeem Israel from bondage, and his memory will be ever-lasting, not only among the Hebrews, his own nation, but also among the other nations who will reverence him for ever. Such favour will I grant unto thee and unto thy posterity, for his brother, too, will be great and obtain the priesthood for himself and for his posterity for ever."

Thus spoke the Lord to Amram, who told his vision to Jochebed, his wife.[1]

Soon the prophetic vision of Amram was realized, for after six months Jochebed gave birth to a son and she suffered no pain, either during the time of pregnancy or in the moment

[1] Beer, *loc. cit.*, p. 31.

of her delivery. And when Moses, the future redeemer of Israel, who was to lead the sons of Israel from the brick-fields of Egypt to the Promised Land of Canaan, was born, the whole house was filled with a radiance like the dazzling splendour of sun and moon. Great was the joy of the mother when she beheld the lovely angelic appearance of her child, and from the miracles which accompanied his birth she knew that he was destined for great things.[1] The parents called the child *Tobia*, God is good, and Amram kissed his daughter Miriam, saying: " Now I see that thy prophecy will be accomplished."

For three months the mother kept her infant concealed, for the emissaries of Pharaoh had not expected her delivery for another three months, but at the end of this time she could no longer conceal her babe from the spying Egyptians. The latter had devised a means by which they could discover the Hebrew new-born babes kept hidden. They used to send their women carrying their own babies into the houses of the Hebrews where they thought an infant might be concealed. Babies usually join the cries of other babies or respond to their cooing. The Egyptian infants were made to cry out, and immediately the Hebrew infants that were kept hidden also raised their voices and betrayed their place of concealment.[2]

" It is better," said Amram, " to expose the child and entrust its fate to Providence, than let our secret be discovered and the boy seized and put to death. The ways of the Lord are many, and He, in His mercy, will protect the child and fulfil the prophecy concerning him." Thus the future redeemer of Israel was exposed in an ark of bulrushes on the waters of the Nile.

This happened on the twenty-first day of the month of Nisan, on the day on which later on Moses and Israel were

[1] *Sepher Hajashar; Pirke de Rabbi Eliezer*, ch. 48; *Sotah,* 12a.
[2] Jellinek, *loc. cit.*; Beer, *loc. cit.*, p. 32

to sing a hymn of praise to God for their redemption from the waves of the Red Sea.

Greatly wondered the angels, and, appearing before the Throne of Glory, thus they spoke: " Need we remind Thee that the child who, on this day of Nisan, is to sing a song of praise unto Thee for rescuing Israel from the waves of the Red Sea, hath to-day been exposed on the waters? Shall he find his death to-day in the sea?"[1]

According to another version it was the sixth day of the month of Sivan on which the ark of bulrushes containing the infant redeemer was exposed, the day on which the Law was to be revealed on Mount Sinai. And the ministering angels appearing before the Lord thus spoke: " Lord of the Universe, shall the great mortal who is to reveal Thy Law on Mount Sinai perish to-day in the sea?"

But a voice from the Throne of Glory replied: " Ye know well that I see everything! What hath been decided in My counsel, the efforts and contrivings of men will never alter. Those who lead others to perdition for the sake of their own safety, using malice and intrigues, never prevail, nor do they attain their end. But those who put their trust in Me in the hour of peril are saved whenever they least expect it, and their distress is speedily changed into sudden and unlooked-for happiness. My omnipotence will reveal itself in the fate and fortunes of the infant now floating on the waves."[2]

Thus spoke the Lord, and He sent one of his numerous agents to rescue the future redeemer of Israel from the waves of the sea.

Melol, the King of Egypt, had only one daughter named Thermutis or Therbutis, known also as Bithia or Bathia, the daughter of God, and whom he loved greatly. The princess was childless and always yearned for a son who could one day inherit the throne of her father. Of a pious disposition, Ther-

---

mutis also suffered greatly on account of the idol worship that prevailed at the court of Egypt, and she frequently sought an occasion to escape from her father's palace, so as not to be a witness to the impurity and wicked ways practised by the King and his suite.

Now it came to pass that in those days the Lord sent an unbearable scorching heat upon Egypt, so that all the inhabitants suffered with leprosy and boils. They all sought relief from their pains in a bath in the Nile. Thermutis, too, was among the sufferers, but having found no relief in the warm baths prepared in her apartments, she decided to try the baths in the Nile.[1] Accompanied by her maids, the princess was walking along the banks of the Nile, suffering both mentally and physically, when she beheld the little ark, wherein lay the future redeemer of Israel, floating on the surface of the waters. Thermutis naturally supposed that the ark contained one of the children exposed at the royal command, and sent one of her maids to fetch it. The maids protested, pointing out that the princess at least ought to observe the royal decree, even if it was unheeded by others. Scarcely, however, had these Egyptian maids raised their voices in protest, than the angel Gabriel appeared and punished them. The earth opened her mouth, swallowed them up, and they all disappeared from the surface, one maid alone, faithful to the princess, remaining for her service.[2]

The princess now stretched out her arm to take the little ark, and in a miraculous manner her arm was lengthened to such an extent that she succeeded in grasping the little ark swimming at a distance of 60 ells. As soon as Thermutis had touched the ark, her affliction departed from her, her leprosy disappeared, and she was suddenly restored to health.[3]

On opening the ark and beholding the radiantly beautiful

[1] Jellinek, Beth-Hamidrash, Vol. II; Josephus, loc. cit.; Book of Jubilees, XLVII, 4.
[2] Sotah, 12b; Exodus Rabba, section Shemot.
[3] Exodus Rabba, ibid.; Targum Pseudo-Jonathan, Exodus, 2, 10.

baby, she felt as if she were looking upon the radiance of Divine Glory.[1] Knowing that the babe was one of the Hebrew children and suddenly remembering her father's decree, the princess was on the point of throwing the ark back into the Nile and of abandoning the infant to his fate. But at this moment the angel Gabriel once more appeared, gave the child a blow and caused it to cry aloud and to continue weeping piteously.

The heart of Thermutis was touched; a wave of compassion for the little innocent swept over her, and even a feeling of motherly tenderness stirred in the bosom of the childless princess.[2]

Deciding to save the child, in spite of her father's cruel decree, she called one of the Egyptian women to nurse the boy. The future redeemer of Israel, however, who was to speak face to face with the Lord, refused to take milk from any of the Egyptian women. The Lord had so ordained it that none of the women of Egypt could boast afterwards of having been the nurse of the Elect of the Eternal.[3]

It was at this moment that Miriam, who had been watching the scene from a distance, stepped forward, and with the permission of the princess called Jochebed, the child's own mother. And thus the rescued child was returned to his mother's arms, and Jochebed, one of the midwives who had disobeyed the cruel decree of Pharaoh, was rewarded by the Lord for her heroic action, for the Lord never forgets the merits of those who put their trust in Him.

On the very day on which the babe who was one day to redeem Israel from bondage was rescued, the astrologers appeared before Pharaoh, and thus they spoke:

"Long live the King! We bring thee glad tidings, for we have read in the stars that the boy destined to redeem Israel

---

[1] Philo, *De Vita Mosis*, II.
[2] *Midrash Abkhir*, in *Yalkut*, § 166; *Exodus Rabba, ibid.*
[3] *Sepher Hajashar*; *Sotah*, 12b; see also Jellinek, *Beth-Hamidrash*, Vol. II, pp. 1–11, and Vol. I, pp. 35–57.

and to bring calamity upon Egypt has met his fate in water. No longer needst thou fear him, O great King."

Thus spoke the astrologers who had been misled by a vague vision, for they had read in the stars that Moses was to die one day on account of water, and it meant that his death was decreed because he had disobeyed the command of the Lord with reference to the waters of Meribah. Pharaoh, however, satisfied with the tidings brought to him by his astrologers, recalled his decree, and the new-born babes of Israel were saved from drowning.[1]

It was on account of the merits of Moses that all the male children begotten on the same day with him were saved from drowning, and it was no vain boast on the part of the redeemer of Israel, when he afterwards said: " The people that went forth out of the water on account of my merits are six hundred thousand men ".[2]

Moses remained with his parents for two years. His father called him Heber, and his mother Jekuthiel, whilst the people of Israel called him Shemaiah ben Nethanel. All Israel knew that the child was destined to deliver them from bondage, and that in his days the Lord would listen to their prayers, and through Moses give them the Law.[3]

When two years had elapsed, Jochebed brought the child to the royal palace and handed it over to the daughter of Pharaoh.

Thermutis, attracted by the supernatural beauty of the boy she had rescued, grew greatly attached to him and conferred upon him the name of Moses, not only because she had drawn him out of the water, but because one day he was destined to draw Israel out of Egypt, and a voice from Heaven called and said to the pious princess:

" Daughter of Pharaoh! Because thou didst have compassion

[1] *Exodus Rabba*, *ibid.*; *Sotah*, *ibid. Pirke de Rabbi Eliezer*, ch. 48; see also Grünbaum, *loc. cit.*, p. 154.   [2] *Numbers*, 11, 21.
[3] Jellinek, *Beth-Hamidrash*, Vol. II, pp. 1–11; *Sepher Hajashar*, *Megillah*, 13a.

upon a child not thine own, and didst call it *thy* son, thou art henceforth *My* daughter, and thy name shall be Bithia (or Bathia), daughter of God."

Her reward for rescuing Moses was great, for Bithia never tasted death, being one of those who entered Paradise alive.[1] In order to be able to maintain that the child was her own son, Bithia had even pretended for some time previously that she was pregnant, and on the day on which the child had been brought to her from his parents' house, it was announced that the princess had been delivered.

Moses was educated and brought up with the royal princes, and his foster-mother, who had adopted him as her own son, constantly kissed and caressed him, never letting him leave the palace or allowing him to be out of her sight. His loveliness was so great, and his beauty so attractive, that all were desirous of seeing him, and whoever set eyes on the boy could not turn their gaze away. Those who met him when he was being carried along on the road would turn and gaze at the wondrous child, feasting their eyes on its supernatural beauty and loveliness. Not only physically, but also mentally was Moses a wonder-child, for his understanding was beyond his years, and in his infancy he already proved that once grown to manhood he would perform great deeds.

Delighted with the extraordinary beauty and gifts of her foster-son, the princess could no longer keep her secret from her father.[2] When Moses was in his third year, she brought the child to the King, and thus she spoke:

" My royal Father! before thy assembled court I confess that this child of such wondrous beauty and noble mind is not my own son. Through the bounty of the River Nile I have received him as a precious gift, and I have adopted him as my son, so that he may one day inherit thy throne

[1] *Leviticus Rabba*; *Yalkut*, § 166; see *Pirke de Rabbi Eliezer*, ch. 48; Grünbaum, *loc. cit.*, p. 154.   [2] *Sepher Hajashar*.

and kingdom." Thus speaking, Bithia, or Thermutis, put the infant in her father's arms.

Pharaoh loved his daughter greatly and would not contradict her wishes, but he was also attracted by the magnetic beauty of Moses, so that he took the child, kissed and hugged it, keeping it close to his breast. Moses thus became the recognized heir to the throne of Egypt.

Now it happened one day, when Moses was three years old, that Pharaoh was seated at the royal table. To his right sat his Queen Alpharanith, and to his left his daughter Bithia with the child in her lap. The princes of the realm and all the royal counsellors, among them Balaam, the son of Beor, and his two sons, stood about the King. Then Moses stretched out his hand, caught the royal crown and placed it on his own head. He thereupon threw it on the ground and alighting from his foster-mother's knee trampled it under his feet.[1] Great was the dismay of the King and his counsellors. Such an action on the part of the child could only augur evil to the King and to the safety of the realm.

"What is your opinion, O my counsellors," said the King, "and what shall be done to this evil child who has taken the royal crown from our head and trampled it under foot?"

Thus spoke Pharaoh, and immediately, Balaam, the son of Beor, rose up, and thus he spoke: "Long live my Lord and King! Dost thou not remember thy dream which thou hast once dreamed, and the interpretation thereof of thy servant? Remember, O King, that this child is one of the Hebrew race, and, endowed with more wisdom and cunning than other children of his age, he has acted with deliberation and purposely. His great aim is, when he is old enough, to take the crown from thy head, to tread thy power under his feet, and to bring Egypt under the sway and dominion of the

[1] *Sepher Hajashar*; *Yalkut*, § 166; Jellinek, *Beth-Hamidrash*, Vol. II, pp. 1–11, and Vol. I, pp. 35–57; see also Beer, *loc. cit.*, p. 39; Grünbaum, *loc. cit.*, pp. 156–158; Josephus, *Antiquities*, II.

Hebrews. His ancestors already have constantly endeavoured to rule over kings and nations and have realized their efforts by intrigues and cunning. Thus Abraham defeated the armies of Nimrod and conquered a portion of his kingdom which was the land of Canaan. Isaac became more powerful than the King of the Philistines, whilst Jacob took from his brother Esau his birthright and blessing, and grew rich at the expense of Laban. As for Joseph, he arrived in this land of Egypt as a slave, and was cast into prison by his master, but he subsequently rose to the highest dignities and became the actual ruler of Egypt. He invited his father and brethren to come over and dwell in the land of Goshen. He gave them the best of this land and kept them at the expense of the country. We may expect a similar attitude on the part of this child who is already treating the royal crown and the royal dignity with contempt. The day will come, O King, when this evil child will tear the crown from thy head and enslave thy people. My advice, therefore, is to slay him at once and thus save Egypt from perdition."[1]

Thus spoke Balaam who had read in the stars that Moses would one day cause the downfall of Pharaoh and the misfortune of the country, but Pharaoh still hesitated to put the child to death.

"Before I decide what shall be done with this child," said Pharaoh, "I will summon all the nobles of my realm and all the wise men of Egypt, and take their counsel."

Thereupon the nobles and counsellors and wise men of Egypt were summoned into the royal presence. The King related unto them what had happened and also what advice had been given by Balaam.

Many nobles agreed with Balaam, some advising that the child be slain with the sword, whilst others were of opinion that he be burnt with fire. Thereupon the Lord sent his angel

[1] See note. p. 227.

Gabriel, who took the shape and form of an old man and mingled with the counsellors of Pharaoh.[1]

According to another version, it was not the angel Gabriel, but Jethro, a member of the royal Privy Council, who was still in Egypt, who prevented the execution of Moses.

" Do not listen, O King," said the angel Gabriel, " to the advice of thy counsellors to slay the child. It will be innocent blood that thou wilt shed, for this child is still young and without discerning. He knows not what he is doing. Before thou dost sentence so young a child to death, it is only just that thou shouldst prove whether his understanding and wisdom are really so great as Balaam, the son of Beor, pretends, and whether his action is the result of design. May it therefore please the King to command that two bowls be brought here, one filled with gold and precious stones, and the other full of live coals. We shall then see whether the child is wiser than befits his age. If he stretches out his hand and takes the gold and precious stones, then he is certainly endowed with wisdom and understanding beyond his years and must have acted with design. He therefore deserves death, but if he grasps the live coals, then it is evident that he is devoid of reason and discerns not between good and evil. His action therefore was only the result of a childish fancy and he is innocent of purpose."

Thus spoke the angel Gabriel, disguised as an old man and one of the wise men of Egypt, and his advice pleased the King greatly. Orders were immediately given that two basins be brought, one full of gold and precious stones, and the other full of live coals.

When the bowls were brought in and placed before Moses, he stretched out his hand and was on the point of taking hold of the jewels, but Gabriel, who had become invisible, caught his hand and directed it towards the live coals. Moses burnt

[1] Jellinek, *Beth-Hamidrash*, Vol. II.

his fingers, and putting them into his mouth burnt his tongue and lips, so that he became slow of lips and slow of tongue (*Exodus*, 4, 11).[1]

The King and his counsellors, now convinced that the child had acted without design when he thrust Pharaoh's crown upon the ground and trampled upon it, decided that no harm should be done unto Moses. Bithia, Pharaoh's daughter, henceforth took great care that her beloved foster-son was kept far away from those who constantly tried to harm him. Moses was educated with love and care in the royal palace, in Bithia's private apartments, and the Lord inspired Pharaoh with love and affection for the son of Amram and Jochebed, so that he always refused to listen to those of his counsellors who strove to destroy the future redeemer of Israel.

Bithia spared no costs to have her foster-son educated as befitted a royal prince. Masters were brought from neighbouring lands who taught the child all sciences and instructed him in the vast learning and wisdom of the Egyptians, so that the boy soon surpassed all his masters in learning and knowledge. It is said that the sons of Balaam, Jannes and Jambres, were his tutors in his early age.[2] Moses acquired knowledge so easily that it seemed as if he were only recalling to his mind instruction which he had already learned before. And so the boy Moses was highly respected by the court of Pharaoh, and the people looked upon him as their future sovereign.[3]

THE JEWELS AND THE LIVE COALS

Quem dum quadam die Terimith obtulisset Pharaoni, ut et ipse eum adoptaret, admirans rex pueri venustatem, coronam, quam tunc forte gestabat, capiti illius imposuit. Erat autem in ea

---

[1] *Sepher Hajashar*; *Exodus Rabba*, section *Shemot*; Jellinek, *Beth-Hamidrash*, Vol. I and Vol. II; see also *Sotah*, 11a; *Sanhedrin*, 106; see also Grünbaum, *loc. cit.*, pp. 158–159.
[2] Abulfaraj, *Histor. Dynast.*
[3] See for the whole chapter, Lewner, *Kol Agadoth*, Vol. II, pp. 4–7.

Ammonis imago fabrefacta. Puer autem coronam projecit in terram, et fregit. Sacerdos autem Helipoleos a latere regis surgens, exclamavit: Hic est puer, quem nobis occidendum Deus monstravit, ut de caetero timore careamus, et voluit irruere in eum, sed auxilio regis liberatus est, et persuasione ejusdam sapientis qui per ignorantium hoc factum esse a puero asseruit. In cujus rei argumentum cum prunas allatas puero obtulisset, puer eas ori suo opposuit, et linguae suae summitatem igne corrupit. Unde et Hebraei impeditionis linguae eum fuisse autumant.

Comestor, *Historia Scholastica, Exodus*, Cap. V (see Migne, *Patrologia*, Vol. 198, p. 1144).

THE ROYAL CROWN AND THE BURNING COALS

An time after ðat ðis was don,
  She brogte him bi-foren pharaon,
And ðis king wurð him in herte mild,
So swide faiger was ðis child;
And he toc him on sunes stede,
And his corune on his heued he dede,
And let it stonden ayne stund;
ðhe child it warð dun to de grund.
Hamonel likenes was ðor-on;
ðis crune is broken, ðis is misdon.
    Bissop Eliopoleos
  Sag ðis timing, and up he ros;
" If ðis child," quad he, " mote ðen,
He sal egyptes bale ben."
If ðor ne wore helpe twen lopen,
ðis child adde ðan sone be dropen;
ðe king wið-stod and an wis man,
He seide, " ðe child doð als he can;
We sulen nu witen for it dede
ðis witterlike, or in child-hede;"
He bad ðis child brennen to colen
And he toc is hu migt he it ðolen,
And in hise muth so depe he is dede
His tunges ende is brent ðor-mide;

&thornor-fore seide de ebru witterlike
&thornat he spac si&thornen miserlike;

The Story of Genesis and Exodus, Edited by Richard Morris,
London, 1865. Early English Text Society, Vol. VII,
p. 75, ll. 2633–2658.

MOSES AND THE GLEAMING COALS

Cordelamor

Je prens grant plaisir et lyesse
A voir cest enfant gracieux.

La Fille

Aussi est il gent et joyeux
Et de rien qui soit ne s'estonne.

Le Roy Cordelamor

Je luy vueil mettre ma couronne
Sur le chef, ou le dieu Hamon
Est figuré, que tant aymon.
En signe d'amour je luy mets.
> [*Icy Moyse prent la couronne et la jecte
> contre terre, et la ront en piéces.*

Le Premier Medecin

Sire, ne me croyez jamais
Se cest enfant que voyez cy
Ne met toute Egipte en soucy;
C'est celuy, tresredoubté sire,
Que Dieu nous demonstra occire,
Et si doit le régne abesser
D'Egipte, detruire et casser.
Par quoy plus endurer n'en puis,
Et de fait deliberé suis
Le mettre tout soudain a mort.

Le Second Medecin

De l'occire auriez grant tort.
S'il a mal faict, c'est ignorance;
Ce qu'il a faict luy vient d'enfance,
Tout clérement le prouveray.

Le Premier Medecin

Par noz haulx Dieux je le tueray,
Car autrement il regnera
Et toute Egipte destruira;
Brief de le tuer ay envye.

Moyse

Ma dame, sauvez moy la vie;
Vela qui me veult mettre a mort.

Cordelamor

Si ne vous vueil je pas permettre
De luy faire aucun desplaisir.

Therimit

Entre mes bras le vueil saisir,
Affin que on ne luy face mal.

Le Premier Medecin

Ung jour sera le principal
Des Ebrieux, je le vous dis franc,
Et sera respandu le sang
Des Egiptiens de sa main.

Le Second Medecin

Si vous debatez vous en vain;
Je vous ay ja dit en substance:
Ce qu'il a faict ce n'est qu'enfance.
Qu'i soit vray, je le prouveray.
Des charbons luy presenteray

Tous ardens, et puis on verra
Que c'est que des charbons fera.
Esprouvons ung petit ce point.

CORDELAMOR

Or sus donc, ne differez point.
A charbons vifz luy presenter.
    [*Il fault des charbons vifz et qu'il y en ait ung faint.*

LE SECOND MEDECIN

Moyse, il fault diligenter
De vous venir ung peu esbatre.

MOYSE

A cela je ne vueil debatre;
Tous jeux nouveaux me semblent bons.
Et que sont ce icy?

LE SECOND MEDECIN

                Des charbons
Que j'ay icy faiz arrenger.

MOYSE

J'en vueil taster, j'en vueil manger;
Ilz me semblent beaux, par mon ame.
    [*Icy met le charbon en sa bouche, et puis dit en
        plurant:*
Helas! m'amye, helas! madame,
J'ay la bouche toute affolée.

THERIMIT
Qu'esse?

MOYSE

            J'ay la langue bruslée.
En me jouant, en m'esbatant
Je me suis bruslé.

THERIMIT

Mon enfant,
Ton enfance tu monstres bien.

J. de Rothschild, *Le Mistère du Viel Testament*, Tome III,
p. 251, ll. 22958–23017.

MOSES AND THE GLEAMING COALS

De Moyse autem parvulo dicunt Hebrei quod coronam quam
Pharao in capite ejus posuit in terra projecit videns in ea ymaginem
Jovis, et voluit Pharao interficere eum eo quod sapientes Egypti
dixerunt regi quod puer ille destrueret Egyptum. Quidam autem
liberavit eum dicens. Videamus si ex infantia fecit; et allatis car-
bonibus incensis, posuit in ore suo et lingua ejus lesa est unde impe-
dite linguae factus est ad loquendum.

The Exempla of Jacques de Vitry, Edited by Th. F. Crane
London, 1890, p. 131, CCCXIII.

CHAPTER XVIII

The Youth and Education of Moses

The virtuous prince—Moses conquers his passions—He avoids pleasure and sin—His visits to Goshen—The golden chain and the family ties—Love and gratitude—The toiling Hebrews—The sad prince—His animosity towards Balaam—His sympathy with the labourers—Moses comforts the Hebrews—Everything is liable to change—The escape of the wizard and his sons—The office of Moses—His request to the King—A day of rest for the labourers—The Sabbath—The gift of Moses—A new decree—The toll of bricks and the babies built in the wall—The cruel taskmasters and the weeping mothers—The beautiful Salomith and the Egyptian taskmaster—The dishonoured wife—The anger of the husband—The righteous indignation of Moses and his hesitation to mete out justice—The heavenly court and the voice from the Throne of Glory—The Ineffable Name, and the death of the Egyptian criminal—The silent sand on the seashore—A secret divulged—The repudiated wife, and the talk of the neighbours—The quarrelsome brothers—The sin of Israel: tale-bearing and back-sliding—The complaint of the nobles of Egypt—The arrest of Moses—The appeal of the angels—The promise of the Lord—The miracle at the scaffold—The ivory neck—Gabriel beheads the executioner—The King's guards stricken with blindness and dumbness—The escape of Moses.

Moses had now grown up, and as he advanced in years, and his knowledge, wisdom, and understanding increased, he constantly strove to conquer all his passions and evil inclinations and to lead a life of virtue and purity. The luxurious life at the court of Egypt offered the young foster-son of the princess many temptations, but Moses persistently refused to be lured by pleasures and sin. Upon his brow he wore the royal diadem, but his heart was full of noble and pure sentiments, and great thoughts filled his mind. He conquered all the passions to which idle youth, reared in opulence and luxury, will easily fall a prey, so that all his friends wondered greatly at his conduct and readily believed that the soul of the young Hebrew was not human, but divine, and that even his body was composed of divine elements. Moses never lived or acted like other mortals, for he excelled all men in noble and elevated sentiments. He spoke what he thought, and acted according to his words.

As the adopted son of Princess Bithia, as the acknowledged heir to the throne of Egypt and successor of Pharaoh, he had reached the summit of earthly greatness, for he was everywhere considered as the heir-apparent, and often called the young king. But Moses was not dazzled by his brilliant prospects and never forgot his extraction, his race, and his ancestors. From his mother Jochebed, whom he was in the habit of visiting, he had learned his true origin, and he knew that he was not an Egyptian, but a Hebrew who had been saved miraculously from the waters, and that the princess was only his foster-mother. He knew that Amram and Jochebed were his real parents, Aaron and Miriam, his brother and sister, and the toiling Hebrews, his brethren. Upon his white brow he wore the diadem, the sign of Egyptian royalty, but in his heart he harboured deep affection and love for his own kith and kin, for the suffering slaves and the toilers in the brickfields of Egypt. The bond which attached the young prince to his own family and people was stronger than the golden chains and necklace he wore as Prince of Egypt and which were the symbol of his close relation to the throne. And yet Moses was too noble to forget his benefactors, or to diminish the love and gratitude he owed them. Loving his real parents, he was yet deeply attached to Pharaoh, and especially to his foster-mother Bithia, whose love he never forgot, even in those moments when, in the interest of his people, he was compelled to declare war on Pharaoh. His sentiments of gratitude towards Pharaoh, and even his affection for the ruler of Egypt, would scarcely have undergone a change had it not been for the fact that his eyes were opened, when he beheld the oppression of the Hebrews.[1]

Daily Moses went out to Goshen to visit his parents and relations, and he was surprised to notice how the Hebrews were groaning under the heavy yoke which was being pressed on their necks, and how they were being compelled by their cruel taskmasters to labour without a respite. Moses asked the reason of this cruel oppression and learned that it was the result of the advice given to Pharaoh by Balaam. He learned how it had come to pass that the Hebrews were now groaning under such heavy burdens, and also how Balaam had sought to destroy Moses himself when he was still in his infancy. This was news indeed for Moses who had been ignorant of these facts. The information filled his heart with indignation and sadness. He felt sad to find himself unable to love Pharaoh as he had loved him before, and could not forgive him his cruel treatment of his brethren. As for Balaam, Moses' indignation and his animosity towards the wizard knew no bounds, but greater still were his sufferings when he saw the toiling labourers and felt that he was not strong enough to rescue them from bondage or even to take them under his protection and at least ease their burden. " Alas," he cried bitterly, " I had rather die than witness the affliction of my brethren."

He took off the golden chain which he wore round his neck, the sign of his princely position, and mingling with the toilers tried to help them and lighten their burden. He noticed how feeble old men and even women were groaning under loads too heavy for them, and he took the loads and placed them on the shoulders of the young and strong, thus making each labour and toil according to his strength, which was already a step towards lightening the sufferings of the slaves. To the Egyptian overseers and taskmasters it seemed, however, as if Moses was acting thus in the interests of the King, so as

---

[1] *Sepher Hajashar*; *Exodus Rabba*, section *Shemot*; Beer, *loc. cit.*, pp. 42–43.

to have the work of building executed sooner. Moses availed himself of his influence over the overseers to diminish their cruelty towards the slaving Hebrews. As for the latter, he tried to comfort and console them.

" My dear brethren," he said, " bear your present hard lot, but be of good cheer and lose not your courage. Better times will soon follow upon the gloomy days of the present, and then suffering and sorrow will change into joy. The world is always full of change, a blue sky follows black clouds, and the storm is succeeded by fair weather."

Thus spoke Moses, doing his best to cheer up his brethren by words of encouragement and consolation, but in his own heart he desponded and could neither forget nor forgive the cruel oppression of his brethren. Balaam he considered as the real culprit and author of the cruel oppression and suffering of his people, and he meditated how he could prevail against this wicked counsellor of Pharaoh.

The magician evidently noticed Moses' change of attitude towards himself, and knew what was in the Hebrew's mind. Fearing the influence of the adopted grandson of the King, who was influential enough to do him harm, Balaam, accompanied by his sons, Jannes and Jambres, left the court of Egypt and escaped to Ethiopia.

Moses in the meantime rose higher and higher in the favour of the King who appointed the lad to the office of introducing distinguished and illustrious foreigners into the royal presence. The whole aim, however, of the future redeemer of Israel was to relieve his people from their terrible burden and suffering and redeem them if possible from bondage. As yet, he was an outsider, for he had not thrown in his lot with his people; but he made use of his influence at the court of Pharaoh to lighten the intolerable burden of his brethren.

One day Moses appeared before Pharaoh and said: " Long

live the King! I have a small favour to ask from your Majesty, will it be granted unto me?" and Pharaoh answered:

" Speak, my son, for I am ready to grant thee any request."

" Sire," said Moses, " it is well known that even the slaves, condemned to constant labour, are granted at least one day in the week on which they are allowed to rest, so that their strength may not be exhausted and their work may not become unsatisfactory and even useless. Now I have noticed during one of my inspections in the land of Goshen that the Hebrews toiling there are given no day of rest. All the week, from dawn till dusk, they work incessantly and know no rest. Such a forced labour, O King, is not profitable to thee, for their strength being exhausted they proceed rather slowly with the building and their work is inferior. Grant, therefore, my request, O King, and give them a day of rest on which they may be able to recruit their strength and, refreshed, start their labour on the following week."

Thus spoke Moses, and Pharaoh replied:

" Thou has spoken well, my son, and I readily grant thee thy request. Which day dost thou think is the best to be given to the Israelites as a day of rest?"

" The seventh day of the week is the most appropriate day of rest, for on this day, consecrated to the planet Saturn, work is anyhow not crowned with success."

" Thy wish is granted," said the King, " and thou mayest inform all the overseers and taskmasters of my royal wish, and make known unto them that henceforth the Hebrews are to cease work on the seventh day, which will be their weekly day of rest."

In blithe spirits Moses left the royal presence and hurried to Goshen to announce the glad tidings to his brethren. Great was the gratitude of the children of Israel for this noble deed of Moses, who had obtained for them at least one day of rest in every week, and they never forgot this boon. The seventh day of the week, the Sabbath, is still praised after many centuries as the " Gift of Moses ".[1]

In the meantime, however, the number of the Hebrews increased considerably, for the decree of Pharaoh to cast all the new-born children of the Hebrews into the Nile had been withdrawn soon after the birth of Moses. This fact once more raised the fear of the Egyptians and of their ruler, so that Pharaoh issued a new law calculated to put a stop to the increase of the subject nation.

It was decreed that every Hebrew had to deliver by sunset a number of bricks imposed upon him by the Egyptian task-masters. If even one brick was short, then the youngest child of the Hebrew labourer who had not made up his toll of bricks was seized and built into the wall in the place of bricks. Such a cruel decree was executed by the Egyptian taskmasters with great alacrity, and they no longer respected the most sacred bonds of the Hebrew families. It often happened that one of the Hebrew slaves, labouring in the brick-fields, could not make up the toll of bricks imposed upon him, and then the ruthless overseers penetrated into his house and snatched away his beloved child from the arms of the weeping and desperate mother. Alive the child was built into the walls.

The Hebrew labourers were furthermore arranged in groups, each group of ten placed under one Hebrew overseer, and ten such overseers were controlled by one Egyptian task-master. It was the duty of the Hebrew overseers to wake the men placed under their control early before dawn and to bring them to their work. Whenever one man was missing, the Egyptian taskmaster called at once the Hebrew overseer and bade him produce the man not at his post without delay.

Now it happened that one of these Hebrew overseers had a wife, Salomith by name, the daughter of Dibri from the

---

[1] *Exodus Rabba*, section *Shemot*; *Sepher Hajashar*; Beer, *loc. cit.*, pp. 43–45; see also Lewner, *loc. cit.*, pp. 8–9.

tribe of Dan, who was beautiful of face and figure and faultless
in body. The Egyptian taskmaster had long noticed her beauty
and a wild passion entered his heart. He thought of means
how to possess this beautiful Hebrew woman. One morning
therefore, before dawn, the Egyptian taskmaster appeared at
the house of the Hebrew overseer and bade him arise and
call the men under his control. Not suspecting any guile, the
husband of the beautiful Salomith quickly arose and went
out to wake and call his men. The Egyptian taskmaster had
in the meantime concealed himself in a dark corner, and as
soon as the husband had left the house he re-entered and took
the place of the husband by the side of the beautiful woman.
After a while the Hebrew overseer, having called his men,
returned, and was surprised to see his taskmaster coming out
of his house.[1]

" With what intent had this Egyptian come back here
in my absence?" he asked his wife, who was still sunk in
slumber.

In great dismay Salomith exclaimed: " Woe unto me! What
is it thou sayest, my husband? The taskmaster has been here,
and in thy absence? I thought that thou hast never left this
room."

Thus lamented the poor woman, and her husband knew
that the Egyptian had dishonoured his unsuspecting wife.
During the morning he cast furious glances at his Egyptian
tormentor, and the latter guessed that the Hebrew had found
out the truth. He therefore was more cruel than usual towards
the man he had sinned against, and not only laid heavier tasks
upon him, but subjected him to more than one bastinado during
the day.

Now it happened that Moses drew nigh at this moment.
The Hebrew, perceiving Moses, the heir to the Egyptian throne,

---

[1] *Exodus Rabba*, section *Shemot*; *Midrash Agadah*, ed. Buber, Vol. I, p. 125; see Beer,
loc. cit., pp. 46-47.

whom he knew to be merciful and just and always ready to take up the cause of his toiling and suffering brethren, hastened and complained to him of the cruel treatment of the Egyptian taskmaster. He also related unto Moses how his tormentor had dishonoured his wife. Moses' anger was kindled against the Egyptian, but a wave of pity and compassion for the Hebrew filled his heart.

" Lord of the Universe," he cried, " where is Thy promise to Abraham that his children will be as many as the stars in Heaven? They are now being slowly tortured and put to death by their tormentors." He looked round to see whether any other labourer would come forth, and in a moment of righteous indignation avenge the misdeed and cruel injustice of the Egyptian. But none came forward, for the suffering labourers no longer dared to protest, however cruel the conduct of their oppressors had become. Burning with indignation, and swayed by a deep sense of justice, Moses raised a spade and was on the point of smiting the Egyptian on the head, when he suddenly hesitated.

" Lord of the Universe," he said, within himself, " I am about to kill this man, and yet what right have I to take his life? He is a criminal just now who deserves severe punishment, but how do I know whether he will not repent one day and atone for his wicked ways by just and pious deeds? Have I read the future to know that this man will not bring forth children who will walk in the ways of the Lord, be merciful and just? and even if it were not so, who am I to dare force the arm of Providence, to punish when vengeance is the Lord's alone?" Thus thought Moses within himself, and lo! the heavenly heights were suddenly revealed unto Moses, the heavens opened before him, and his eyes witnessed the mysteries of the world below and of the worlds above. He saw the ministering angels surrounding the Throne of Glory and the heavenly court was sitting in judgment over man.

And Moses heard a heavenly voice calling unto him: " Thy scruples, O Moses, just as they are and inspired by noble sentiments, are out of place in this case. Justice should take its course. Know that this Egyptian who has committed adultery and manslaughter many a time and was on the point of slaying the man against whom he has sinned, will never repent, but persist in his evil ways. Neither he nor his children will ever do righteously, but only work evil. Wert thou even to give him now his life until the end of days, none of his seed will ever commit any just and meritorious deed which would wipe out his wickedness. The future is an open book to the omniscience of the Almighty. This man has deserved death, and thou, Moses, hast been called hither to execute the decree of Providence."

No longer did Moses now hesitate to slay the Egyptian, so as to save the Hebrew from a certain death which would sooner or later be his fate. But before raising his hand to smite the Egyptian, Moses called on the name of the Most High, so as to strengthen himself in his purpose. Scarcely had the Ineffable Name left his lips and the sound reached the ears of the Egyptian, when the latter fell down to the ground and died, even before the hand of Moses had touched him. Not with his hand but with a word of his mouth did Moses kill the Egyptian criminal.[1]

Moses, however, knew that his deed, although morally justified, would be legally condemned in Egypt, and that were it to be bruited abroad he would incur the wrath of the King, and the consequences would be fatal. He therefore decided to conceal the deed. Turning to the Hebrews, who alone were present and had crowded round their comrade whom Moses had thus rescued, the future redeemer of Israel thus spoke unto them:

[1] *Exodus Rabba*, section *Shemot*; Beer, *loc. cit.*, pp. 46-48; see *Sepher Hajashar*; Jellinek, *loc. cit.*, Vol. II, pp. 1-11; see also *Pirke de Rabbi Eliezer*, Ch. 48; Grünbaum, *loc. cit.*, p. 160.

" My brethren, remember the promise once made by the Lord unto your forefathers: *Ye shall be like the sand on the seashore*. Just as the sand falls and makes no sound and is silent when it is pressed by the foot of man, so may ye be silent and make no sound concerning this deed which shall remain a secret never to be divulged."

Unfortunately, however, the deed remained not long a secret. It was bruited abroad, and Moses soon found that his deed was known not only to his own people, but also to the Egyptians. He had returned to the palace, whilst the Hebrew whom he had rescued went home to inform his wife that according to an old Hebrew custom he was compelled to separate from her and to send her away, as another man had approached her. The poor woman hurried to her relatives and asked them to intercede on her behalf. In vain, however, did the latter plead and even threaten, for the husband remained adamant. The matter was thus being talked about, and so the whole story in all its details, including Moses' punishment of the Egyptian, became known to all the Hebrews. Thus Dathan and Abiram, two brothers, the sons of Pallu, of the tribe of Reuben, who were known for their quarrelsome character and their contentiousness, learned of what had occurred. On the following day the Hebrews began to talk on the event of the previous day, some of them maintaining that the husband had acted wisely in repudiating his wife, whilst others blamed him. Dathan and Abiram began to discuss the matter, and a scuffle ensued.

Moses was just approaching when he saw Dathan raise his hand to deal Abiram a deathly blow, and he exclaimed:

" Why art thou acting so wickedly as to lift up thy hand against thy brother? He is no better than thou, but thou art a villain to deal him a blow!"

Insolently Dathan turned against Moses and cried:

" And what business hast thou, beardless youth, to interfere! Dost thou imagine because thou art the foster-son of the Princess that thou hast a right to be a judge over us and command us? We know that thou art the son of Jochebed and hast no right to rule over us. We will make known what thou didst do unto the Egyptian whom thou didst slay with the sword of thy mouth, by pronouncing the name of God. Dost thou intend to slay us, too, in the same manner?"

Thus spoke Dathan, and Moses was greatly affected by his taunts. " Alas," he cried, " it is now clear to me why such heavy burdens have been laid upon the shoulders of my people. I have wondered in my heart what crime my brethren could have committed to be punished thus and be oppressed so mercilessly. Now I know that their great sin is tale-bearing and back-sliding."

His rebuke, however, had no effect upon the wicked pair, Dathan and Abiram. They betook themselves to the King and informed him of what had happened and how Moses had slain the Egyptian and buried his body in the sand.

Their words made an impression upon Pharaoh and kindled his wrath. It was not so much that the adopted son of his daughter had slain an Egyptian, as the fact that the young man seemed to be opposed to his wishes and to disregard his decrees. For some time already the nobles of the land had been complaining against Moses, pointing out to Pharaoh that the acknowledged heir to the throne was an enemy of the King and of the country. " The friends of the King," they said, " are not his friends, and he associates with the enemies of his Majesty. He hates the men whom the King honours and loves, and befriends those whom the King hates. Such conduct," urged the magnates, " only proves that the young man harbours evil thoughts and is only waiting for a suitable opportunity to do away with the King and seize the power." Pharaoh, who had always been favourably disposed to Moses, now made up his mind to get rid of him, and he issued an order to arrest the

foster-son of Bithia. Accused of homicide, Moses was condemned to death by the sword.[1]

At that moment the ministering angels appeared before the
Throne of God and thus they spoke: " Lord of the Universe!
Moses, whom Thou didst called the familiar of Thy house,
is lying under restraint, awaiting death by the executioner's
hand! He is on the point of being led to the scaffold!"

But the Lord replied:

" Be assured, my angels, that I will espouse the cause of
my faithful servant and that no harm will be done unto him
who is to redeem my people from bondage." [2]

Thus spoke the Lord, and indeed a miracle happened when
the son of Amram was led to the place of execution and mounted
the scaffold. The sharp sword was set ten times upon his neck,
but every time it slipped away, for the neck of Moses had
become as hard as ivory. Thereupon the Lord sent down the
angel Gabriel who assumed the shape and form of the Royal
Executioner, whilst the latter was changed into the form of
Moses. Gabriel, seizing the sword destined to slay Moses,
beheaded the executioner, whilst Moses escaped.

In vain did Pharaoh, who soon perceived that the intended
victim had escaped, order the pursuit of Moses. The King's
guard were momentarily stricken with blindness and dumbness,
so that they could neither see his flight, give information about
his abiding-place, nor get at him.

An angel had in the meantime carried away Moses to a spot
far away from Egypt, at a distance of a forty days' journey, so
that he was safe from pursuit and out of reach of the wrath of
Pharaoh.[3]

---

[1] *Exodus Rabba*, section *Shemot*; see also Beer, *loc. cit.*, pp. 48–50; Lewner, *loc. cit.*,
pp. 9–10.   [2] Beer, *loc. cit.*, p. 51.
[3] *Sepher Hajashar*; see also Jellinek, *loc. cit.*, Vols. I and II; Lewner, *loc. cit.*, p. 10.

CHAPTER XIX

The King of Ethiopia

The war between Ethiopia and Aram—Kikanos, King of Ethiopia—
Balaam is appointed Regent—The treachery of the wizard—The impregnable city—The poisonous serpents—The return of Kikanos—The long
siege—The arrival of Moses—The majestic stranger—Moses is appointed
Commander-in-Chief of the Ethiopian army—The death of Kikanos—The
new king—The men of Ethiopia, and the counsel of Moses—The story of
the serpents and the storks—The triumphant entry into the capital—
Adoniah, the wife of Moses—The rebellion of the men of Aram—Moses
rules over Ethiopia—The jealous nobles—The speech of the Queen—A
neglected wife—Monarchos, the son of Kikanos—The dethroned king—
Moses leaves Ethiopia.

Now it happened in those days that a war had broken out
between the King of Ethiopia and the children of the East and of
Aram. Kikanos, the King of Ethiopia, went out at the head of a
mighty army against the enemy whose hosts were as numerous
as the sand of the sea shore. Before leaving his capital city
of Saba, or Meroe, Kikanos entrusted the country to Balaam
and appointed the magician and his two sons as regents during
his absence.

The wily wizard, however, powerful magician that he was,
succeeded in bewitching the people by his enchantments and
persuaded them to forget their allegiance to the King. The
inhabitants deposed Kikanos and chose Balaam as their King,
appointing his two sons as Commanders-in-Chief of the
armies.

The city of Saba was already almost impregnable, surrounded as it was by the Nile and Astopus, or Astaboras, but

Balaam took steps to make the city absolutely unapproachable, so as to prevent Kikanos from entering it on his return. He raised the walls of the city on two sides, and dug numerous canals on the third side, between the city and the Nile. Into these canals he let run the waters of the rivers, so that none could approach the city of Saba even after crossing the rivers. As for the fourth side, Balaam, thanks to his magic power and his enchantments, assembled poisonous serpents which were very numerous on the roads between Egypt and Ethiopia.

In the meantime Kikanos, having subjugated the nations of the East, returned to Ethiopia. Great was his surprise, when he found the new city walls and ramparts and the barred gates.

" No doubt," said he, " the inhabitants have raised these walls and fortified them so as to protect themselves against an attack by the Kings of Canaan."

Soon, however, he found that such was not the case. The guards refused to open the gates to him and to his army. " Balaam," they replied, " is now our rightful king, and we have instructions not to open the gates to King Kikanos and his army."

In vain did Kikanos make several attempts to enter his capital by force. The vessels and rafts transporting his men were submerged by the wild rushing and swirling waters of the canals, and he lost many men. His attempts to enter the city from the side protected by the snakes and scorpions also failed, for the reptiles killed a great number of his men. Nothing remained for the King to do but to lay siege to his own city, and for nine years he surrounded it, so that none could either leave or enter it.

It was at this time that Moses, a fugitive from Egyptian justice, appeared in the camp of King Kikanos. His majestic and noble appearance, his radiant beauty, and his extraordinary strength struck Kikanos and his men and exercised a great attraction upon them. Gladly they received Moses in their midst, and soon afterwards the King, in whose eyes Moses had found favour, appointed the son of Amram as his counsellor and Commander-in-Chief of his armies.[1]

The siege had lasted nine years, when Kikanos fell sick and died after a seven days' illness. The men of Ethiopia, weary of the long siege and despairing of ever taking the city and entering their homes, were now at a loss what to do. They decided to set a king over themselves who would counsel them and decide their conduct in the future. None was found more fit to occupy the vacant throne than Moses, the handsome and majestic stranger from Egypt. Stripping off their upper garments, the men of Ethiopia made a sort of throne and set Moses upon it. The trumpets were blown, and Moses was proclaimed King of Ethiopia, Adoniah, the widow of Kikanos being chosen as his wife. This happened 157 years after the arrival of Jacob and his sons in Egypt, when Moses was twenty-seven years of age.

On the seventh day after the proclamation, the people and the nobles appeared before their new king, and thus they spoke: " We have come, O King, to ask thy counsel. Tell us how to proceed so as to hasten the fall of the city which we have been besieging for many years."

Thus spoke the people and nobles of Ethiopia, and Moses replied: " For nine years ye have been besieging this city, but ye will never take it unless ye hearken unto my words. Now this is my counsel, and if ye do my bidding, the city will soon be delivered into our hands, and we will enter its gates triumphantly.

" Make it known in the camp," continued Moses, " that the King commands each man to go to the forest and there to fetch a fledgling from the nests of the storks. He who will not

[1] *Sepher Hajashar*; Jellinek, *loc. cit.*, Vol. II, pp. 1–11; cf. Gaster, *The Chronicles of Jerahmeel*.

obey the King's command shall die, and all his belongings shall be taken by the King."

The men of Ethiopia did as they had been bidden, and each man brought a young stork. Moses thereupon bade them rear the fledglings until they had grown up, and then ordered his men to starve the birds for three days. On the third day, he led his army, prepared for battle, against the city, each man holding his trained stork in his hand. When they had reached the spot which Balaam had filled with poisonous serpents and snakes, Moses ordered his men to send forth the storks upon the reptiles. The trained and hungry birds swooped down upon the snakes and destroyed them, so that the way to the city became clear. The Ethiopian army, led by Moses, thereupon rushed the city, and subdued it. They killed all those who offered any resistance, whilst none of Moses' men died. Balaam, his two sons, Jannes and Jambres, and his eight brothers, managed to escape, thanks to their magic art. They flew through the air and betook themselves once more to Egypt, where Balaam took service at the court of Pharaoh.

Moses had thus delivered the city and the Ethiopian army, and led them to victory. Great was the gratitude of the people to their king who had saved them from destruction, thanks to his good counsel and courage. They confirmed him in his kingship, set the royal crown upon his head, and gave him the widow of Kikanos as wife, the lady willingly offering her hand to the handsome king. Even as King of Ethiopia, Moses continued to fear and love the God of his fathers and never strayed from the path of virtue and righteousness, either to the right or to the left.[1]

The children of the East and the men of Aram, having heard of the death of King Kikanos, made an attempt to shake off the Ethiopian yoke, but Moses went forth with a mighty army

[1] *Ibid*; see also Beer, *loc. cit.*, pp. 51–54; Lewner, *loc. cit.*, pp. 11–14.

and quickly subdued the rebellious nations. Thus Moses
ruled over Ethiopia for forty years. The whole country honoured
and loved the King, the pillars of whose throne were right,
integrity, and justice.

There were some nobles, however, who could not forget
that their King was not of their own race, but a stranger and
an alien in their midst, and a party was formed for the purpose
of deposing Moses. They succeeded in gaining the ear of
Queen Adoniah, who was Moses' wife only in name, for never
had he approached the heathen woman, nor turned his eyes
towards her. One day, therefore, in the fortieth year of his
reign, when Moses was seated upon his throne, his wife before
him, and all the nobles surrounding him, the Queen rose up
and thus she spoke:

" Men of Ethiopia! Forty years have now elapsed since ye
appointed this husband of mine as your King and ruler. Great
are his merits and the services he has rendered to our country.
But know ye, people and nobles of Ethiopia, that he is a stranger
in our midst. Never has he worshipped the gods of the Ethiopians, and never has he approached me, his lawful wife. I
therefore think that it will be more seemly and right to appoint
my son Menacham (or Monarchos), who has now grown up,
as your rightful king. He is the son of Kikanos, one of your
own race, and not a stranger, a subject of the King of
Egypt."[1]

Thus spoke the Queen, and in silence the people and nobles
listened to her words. Their attachment to their ancient royal
house, to the memory of Kikanos and his seed, was deep, but
their love and veneration for Moses prevented them from
paying immediate heed to the words of their Queen. A popular
assembly was at last convened, and the question of the abdication of the King and the crowning of Monarchos was dis-
cussed. The counsels of the partisans of Monarchos at last

prevailed, and he was crowned King, Moses being invited to abdicate in favour of the son of Kikanos.

Willingly did the son of Amram yield to the wishes of the people, and without regret he left the country and the men of Ethiopia, who dismissed him with great honour and rich presents.[1]

[1] *Ibid.*

CHAPTER XX

At the Well of Midian, or the Marriage of Moses

The weary traveller—The high-priest of Midian—The futility of idol worship—The abdication of the high-priest—The anger of the Midianites against Jethro, or Reuel—The ban—The rude shepherds and the daughters of the high-priest—A scene of violence—Moses interferes—The gallant Egyptian—The gratitude of the modest maidens—Zipporah falls in love with the handsome stranger—Reuel is afraid of trouble—Moses is cast into a pit—The kindness of Zipporah—Her stratagem—She remains at home and takes care of the house—The prosperity of Jethro, or Reuel—The numerous suitors—The wonderful staff in the garden—The story of the sapphire rod—Zipporah reminds her father of the prisoner—With God all things are possible—Moses is set free—His prayer in the garden—He uproots the staff in the garden—The amazement of Jethro—A prince in Israel—Another version of the marriage of Moses and Zipporah—The maiden's confession—The test of the suitors—The devouring tree—Moses asks the hand of Zipporah—The test—The wonderful rod and the anger of Jethro—Moses set free after seven years—Jethro kisses Moses and blesses the Lord—The united lovers—The faithful shepherd—The story of the white wolf—The story of the dove and the hawk—Angels in disguise—The thirsty kid and the loving shepherd—" Thou shalt pasture the flock of God "—The story of the three travellers and the dropped money-bag—The murder of the innocent—The amazement of Moses—His prayer to God—The reply of the Lord—The mysterious workings of Providence—Divine justice—The ways of the Lord are inscrutable—A Jewish legend in European literature—A poem by Jami—Gellert's " Das Schicksal "—Parnell's " Hermit "—The *Gesta Romanorum*.

Sixty-seven years of age was the future redeemer of Israel, when he journeyed through the desert towards Midian, not daring to return to Egypt. It was a hot day when, towards noon, Moses reached a well outside Midian, where he sat down to rest from the fatigues of his weary journey. It was here that he met the daughters of Jethro, or Reuel, and among them Zipporah, his future wife.

Jethro, or Reuel, who had returned to Midian after leaving the court of Pharaoh, had risen to the dignity of high-priest and prince of the country. Soon, however, he became convinced of the futility and vanity of idol worship, and his priestly dignity became repugnant to him. He decided to give up his office and ask the people to entrust it to someone else. He dared not, however, confess his hidden motives to the people, and therefore pretended that only old age compelled him to give up his sacred duties.

" I am old," said Jethro to the representatives of the people, " and can no longer fulfil my duties. Choose, therefore, someone in my place." Thus speaking, he handed over to the representatives of Midian all the holy vessels appertaining to the idol worship, and divested himself of his sacred garments.

The people appointed a new high-priest, but they suspected Jethro of heretic views. In great fury they pronounced the ban against their former high-priest and decreed that none should render him any service, pasture his flocks, or help him in any way.

Jethro, whose entire wealth consisted in flocks, was greatly embarrassed when all the shepherds left his service. There was nothing for him to do but to bid his seven daughters undertake the task of pasturing his flocks, and of leading them daily to the watering troughs.

Water was scarce in those regions, and the maidens, afraid of being prevented by the shepherds from watering their flocks, hastened to the watering troughs early before the other shepherds had made their appearance. Scarcely, however, had the daughters of Jethro filled the troughs, than the shepherds appeared, and unceremoniously drove away the feeble shepherdesses, watering their own flocks from the troughs the latter had filled with great trouble.

It was such a scene of rudeness and violence that Moses witnessed on the day he had reached the well outside Midian. Full of indignation, the former King of Ethiopia rose up and hastened to the protection of the maidens, whom the shepherds had thrown into the water, intending to kill them. Burning with righteous anger, Moses interfered, rebuking the shepherds for their rudeness and violence.

"In the name of Divine justice," he cried, "which is exercised even in the desert, and in the name of the Almighty who has sent me to deliver these innocent maidens, I swear unto you that I will not permit you to do them any harm."

The shepherds, both afraid and ashamed, drew back.

Moses thereupon dragged the daughters of Jethro out of the water, filled the troughs and gave first the herds of the maidens to drink, and then the flocks of the shepherds. When Moses let down the pitcher to draw the water and fill the troughs, the water leaped up and flowed in such abundance that one bucketful was sufficient to water the herds of Jethro and also of the other shepherds. It was the same well at which Jacob had once met Rachel, and which had been created in the twilight of the first Sabbath eve.[1]

Although reared in modesty, the daughters of Jethro did not hesitate to address the stranger and to thank him for his kind assistance. "Do not thank *me*," said Moses, "but thank that Egyptian whom I killed and on account of whom I had to flee from Egypt."

Great was the astonishment of Reuel, or Jethro, when he saw his daughters return so soon on that day, and when he heard their tale he bade them go and invite the stranger to their house. Zipporah, who had at once attracted the attention of Moses, and who, in her turn, had also fallen in love with the handsome stranger, hastened to do her father's bidding. Amazed at the handsome appearance and majestic bearing of the

[1] *Pirke de Rabbi Eliezer*, Ch. 40.

stranger, Reuel asked him whence he came. " My daughters
tell me that thou art an Egyptian." Moses, without admitting
that he was an Egyptian, but also without asserting that he
was of the Hebrew race, related unto Reuel that he hailed
from Egypt, and that he had been compelled to leave the
country. " I have since been King of Ethiopia," he added,
" but was compelled to abdicate."

Reuel began to consider the matter, and wondered why his
guest had been forced to leave both Egypt and Ethiopia. " He
may have been guilty," thought the ex-high-priest of Midian,
" of an act of high treason, and if I give him shelter and protection, I may find myself in trouble and embroil myself with
Pharaoh and with the men of Ethiopia who have wrested the
kingdom from him. Besides, I may incur the further displeasure
of my own countrymen, the men of Midian, who are already
hostile unto me, if I venture to harbour this somewhat mysterious stranger. I will not deliver him unto the King of Egypt,
but I will put him in prison." And thus Reuel bound Moses
with chains and cast him into a dungeon.[1]

Soon Reuel, who was constantly thinking of reconciliation
with his countrymen, forgot all about Moses, who would have
perished in the pit had it not been for the love the gentle and
fair Zipporah bore him. She had loved Moses from the very
moment she had set eyes upon him, and could never forget
his kindness to herself and to her sisters, when he saved them
from the shepherds of Midian. She thought of ways and means
how to provide the prisoner, not only with food and drink,
but also with various dainties and to lighten his confinement.
One day Zipporah came to her father and thus she spoke to
him:

" Thou hast no wife, but seven daughters, and if we all
go out to pasture and water thy flock there remains none at

---

[1] Jellinek, *Beth-Hamidrash*, Vol. II, pp. 1–11; *Sepher Hajashar*; see also Beer, *loc. cit.*,
pp. 56–59; Lewner, *loc. cit.*, pp. 16–17.

home to look after thy house. If it were thy will to hearken to my voice, then I would advise thee to send out my sisters to tend the herds and I will remain at home and take care of thy house. If not, then let me go abroad and tend the flock, whilst my sisters remain at home and take care of thy house."

And Reuel replied: " Thou hast spoken well, my daughter, and henceforth thy sisters shall go abroad and tend the herds, whilst thou wilt remain in the house and take care of it."

And thus Zipporah remained at home, and could find many an opportunity to provide Moses with food and drink and even with all sorts of dainties. In return for which the prisoner, who knew that she was his destined wife, instructed her in the law of the Most High.

Thus seven years, and according to others ten years, had passed. Reuel had long forgotten the existence of Moses whom he had once cast into the dungeon. He had reconciled himself with his countrymen, and had been restored to his former rank and position.

He had grown prosperous, and princes and magnates came to ask his daughters in marriage. It was especially the noble and fair Zipporah who had many suitors for her hand. She loved Moses in secret, but she dared not confess it to her father, for fear that, remembering the existence of the stranger, he would put him to death. Zipporah was therefore happy when she heard on what condition her father had promised to grant the hand of his daughter.

There was a tree in Jethro's garden, a staff he had once planted there and which no one could pluck up or even touch. The story of this staff runs as follows: It was a staff made of sapphire which the Almighty had created in the twilight of the first Sabbath eve.[1] When Adam was driven out of the Garden of Eden, he carried this staff with him, as one of the gifts he had received from the Creator. He handed it to Enoch,

---

[1] *Pirke de Rabbi Eliezer*, Ch. 40; *Abot di Rabbi Nathan*, ed. Schechter, p. 48a.

ZIPPORAH BRINGS SUCCOUR TO MOSES IN THE PIT

who transmitted it to Noah, who again handed it to Shem. The staff reached Abraham, who transmitted it to his son Isaac. The latter gave it to Jacob, who brought it with him to Egypt and handed it to his son Joseph. When the Viceroy died, the Egyptians pillaged his house and took away this sapphire rod which they brought to Pharaoh. Reuel, who was one of the counsellors of Pharaoh, saw this rod and made up his mind to possess it. His desire was so great that he did not hesitate to steal it and carry it away when he left Egypt. He planted the rod in his garden, and no one could uproot it or even approach it.

Now Jethro, or Reuel, made it known all over the country of Midian that he who could pluck up this staff would take Zipporah to wife.

Thereupon the strong chiefs of Midian, the sons of Keni and all the mighty men of Ethiopia whom the fame of Zipporah's beauty had reached, and who were anxious to win her, came and tried to uproot the staff, but without avail.[1] Thus the staff remained in Jethro's garden, whilst his fair daughter was free from the importunities of her numerous suitors.

It was time, however, she thought, to liberate Moses from prison and perchance her father would give her to him to wife. One day therefore she approached Reuel and thus she spoke unto him:

" Many years ago thou didst cast into dungeon a stranger who hailed from the land of Egypt. Wilt thou not seek and inquire for him? He is crying and praying to his God, and there is a sin upon thee. Now wilt thou send forth and fetch him?" Thus spoke Zipporah, but Reuel replied:

" Whoever has heard that a man who has been without food or drink for so many years could still be alive?"

Zipporah, however, said that with God all things were possible.

---

[1] *Pirke de Rabbi Eliezer* Ch. 40; *Yalkut*, §§ 168 and 173.

" Hast thou not heard, my father, that the God of the Hebrews is great and powerful, and that at all times He works many wonders in favour of his people? He delivered Abraham the Hebrew from the furnace of the Chaldæans, and Isaac from the knife of his father. He protected Jacob when he wrestled with the angel at the brook of Jabbok, and He has done many wonders even for this man whom thou didst cast into prison, for He saved him from the river of Egypt and from the swords of Pharaoh and of the children of Cush. Could He not also have saved him from death by hunger and delivered him from the dungeon in which he lieth?"

Thus spoke Zipporah, and Reuel was at last persuaded and consented to go and see whether Moses was still alive. He was surprised to find Moses not only alive, but standing erect and praying to the Almighty. Immediately he set him free, cut his hair, gave him a change of garment, and set food before him.

Moses thereupon went out into Reuel's garden, which was at the back of the house, to pray to the Lord and to give thanks to Him for the many wonders He had done unto him. Then he lifted up his eyes and suddenly beheld the sapphire staff planted in the ex-high-priest's garden. Approaching this wonderful staff he saw that the Ineffable Name, the name of the Most High, was engraved upon it, and he stretched out his hand to take it. Moses uprooted the staff as easily as one lifts up a branch in a dense forest, and it became a rod in his hand. When Reuel came into the garden and saw the staff in Moses' hand, he was amazed, for none had hitherto been able to uproot or even to touch it.

" This man," said Jethro, " is called upon to be a great man and a prince in Israel." He immediately gave him his daughter Zipporah to wife, whose secret wish had thus been fulfilled.[1]

[1] *Sepher Hajashar*; Jellinek, *Beth-Hamidrash*, Vol. II, pp. 1–11; Gaster, *The Chronicles of Jerahmeel*, pp. 120–121; see also Grünbaum, *Neue Beiträge*, p. 163; Beer, *loc. cit.*, pp. 60–62.

The story of the marriage of Moses and Zipporah and of the rod of Moses is told somewhat differently in the *Midrash Vayosha*. It is Moses himself who relates the story to the children of Israel, after giving an account of his birth, of his upbringing, his escape from Egypt and sojourn in Ethiopia. When he arrived at the well of Midian and had saved the seven daughters of Reuel from the cruel shepherds and watered their flocks, he saw Zipporah and noticed her modest and pious demeanour. He then knew that she was different from all the others. He spoke to her and proposed marriage unto her. Zipporah, struck by the appearance of the handsome and majestic stranger, however, replied:

" Alas, noble stranger, I cannot be thy wife, for never wilt thou be able, in spite of thy courage and thy strength, to carry out the condition imposed by my father and to stand the test by which he tests all the suitors for my hand. In his garden he has a tree, and he asks every suitor for my hand to uproot it, but none has as yet been able to do so. As soon as a would-be suitor approaches this tree and touches it, it devours him."

Moses asked the maiden whence her father had this wonderful tree, to which Zipporah replied that it was really the rod which the Lord had once created and given to Adam. Reuel, who had been one of the astrologers of Pharaoh, had seen the staff, stolen it and brought it to Midian. Upon this staff was engraved the Ineffable Name and also the ten plagues which the Lord was one day to bring upon Egypt. For many days and years the wonderful staff had remained in Reuel's house, when one day he took it into his hand, went out into his garden and there stuck it into the ground for a while. When he returned to fetch it, he found that his attempt to draw it out again failed. The staff had sprouted and was bringing forth blossoms. Thus the staff remained in Reuel's garden and he tested with it all those who came to marry one of his daughters. He insisted upon their pulling the staff out of the ground, but everyone fell a victim to the devouring tree.

All this Zipporah, in great distress, related unto Moses, for she would willingly have become then and there the affianced wife of Moses. The maidens thereupon went home, and Moses accompanied them. Their father, astonished at their speedy return from the well, asked them the cause. They replied that an Egyptian had delivered them from the rude and cruel shepherds, and had watered their flocks.

" I heard them describe me as an Egyptian," Moses is supposed to have said afterwards to the children of Israel; " I heard them calling me an Egyptian, and yet I did not step forward and loudly proclaim my Hebrew birth. God has punished me for this, and I am not permitted to enter the Holy Land." Because he had not protested when he was described as an Egyptian, he had to die outside of Canaan.

And when the daughters of Reuel informed their father that a kind Egyptian had saved them on that day, the ex-high-priest of Midian said unto them: " Go and call the man, who has done to you such a valuable service, to come into our house that he may eat bread at our table."

And when Moses had entered Reuel's home and partaken of food, he spoke to his host at once on the subject of Zipporah whom he wished to take to wife.

Reuel replied: " I will give her to thee, if thou wilt uproot the rod which is in my garden, and bring it to me."

Moses went out into the garden, found the sapphire rod, and, having easily pulled it out, brought it to Reuel. When the latter saw the rod in Moses' hand, he at once knew that he was that man, the great Prophet of whom it had been prophesied by the wise men of Egypt that he would one day arise and destroy the whole land of Egypt. His wrath was kindled against Moses and he seized him and cast him into a pit in his garden, where he expected he would find his death.

But Zipporah loved Moses and said unto herself: "How can I allow this just and perfect man to die such a death?" and she thought of a way how to save him. She therefore approached her father and thus spoke unto him. "Would it be thy will, my Father, to hearken unto my advice. Thou art a man who has no wife but seven daughters who are compelled to tend thy flocks. Now, if thou dost desire that my sisters preside over thy household, then I shall go with the herds, otherwise let my sisters go abroad with the herds and I will take care of the house."

And Reuel replied: "Thou hast spoken well, my daughter, and henceforth thou shalt remain at home and take care of my house and of all that there is therein."

And from that day Zipporah was able to provide Moses with food and drink and even with all sorts of dainties. Thus seven years had passed, and then Zipporah again spoke to her father: "Dost thou remember that once upon a time thou didst cast into the pit a stranger who came to our house and uprooted the staff in thy garden? Now thou didst commit a great sin, and would it were thy will to open the pit and see whether the man be still alive or dead. If he is dead after these many years, then throw his corpse away so that it does not rot in thy house. Should he, however, be still alive, then thou must know that he is a perfect saint."

And Reuel said unto Zipporah: "My daughter, thou hast spoken well, but dost thou remember the name of that man?"

"His name," replied Zipporah, "was Moses, the son of Amram."

Thereupon Reuel went out and uncovering the pit called aloud: "Moses! Moses, son of Amram!" and Moses replied: "Here am I." Thereupon Jethro drew him up, kissed him upon the head and thus he spoke: "Blessed be the Lord who hath guarded thee in the pit for seven years. I now acknowledge that He is the Lord who slayeth and reviveth, and I also acknowledge that thou art one of the perfect and just men. Through thy hand Egypt will one day be destroyed, and through thy hand the Lord will redeem Israel from Egypt and drown in the sea Pharaoh and his army."

Thus spoke Jethro and he gave Zipporah to Moses as wife.[1] Moses was now tending the flocks of his father-in-law Jethro, and very true and faithful was he in the discharge of his duties. One day, when pasturing his herd in the desert of Midian, an angel suddenly appeared to him in the disguise of a white wolf.

" Peace unto thee, O man of God," said the white wolf.

In amazement the future redeemer of Israel looked up and contemplated the speaking beast.

" Man of God," continued the white wolf, " I am hungry and no food has passed my mouth for many days. Give me one of thy lambs that I may appease my hunger and not die."

Having somewhat recovered from his first fright Moses said: " How is it that thou art able to speak with a human tongue? The beasts have not been endowed with speech by the Creator of the Universe!"

To which the white wolf replied: " Dost thou wonder that an animal speaketh? One day the Law will be given through thee, and thou wilt thyself relate the story of the golden calf which will open its mouth and speak, and the story of the speaking ass of Balaam. I wonder at thy asking me such a question. Hasten now to give me one of thy lambs that I may appease my hunger and then go my way to fulfil the will of my Maker."

Thus spoke the white wolf, but Moses replied: " I am only a hired labourer and have no right to dispose of the property of my master. The flocks belong to my father-in-law,

---

[1] *Midrash Vayosha* (Jellinek, *Beth-Hamidrash*, Vol. I, pp. 35–57); see also Wünsche, *Ex Oriente Lux*, Vol. II, p. 43; cf. Lewner, *loc. cit.*, pp. 21–22.

Jethro, and without his permission I cannot give thee even the smallest lamb, however great thy hunger. When the Patriarch Jacob tended the flocks of his father-in-law Laban, he served him faithfully and watched over his herds with such loving care that none was ever lost. He was devoured by heat during the day and suffered from cold during the night." (*Genesis*, 31, 40.)

The white wolf seemed to grow impatient. " Have I come here," he replied, " to listen to thy arguments? If thou dost refuse to give me one of the lambs wherewith I may appease my hunger, without first consulting thy father-in-law, then hasten and ask his permission."

" I cannot grant thy request," replied Moses, " for I am only a hired labourer and have no right to leave my work without the consent of my master. If I leave the herds, who will look after them and protect them from the wild beasts of the desert: lions, panthers, and wolves, dumb or speaking? There are many such beasts of prey around here besides thee."

But the wolf replied: " Fear not for thy flocks, I will look after them and protect them against any beasts of prey. As for myself, I swear unto thee by the living God that I will devour none of them. Should I be guilty of any robbery, thou mayest call me one belonging to the tenth generation which is more wicked than the generation of the flood, or that of the tower of Babel."

Thus spoke the white wolf, and Moses had compassion with him and hastened to find his father-in-law, to whom he related all that had occurred.

And Jethro said: " Give the hungry white wolf one of my best sheep, that he may appease his hunger."

In blithe spirits, Moses returned to announce the glad news to the waiting beast, whom he beheld from a distance patiently guarding the flock.

" Take one of the best lambs," said Moses, " and appease

thy hunger." But scarcely had he spoken these words, than the white wolf suddenly disappeared.[1]

A similar story, wherein, however, the animal appealing to the sense of pity of the future redeemer of Israel is a hawk, is told in the *Tuti-Nameh*.

One day a dove suddenly came flying to Moses, imploring his protection. " O prophet of God," cried the dove, " a fierce enemy is pursuing me and would that it were thy will to give me protection."

Touched by this pitiful appeal, Moses offered a refuge to the homeless bird, taking it under his garment.

Suddenly the pursuing hawk appeared, and thus spoke unto Moses: " O Moses, I am tormented by the gnawing pangs of hunger, and in vain am I searching for food. Hast thou any right to deprive me of my rightful prey and thus increase my torments? Man of God, hand over unto me the dove thou hast taken to thy bosom, and let me appease my hunger."

But Moses replied: " Is it food in general, any food, thou seekest, or just this dove? If it is food thou art after, then I will do my best to give thee satisfaction, but if it is this dove thou wishest to devour, then I will not let the bird go. It is under my protection, and under no condition will I betray its trust."

Thus spoke Moses, and the hawk replied: " Man of God! It is only food I am seeking, no matter whether it be this dove or anything else that will appease my hunger." Thereupon the future redeemer of Israel cut from his holy limbs a piece of flesh, equivalent in weight to that of the dove, and gave it to the hawk saying: " Here is thy nourishment."

" O prophet of God," said the hawk, " I am no hawk at all but the angel Michael, and the dove thou hast so lovingly taken care of is the angel Gabriel. We have only come to

---

[1] *Hagoren*, Vol. VIII, p. 21 (*Maasse al dor haassiri*); *Jewish Quarterly Review*, New Series, Vol. II, pp. 339–364; see also Bin Gorion, *Der Born Juda's*, Vol. III, pp. 16–17.

test thee and to make manifest thy generosity, noble mind, and magnanimity." Thus speaking, both hawk and dove disappeared.[1]

Another time it happened that a kid had left the flock and escaped over valley and hill. It finally stopped at a mountain stream and drank to appease its thirst.

" Poor little kid," said Moses, " so it was thirst that made thee run so swiftly in search of a water course. Poor, tired little one, I knew it not when thou didst run away from me. And now thou must be weary and tired out from thy long run."

Thereupon Moses, the kind and loving shepherd, took the little kid, laid it upon his shoulders and carried it back to the flock.

And the Lord said: " Thou hast patience and forbearance with a little kid, and hast shown compassion with the flock belonging to a man. Thou shalt therefore pasture the sheep of God and be the shepherd of Israel, My flock." [2]

AT THE WELL

Another legend of Moses runs as follows: He was in the habit of roaming about in the country, and, whilst feeding his flock, he gave free play to his meditation, for his mind was busy with great thoughts and with his impending mission to redeem Israel from bondage, to lead them from the brick-fields of Egypt to the land flowing with milk and honey. Moses preferred solitary places where, undisturbed, he could meditate over the ways of God and the laws of nature, and where the spirit of the Lord of the Universe often came over him. One day, the prophet had reached such a spot and sat down under a tree not far away from a well which he could overlook. He was ruminating and meditating in his usual manner, when

[1] *Tuti-Nameh*, German transl. by G. Rosen, 1858, Vol. II, pp. 32–33; see also Bin Gorion, *loc. cit.*, pp. 244–245.
[2] *Exodus Rabba*, section *Shemot*.

suddenly he saw a man approaching the well, drinking from it and then continuing his way. The traveller had not noticed that he had dropped a money-bag whilst drinking from the well. Soon afterwards another traveller appeared who likewise approached the well and slaked his thirst. He noticed the money-bag, picked it up and departed joyfully. Thereupon a third traveller appeared, quenched his thirst at the well and lay down to rest.

In the meantime, the first traveller had found out his loss and thought that he had no doubt dropped his money-bag at the well. He hurried back to the well where he found the resting man.

" Didst thou find a money-bag here, which I dropped whilst bending down to drink from the well?"

" I have seen no money-bag," replied the traveller, " I came here, quenched my thirst, had some food, and am now resting awhile before continuing my way, but never have I set eyes upon any money-bags."

" If thou hast been resting here for a little while," said the first traveller, " then thou must surely have found my money-bag which I lost here."

" My friend," replied the other, " I found *no* money, and thou must have lost thy bag somewhere else or perhaps didst not lose it at all."

" Thou art a thief," cried the first traveller in a rage, " and I command thee immediately to return my money."

Accused of theft, whilst knowing himself to be innocent, the third traveller waxed wroth and in angry tones repudiated the accusation of the stranger. From high words the two men soon came to blows, and a mighty quarrel ensued.

Moses, awaking from his meditations, hastened to the spot to pacify the men, to explain how matters stood and to exculpate the innocent man. But the prophet came too late. In his fury the man who had lost his money killed the third traveller whom he accused of theft, but realizing what he had done, he took to flight.

Compassion filled the heart of the future redeemer of Israel, and tormenting thoughts crowded his brain. Raising his hands to Heaven, he called in his agony to the Lord and entreated the Most High to explain unto him the mysterious workings of fate and why a benevolent God had permitted such unjust deeds to take place.

"Lord of the Universe," spoke Moses, "can it be Thy will to punish the innocent and let prosper the guilty? The man who hath stolen the money-bag is enjoying wealth which is not his, whilst the innocent man hath been slain. The owner of the money, too, hath not only lost his property, but his loss hath been the cause of his becoming a murderer. I fail to understand the ways of Providence and workings of Divine justice. O Almighty, reveal unto me Thy hidden ways that I may understand."

Thus prayed Moses in the agony of his soul, and a voice from Heaven replied: "Thou deemest My decrees unjust, and canst not understand My ways, but the human mind cannot always conceive the Divine measures and the mysterious workings of Providence. Know then, O Moses, that the man who lost the money-bag, though God-fearing and pious himself, had inherited the money from his father who had robbed it from the father of the man who found it now. The finder hath thus come into his own again, and regained his property. The man who was slain, although not guilty of theft, was only apparently an innocent man. In years gone by, he had slain the brother of the man who has killed him now. He was never punished because none had witnessed the bloody deed. The blood of the victim, crying for vengeance, hath now been avenged. Know then, O Moses, that I ordained it that the murderer should be put to death by the brother of the victim, whilst the son should find the money of which his father had once been robbed. My ways are inscrutable, and often the human mind wonders why the innocent suffer and the wicked prosper." [1]

This legend, which is of Jewish origin, is referred to in a somewhat different version in an article in *The Spectator*, where " a Jewish tradition " concerning Moses is related:

" That great Prophet, it is said, was called up by a voice from Heaven to the top of a mountain; where, in a conference with the Supreme Being, he was permitted to propose to Him some questions concerning His administration of the universe. In the midst of this Divine colloquy he was commanded to look down on the plain below. At the foot of the mountain there issued out a clear spring of water, at which a soldier alighted from his horse to drink. He was no sooner gone than a little boy came to the same place and, finding a purse of gold which the soldier had dropped, took it up and went away with it. Immediately after this came an infirm old man, weary with age and travelling, and having quenched his thirst, sat down to rest himself by the side of the spring. The soldier, missing his purse, returns to search for it, and demands it of the old man, who affirms he had not seen it, and appeals to Heaven in witness of his innocence. The soldier, not believing his protestations, kills him. Moses fell on his face with horror and amazement, when the Divine Voice thus prevented his expostulations:

" ' Be not surprised, Moses, nor ask why the Judge of the whole earth has suffered this thing to come to pass. The child is the occasion that the blood of the old man is spilt; but know that the old man whom thou sawest was the murderer of the child's father.' " [2]

This legend forms the subject of a graceful poem by Gellert

---

[1] *Megillath Esther*, in *Zeena Urena*, quoted by Grünbaum, in his *Judisch-Deutsche Chrestomathie*. Leipzig, 1882, pp. 215–218; see also *Jewish Quarterly Review, loc. cit.*, pp. 350–351; Bin Gorion, *loc. cit.*, pp. 23–25.

[2] *The Spectator*, No. 237.

entitled " Das Schicksal ". It has been pointed out [1] that the fable
is of Oriental origin, and that it bears a striking resemblance
to one written by the Persian poet Jami, contained in his
Subhat ul Abrar. Jami's poem was translated into English
and published in the *Journal of the Asiatic Society of Bengal*.[2]
Whether Gellert derived his story from *The Spectator* or not
is of secondary interest to us. What is more important is the
fact that this Oriental legend has made its way into European
literature, such as Gellert's " Das Schicksal " and Thomas
Parnell's " Hermit ".

> The Maker justly claims that world He made,
> In this the right of Providence is laid;
> Its sacred majesty through all depends
> On using second means to work his ends:
> 'T is thus, withdrawn in state from human eye,
> The power exerts his attributes on high,
> Your actions uses, nor controls your will,
> And bids the doubting sons of men be still.
> What strange events can strike with more surprise,
> Than those which lately struck thy wondering eyes?
> Yet, taught by these, confess the Almighty just,
> And where you can't unriddle, learn to trust.

Thomas Parnell, " The Hermit ".[3]

The legend is also found in *Thousand and One Nights* [4]
and in the *Gesta Romanorum*,[5] and Thomas Parnell most
probably based his poem upon the story in this Latin collection.[6]

---

[1] *Z.D.M.G.*, 1860. [2] 1860, pp. 13–15.
[3] S. Johnson, *English Poets*, 1790, Vol. XXVII, p. 81. [4] Lane, II, 577–578.
[5] *Gesta Romanorum*, ed. Oesterley, Berlin, 1872, Ch. 80 (72), p. 396; see also Ch. 127.
[6] See also Gaston Paris, " L'Ange et l'Ermite, étude sur une légende religieuse " in *La Poésie du Moyen Age*, Paris, 1885, pp. 151–187; cf., however, Vol. III of the present work, chapter on the Prophet Elijah.

DIVINE JUSTICE

One day spake Moses in his secret converse with God,
" Oh thou all-merciful Lord of the World,
Open a window of wisdom to my heart,
Show me thy justice under its guise of wrong."
God answered, " While the light of truth is not in thee,
Thou hast no power to behold the mystery."
Then Moses prayed, " O God, give me that light,
Leave me not exiled far away from truth's beams."
" Then take thou thy station near yonder fountain,
And watch there, as from ambush, the counsels of my power."
Thither went the prophet, and sat him down concealed,
He drew his foot beneath his garment, and waited what would be.
Lo from the road there came a horseman,
Who stopped like the prophet Khizr by the fountain.
He stripped off his clokes and plunged into the stream,
He bathed and came in haste from the water.
He put on his clothes and pursued his journey,
Wending his way to mansion and gardens;
But he left behind on the ground a purse of gold,
Filled fuller with lucre than a miser's heart.
And after him a stripling came by the road,
And his eye, as he passed, fell on the purse;
He glanced to right and to left, but none was in sight;
And he snatched it up and hastened to his home.
Then again the prophet looked, and lo! a blind old man
Who tottered to the fountain, leaning on his staff,
He stopped by its edge and performed his needful ablutions,
And pilgrim-like bound on him the sacred robe of prayer.
Suddenly came up he who had left the purse,
And left with it his wits and his senses too,
—Up he came, and, when he found not the purse he sought,
He hastened to make question of the blind old man.
The old man answered in rude speech to the questioner,
And in passion the horseman struck him with his sword and slew
    him.

When the prophet beheld this dreadful scene,
He cried, " Oh Thou whose throne is highest heaven,
It was one man who stole the purse of gold,
And another who bears the blow of the sword.
Why to that the purse and to this the wound?
This award, methinks, is wrong in the eye of reason or of law."
Then came the Divine Voice, " Oh thou censurer of my ways,
Square not these doings of mine with thy rule.
That young boy had once a father,
Who worked for hire and so gained his bread;
He wrought for that horseman and built him his house,
Long he wrought in that house for hire,
But ere he received his due, he fell down and died,
And in that purse was the hire which the youth carried away.
Again, that blind old man in his young days of sight.
Had spilt the blood of his murderer's father;
The son by the law of retaliation slays him to-day,
And gives him release from the price of blood in the day of retri-
  bution.

Jami, in Subhat ul Abrar, translated from the Persian by
G. B. Cowell, in Journal of the Asiatic Society of Bengal,
1860, pp. 13–15).

CHAPTER XXI

The Divine Mission, or the Humble Shepherd

Heavy tasks are laid upon the Hebrews—Moses at Horeb—The burning bush—Moses remembers his duties—The voice of Amram—The modesty of Moses—Elohim, Zebaoth, and Adonai—The honour of the elders—Punishment for slander—Believers and sons of believers—Jethro's consent—Satan in the guise of a serpent—Zipporah and Eliezer—The meeting of the brothers—Aaron's reward—The anniversary of the King of Egypt—The royal palace—The lions gambolling like dogs—The amazement of the kings —The message of the sons of Amram—The Chronicles of Egypt—The names of the gods—The living among the dead—How old is your god? —The strength of the Lord—Balaam's advice—Brine to Spain and fish to Accho—Straw to Ephraim—Moses and the magicians—The miraculous rod —Pharaoh's terror—The sheep between the wolf and the shepherd— The cry of Moses—The faith of the Patriarchs—The ten plagues—The first Passover—The slaying of the first-born—Pharaoh in search of Moses— The pleading of Bithia—Children of Israel, you are your own masters— The march towards a new destiny.

In the meantime the children of Israel were sighing under their heavy yoke in Egypt, for the new King, instead of lightening their toil, had put new and heavier tasks upon their shoulders. The Lord now remembered His covenant and decided to hasten the hour of redemption.

Now one day, when he was guarding the flocks of his father-in-law Jethro and wandering through the desert, Moses came to Mount Horeb. Moses always used to lead his sheep to open places, so as to prevent them from pasturing in private property. It was thus that he came in his wanderings to Mount Horeb. Here a wonderful sight was offered to his gaze. Mount Horeb began to move at his approach, coming to meet him, and only stood still when Moses placed his foot on it. He further saw a blazing flame enveloping the upper part of a bush, but never consuming it.

Moses looked at the thorn bush and its low appearance, and he said to himself: " The thorn bush is like Israel, whose symbol it is, for like the bush Israel, as compared with other nations, is lowly indeed, being in exile."

And whilst such thoughts were crowding the brain of the Prophet, and his heart was aching for his people, lo! a blazing flame enveloped the upper part of the bush, but neither did it consume it nor did it prevent it from bearing blossoms.[1]

Moses approached the bush and he heard a voice saying: " Just as the fire hath not consumed the bush, so Israel will never be destroyed, for the fire which will threaten it will be extinguished, and suffering and oppression will never put an end to this nation."

Suddenly Moses remembered his duties and turned from the wonderful sight, little inclined to be interrupted in his work for which he received wages. The sight offered to his gaze became, however, more wonderful, so that it startled him completely, and he decided to investigate it more closely. It was then that the Lord spoke to him again.[2]

Not wishing to startle Moses, who was still unused to the appearance of God and to prophetic missions, the voice addressing him sounded like the voice of his father Amram.

It called: " Moses, Moses!"

" Here am I, my father," he said. But the voice replied:

" I am not thy father, I am the God of thy father, the God of Abraham, Isaac, and Jacob."

Great was the joy of the son to hear his father mentioned together with the Patriarchs, and even first, but he covered his

---

[1] *Exodus Rabba*, section *Shemot*.   [2] *Ibid.*

face before the Divine glory to which he was not yet accustomed.

"Who am I," said he, "to dare look at the Divine Glory?"

And the Lord said: "Because thou hast been so meek and modest, therefore wilt thou dwell forty days and forty nights on the mountain, and thy face will so shine that men will fear to look at thee."[1]

The Lord had appeared to Moses in the midst of a thorn bush also for another reason. The thorn bush is the symbol of sorrow and of distress, and it was fitting that He should convey His message there, because He saw how Israel dwelt in sorrow and distress, and He dwelt with them.[2]

"Come," said the Lord, "I will send thee unto Pharaoh to deliver the people of Israel."

But Moses replied: "Lord of the Universe! Who am I to go to Pharaoh, and how can I accomplish such a mission as to bring the children of Israel out of Egypt? How could I alone minister to the people? Where shall I take food and drink for them? How shall I be able to protect them against the heat of the scorching sun, against storm, hail, and rain? How shall I be able to provide for the pregnant women, the women in child-birth, the new-born babes, and the little children?"

But the Lord replied: "I will be with thee, and will provide the little ones with food."

"But how can I go to Pharaoh," said Moses, "who is mine enemy and seeketh to hurt me, lying in wait to take my life?"

But the Lord said: "There is no need for thee to fear any man, either Pharaoh or anyone else, for I shall be at thy side."

Moses still objected and declined his mission. "Lord of the Universe!" he said, "when I come to the children of

[1] *Exodus Rabba*, section *Shemot*; *Berachoth*, 8; cf. Lewner, *loc. cit.*, pp. 22–24.
[2] *Pirke de Rabbi Eliezer*, Ch. 40; *Midrash Tanchuma, Exodus*, § 14; *Yalkut, Psalms*, § 843; *Exodus Rabba*, section *Shemot*.

Israel, and they will ask me: ' Who sent thee?' what can I say? I shall not be able to tell them Thy name."

" Dost thou desire to know My name?" said the Lord. " Know then that My name is according to My acts. *Elohim* is My name when I judge My creatures; and I am the Lord of Hosts, *Zebaoth*, when I lend strength to men in battle, enabling them to rise and conquer their enemies; I am *Yahveh* or *Adonai*, when I have mercy upon My creatures; and I am *El Shaddai*, when I am the Lord of all strength and power. But unto the children of Israel thou wilt say: ' The Lord who hath saved you from evil in the past, will deliver you from Pharaoh, redeem you from the Egyptian bondage and also from the suffering which will be your lot in days to come.' "

" I know," said Moses, " that everything is possible to Thee, but how can I reveal unto Israel their future suffering, when they are still sighing under the yoke of Egypt?"

" Thou hast spoken well," replied the Lord, " and thou needst not tell them this, but say to them that I will redeem them from their present bondage[1] Assemble first the elders of Israel, for the honour of the elders of a people is great in Mine eyes, and they will listen unto thee. Pharaoh will be obdurate, but do not fear, for in the end he will let the people go, and they will not leave the country empty-handed." [2]

" But the Israelites will not believe me," again pleaded Moses.

" No," replied the Lord, " thou art mistaken, for the children of Israel are great believers, the sons of believers; they are the sons of Abraham who was a great believer, and they will believe thee too."

God then bade Moses cast his rod upon the ground, and it became a serpent, and then He bade him put his hand in his bosom, and it became leprous, as white as snow. This was to

---

[1] *Exodus Rabba*, section *Shemot*; cf. Lewner, *loc. cit.*, pp. 24-25.
[2] *Exodus Rabba*, ibid.; *Berachoth*, 10.

indicate to the Prophet that because he had slandered the children of Israel, accusing them of lack of faith, he deserved to be punished with leprosy, even as the serpent had once been punished for being slanderous.[1]

" Lord of the Universe!" once more pleaded Moses, " when Lot was made a captive, Thou didst send one of Thy angels to save him, whilst in the case of Hagar, Abraham's bond-woman, five angels came to rescue her. Do the children of Abraham deserve less? Why shouldst Thou not send Thy angels to redeem them, instead of sending me who am only a poor mortal? And even if it is Thy will to send a man who will be the redeemer of Israel, my brother Aaron is greater than myself, and more worthy to be chosen as Thy messenger."

" Thy brother Aaron will be thy companion," replied the Lord, " and he will never be jealous of the honour vouchsafed unto thee." [2]

Meek and humble though he was, Moses yielded at last to the command of the Most High, and accepted the great mission, still feeling in his heart that he was unworthy to undertake it. He now hastened to acquaint his father-in-law with his purpose, for he had promised never to leave Midian without the latter's permission. Jethro at first objected to Moses taking his wife and children with him.

" The suffering of those who are in Egypt is already great, and God is sending thee to redeem them; why then shouldst thou take more hither?"

Thus spoke Jethro, but Moses replied:

" Should my wife and sons remain in Midian and not hear the voice of God on Mount Sinai, when the Lord will come to give the Holy Law?" Jethro then gave his consent, and Moses, taking his wife and children with him, went forth on his return journey to Egypt.[3]

---

[1] Exodus Rabba, 3; cf. also Pirke de Rabbi Eliezer, Ch. 40.
[2] Ibid. [3] Exodus Rabba, 4.

He mounted the ass which had once borne Abraham when he rode to Mount Moriah, there to sacrifice his son Isaac, and upon which the Messiah will one day ride when he appears at the end of days.[1]

His faith, however, and enthusiasm were not great at this moment. He was still afraid lest he would be scorned by the Israelites who would not believe in him and in his mission. For this lack of faith in the Lord, Moses was punished. On the road to Egypt, Satan appeared to him in the guise of a serpent and swallowed up his body down to his feet, but he was saved by his faithful wife Zipporah. She knew that this was a punishment because their second son had not yet been circumcised, Jethro having made it a condition that one half of the children should be Israelitish and the other Egyptian. Swiftly Zipporah took a sharp flint stone, circumcised their son Eliezer and touched the feet of her husband with the blood of circumcision. Immediately a heavenly voice called out: " Spew him out," and the serpent obeyed.[2]

On the very day on which Moses was travelling through the desert, accompanied by his wife and children, the voice of the Lord fell upon the ears of Aaron the Levite in distant Egypt. Aaron was walking along on the banks of the Nile, when the Lord appeared to him and bade him go out and meet his brother. He hastened to obey the will of the Lord, and the meeting of the brothers was a happy one. After embracing his brother, Aaron lifted up his eyes and saw Zipporah and her children.

" Who are these?" he asked.

" They are my wife and my sons," replied Moses.

At this Aaron was displeased, and advised his brother to send them back to Midian.

" Our sorrow is already great enough, on account of those

---

[1] *Pirke de Rabbi Eliezer*, Ch. 2.
[2] *Exodus Rabba*, 5; Jellinek, *Beth-Hamidrash*, Vol. I, pp. 35-37; *Nedarim*, 31b-32a; see also *Book of Jubilees*, XLVIII, 2.

who are in Egypt, why dost thou bring more to the land?"
Thus spoke Aaron who realized that the mission Moses was
engaged upon would be both long and perilous, and he wanted
him to be care-free and not bothered by the presence of wife
and children. Moses subsequently sent his wife and children
back to the house of his father-in-law where they remained till
the day when Israel was delivered from the hand of Pharaoh.[1]

And because Aaron had not been envious of the honour
and distinction vouchsafed unto Moses, his younger brother,
who had been elected to be the redeemer of Israel, the Lord
rewarded him afterwards by placing upon his breast the *Urim*
and *Thummim*, and raising him to the dignity of High-Priest.

Arrived in Egypt, the brothers immediately assembled the
elders of Israel and announced to them the glad tidings. With
the elders came the aged daughter of Asher, Serah, whom
Jacob had once blessed with life eternal. She knew the very
words which the redeemer coming to deliver Israel would use,
as the secret had been revealed unto her by her father. When
she heard the words Moses spoke, she knew at once that he
was indeed the redeemer sent by God.[2]

Moses and Aaron now invited all the elders of Israel to
accompany them to Pharaoh. The elders started out with the
leaders, but stealthily, on their way, they dropped off, one by
one, and two by two, so that when at last the sons of Aaron
reached the palace, they were alone.

And the Lord said: " Since ye have acted thus and abandoned my messengers, ye will be punished."

When the hour, therefore, came for Moses to receive the
Law on Mount Sinai, the elders of Israel were not permitted
to accompany him, and to ascend the holy mountain, for they
were told to tarry at the foot of the mountain and to wait until
Moses returned.[3]

---

[1] *Mekhilta Yitro*, ed. Venice. p. 22a; *Midrash Agadah*, ed. Buber, Vol. I, p. 150; see
also *Exodus Rabba*, 4, where Jethro raises the same objection.   [2] *Exodus Rabba*, 5.
    [3] *Ibid.*, and *Midrash Tanchuma*, ed. Buber, *Exodus*, p. 13; cf. Lewner, *loc. cit.*, pp. 28–29.

The day on which Moses and Aaron first appeared in the presence of Pharaoh happened to be the anniversary of the King. All the kings of the earth came on this occasion to do homage to Pharaoh and to bring him crowns, for he was the ruler of the whole world. Now the servants of the King came and announced that two old men were standing outside asking to be admitted.[1] The palace of Pharaoh had 400 doors, 100 on each side, and each door was guarded by 60,000 valiant soldiers. But Moses and Aaron penetrated into the palace, led by the angel Gabriel, who brought them in, unobserved by the guards. When the two leaders of Israel explained to Pharaoh their Divine mission, he not only drove them out of his presence, but was furious against the guards who had admitted them. They were severely punished, some slain, and others scourged. New guards were put in their place, receiving the instruction not to admit the two old men. The next morning Moses and Aaron were once more in the presence of Pharaoh, and none of the new guards could explain how they had been able to effect their entrance.[2]

Another version of the appearance of Moses and Aaron before Pharaoh runs as follows: At the gate of the royal palace there were stationed two lions, and no one durst approach the door, for fear of being torn to pieces. Only when the magicians came and led the beasts away, could a visitor penetrate into the palace.

When the keepers heard that Moses and Aaron were coming, they let the beasts loose, as they had been advised by Balaam and the other magicians of Egypt, so that the lions might devour the two brothers. But when the sons of Amram approached the gate, Moses raised his rod, and the lions joyously bounded towards him and his brother, gambolling round them like dogs round their masters, and followed them wherever they went.[3] When the brothers came into the presence of

[1] *Yalkut, Exodus*, § 181; *Exodus Rabba*, 5.   [2] *Sepher Hajashar.*
[3] Jellinek, *Beth-Hamidrash*, Vol. II, pp. 1-11.

Pharaoh, the kings and magnates and sacred scribes trembled exceedingly and started up in awe. Moses and Aaron resembled the ministering angels, their stature was like that of the cedars of Lebanon, the pupils of their eyes were like the spheres of the morning star, their beards were like palm branches, and the radiance of their countenances was like the splendour of the sun. In his hand Moses held the wonderful sapphire rod, and the speech of the sons of Amram was like fiery flame.

Great was the awe of all present, and the kings took off their crowns and prostrated themselves before Moses and Aaron. Pharaoh sat and waited for the two to speak. " Perchance they have brought me gifts or a crown," thought he. " Who are you," he queried, " and what is your request?"

" We are the messengers of the Most High; the God of the Hebrews hath met us and He requests thee to let His people go a three-days' journey into the wilderness to sacrifice unto Him."

When Pharaoh heard these words, he waxed wroth and said: " Who is your God that I should listen unto Him? Hath He sent me a crown or a present? Ye have only come to me with words! I know not your God, and I will not grant His request."

Thereupon Pharaoh ordered the chronicles to be fetched from the royal archives so as to find out whether the name of the God of the Hebrews was recorded among the names of the gods of other nations. And the scribe read unto him: " The God of Moab, the God of Ammon, the God of Zidon," but he could not find the God of the Hebrews recorded in the chronicles of Egypt. He could not find the name of the Lord, of the God of the Hebrews, among the other gods recorded in the book of chronicles, for he was seeking for the living among the dead, the Eternal among the perishable.

But Pharaoh said:

" I do not find the name of your God in my books. Tell

me, is He young or old? How old is He? How many cities hath
He captured? How many countries hath He made subject to
Himself? How many nations hath He subdued? How long is
it since He ascended His throne?"

And Moses and Aaron replied: " The strength and power
of our Lord fill the whole world. He was before the world was
created, and He will be till the end of days. He created thee
and breathed into thee the spirit of life."

" And what is His occupation?" asked Pharaoh, whereto
Moses and Aaron replied:

" He stretched out the heavens and laid the foundations
of the earth; His voice heweth out flames of fire; He uproots
mountains and breaks rocks. His bow is fire, and His arrows
are flames. His spear is a torch, His shield a cloud, and His
sword a lightning flash. He created the hills and the mountains
and covered the earth with grass. He sends down dew and
rain upon earth, causes plants to grow, and sustains life. He
forms the embryo in the womb of the mother and sends it
forth as a living being."

" Ye lie," cried Pharaoh, " when ye say that your God
created me, for I am the master of the Universe and I created
myself, and also the River Nile." [1]

Then Pharaoh said unto his wise men: " Have ye ever
heard the name of the God of these people?"

And the wise men of Egypt replied: "We have heard of Him
that He is the son of wise men and the son of ancient kings."

And the King of Egypt said unto Moses: " I know not
your God, and I will not send away your people." [2]

Thereupon Pharaoh sent for the magicians of Egypt and
related unto them what had occurred, and how Moses and
Aaron had penetrated into the palace in spite of the lions,
and what request they had made.

[1] *Exodus Rabba*, 5; *Yalkut*, § 181; *Midrash Tanchuma*. ed. Buber, *Exodus*, p. 19; *Midrash Agadah*, ed. Buber, Vol. I, p. 133; *Sepher Hajashar*; cf. Lewner, *loc. cit.*, pp. 29-31.
[2] *Exodus Rabba*, 5; *Yalkut*, § 181.

" How could these men," asked Balaam, " enter the palace without being torn by the lions?"

" The beasts," replied the King, " did do them no harm, but fawned upon them and gambolled like so many dogs joyously running to meet their masters."

" Then they must be magicians like myself and the other wizards of Egypt," said Balaam, " and, if it please the King, let these men be fetched again, and we will test their powers."

Moses and Aaron were summoned before the King, now surrounded by Balaam and the other magicians of Egypt. In his hand Moses carried the rod of God.

Pharaoh then said unto them: " Who will believe ye, that ye are sent by the God of the Hebrews? Show us a miracle."

Then Aaron cast his rod and it became a serpent.

Pharaoh then called his magicians and they did likewise. Then the King laughed aloud and mocked them.

" Verily," he said, " this is but little proof of the greatness and power of your God. This is but poor magic for Egypt, a country steeped in the art of magic. Our little children can do this."

He then ordered little children to come before him, and also his own wife came, and they all cast their rods which turned to serpents.

" It is customary," continued the King, " to bring to a place merchandise of which it is in need, but you seem to bring brine to Spain and fish to Accho."

Then Jannes and Jambres, the two magicians, mocked Moses and Aaron and said: " Are you carrying straw to Ephraim?"

But Moses replied: " One carries vegetables to a place of many vegetables." [1]

Thereupon the serpent of Aaron swallowed up all the other

---

[1] *Exodus Rabba*, 9; Jellinek, *loc. cit.*, Vol. II, pp. 1-11; *Sepher Hajashar*; cf. Lewner, *loc. cit.*, pp. 33-34; Bialik, *Sepher Haagadah*, Vol. I, pp. 55-57.

serpents. This miracle, too, produced but a small impression upon the Egyptians.

" It is only natural," said Balaam, " that a living thing should devour another living thing, and one serpent swallow other serpents. If thou wishest us to admit that the spirit of God is in thee, then cast thy rod upon the ground, and whilst it is still wood, let it swallow up our rods of wood."

Aaron did as he had been bidden, and his rod of wood swallowed up the wooden rods of the Egyptians. The bulk of the rod, however, remained as before.[1]

When Pharaoh saw this miracle, terror seized him, and he was afraid lest Aaron's rod would swallow him up too. But in spite of his fear, he remained obdurate.[2] The result of the request made by Moses and Aaron to Pharaoh was that he made the lot of Israel even heavier, and that their suffering increased. This extreme suffering of his people distressed the Prophet greatly, and his heart grew heavy. It was then that he took his wife and children back to Midian, so as to be free to devote all his time to the work of redeeming his people. On his return to Egypt, he still found that his people were sighing under a reign of terror, and his spirit almost rebelled. His people were like a sheep that had been carried away by a wolf. The shepherd rushed after the wolf to snatch the sheep and save it from the jaws of the beast of prey; he pulled it one way, whilst the wolf pulled it the other way, and thus the poor sheep was torn to pieces. Such was the position of Israel between Moses and Pharaoh, and two of the Israelitish officers, Dathan and Abiram, did not hesitate to tell Moses so, when he returned to Egypt from Midian.[3] Moses' spirit almost rebelled, and he uttered words which were a challenge to the Most High.

" Lord of the Universe," he cried, " why is the nation of Israel suffering more than all the other nations in the world?

[1] Jellinek, loc. cit.
[2] Exodus Rabba, 9; Midrash Agadah, ed. Buber, p. 136; cf. Lewner, loc. cit., pp. 33–34.
[3] Exodus Rabba, 5.

Is it really because Abraham had once asked for a sign and
said: ' Whereby shall I know that I shall inherit the land?'
and had thus been guilty of a lack of faith? Is it for this that
Thou hast decreed that his seed shall be a stranger in a land
which is not theirs and be in bondage there? Then, why hast
Thou compassion with the children of Esau and of Ishmael,
who are also of the seed of Abraham? Why are *they* not in
bondage, but are living peacefully in their own lands and are
not aliens and slaves among strangers? And now the position
of Israel is desperate, and its sufferings are cruel to the extreme,
' for living children are immured in the walls of the buildings '."

Thus cried Moses, in the agony of his soul, and at that
moment the angel of Justice approached and said: " Lord of
the Universe! for such audacious words Moses deserves to
be punished."

But the Lord forgave Moses, for He knew that only out
of his great love for his people and his compassion with the
sufferers had he uttered such words.[1]

The Lord nevertheless rebuked Moses and said: " Alas
for the departed and who no longer are here! Many a time did
I appear and manifest myself to Abraham, Isaac, and Jacob,
under my name of *El Shaddai*, but never did they venture
to question My acts, or ask for My name.

" I spake unto Abraham: ' Walk throughout this land, for
unto thee will I give it ', but when the time came for him to
bury his wife Sarah, he found no resting place for her until
he had bought and paid for it four hundred silver shekels. And
yet he never questioned My words or promise.

" I said unto Isaac: ' Dwell in this land, and I will be with
thee and bless thee '. When his herdsmen required water
they found none but had to strive for it. And yet he did not
question My words, nor did he find fault with me.

" I spake unto Jacob: ' The land whereon thou liest, to

---

[1] *Exodus Rabba*, 5–6.

thee will I give it ', but when he looked for a piece of ground where to pitch his tent, he found none and had to buy it for a hundred pieces of silver. And yet he never questioned My acts nor did he find fault with Me. None of them ever asked to know My name. Thou alone didst at first ask to know My name, and now thou sayest: ' Thou hast not saved Israel '. Well, now thou shalt see what I will do unto Pharaoh. Thou wilt witness the war against Pharaoh and his punishment, but thou wilt not be permitted to witness and be present at the war of the thirty-one kings of Canaan." [1]

Ten plagues did the Lord bring over the land of Egypt, but Pharaoh remained obdurate until the Lord slew the first-born. It was midnight, when Pharaoh awoke from his sleep and heard the commotion and tumult. Cries and wailing filled the air, and pale and haggard his servants came to inform the King of the calamity that had befallen the country.

Pharaoh arose, and, accompanied by his daughter Bithia and his servants, went forth to seek Moses and Aaron. He did not expect Moses to come again to him, for he knew that the latter had never uttered an untruth, and had he not said: " I will see thy face again no more "? With great difficulty did Pharaoh find the abode of the son of Amram, the leader of the Israelites who was to deliver them from bondage, for neither in palace nor in mansion did the son of Amram, the redeemer of Israel, dwell, but humbly among his people. And when Pharaoh at last discovered the dwelling place of Moses, he knocked at the door and called aloud: " Moses, Moses, my friend, pray to the Lord on our behalf."

Moses and Aaron were at that moment celebrating the first Passover, and when they heard the voice of Pharaoh, Moses asked: " Who art thou and what is thy name?"

" I am Pharaoh," replied the King, " Pharaoh who stands here in humiliation."

---

[1] *Sanhedrin,* 111a.

"Why dost thou come thyself?" again asked Moses. "It is not the custom of kings to come to the doors of common people."

"I entreat thee, my lord," said Pharaoh, "come and pray for us, intercede on our behalf, for the whole population of Egypt will soon be dead."

"I cannot leave the house," said Moses, "for the Lord hath commanded us not to go out until the morning."

"Then step up to the window, and speak to me," pleaded Pharaoh."[1]

Moses stepped up to the window, and saw Pharaoh and his daughter Bithia who began to reproach him for his ingratitude.

"Why hast thou brought this evil upon us?" she cried. "I have brought thee up and been kind to thee and saved thy life many a time!" Thus cried Bithia, whereto Moses replied:

"Ten plagues did the Lord bring upon Egypt; hath any of these affected thee? Thou hast been spared, because the Lord remembered thy great merit and thy good deeds."

Bithia acknowledged that no evil had accrued to her personally, but she could witness no longer the great calamity that had befallen the country and the plight her people were in.

"I warned thy father," said Moses, "but he would not hearken unto my words."[2]

Thereupon Pharaoh stepped nearer and said: "Thou didst say yesterday that all the first-born in the land of Egypt shall die, but now nine-tenths of the people are already dead."

And Moses said: "Thou art a first-born thyself, but thou wilt be spared and not die, and in spite of all that has happened, I will teach thee something and thou wilt learn. Raise thy voice and shout aloud: 'Children of Israel! Ye are henceforth your own masters, arise and depart from among my people.

---

[1] Jellinek, *Beth-Hamidrash*, Vol. I, pp. 35–57.
[2] *Sepher Hajashar*; *Midrash Shokher Tob*, Ps., 68.

Hitherto ye were the slaves of Pharaoh, but now ye are in the power of the Eternal. Go and serve the Lord, your God!' "

Pharaoh obeyed, and, raising his voice, repeated three times the words Moses had dictated to him. And the Lord caused the voice of Pharaoh to be heard all over the land of Egypt.[1] The people heard and knew that the hour of redemption was at hand. Then Pharaoh insisted upon the Israelites leaving at once, in the darkness of the night, but Moses replied:

" Are we thieves or burglars that we should sneak away under cover of darkness? The Lord hath commanded us not to leave our houses until the morning, and we will depart from the country, holding our heads high, and before the whole of Egypt.[2] But why dost thou so insist upon our leaving at once?" he asked.

" Because I am a first-born myself," replied Pharaoh, " and I fear lest I, too, will die."

" I told thee already," said Moses, " that thou needst not fear for thy life, for thou art destined for greater things. Thou wilt live to manifest to the greatness of God." [3]

And thus the slaves, the labourers in the brickfields of Egypt, left the country, redeemed from bondage, and began their long march towards their new destiny.

[1] Jellinek, *loc. cit.*
[2] *Midrash Tanchuma*, ed. Buber, p. 52; *Midrash Agadah*, ed. Buber, p. 142, cf. Bialik *loc. cit.*, p. 61.
[3] Jellinek, *loc. cit.*; cf. also Lewner, *loc. cit.*, pp. 40–42.

CHAPTER XXII

The Redemption, or the Passage through the Red Sea

Uzza, the tutelary angel of Egypt—His contention with Michael—Michael's reply—The Lord espouses the cause of Israel—The situation of the people—The four parties—The prayer of Moses—Moses and the disobedient sea—The tribes of Benjamin and Judah enter the cleft sea—Their reward—Gabriel and the turbulent waters—The twelve channels—Food out of the water-walls—The pillar of cloud and the pillar of fire—Uzza pleads for the Egyptians—The heavenly judges—Uzza and Gabriel—The brick wherein a Hebrew child had been immured—The Lord upon His Throne of Justice—Pharaoh in the waves of the sea—Gabriel tortures him for fifty days—Pharaoh as King of Nineveh—Pharaoh at the gates of hell—The fear of the Hebrews—The Egyptians floating on the surface of the waters—The quarrel between the sea and the earth—The Israelites intone a song of praise—The angels are commanded to wait—The precedence of the women of Israel—The wealth of the Egyptians.

When the Israelites had left Egypt, Uzza, the tutelary angel of the Egyptians, appeared before the Lord and thus he spoke: "Thou didst decree and foretell unto Abraham that his descendants, the people of Israel, shall be held in bondage for a period of four hundred years. Now my people, the Egyptians, have had dominion over the nation of Israel only for eighty-six years. The Israelites are therefore still bound to serve the Egyptians for another three hundred and fourteen years."

Thus spake Uzza, the tutelary angel of the Egyptians, and the Lord called unto Michael, the tutelary angel of Israel, and said unto him: "Contend with Uzza, answer his arguments, and save Israel from his hands."

Michael replied: "Israel has never sinned, either to thee

286

or to thy nation, and has been condemned to serve the Egyptians only because Abraham had once uttered the words: ' Whereby shall I know that my children shall inherit the land?' On account of the Patriarch's lack of faith, the duty of serving thy nation was laid upon my people. But the Lord only said: ' Thy seed shall be strangers in a country which is not their own.' And they have indeed been strangers in Egypt ever since the date of Isaac's birth, and the period of four hundred years has now elapsed." Thus spoke Michael in defence of Israel.

When Uzza heard these words, he found no answer and was silent.[1]

In the *Midrash Vayosha* a somewhat different version is given: Uzza said that he had a suit with the nation of Israel, and if it seemed well to the Lord, let Him summon Michael to contend with him. Michael knew not how to contradict the words of the tutelary angel of Egypt, and the Lord Himself pleaded and espoused the cause of Israel, bringing Uzza to silence.[2]

When the Israelites saw the mighty hosts of Pharaoh and the detachments of the Egyptian army approaching, they were greatly afraid. Great terror seized them, and they said unto Moses: " What have we done? Now Pharaoh will wreak terrible vengeance upon us for the death of the first-born. If we march into the desert, we shall be torn by wild beasts; if we advance into the sea, we shall be drowned; and if we return to Egypt, our sufferings will now be greater than ever."

Desperate indeed was the situation of the people. The sea was in front of them, the desert, full of wild beasts of prey, to the right and to the left, and the advancing army of Egypt behind them. They were contending among themselves what it would be best to do and were divided into four opinions.

One party, the tribes of Reuben, Simeon, and Isachar, said:

---

[1] *Midrash Abkhir*, quoted in *Yalkut*, § 241.
[2] Jellinek, *Beth-Hamidrash*, Vol. I, pp. 35–57.

" It is better to be drowned in the sea than return and fall into the hands of the Egyptians, our implacable enemies and oppressors, who will now deal with us mercilessly." Another party, the tribes of Zebulun, Benjamin, and Naphtali, were in favour of returning to Egypt and trusting in the Lord. A third set, the tribes of Judah and Joseph, advised an open battle with the Egyptians; whilst the fourth party, the tribes of Dan, Gad, and Asher, said unto Moses: " Let us shout and raise a great clamour and noise and thus intimidate the Egyptians and frighten them."

But Moses silenced all the parties.

" Ye will see the Salvation of the Lord to-day," he said, " but the Egyptians ye will see to-day for the last time and never again. As for fighting, the Lord will fight for ye, whilst ye yourselves shall hold your peace, pray to the Lord and glorify Him."

And the Israelites remembered the words of Jacob, when he blest his sons: " It is not for Israel to fight and use weapons of war. Prayers are its swords, and supplications its bows."

Then the people uttered a loud prayer to God, and cried: " Lord of the Universe! Help us!" And the Lord hearkened unto their prayers. Moses, too, cried to the Lord and prayed: " Lord of the Universe! Succour the people whom Thou hast led out of Egypt and let them not fall into the hands of their pursuers."

But the Lord replied: " Do not pray now, but command the people to advance towards the sea."

Moses was amazed: " How can they pass the sea?" he cried. " They will be drowned."

" Thou hast little faith," replied the Lord. " Have I not once commanded the waters to gather in one place, and the dry land to appear, and all for one man, Adam? Should I not do the same for the sake of this multitude, the seed of Abraham, Isaac, and Jacob?"

At the command of God, Moses lifted up his rod and stretched his hand over the sea, commanding it to divide. But the sea asked: " Who art thou that hast come to cleave my waters?"

" I am the messenger of God," replied Moses, " and I command thee to do my bidding."

Still the waters refused to obey and divide.

Moses lifted up his rod and said: " Look at the rod in my hand, the rod given to me by the Almighty."

The sea, however, still continued to be perverse and refused to obey.

Thereupon the strength of the Lord appeared at the right hand of Moses, and immediately terror seized the sea and it began to skip and flee.

" For hours," said Moses, " have I been bidding thee to divide, but thou didst not hearken to my command, and now thou art suddenly running away."

" I am not fleeing before thee, son of Amram," replied the sea, " but before God, the Lord of the Universe, the Master of all created things." [1]

Israel now approached the cleft sea and stood before it. When the people saw the black mud at the bottom of the sea, they hesitated to enter it.

The men of the tribe of Reuben said: " In Egypt we used to sink in mud, and now Moses has brought us here to enter the sea and to sink again in black mud."

The tribe of Simeon, too, refused to enter the sea, and none of the other tribes showed any readiness to venture upon the muddy soil.

But the tribe of Benjamin sprang into the sea, followed by the tribe of Judah, and all the other tribes followed their example.

---

[1] *Exodus Rabba*, 21; *Sepher Hajashar*; *Mekhilta*, ed. Venice, p. 12b; quoted in *Yalkut* § 234.

And the Lord said: " As the tribes of Benjamin and Judah have shown their trust in Me, therefore shall they be rewarded. In the allotment of Benjamin, the Temple will once stand, and from Judah will issue kings who will rule over Israel."[1]

Another version runs as follows: When Moses commanded his people to advance, they approached the sea, but suddenly fear seized them, and they turned backwards, afraid lest the waters would swallow them up. But the tribe of Judah sanctified the Lord and entered the waters first, led by Nachshon, the son of Judah, and all Israel followed them.[2]

In the meantime the Egyptians approached and saw Moses, his rod in his hand, and the Israelites passing the cleft sea.

Although the waters had divided at the command of God, they were still rather turbulent and ready to sweep over Israel and to drown the nation, but Gabriel preceded the tribes and held back the waters. Turning to the wall of water on the left, the angel said: " Do not touch Israel, and beware of attempting to destroy them, for in times to come, they will wind the phylacteries about their left hand." He then turned to the wall of water on the right and said: " Beware of touching Israel who are going to receive the law which will be given unto them by the right hand of the Holy Lord."

And the waters obeyed and kept back.

But Sammael, who is Satan, was busy raising accusations against Israel. He appeared before the Lord, and said: " Lord and Judge of the Universe! the people of Israel have worshipped idols in Egypt "; but the Lord replied:

" If they have done so, they did it involuntarily and because heavy tasks had been laid upon their necks, and I have forgiven them."[3]

[1] *Exodus Rabba*, 27; *Mekhilta, ibid.*; quoted in *Yalkut*, § 234; Jellinek, *loc. cit.*, Vol. I, pp. 35-57; cf. Lewner, *loc. cit.*, pp. 47-48.
[2] *Pirke de Rabbi Eliezer*, Ch. 42; see also *Sotah*, 36b-37a; *Midrash Shokher Tob, Ps.*, 76, 1.
[3] *Midrash Abhkir; Exodus Rabba*, 21; cf. Lewner, *loc. cit.*, pp. 48-49.

GABRIEL PROTECTS THE TRIBES DURING THEIR PASSAGE
THROUGH THE RED SEA

Many miracles were wrought for Israel during their passage through the Red Sea. The waters were congealed and made into twelve channels or valleys, one for each of the tribes who walked along them. There were walls of water between the different paths, but the water was clear and transparent as glass, so that each tribe could see the others. Whatever their hearts desired, the Israelites found in the middle of the sea. There was sweet water to slake their thirst, and delicious food grew on the water walls. The Hebrew women were following their husbands, carrying their children in their arms, and when a child cried, the mother had only to stretch out her hand and pluck an apple, a pomegranate, or any other fruit to quiet the crying babe.[1]

The Egyptians, seeing the Israelites passing through the cleft sea, prepared to follow them, but suddenly turned back, afraid lest the waters would swallow them up. Thereupon an angel of the Lord appeared before them in the shape of a man riding on a mare, and the horse on which Pharaoh rode neighed, ran and entered the sea, and the Egyptians immediately followed their king.[2]

The Lord then fought against the pursuing Egyptians with a pillar of fire and a pillar of cloud. The pillar of cloud turned the soil and clay into mire, whilst the pillar of fire heated this mire so that the hoofs of Pharaoh's horses dropped off, and the wheels of his chariots fell off and were burnt to ashes.

And when Uzza, the tutelary angel of the Egyptians, saw the great distress his nation was in, and how his people were on the point of being drowned in the sea, he came before the Lord, ready to defend the Egyptians and to plead their cause.

" Lord of the Universe," he pleaded, " Thou art called up-

---

[1] *Exodus Rabba*, 21; *Pirke de Rabbi Eliezer*, Ch. 42; *Yalkut* to 2 *Samuel*, 20, § 152; cf. also Grünbaum, *Neue Beiträge*, p. 167, and see Friedlaender's edition of *Pirke de Rabbi Eliezer*, p. 331, note 6.

[2] *Pirke de Rabbi Eliezer*, Ch. 42; *Abot di Rabbi Nathan*, ed. Schechter, Ch. 27, p. 42a; see also Jellinek, *loc. cit.*, Vol. I, pp. 35–57; Gaster, *The Chronicles of Jerahmeel*, p. 160 (LIV, 9); Grünbaum, *Neue Beiträge zur semitischen Sagenkunde*, p. 166.

right and just in Thy judgment; there is no wrong before Thee, no bribery, and no respect for persons. Why then dost Thou judge my children to-day not according to their actions, for they do not deserve the punishment of drowning? Have my children drowned any of Thine? Have they massacred or slaughtered them? All that the Egyptians did was merely to impose slavery upon the children of Israel, and the latter have received their wages for this work, for they carried away with them the silver and golden vessels of the Egyptians."

Thus pleaded Uzza, and the Lord bade all the heavenly judges and members of the celestial court assemble in His presence. " Judge," said the Lord, " between me and the angel Uzza, the tutelary angel of the Egyptians, who hath come to plead the cause of his nation. There was a famine in Egypt in days gone by, and I sent Joseph to the country. He came and saved the people from death by hunger and ruled over them; and all the Egyptians swore allegiance to Joseph and were his slaves. Now when my children came down to Egypt, the Egyptians soon forgot their benefactor Joseph and laid heavy tasks upon his kith and kin, condemning them to such hard labour that in their agony they cried unto Me, and their prayers have ascended to Heaven. I heard their bitter groans, and I sent my faithful servants, Moses and Aaron, who asked Pharaoh, in My name, to let the people of Israel go. He refused to do so, but was compelled to let them go, when I sent ten plagues upon him. And now he is pursuing my children, ready to destroy them." Thus spake the Lord, and the members of the celestial court replied unanimously: " Just is the Lord in all His ways, and the Egyptians deserve to perish in the sea."

But Uzza still continued to plead the cause of the Egyptian: " I know and admit," he said, " that my nation hath deserved heavy punishment, but Thou, Lord of the Universe, art merciful and full of pity for Thy creatures; may it be Thy

will to deal with the Egyptians according to Thy mercy."
Thus pleaded Uzza, the tutelary angel of Egypt, and the
Lord was almost on the point of letting mercy prevail.

But Michael spread his wings and swiftly flew to Egypt
whence he fetched a brick wherein a Hebrew child had been
immured. He held up this brick and thus he spoke: " Lord
of the Universe! Wilt Thou have mercy upon this nation which
has been cruel, torturing and massacring the innocents?"

Uzza saw the incriminating brick in Michael's hands,
heard his words, and he was silent.

Thereupon the angel Shaftiel came up and thus he spoke:
" Lord of the Universe! Wilt Thou have compassion upon
such a nation?"

The Lord then seated Himself upon the throne of judgment
and allowed justice to have its course, and it was decreed that
the Egyptians should receive their well-deserved punishment.
The waters surged upon the army of Pharaoh, the sea began
to seethe, black clouds gathered under the sky, the stars were
darkened, and the Egyptians began to sink.[1] They all perished,
with the exception of Pharaoh.

Pharaoh was being tossed about in the waves of the sea,
when he heard the children of Israel raise their voices to praise
the Lord, rendering thanks to Him for His great wonders. " I
believe in Thee, O God," he cried. " Thou art righteous, and
I and my people are sinners. I acknowledge that there is no
God beside Thee in all the world."

Gabriel immediately descended, laid an iron chain upon
Pharaoh's neck, and thus he spoke unto him: " Thou art a
sinner! Yesterday only thou didst deny the Lord, and didst
say: ' Who is the Lord that I should hearken unto Him?'
But to-day, tossed about on the waves of the sea, thou art ready
to repent!" Thereupon the angel let Pharaoh drop into the

---

[1] *Exodus Rabba*, 22–23; *Midrash Abhkir*; quoted in *Yalkut*, § 241; cf. *Pirke de Rabbi
Eliezer*, Ch. 43: *Targum Pseudo-Jonathan* to *Exodus*, 24, 10; Jellinek, *loc. cit.*, Vol. I, pp.
35–57; see also Bialik, *loc. cit.*, pp. 63–64, and Lewner, *loc. cit.*, pp. 49–51.

depth of the sea where he kept him securely, torturing him for fifty days. At the end of the time, Gabriel carried Pharaoh to the city of Nineveh where he became King. He ruled over Nineveh 500 years, and was King when Jonah came to announce the overthrow of the city on account of the wickedness of the inhabitants. It was Pharaoh, then King of Nineveh, who covered himself with sackcloth and ashes and proclaimed once more that there is no God beside the Lord, whose judgments are faithful and whose words are true.

Pharaoh never died, for it had been decreed that he should live eternally. His station is at the gates of hell, where he receives the kings and rulers of the nations whom he rebukes for their wickedness and their lack of knowledge of the Lord:

"Ye ought to have learned wisdom from me," he says unto them. "I, too, once denied the Lord and would not hearken unto His voice. He sent ten plagues upon me and upon my country, and hurled me to the bottom of the sea. He kept me there for fifty days, at the end of which He released me, so that I was compelled to believe in him." [1]

Although they had miraculously escaped danger, the Israelites were still afraid that the Egyptians, having passed the sea like themselves, were still alive. Pharaoh, they feared, would soon be upon them again. But the Lord commanded the sea, and it cast out the corpses of the enemy who were floating on the surface of the waters like skin bottles. Then a north wind blew and cast them out opposite the camp of Israel who recognized all the officials of Pharaoh. "These were the officials," they said, "and these the taskmasters who laid the heavy burdens upon us." [2]

With regard to the corpses of the Egyptians, there ensued a mighty quarrel between the sea and the earth. The sea said:

[1] Jellinek, loc. cit., Vol. I, pp. 35–57; Vol. II, pp. 1–11; see also Gaster, The Chronicles of Jerahmeel, p. 128 (XLVIII, 12) and p. 37 (XVI, 5).
[2] Pirke de Rabbi Eliezer, Ch. 42.

" I will wash ashore all these corpses so that they might not defile my waters," and it cast them upon the shore.

But the earth replied: " I will not take all these corpses, for when I once sucked up the blood of Abel, a terrible curse was pronounced against me by the Lord. I tremble when I think of the curse that will fall on me if I receive all these slain." Thus spoke the earth, and cast the dead Egyptians back into the sea.

But the Lord, remembering Pharaoh's repentance and his words wherein he acknowledged God and His justice, decided that as a reward for this the Egyptians should not remain unburied. He bade the earth swallow up all the corpses of the Egyptians and grant them burial.[1]

When the Israelites were quite convinced that the Egyptians had been drowned and that they had been indeed delivered from bondage, they prepared to sing a song to the Lord and to sound His praises. All the angels then assembled, ready to intone their song, too, but the Lord bade them wait.

" Let Israel sing first," He said.

And the spirit of the Lord came over the children of Israel, so that sucklings dropped their mothers breasts, raised their eyes to heaven, opened their mouths, lifted up their voices, joined in the song and sounded the praises of God. When the men had completed their song, the angels once more wanted to raise their voices, but God once more bade them tarry awhile. " It is the turn of the women of Israel now," he said.

The angels began to murmur. " Is it not enough that the men have come before us? Shall also the women precede us?"

But the Lord replied: " Let the children of man sing first, for they are mortal and may die before having completed their song; ye are eternal and will have many an opportunity to intone a song." [2]

---

[1] *Mekhilta*; see Jellinek, *loc. cit.*, Vol. I, pp. 35–57; *Pirke de Rabbi Eliezer*, Ch. 42.
[2] *Sotah*, 30b; *Exodus Rabba*, 23; *Yalkut*, § 241; *Midrash Tanchuma*, ed. Buber, p. 61; cf. Lewner, *loc. cit.*, p. 52.

The sea had not only cast out all the Egyptians, but also their horses, and plenty were the jewels and pearls upon the men and the beasts. Not only all these ornaments, but also the treasures it contained did the sea cast out upon the shore. The liberated slaves collected vast wealth, but with the wealth their greed also increased. When Moses urged them to proceed now, they would not listen unto him, unable to tear themselves away from the seashore. Moses, whose great aim was to lead his people to Sinai, there to receive the Divine law, and hence bring them to the Promised Land where they could practise it, lost patience.

" Do you imagine," he cried, " that the sea will for ever cast out upon the shore precious stones, gems, and pearls?" [1]

---

[1] *Exodus Rabba*, 24; *Midrash Agadah*, ed. Buber, p. 63; see Lewner, *loc. cit.*, pp. 52–53.

CHAPTER XXIII

From the Red Sea to Sinai

In the wilderness of Shur—The miraculous food—The angels grinding the mills—The tables of congealed dew—The rivers running through the land of the heathen nations—The wonderful flavour and taste of the manna —The perfume and fragrance—The heavenly food helps to settle doubtful points—The disputed slave—At Rephidim—Amalek, the first enemy of Israel—The jealousy of the nations—The Lord rebukes them—Eliphaz and Amalek—The hatred of Esau—An army of magicians—The faithful leader of the people—A stone as a seat—Jethro's letter to Moses—Zipporah's regret—Her reward—The sanctification of the nation—They become physically and mentally perfect—The Lord offers the Torah to the heathen nations—Their refusal—The quarrel of the mountains—Mount Sinai chosen as the holy spot on account of its humility—The Torah and the women of Israel—The bondsmen of Israel—The Patriarchs and the little children—The wonders accompanying the Revelation—The Divine voice —The fear of the people—The dead revived—The Torah and the dew of life—The heathen kings and Balaam—Moses in Heaven—Kemuel, the heavenly porter—Hadarniel and Sandalphon—The murmur of the angels— Moses contends with them—What avails the Torah to you?—The laws of the Torah for men and not for angels—The Law written in black fire— Moses and Rabbi Akiba—The martyrdom of the learned Rabbi—Satan and the Torah—Earth, sea, and abyss—The modesty of Moses—The Law of Moses—Satan and the Israelites—The bier of Moses between heaven and earth—The sin of Israel—Jannes and Jambres—Aaron and Hur—The jewellery of the women—The women refuse to deprive themselves of their ornaments—The magic golden plate—Sammael and the golden calf—Get thee down from thy greatness—Moses and the angel Yefefiyah—The anger of the prophet—The punishment of the sinners—The golden lips—The five angels of destruction—Peor and the burial place of Moses.

Into the wilderness of Shur the people now followed Moses. The wilderness was full of serpents and scorpions, but the pillar of cloud made the way of the people even, and the snakes and scorpions not only did them no harm but fled at the approach of the Israelites, hiding in holes. The wonders and miracles wrought in favour of the Chosen Race during their life in the wilderness were many. They fed on heavenly food called manna.

Miraculous was its origin, miraculous the manner in which it came down from Heaven, and miraculous its taste and flavour. Created on the second day of creation, manna, or the food of the angels, is ground by the angels in mills standing in the third heaven called *Shekhakim*. Moses saw the mills and the angels grinding the manna, when he ascended to Heaven to receive the Law. Before the manna descended upon earth, a north wind used to pass over the desert, sweeping it of the dust, whilst a rain immediately came and washed the ground clear. Then a dew came down which the wind turned into a hard substance, forming tables two ells high. The sun, casting its rays upon these tables of congealed dew, made them glisten and sparkle, wonderful to behold, and upon these tables the manna then descended. Then the dew again came down, forming a sort of cover for the manna to protect it from dust.

For two hours the manna, or food of the angels, lasted every day, and after that time it melted away and streams of it ran through the desert into the lands of the nations.

The heathen nations made attempts to drink out of these rivers, but the water tasted bitter unto them. Whenever they caught a roe that had drunk out of these streams, killed it and partook of its flesh, it had a delicious flavour, so that they exclaimed: " Happy are the people that are in such a case."[1] The flavour of the manna was not less miraculous, for this heavenly food had the taste of milk and honey and of cakes made of fine flour, dipped in oil and honey. But there was more in it. The manna had the flavour of any dish a man desired to eat, and when he partook of the manna it tasted

[1] *Yoma*, 75a; *Midrash Agadah*, ed. Buber, p. 148; *Midrash Tanchuma*, ed. Buber, p. 67; *Midrash Abkhir*, quoted in *Yalkut*, § 258.

exactly like the food he fancied, so that he felt as if he were partaking of that particular food. When children partook of the manna, it tasted to them like milk, and they exclaimed: " How delicious the milk we have drunk to-day!" whilst the youths said: " How delightful the honey to-day!" Old men used to say: "We have never eaten such excellent bread in all our lives." When men wished to eat meat, or a bird, then manna tasted like meat to them.

The perfume and fragrance of the manna were wonderful, but on the Sabbath, when a double portion came down on the preceding day, its taste, flavour, and fragrance were even a thousand times more wonderful. It was no trouble whatever to gather the manna, and those who were too lazy to go out, found it at the entrance of their tents, and even whilst lying upon their beds, they had only to stretch out their hands, take the manna, and eat it.[1] The manna came down in such abundance that it would have been sufficient for many nations to feed on it, and yet, when the Israelites measured it, it only contained the measure required for each individual.

Another peculiarity of this heavenly food was that it served to settle sometimes doubtful points, as, for instance, to prove the truth or falsehood of a statement.

One day two men came before Moses: " My neighbour," said the first, " has stolen my slave."

" This is a lie," cried the other, " I never did steal thy slave, I bought him from thee."

" Return to your tents," replied Moses, " and to-morrow I will give judgment."

On the morrow they counted the measures of the daily ration of manna required for each household, and lo, the daily ration required for the disputed slave came down before his first master's tent. It was a clear proof that the slave still belonged to him and had never been sold. Moses consequently

[1] *Yalkut*, § 258.

commanded the thief to return the property to the rightful owner.[1]

At Rephidim the first enemy of Israel moved against them with armed forces. The heathen nations saw from afar the manna descending and rising to great heights, and they witnessed the great miracle the Lord had wrought for Israel by sending down to them heavenly food.

The kings and people grew jealous, and said in their hearts: " Let us go out, meet Israel, destroy the nation and wipe out its very name."

But the Lord replied: " Ye are jealous of my children! Many of you are living in peace and prosperity in your own countries, and Israel never envies you nor does she grow angry. Scarcely, however, have ye noticed that the slaves of yesterday have been set free, that the labourers in the brickfields of Egypt are advancing towards Canaan, the land promised to their ancestors as their national home, than ye already envy this nation its possible peace and prosperity. Ye already hate Israel and are thinking of means how to destroy the people oppressed."

Thus spoke the Lord, but, on account of Israel's lack of faith at Rephidim, He turned Amalek against them. Amalek was the son of Eliphaz, the son of Esau, and when he saw the great favours bestowed upon his kinsmen, the seed of Jacob, he grew jealous. His father Eliphaz advised him to make friends with this favoured nation and to go out into the wilderness and render them services, but Amalek only waxed wroth with his father. He sent messengers to many heathen nations and invited them to join him in his expedition and fight Israel. The heathen nations, however, declined to make war upon Israel, for whom the Lord had wrought so many miracles. And so Amalek went out alone, rapidly moving in one night over a distance of 400 parasangs.[2]

[1] Yoma, 75a; Midrash Agadah, ed. Buber, p. 148; cf. Lewner, loc. cit., pp. 55-56.
[2] Yoma, 75a; Mekhilta, ed. Venice, p. 20b; Midrash Tanchuma, section Ki-Teze; Pirke de Rabbi Eliezer, Ch. 44.

Whilst the other nations were afraid to wage war against Israel who had been chosen by the Lord, Amalek, who had inherited the hatred of his grandfather Esau for the seed of Jacob, marched against them. He acted treacherously before openly attacking them. From the archives of Egypt he had procured himself the list of the tribes, and, acquainted with their names, he stationed himself with his men before the camp of Israel and invited them by their names to come and do business with him. Suspecting no guile, many Israelites answered the call and were treacherously slain by Amalek.[1]

Being a magician himself and accompanied by a vast army of wizards and enchanters, Amalek knew exactly the hour of death of each individual and attacked them accordingly.[2] He also mutilated the bodies of the Israelites and jeered and mocked at and made sport of the covenant of Abraham.[3]

Amalek was defeated in battle by Joshua, the son of Nun, but only with the aid of Moses, who lifted up his hands heavenwards and prayed to the Lord. Unable to stand all the while with raised arms, Moses was compelled to sit down for a while. At that moment his servant came and offered to bring him a cushion or a comfortable seat, but Moses waved him away. He would not sit down upon a comfortable seat, he, the leader, whilst Israel, his people, were in distress and fighting a desperate foe.

" Bring me a stone," he said, " and thereupon will I sit and pray."[4]

When Jethro, the father-in-law of Moses, heard of all that had occurred, how the Israelites had been led out of the land of Egypt, and passed the Red Sea, he decided to set out for the desert. He sent a messenger to Moses, announcing his

---

[1] *Midrash Tanchuma*, section *Ki-Teze*; *Pesikta* (1868), 3, p. 26b; *Pesikta Rabbati*, ed. Friedmann, 52a.

[2] *Yalkut Reubeni*; see also, Gaster, *The Chronicles of Jerahmeel*, XLIII, 13.

[3] *Pesikta*, 3, 27b.

[4] *Midrash Tanchuma*; *Taanith*, 11; *Mekhilta*, ed. Venice. p. 21; *Yalkut*, § 265; *Midrash Agadah*, ed. Buber, p. 149; cf. Lewner, *loc. cit.*, pp. 56–59; Bialik, *loc. cit.*, pp. 66–67.

arrival. Some say that he arrived at the camp of Israel but could not enter it, because it was surrounded by a pillar of cloud. He then wrote a letter to Moses, tied it to an arrow and shot it into the camp. In his letter he begged Moses to come out and meet him.

"If I am unworthy of this honour," wrote Jethro, "then come out for the sake of thy wife Zipporah and thy two sons whom I have brought with me."

And the Lord said unto Moses: "Go out and meet Jethro and treat him kindly, for Israel should be kind to and love strangers and aliens, even as I do."

Moses, accompanied by Aaron, Nadab, Abihu, and seventy elders, came out to meet Jethro and did him honour.

When Jethro heard all the miracles, he rejoiced, but he was also grieved at the destruction of his former co-religionists the Egyptians, and felt a sting in his flesh. He blessed, however, and praised the Lord, and acknowledged His greatness.

As for Zipporah, when she heard how the women of Israel had intoned a song and sounded the praises of God, she was sorry not to have been present on this occasion and joined the women of Israel. And the Lord said: "As Zipporah has been grieved on this account, she shall be rewarded and her soul will one day be in Deborah, the prophetess, who will sing a song of salvation and redemption." [1]

The great day was now approaching, the day on which the Lord was to give the Law to Israel on Mount Sinai.

The Law was not proclaimed to Israel immediately after the exodus and their deliverance from Egypt, because they were still steeped in idol worship. The Lord, therefore, waited until the bricklayers of Egypt had grown accustomed to liberty and divine miracles.

They had partaken of heavenly food, witnessed the miracles

---

[1] *Exodus Rabba*, 27; *Midrash Tanchuma*, ed. Buber, p. 73; *Midrash Agadah*, ed. Buber, p. 150; *Mekhilta*, ed. Venice, p. 22b; *Yalkut*, § 268; see also *Seder Hadorot*.

of God, shaken off the materialism of Egypt, and become more worthy of receiving spiritual nourishment. The manna, the quails, and the well were gifts bestowed upon Israel as a preliminary to the great treasure to be handed to them at the foot of Sinai.[1]

Mentally and physically the people became more worthy of receiving the Law. At the time of the exodus there were many mutilated, sick, maimed, and lame persons among the Israelites, in consequence of their hard labour in Egypt and the accidents connected with such work. But the Lord commanded the ministering angels, and they descended upon earth, healed all the sick and made whole all the halt. The whole nation became perfect, physically and mentally.

Before, however, giving the Torah to Israel, the Lord at first offered it to the Gentiles who unanimously refused it. The Lord did act thus, so that the heathens might not pretend hereafter that they would have accepted the Law had it only been offered unto them.

God, therefore, approached the sons of Esau and said to them: " Will ye accept the Law?"

But they asked by way of a reply: " What is written in this Law?"

" It is written therein," said the Lord, " ' Thou shalt do no murder '."

And the sons of Esau replied: " We cannot accept Thy Law, for when Isaac once blessed our father Esau, he said: ' By the sword shalt thou live!' We are men of war and live by our swords, killing our enemies and robbing them. If we accept the Torah, we shall thus have to abandon the blessing bestowed upon us."

The Lord thereupon turned to the sons of Ammon and Moab.

" Will ye accept the Law?" he said.

[1] *Midrash Echa Rabba*; cf. Bialik, *loc. cit.*, pp. 67–68.

" And what is written therein?" they asked.

" It is written in the Law: ' Thou shalt not commit un-chastity '."

But the sons of Ammon and Moab replied: " We owe our very origin to unchastity, and we cannot accept Thy Law."

The Lord thereupon approached the sons of Ishmael and said unto them: " Will ye accept the Law?"

But the sons of Ishmael replied: " What is written therein?"

" It is written in the Law," replied the Lord: ' Thou shalt not steal '."

When the sons of Ishmael heard these words, they replied: " We cannot give up the laws and customs of our fathers who have always lived and thriven on theft and robbery. Did they not once steal Joseph out of the land of the Hebrews and sell him to Egypt? We cannot accept Thy Law."

The Lord thereupon offered the Torah to the Canaanites, and they, too, asked: " What is written in this Torah?"

" It is written therein," replied the Lord: " ' Thou shalt have a right measure and a right weight '."

But the Canaanites refused the Law which contained such injunctions.

The Lord thereupon sent messengers to all the heathen nations of the world, offering them the Torah, but all refused it.

Then the Lord revealed himself to the people of Israel, and they replied: " All that the Lord hath spoken, we will do and be obedient." [1]

And at that moment sixty myriads of ministering angels came down and crowned each Israelite with two crowns, one for the words: " We will do ", and the other for the words: " We will be obedient." [2]

Before giving the Torah to the Israelites, the Lord also

[1] Midrash Shir-Hashirim; Mekhilta, ed. Venice, p. 25a–b; Yalkut, § 286; Exodus Rabba, 27; Pesikta Rabbati, ed. Friedmann, 21. p. 99b; cf. Lewner, loc. cit., pp. 60–61.
[2] Sabbath, 88.

said unto Moses: " Go and speak to the daughters of Israel, make known to them the contents of the Torah and ask them whether they will accept it." Thus the women were asked first, because, as a rule, men follow the counsel of women.[1]

And when the mountains heard that God intended to reveal the Law upon one of them, they began to quarrel among themselves and to contest for the great honour. Each was anxious to be chosen as the spot where the Glory of the Lord would be revealed. Mounts Tabor, Hermon, and Carmel, all rushed forward and claimed the honour. A mighty dispute thus ensued between the contesting mountains, a dispute settled only by God Himself.

" Do not quarrel," said the voice from Heaven, " for Mount Sinai has been chosen as the spot for the delivery of the Law. I have measured all the mountains and My choice hath fallen on Mount Sinai, because it is lower than all of ye, and humbler, and the Lord loves humility. Upon all ye proud mountains, on account of your height, idols have been worshipped, and ye are unworthy to be the holy spot where the Law will be delivered. Upon Sinai alone the feet of idol worshippers have never trodden, and no heathen sanctuaries have been erected there." [2]

Now Moses sanctified Israel and bade them prepare for the Revelation. At first, however, as he had been requested by the Most High, he assembled the women of Israel and with kindly words explained to them the contents of the Law. " Men, as a rule, hearken to the counsel of women," said the Lord, " and if the women accept My commandments, they will not be able to imitate their mother Eve who, when she sinned, excused herself with the words: ' The commandment had not been given to me, but to my husband alone.' The women, too, will instruct their children in the Law."

[1] *Pirke de Rabbi Eliezer*, Ch. 41; *Exodus Rabba*, 28; *Sabbath*, 87a; *Mekhilta*.
[2] *Genesis Rabba*, 99; *Sotah*, 5a; *Leviticus Rabba*, 23; *Numbers Rabba*, 13.

Thereupon the Lord asked Israel to furnish Him with a guarantee and bring him bondsmen who would stand surety for them that they would observe the Law.

" Who will be your bondsmen?" asked the Lord.

" Our ancestors, Abraham, Isaac, and Jacob, are our bondsmen, and will stand surety for us," replied the Israelites.

But the Lord replied: " And who will stand surety for your forefathers? They lacked faith sometimes, and are moreover already in my debt. I want better bondsmen than these."

" Our children shall be our bondsmen," cried Israel.

The Lord accepted their offer, and thus the children at the mothers' breast and those yet unborn became the bondsmen for Israel that they would observe the Law, and it is the children that God calls to judgment, when the sons of Israel abandon the Law.[1]

Great were the wonders and miracles accompanying the Revelation on Sinai. Mount Sinai rose from the earth and became taller than all the mountains of the world. The heavens opened, and the summit of the holy mount towered into the opening.[2] Nature was hushed, the whole universe stood still, and no creature uttered any sound. Birds did not sing, nor did oxen low; the sea ceased her roaring, the Ophanim their motion, and the Seraphim no longer uttered their " Holy ". A breathless silence prevailed, and there was a stillness never witnessed before and never to occur again. And in the midst of this solemn and supernatural silence, the voice of the Lord resounded, calling: " I am the Lord, your God." The Divine voice travelled from one end of the world to the other, and was heard by all the inhabitants of the earth, by old and young, by the aged and the suckling, by the youth and the maiden. And the Divine voice divided itself into seventy tongues and travelled from one end of the world to the other, so that all

---

[1] *Midrash Chasit*; *Exodus Rabba*, 28; cf. Lewner, *loc. cit.*, pp. 62–63.
[2] *Pirke de Rabbi Eliezer*, Ch. 41; *Exodus Rabba*, 28.

could understand it. Each individual understood it in his own way, according to his individuality and his intelligence. Scarcely had the words been uttered, when they became flame and visible to the whole nation.

When the people heard the Divine voice and the Divine words, they trembled greatly and were alarmed. They rushed forward to the south, for it seemed to them that the voice was coming from the south, and then it seemed to them again as if the voice had come from the north. Then they heard the voice coming forth from all corners of the world, and also from heaven and from earth, and they called out: " Now we know that the glory of the Lord fills the whole universe."

Thereupon the angels of the Lord came down, two angels for each Israelite, brought unto them the Invisible Word and explained unto them its sanctity, and the reward and punishment awaiting every one who will either observe or disobey the Word. The angels thereupon having warned each Israelite, asked everyone separately: " Wilt thou accept the word of God?" and each answered: " Yea." Thereupon the angels kissed each Israelite, and the word returned to the Lord who engraved it upon the Tables.[1]

When the first commandment was uttered, and the flames, thunder and lightning increased, the people were so alarmed and so frightened that their souls fled from them. Immediately, the Torah appeared before the Lord and said: " Lord of the Universe, Thou hast given me to the living and not to the dead. Thou hast given me to man that he may live and prolong his days upon earth, and behold! they are all dead. Restore them to life, and give them strength to listen to Thy word." Thus spake the Torah, and for the sake of the Torah, the Lord let fall upon the Israelites the dew of Heaven, the dew that is destined to revive the dead, and their souls returned unto them and they came to life again.[2]

[1] *Exodus Rabba,* 29; *Midrash Shir-Hashirim.*   [2] *Exodus Rabba,* 29.

The great light, thereupon, emanating from Mount Sinai, filled the whole world, and the Voice was heard by all the inhabitants. And when the heathen nations heard that Voice, the kings trembled upon their thrones, and came to Balaam to ask for an explanation. " What is that awful voice we hear, those rumblings and peals of thunder that accompany it? Is it possible that God is bringing another flood upon the world?"

" No," replied the wizard, " the Lord has once promised that He would never visit the world with a flood."

" Perchance," said the kings, " He intends to destroy the world by fire?"

But Balaam replied: " Such is not the case. The light ye see, and the voice ye hear are the result of another cause and of a great event. The Lord is bestowing His Torah upon the people of Israel."

And when the kings of the heathen nations heard these words, they were quietened, and returned each to his country and to his kingdom.[1]

Now Israel withdrew from Mount Sinai, as they could no longer stand the awful vision, and implored Moses to receive himself the Law and to communicate it to them afterwards. Their wish was granted, and Moses alone ascended the holy mountain, where he remained for forty days.

For seven days Moses remained on the mountain, and then he ascended to Heaven, there to receive the Law. At that moment a cloud appeared before him, but he knew not whether to ride on it or only to take hold of it. Whilst he was thus deliberating, the cloud suddenly opened and Moses having entered it, it carried him aloft. He thereupon walked along on the firmament, even as a man walks upon earth. Suddenly the angel Kemuel, the heavenly porter who is appointed over 12,000 angels guarding the gates and portals of Heaven.

[1] *Yalkut*, § 286; *Mekhilta*, p. 25a; *Zebachim*, p. 116a.

approached him and harshly inquired: "What dost thou here, son of woman, and how darest thou walk among the angels, and art not afraid of their consuming fire?"

"I am the son of Amram," replied Moses, "and have come here by the command of the Most High to receive the Law."

But Kemuel wanted to destroy Moses, and the Prophet called upon the Name of God. Immediately a great fear seized the angel Kemuel and he fled from Moses a distance of 13,000 parasangs (according to another version, Moses destroyed Kemuel and wiped him out of existence).

The cloud then carried Moses higher up until he reached the angel Hadarniel, an angel from whose mouth issue 12,000 flashes of lightning with every word he utters. When Moses beheld Hadarniel, a terrible fear seized him and he could not utter a word, tears only flowing from his eyes. But the Lord had mercy upon Moses and rebuked Hadarniel. The angel thereupon said unto Moses: "I will go before thee, O son of Amram, and show thee the way, even as a pupil goes before his master." He led the son of Amram until he reached the spot where stood the angel Sandalphon, and then he spoke to Moses, saying: "I cannot go farther lest I be consumed by the fire of Sandalphon."

When Moses heard these words and beheld the angel Sandalphon, he was greatly frightened, and tears once more flowed from his eyes. He prayed to the Lord and besought his mercy, and God had compassion upon Moses and stood before him till he had passed the fire of Sandalphon. Moses then came to the river of fire called Rigyon, but the Lord took Moses, drew him across the river of fire and brought him into the vicinity of the angels who surround the Throne of Glory and who are mightier and stronger than all the other ministering angels. They wished to scorch Moses with their fiery breath, but God spread the radiance of His Glory upon Moses and strengthened him, so that the fiery breath of the angels could not harm him.[1]

As soon as the angels became aware that Moses had ascended to Heaven to receive the Law, they murmured and complained at this.

But the Lord said to Moses: " Answer them and prove unto them that the Torah avails them not."

" How can I answer them?" cried Moses. " They will consume me with their fiery breath."

" Take hold of My Throne of Glory," replied the Lord, " hold on tight to it and answer them."

Thus strengthened, Moses argued with the angels and said: " What avails the Torah to you? In the Torah it is written: ' I am the Eternal, thy Lord, that hath led thee out of the land of Egypt and out of the house of bondage.' Have you ever been slaves in Egypt and redeemed?

" It is again written in the Torah: ' Thou shalt have no other Gods beside Me.' Are you dwelling among the heathen nations and are there idolaters among you, you who witness the Glory of God, His greatness, and strength?

" It is written in the Torah: ' Thou shalt not utter the name of the Eternal in vain '. Are you engaged in business that you have to be taught concerning oaths?

" It is written in the Torah," Moses continued: " ' Remember to keep the Sabbath holy '; now is there work among you that you need rest?

" It is written in the Torah: ' Honour thy father and mother '. Have you any parents to honour?

" It is further written in the Torah: ' Thou shalt not kill, thou shalt not commit adultery, thou shalt not steal, thou shalt not covet '. Are there murderers among you, are there women among you, is there money in heaven or private pro-

---

[1] *Exodus Rabba*, 28; Gaster, *The Chronicles of Jerahmeel*, pp. 144–147 (LII, 1–8), and *Journal of the Royal Asiatic Society*, 1893, pp. 588–590.

perty? Are there houses or fields or vineyards in Heaven which you might covet, if you are not taught by the Torah that it is a sin?"

Thus argued Moses, and when the angels heard his words, they agreed that the Lord was right in deciding to deliver the Law to Israel, and they called out unanimously: "Eternal, our Lord, how mighty is Thy name in all the earth! Thou who hast extended Thy glory over the heavens." [1]

When Moses reached Heaven, he beheld the Law written in black fire upon skins of white fire, and he also beheld the Lord seated upon the Throne of Glory and occupied in adding and ornamenting the letters of the Torah with crowns. He asked:

"Why art Thou now adding these crown-like ornamentations to the letters?" Whereto the Lord replied:

"In days to come there will be born a man named Rabbi Akiba, a scholar in Israel, full of knowledge and wisdom, to whom the secret of these dots and ornamentations will be revealed. He will interpret them, basing upon their interpretation numerous laws and injunctions."

"If it is Thy will," said Moses, "may I be permitted to behold this wise man?"

"Look behind thee," said the Lord.

Moses did as he was bidden, and lo, he saw a house full of students, sitting at the feet of a master who was explaining unto them the secrets and mysteries of the Torah. Moses heard their discussions, but could not follow them and was greatly grieved. Thereupon he heard the disciples asking their master: "Whence dost thou know this, O our master?" and Rabbi Akiba replied: "What I have told you has already been explained to Moses, the son of Amram on Mount Sinai." When Moses heard these words, he was content.

In his modesty, however, the Prophet turned to God, saying:

[1] *Sabbath*, 88b–89a; Gaster, *loc. cit.*, p. 147 (LIII, 9).

" Lord of the Universe! Thou wilt one day create a man like Rabbi Akiba who will excel me in knowledge and wisdom; why dost Thou not give the Torah to Israel through him instead of me?"

But the Lord replied: " Such is my decree."

" Lord of the Universe," said Moses again: " Thou hast shown me this man and I have beheld his great learning, may I also be permitted to see the reward awaiting him?"

And the Lord replied: " Look behind thee."

Moses looked, and horror seized him. He saw cruel men seizing the erudite and holy Rabbi and tearing his flesh from his body with sharp iron instruments. In the agony of his soul, Moses cried: " Lord of the Universe! Is this the reward meted out to the holy man for his great erudition?"

The Lord answered: " Be silent, for such is my decree; but as thou hast shown thy modesty, thou shalt be rewarded, and I will make thee excel in wisdom all other men." The Lord then opened the treasures of wisdom and bestowed upon the son of Amram forty-nine parts, one part only remaining for the rest of the world, so that the Prophet became wiser than all other men. And all the mysteries of creation were revealed unto Moses, and he read in the future as in an open book.[1]

When Moses had received the Torah and was about to descend upon earth, Satan appeared before the Throne of Glory and thus he said: " Lord of the Universe, where is the Torah?"

" I gave the Torah to earth," replied the Lord.

Immediately Satan betook himself to earth and asked: " Where are the whereabouts of the Torah?"

Whereto earth replied: " The Lord knows of its course. He looketh to the end of the earth and seeth under the whole heaven."

---

[1] *Menachot*, 29b; *Leviticus Rabba*, 26; *Exodus Rabba*, 41; cf. Lewner, *loc. cit.*, pp. 69–71.

Satan then betook himself to the sea, and asked for the Torah, but the sea replied: " It is not with me."

He turned to the abyss, but the abyss only replied: " The Torah is not with me."

Satan returned to God and said: " Everywhere have I searched for the Torah, but found it not."

" Go and ask the son of Amram," replied the Lord.

And to Moses Satan at once betook himself.

"Where is the Torah, O son of Amram," asked Satan, " the Torah which God hath given thee?"

" Who am I," answered Moses, " that the Lord should make me a present of the Torah?"

" Moses," said God, " thou art uttering a falsehood."

" Lord of the Universe," replied Moses, " Thou dost possess a rare treasure which delights Thee daily; have I any right to claim it now as my own because Thou didst teach me its contents?"

" Since thou hast been so humble," replied the Lord, " the Torah shall henceforth be named after thee, and shall be known as the Law of Moses." [1]

In the meantime the Israelites were waiting for the return of Moses from the Mount. Satan, now anxious to accuse Israel and to make them forget the first commandment, did his best to lead them astray. Moses had promised the Israelites to come down from Mount Sinai after forty days, and at noon of the fortieth day he had not yet returned. Satan, always eager to lead men astray, and particularly jealous of Israel at that moment, came to the Israelites and asked: " Where is your law-giver, Moses, the son of Amram?"

" He has ascended to Heaven," replied the Israelites.

When Satan saw that they would not listen to his insinuations, he said to the people: " Look up and behold your leader who is dead."

---

[1] *Sabbath,* 89a.

And indeed, midway between heaven and earth, the Israelites beheld a heavy cloud, and on it a black bier on which lay stretched out dead their leader Moses.

Thereupon the rabble, 40,000 in number, who had come out of Egypt with the sons of Israel, led by the two magicians, Jannes and Jambres, came up to Aaron and Hur and thus they said: " The Egyptians among whom we dwelt were in the habit of carrying their gods about with them, uttering hymns and singing before them, and they saw their gods before them. Now Moses is dead, and we ask thee to make unto us a god like the gods of the Egyptians, that we may see it before us." Thus spoke the mixed multitude to Aaron and Hur.

" Tarry awhile," said Aaron and Hur, " Moses will soon come down from the Mount."

But the rabble, led by the magicians Jannes and Jambres, would not listen to them.[1]

Then Hur, the son of Miriam, whose name was also Ephrath, because she was of noble birth, rebuked them, and spoke harsh words unto them: " Ye stiff-necked people," he cried, " have ye already forgotten all the miracles the Lord hath wrought on your behalf?"

Then they rose up and slew Hur.[2] They then turned to Aaron and said: " If thou wilt make us a god, it is well, otherwise we will do unto thee as we have done unto Hur."

When Aaron saw that Hur was dead, he was afraid lest Israel would commit another great sin by killing him, too, and he preferred to grant them their wish, still hoping that in the meantime Moses would return. But Aaron thought: " If I ask the Israelites to bring me gold and silver, they will do so immediately. I will therefore ask them to bring me the jewellery of their wives and their daughters, and as the latter will no doubt refuse to deprive themselves of their ornaments, the

[1] Midrash Tanchuma, section Ki-Tissa; Midrash Agadah, ed. Buber, p. 181; Sabbath, p. 89a; Pirke de Rabbi Eliezer, Ch. 45.   [2] Ibid.

matter will be delayed or fail altogether." Thus thought Aaron, and he bade the people bring him the ornaments and earrings of their wives and daughters.

The men approached the women, but the latter refused to give up their ornaments, saying: " Heaven forbid that we should give our ornaments to make a graven image and thus deny the Lord who has wrought such miracles on our behalf." Thus spoke the women of Israel, and the men at once broke off their own earrings which were in their ears after the fashion of the Egyptians and the Arabs, and brought them unto Aaron.[1]

When Aaron saw that his plan had failed, he raised his eyes to Heaven and said: " Lord of the Universe, Thou knowest my innermost thoughts and the reason why I am doing this." He thereupon cast the ornaments into the fire.

Now, among the ornaments was a golden plate upon which the name of God was written, and upon it was also engraven the figure of a calf. This plate a man named Micah cast into the furnace, and a calf came out.[2] Into this calf Sammael immediately entered, so that it ran about like a living beast and lowed like one.[3]

Aaron was amazed and sorely grieved, when he saw this, and he said unto the Israelites: " Why are you in a hurry to worship your god? I will build an altar unto it, and to-morrow will be a great festival." Aaron thus still cherished the hope of delaying the sin of idol worship, as Moses would certainly return in the meantime. His hope, however, was frustrated, for on the morrow Moses had not yet returned, and the people began to worship the golden calf.[4]

Then the Lord said to Moses who was still in Heaven: " Get thee down from thy greatness, for it is only for Israel's sake that I gave thee greatness and cast honour upon thee. Now that Israel hath sinned and become disloyal to Me, I

[1] Ibid.   [2] Midrash Tanchuma, section Ki-Tissa.   [3] Pirke de Rabbi Eliezer, Ch. 45.
[4] Sabbath, 89; Midrash Tanchuma, section Ki-Tissa.

have no use in thee and there is no reason why I should distinguish thee.[1] Thy people," the Lord said, " whom thou didst lead out of Egypt, have sinned."

And when Moses was allowed to descend from Heaven, he had once more to pass the angels of Fear and of Sweat, of Trembling and Quaking, and he was so filled with horror that he forgot all that he had learned. God then called the angel Yefefiyah, who brought back remembrance to him and handed to him the Torah. Armed with the Law, Moses passed the ranks of all the angels, and they became his friends, giving him presents and revealing to him mysteries. They taught him the secret of the Holy Names, and the angel of Death taught him a remedy against Death.[2]

Moses descended from Heaven, carrying the tables of the Law. The tables carried their own weight so long as the celestial writing was upon them, but when Moses came down and beheld the cymbals, the dances and the calf, he suddenly became aware of the enormous weight of the tables and felt that he could not carry both himself and the tables. He noticed at the same time how all the letters upon the tables were vanishing, so that no celestial writing remained upon them. Amazed, the law-giver stood still contemplating two almost meaningless heavy stones in his hand, uselessly burdening him. He cast them from him and broke them.[3]

Moses' anger was great. He burned the calf, powdered it like the dust of the earth and cast it upon the water. He thereupon made the Israelites drink this water, and the lips of all those who had worshipped the calf and kissed it became golden, so that they could be distinguished from those who had not sinned.[4] The sinners were punished, and Moses ultimately succeeded in appeasing the anger of God.

---

[1] *Berachoth, 32a.*   [2] *Yalkut Reubeni, fol.* 107c.
[3] *Pirke de Rabbi Eliezer*, Ch. 45; *Abbot de Rabbi Nathan*, p. 67a; *Targum Pseudo-Jonathan*; *Exodus*, 32, 19; see *Yalkut*, § 293; cf. Lewner, *loc. cit.*, pp. 76–79.
[4] *Pirke de Rabbi Eliezer*, Ch. 45.

MOSES CASTS FROM HIM THE TABLES OF THE LAW

The Lord had sent down five angels to destroy Israel, they were Wrath, Anger, Temper, Destruction, and Glow of Anger, but Moses hastened to the Cave of Machpelah and there invoked the Patriarchs on behalf of Israel: " If ye are children of future life," he cried, " then stand by me now, in this hour of need, for your children are like sheep given over to slaughter."

The Patriarchs arose and also invoked God who had once promised to multiply their seed as the stars of heaven. God took into consideration the merits of the Patriarchs, and the three angels, *Kezef*, *Af*, and *Hemah* were at once called away, but two of them, Mashit and Haron remained.

Thereupon Moses once more prayed to God, and He held back the angel *Mashit* (Destruction), and *Haron* (Glow of Anger) alone remained. Moses, however, conquered even this last angel. He cast Haron down into the earth and buried him in a spot in the possession of the tribe of Gad, where he remained bound and kept in check by the Prophet. The name of this angel is also *Peor*, for every time when Israel sinned, he tried to rise from the earth, open his mouth and destroy Israel with his breath. But Moses had only to pronounce the name of God, and Haron was at once drawn down beneath the earth.

When Moses died, God buried him opposite to the place where Peor is kept a prisoner. Every time that Israel sins, Peor rises to the upper world, ready to destroy the nation with his breath, but no sooner does he behold the burial place of Moses than he falls back terror-stricken, returning to the depths of the earth.[1]

---

[1] *Pirke de Rabbi Eliezer*, Ch. 45; *Exodus Rabba*, 41; *Midrash Shokher Tob, Ps.*, 7; *Yalkut, Ps.*, 7, § 673; see also *Sabbath*, 55a; *Nedarim*, 32a.

CHAPTER XXIV

In the Wilderness

The revolt of Korah—His ambition—Korah and his wife—The Levites —Moses speaks kind words to the rebels—The parable of the poor widow and her orphaned daughters—The exigencies of the priests—The heavy taxes—The punishment of Korah and his company—On, the son of Peleth— A clever woman—The lady with the streaming hair—The reproach of the Israelites—The plague—The secret taught unto Moses by the angel of death—Death and incense—The foes of Israel—False friends—Amalek and the sons of Esau—The prayer of Israel—The Amorites—The valley of Arnon—The enemy in hiding—The jutting rocks and the caves—The two lepers, Eth and Hav—The miracle of the well—Sihon, King of Heshbon— The offer of peace—Og, the giant—Og and the ark—Og and Sarah the beautiful—The giant's thigh-bone and the gravedigger—Og, a former slave of Abraham—The wonderful bed—The giant's food and drink—The mysterious wall—The mountain and the ants—The leap into the air—The death of Og—The Moabites—Balak and Balaam—The magicians' advice —The seductive maidens—Linen garments and unchastity—Simri and Cozbi—Phinehas the zealot—The war against the Midianites—The flying magician—The death of Balaam.

During the sojourn of the children of Israel in the desert, Moses had much trouble with them, and many revolts embittered his life. Such was the revolt of Korah who, jealous of the greatness of the son of Amram, revolted against him, and incited many of the people. According to Jewish legend it was his wife that excited Korah to revolt against Moses. Korah was of the tribe of Levi, and when Moses commanded the Levites to " cause a razor to pass over all their flesh ",[1] Korah was also compelled to cut his hair and shave. Thereupon his wife said unto him:

" How long will Moses, thy kinsman, laugh and mock at

[1] *Numbers*, 8, 7.

thee? He himself is King, and Aaron, his brother, he has raised to be High-Priest. Not only the children of Israel are compelled to give tithe to the priests, but also the Levites. And now he is humiliating you, treating you as if you had been sheep, commanding you to cut off the hair of your head and to shave, and also to offer you as a wave offering as if you were animals."[1]

Now Korah was an exceedingly wealthy man, possessing vast treasures, gold and silver and precious stones; and being very wealthy he desired also honour.

He thought in his heart: " Am I not the son of Izhar, the son of Kehath, who was the father also of Amram? My father Izhar was a younger brother of Amram, and I am a cousin of Moses and of Aaron. Moses is King, Aaron is High-Priest, and I had always hoped that I would be appointed the Prince of my tribe. But no, Moses has raised to this dignity Eliphaz the son of Usiel, who was a younger brother of my father. He has evidently made up his mind to slight me, and is holding me in contempt, although I am the possessor of vast treasures. I will therefore raise a revolt against Moses and upset all his plans."[2]

Thereupon Korah went from tent to tent and incited two hundred and fifty princes of the congregation, " called to the assembly, men of renown ".

When Moses heard that a conspiracy had been formed against him, he went himself to the tent of Korah and spoke kindly to the rebels.

" My brethren," said he, " I have heard that ye are not satisfied with me, and are accusing me of pride and arrogance. Have you forgotten that I went from Midian to Egypt for your sake, but never asked any reward for all my trouble and my labours? If I am now supposed to be ruling over you, it is not

---

[1] *Numbers*, 8, 11.
[2] *Yalkut,* § 750; *Midrash Tanchuma,* section *Korah*; *Midrash Mishle (Proverbs)* 11.

because I have sought greatness and been ambitious. It is the Lord who has commanded me to be your leader, and I have never done anything except what the Lord has commanded me to do."

Thus spoke Moses, but Korah replied:

" Thou hast done but little for us. Thou hast taken us out of Egypt, where we lived in plenty, but hast not brought us to Canaan, the land thou didst promise to give us."

And when the followers of Korah heard his words, they rose against Moses and were almost on the point of stoning him.

The Prophet was sorely grieved, not because they wanted to stone him, but because they were thus committing a grievous sin against the Lord.[1]

Thereupon Korah went out to the tents of Israel, endeavouring to find followers and partisans for his conspiracy among the people.

" What wrong has Moses done unto thee that thou art so angry with him?" asked the children of Israel. To this Korah replied hypocritically:

" Had it only been a question of myself, of my honour and of my thwarted ambitions, or of the wrong he has done unto me, I would never have said a word and borne all offences silently, without a murmur, but Moses has wronged the whole congregation. He has laid upon all the children of Israel heavy burdens and given them laws which are very severe. Let me tell you what cruel treatment a poor widow living in my neighbourhood has met at the hands of Moses."

" Tell us the story of the poor widow," said the children of Israel, and Korah told them as follows:

" There was a poor man dwelling in my neighbourhood, a man whose days were full of misery, for he suffered great want. When the man died, his widow and her two orphan

[1] *Yalkut, ibid.; Midrash Tanchuma, ibid.*

daughters had only one small field in their possession. This the widow decided to cultivate so as to find sustenance for herself and for her children. But when she started to plough her field, Moses came and said:

" ' Thou shalt not plough thy field with an ox and an ass together.' [1]

" The woman hired an ass only and ploughed her field. When she started to sow, Moses again came and said:

" ' Thou shalt not sow thy field with two kinds of seed.' [2] When she had finished sowing and her field had borne fruit, and the time came to reap, Moses came again and told her not to reap wholly the corners of the field, not to gather the gleanings but to leave them for the poor.

" She obeyed his instructions and brought the harvest into her barn. When the woman was about to thrash the grain, Moses again came and said: ' Give me the heave-offering, the first and the second tithes for the priests.'

" And the poor woman said unto herself:

" ' There is very little to be got out of the field, and it will scarcely yield anything for myself and my two daughters, if I am to pay such heavy taxes and give away a large portion to the priests. I will sell my field and buy unto me two ewes whose milk will nourish us, my two daughters and myself, and out of their wool we shall make clothes unto ourselves.' Thus thought the woman. She sold her field and bought two sheep. When her sheep brought forth young, Aaron, the High-Priest, came and said:

" ' Give me the first-born of thy sheep, for they belong to me, according to the Law, as it is said: " All the firstlings, males that are born of thy herd and thy flock, thou shalt sanctify unto the Lord thy God ".' [3]

" The poor woman handed over the firstlings to the High-Priest. When the time of shearing came and she hoped to be

---

[1] *Deuteron.*, 22, 10.   [2] *Leviticus*, 19, 19.   [3] *Deuteron.*, 15, 19.

able to weave out of the wool garments for herself and her daughters, Aaron came again and demanded his share of the shearing:

" ' Give me the first of the fleece of thy sheep which is the priest's due according to the Law, for it is written: " And the first of the fleece of thy sheep shalt thou give unto him ".' [1] The poor widow did as she was bidden, but she was sorely grieved and said in her heart:

" ' This priest is robbing me constantly and leaves me but little for myself and my children. I will slaughter the two sheep and eat their meat, and the priest will cease to rob me.'

" Thus thought the poor widow in her heart, but scarcely had she slaughtered her two sheep, her only property, than Aaron once more appeared and demanded the shoulder, the two cheeks and the maw as his share.

" ' This is the Law,' he said, ' for it is written: " And this shall be the priest's due from the people, whether it be the ox or sheep, that they shall give unto the priest the shoulder, and the two cheeks, and the maw ".' [2]

" When the poor widow heard these words, she exclaimed:

" ' Woe unto me! I had hoped never to see again the face of this priest who has been robbing me all my life, but lo! he has come again.' In her anger she said in her heart:

" ' I will contrive that neither I nor he shall have anything of the meat of my sheep.' Turning to Aaron, she said:

" ' I cannot give thee the share thou art claiming, for I have devoted the slaughtered sheep to God.' But Aaron replied:

' " If such is the case, then *all* is mine, for everything devoted in Israel belongs to the priest.[3] Such is the Law.' Thus speaking, he seized the two slaughtered sheep and walked away, leaving the widow and her orphan daughters weeping bitterly.

" Thus," concluded Korah, " the priests are always acting,

[1] *Deuteron.*, 18, 4.   [2] *Deuteron.*, 18, 3.   [3] *Numbers*, 18, 14.

despoiling the poor, the widows, and the orphans. When the children of Israel are asking them: why are ye acting thus? they reply: because such is the Law!"

When the people heard these words spoken by Korah, they were very wroth against Moses and Aaron.[1]

Korah and his partisans rebelled against Moses and Aaron, the Prophets of the Most High, but swift punishment was meted out to them. The ground clave asunder, the earth opened her mouth and swallowed up Korah, his followers and their households, and all the men that appertained unto Korah, and all their goods.[2]

One man, however, had a lucky escape, owing his salvation to his wife. His name was On, the son of Peleth. His wife was a clever woman, and when she saw Korah talking to her husband and persuading him to rebel against Moses and Aaron and depose them from both leadership and priesthood, she did not approve of the plot. On had given his promise to Korah to join him, but when the leader of the rebellion had left, and On was discussing the matter with his wife, the latter said to him:

" I do not approve of this plot, and as for thyself, my dear husband, no benefit will ever accrue to thee from the rebellion, whether it be successful or not. If Moses gains the victory and is master, thou wilt be subject to him, and if Korah is successful, thou wilt be subject to him."

" Thou art right," admitted On, struck by the truth of his wife's argument, " but what can I do now? I have given an oath to Korah to join him when he comes to our tent to fetch me, and it is incumbent upon me to keep my oath."

" Do not thou worry," said On's wife, " and leave the matter to me. I will contrive it so that neither Korah nor his followers will dare approach the tent to fetch thee." [3]

---

[1] *Yalkut*, § 750; *Midrash Shokher Tob; Midrash Agadah*, ed. Buber, Vol. II, pp. 116–117.
[2] *Numbers*, 16, 32. [3] *Sanhedrin*, 109b; *Midrash Tanchuma, ibid.*

Thereupon she gave wine to drink to her husband, so that he became intoxicated and fell into a deep sleep. When Korah and his company came to fetch On, the latter's wife uncovered her hair, and, letting her long tresses stream loose, appeared at the door of the tent. None of Korah's company dared approach a woman with uncovered head and streaming hair, and they at once drew back. In vain did they make several attempts to get at On, the son of Peleth, but every time when they saw the woman in this condition they started back.

On awoke from his sleep at the very moment when Korah and his company were being swallowed up by the earth. He heard a tremendous noise and loud clamour, and the bed upon which he slept began to rock. Greatly frightened, he asked his wife what it meant.

"It is the punishment meted out to Korah and to his company for their sin in plotting a rebellion against Moses and Aaron," replied his wife.[1]

When On heard these words, he thanked the Lord who had sent him a righteous and clever wife, to whom apply the words:

"Every wise woman buildeth her house; but the foolish plucketh it down with her own hands."[2]

The sons of Korah, too, had been saved.

The death and destruction of Korah and his company ought to have convinced the children of Israel that Moses was only acting according to the will of God, that he had never usurped the power for himself or arbitrarily invested his brother Aaron with the priesthood. The conviction may have been brought home to the children of Israel, but still they persisted in seeking quarrel with Moses. They now accused him of being responsible for the death of many noble men in Israel.

"Had Moses not excited the revengefulness of the Lord," they said, "the men would not have perished."

---

[1] *Sanhedrin*, 110a; *Pesikta (Sutarta)*, section *Korah*. [2] *Proverbs*, 14. 1.

These words of the children of Israel brought upon them the anger of the Lord.

The wrath went out from the Lord, and the plague began. At this critical moment, Moses remembered the remedy against death which the angel of death had once taught him. When he ascended to Heaven to receive the Torah, the angels had at first objected to Moses' presence in the celestial regions, and had looked upon him as an intruder. In the end, however, they became his friends, bestowed gifts upon him, and taught him many secrets. The angel of death, too, had taught him a remedy how to stay death, and this was to burn incense.

Turning now to Aaron, Moses commanded him to take holy fire from the altar, put incense upon it, and go quickly among the congregation. Unaware of the secret remedy taught unto Moses by the angel of death Aaron was surprised.

" My brother," he said, " hast thou in view my death? Dost thou not remember that my two sons, Nadab and Abihu, died because they had put strange fire into the censers, and now thou commandest me to carry holy fire outside."

" Know, my brother," said Moses, " that whilst thou art thus talking, the children of Israel are dying. Go and do quickly as thou art bidden."

" If such is the case," said Aaron, " and the lives of the children of Israel are at stake, I will carry out thy command, for it is better that I or a thousand like me should be burned, but that Israel might be saved."

Aaron hurried out and stayed the angel of death.[1]

During their wandering in the wilderness the Israelites had to contend with many foes, Edomites, Amorites, and Moabites, Og, King of Bashan, and Balak, King of Moab, all of whom were jealous of the strength of the children of Israel, and sought to harm them.

When Aaron died, the clouds of glory which for forty years

[1] *Pesikta Sutarta*, section *Korah*; *Sabbath*, 89a; cf. *Midrash Agadah*, p. 118.

had covered the site of the camp, vanished, and their disappearance brought terror to the hearts of Israel.

" Now that we are no longer protected by the clouds of glory," they said, " the clouds which made it impossible for our enemies to approach our camp, we shall be harassed by our foes." And indeed, thus it really soon came to pass.

The first foe who now once more came to wage war upon Israel, though not an open but an underhand war, was Amalek, the grandson of Esau. The other sons of Esau, as soon as they learned that Aaron was dead and that the clouds of glory had disappeared, rejoiced greatly and sent word to Amalek requesting him to wage war upon Israel. Amalek was ready to appear once more in the field, especially since Israel seemed to have stumbled and sinned before the Lord. Remembering, however, past experiences, Amalek decided not to go in open warfare against the sons of Israel, but to use craft. His men, therefore, disguised themselves as Canaanites, donned Canaanite costume, and learned to speak the speech of the Canaanites.

" The Lord," said Amalek, " hearkens unto the prayers of Israel and always answers them. Now, when the Israelites will see us and take us for Canaanites they will, no doubt, implore the Lord to come to their assistance against the Canaanites and not against the Amalekites, and we shall thus be saved and will slay them."

Amalek's men, disguised as Canaanites, now concealed their swords in their garments and appeared in Israel's camp.

" We are Canaanites," they said, " and have come to condole with you, for we have heard that a great calamity has befallen you on your way, and that your High-Priest Aaron is dead." Thus spoke the Amalekites, making use of the speech of Canaan, and suddenly fell upon the children of Israel.

But when the latter saw these men dressed like Canaanites and speaking the speech of Canaan, but whose countenances denounced them as Amalekites, descendants of Esau, they prayed unto the Lord as follows: " Lord of the Universe! strange are these men with whom we are now waging war, and strange are their deeds, we do not know whether they are of the nation of Canaan or of Amalek. We pray therefore unto Thee to visit punishment upon them to whichsoever nation they belong."

The Lord hearkened unto the prayers of the children of Israel, stood by them and delivered Amalek into their hands.[1]

One of Israel's foes were the Amorites. When they heard that the children of Israel would soon have to pass through the valley of Arnon, they said to each other:

" Let us go to that valley and there lie in wait for Israel." Now the valley of Arnon was enclosed by two lofty mountains that lay very close together. The Amorites hurried to the valley and hid in the numerous caves on the slopes of the mountains. " When the Israelites," they said, " will penetrate into the narrow defile between the two mountains, we will sally forth, attack them suddenly and thus easily destroy them."

The plan of the Amorites was, however, frustrated by the Lord. Before Israel went the ark which levelled the mountains and smoothed the rough places.

When Israel had reached the valley of Arnon, ascended one mountain and intended to descend into the defile, the two mountains were by a Divine miracle moved so close together that the Amorites were crushed. One mountain was full of caves wherein the Amorites were hiding, whilst the other consisted of pointed, jutting rocks. When the rocks entered into the caves, the Amorites concealed in them were all crushed, and Israel was thus delivered from a dangerous foe.

The Israelites passed on and would never have known what a miracle had just been performed for them by the hand of

---

[1] *Midrash Tanchuma*, section *Chukath*; *Yalkut*, § 764; cf. *Midrash Agadah*, p. 127.

God. But there were two lepers among the Israelites, Eth and Hav, who, according to custom, were following the camp. These two suddenly saw blood flowing from under the mountains and they hurried and informed the people of what had occurred.[1]

According to another source the Israelites learned the fate of the Amorites through the well. The Lord bade the well to flow past the caves and wash out the corpses of the Amorites, and it was thus that the children of Israel discovered the miracle the Lord had wrought for them.[2]

When the Israelites had passed the valley of Arnon, the Lord commanded Moses to wage war against Sihon, King of Heshbon, the Amorite. Before, however, waging war against Sihon, Moses sent him messengers of peace. " The Lord," he said in his heart, " has commanded me to contend in battle against Sihon, but I know that He loves peace and will not be angry with me if I first send messengers of peace to the Amorite." Moses was following the example of the Lord who had sent him to Pharaoh with words of peace before punishing the Egyptians and compelling them to let Israel go.

Sihon, King of Heshbon, refused the peace proposals of the leader of Israel, but the Lord was well pleased with the conduct of His servant.

" Thou hast acted well," He said, " in offering peace before waging war, and in future thou shalt never declare war upon a city, but first urge the inhabitants to surrender in peace."

Another redoubtable enemy of Israel was Og, King of Bashan. Og was one of the giants who had been saved during the flood by clambering upon the roof of Noah's ark.[3] It was he also who had hurried to bring news to Abraham concerning Lot's bondage. Og's motive was not a disinterested one. He

---

[1] *Berachoth*, 54b; *Yalkut*, § 764; cf. *Midrash Agadah*, pp. 128–129.
[2] See *Midrash Tanchuma*, section *Chukath*; *Num*, Rabba, 79.
[3] See Vol. I, Ch. 17.

hoped that Abraham would hasten to the rescue of his kinsman, be killed in battle, and thus would he, Og, be able to get possession of Sarah the beautiful.[1] Og was of a gigantic build, and his strength was enormous. His thigh bone alone is said to have measured more than three miles (parasangs). " I was once a gravedigger," relates one Rabbi in the Talmud, " and I hunted a stag that fled into the thigh bone of a dead man. For three miles did I run after the stag without either catching it or reaching the end of the thigh bone. I made inquiries afterwards and found out that it was the thigh bone of Og, King of Bashan."[2] Og is said to have been a slave of Abraham who subsequently gave him his freedom. One day, when Abraham rebuked him, Og was frightened, and one of his teeth fell out. Out of this Abraham fashioned a bed in which the giant used to sleep.[3] The giant's food and drink were in accordance with his size and strength. He devoured daily a thousand oxen and as many other animals, and his daily drink was a thousand measures of liquid. Such was the giant Og, and it was quite natural that Moses should have hesitated to wage war against him, but the Lord told him not to fear the giant.

Now when Og heard what had happened to Sihon, King of Heshbon, he said unto himself: " It will be easy for me to destroy Moses and the whole camp of Israel." He went up and sat upon the wall of the city with his feet touching the ground.

Moses approached the place of Edrei, reaching the outskirts at nightfall. " Let us pass here the night," he said, " and in the morning we shall attack the city."

Next morning, when Moses looked towards the city, he was amazed.

" Is it possible," he cried, " that during the night the men of Edrei could have built such a high wall?" But when Moses

---

[1] See Vol. I, Ch. 22.   [2] *Niddah*, 24b.   [3] *Yalkut Chadash*, 16b.

looked more closely he saw that it was not a second wall, but Og sitting upon the first wall and darkening the sun with his giant stature.[1]

Og then said in his heart:

" I see that the camp of Israel is three parasangs in circumference. I will therefore tear up a mountain three parasangs wide, lay it upon my head and then hurl it upon Moses and the Israelites and thus crush them." Thus thought Og and carried out his plan.

" Fear not," said the Lord to Moses, " for he is in thy hand."

A miracle now happened which caused Og's death. Ants came and perforated the mountain and it sank over the giant's head. He made an effort to shake it off, but his teeth suddenly grew into tusks, pushed and thrust through the mountain so that the giant, in spite of his efforts, could not draw his head out.

Now Moses was ten cubits in height, and he took a hatchet ten cubits long, leaped into the air ten cubits and hit Og on the ankle. The giant fell down, and Moses was able to slay him.[2]

Moses and the Israelites had also to fight against the Moabites. Balak, King of Moab, a great magician himself, having noticed that the Israelites were conquering their enemies by supernatural strength, decided to call upon Balaam to curse the people of Israel.

Accompanied by his two sons, the famous wizards Jannes and Jambres, Balaam, after some hesitation, set out to curse the people of God. His magic power, however, had no effect on Israel, the nation being protected by the merits of the Patriarchs and by angels. The heathen prophet's curses turned to blessings. Unable to fulfil Balak's wish to curse Israel, the

---

[1] *Deuter. Rabba,* 1; cf. Eisenmenger, *loc. cit.,* Vol. I, p. 389.
[2] *Berachoth,* 54b; *Sepher Hajashar.*

magician gave the King of Moab an advice, counselling him to resort to seduction.

" The God of this people," said Balaam, " hates lewdness and unchastity. Select thou, therefore, pretty women, the handsomest daughters of Moab, and send them out to seduce the sons of Israel to unchastity and then to idolatry. The God of this people will then punish them for their sin."

Thus spoke Balaam, the wicked magician, and Balak, acting upon his advice, proceeded in the following manner. He pitched tents, at the entrance of which old women were offering linen garments for sale.

When the Israelites came to buy the garments, the old women showed them some samples of the goods which they were selling at a cheap price, but invited the men into the interior of the tents where, they said, they would find more beautiful wares. The unsuspecting purchasers, anxious to buy linen garments, went inside, where they were received by young and beautiful women, wearing splendid and costly robes and well perfumed. The sirens of Moab employed all their blandishments and allurements and seduced the men to unchastity and then to idolatry, making them worship the idol of Peor. It was thus that Israel sinned at Shittim in consequence of the wicked counsel of Balaam the magician.

The heathen prophet, however, was very soon punished for the harm he had thus done to Israel. When Phinehas, the son of Eleazar, had slain Simri, the prince of the tribe of Simeon, and Cozbi, the woman with whom he had sinned, and who was a daughter of Balak himself, the Israelites were commanded to wage war against the Midianites. Balaam was with that nation helping them against Israel. Resorting to witchcraft, he flew in the air, but Phinehas held up the pure gold plate upon which was engraved the ineffable name, and Balaam fell to the ground. In vain did the magician plead for his life. " Thou dost deserve death," said Phinehas, " for in addition to thy evil deeds in the past, as one of Pharaoh's counsellors, thou art responsible for the death of 24,000 Israelites who had been lured to sin by thy wicked counsel." Thus the great magician, who is supposed to have been none other than Laban, met his death.[1]

[1] *Targum Pseudo-Jonathan, Numbers,* 22, 22; 23, 9, 10, 23; 24, 25; 31, 8; *Numbers Rabba,* 20; *Midrash Tanchuma,* section *Balak; Sanhedrin,* 106b; *Sepher Hajashar;* Philo, *De Vita Moysis,* I, 48; 54–56; Josephus, *Antiq.,* IV, 6, 2; 6–9; see also *The Samaritan Book of Joshua,* Ch. 3 and 4; Hamburger, *Real-Encyklopädia, s.v. Balaam;* cf. for the whole chapter, Lewner, *Kol Agadoth.* Vol. II, pp. 98–110; 120–130.

CHAPTER XXV

The Death of Aaron, or Aaron the Peacemaker

Moses is commanded to prepare Aaron for his death—The grief of Moses—He changes his usual custom—The difficult passages of the Law —The book of *Genesis*—The wonders of the Creator—The sin of Adam— The sentence of death—Human destiny—Moses talks of death—The walk to Mount Hor—Aaron is honoured—The joy of the children of Israel— The popular High-Priest—Aaron the Peacemaker—Nabal the son of Birshah—The women praise Aaron—On Mount Hor—The light of God— Moses is embarrassed—The mysterious cave—The couch spread out by celestial hands—Aaron mentions the word of death—Moses consoles his brother—The soul lured away by a Divine kiss—The return of Moses and Eleazar—The anger of the children of Israel—Satan among the people— The prayer of Moses—The bier of Aaron is carried in mid-air by angels— The grief of the people—The disappearance of the clouds of glory—The sun and the moon reappear.

When the day arrived for Aaron to die, the Lord said unto Moses:

" The time has now come for thy brother Aaron to be gathered to his people. Go thou now and tell him to prepare for death. Console him, however, and say that even if he is doomed to die, his sons will inherit his High-Priesthood." Moses was sorely grieved when he heard these words, and he wept passionately all the night. When dawn broke, he betook himself to Aaron and called: " Aaron, Aaron, come out."

The High-Priest hurried out of his tent and was astonished to see his brother standing at the door. It had been the custom for Aaron and the elders to appear every morning before Moses to give him greeting. Aaron was therefore surprised to see his brother making a change in the usual custom.

" I have studied the Holy Law all the night," said Moses,
" and finding some difficult passages I came hither to ask thee
to elucidate them, perchance thou wilt be able to explain them
unto me."

" Tell me what it is about?"

" I have not tasted any sleep this night," said Moses, " and
I no longer remember the difficult passages, but I do know
that they are in the book of *Genesis*."

Aaron fetched the book of *Genesis* and they began to read
it. They read the section relating the creation of the world,
and both exclaimed:

" How wonderful are the works of the Lord and how great
His wisdom with which He created the Universe!"

When they came to the section relating the creation of
Adam, Moses said:

" What can I say with regard to Adam who brought death
into the world?"

" Such is the will of the Lord," said Aaron. " God had
placed Adam and his wife in the Garden of Eden and bestowed
upon them benefits such as He has not bestowed upon mortal
man ever since, but as they sinned, they were expelled from
the Garden of Eden, and death was decreed upon man. Such
is the end of man."

" And such will be our end," added Moses, " although
I carried off a victory over the ministering angels, and thou
didst ward off death and stay the hand of the angel of death.
How long have we still to live? A few years, perhaps." Thereupon Moses began to speak about death.

Aaron listened and wondered.

" Moses," he said, " why art thou talking so much about
death to-day?"

Moses did not reply, but when Aaron insisted, he answered
evasively:

" The Lord has bidden me to make a communication to

thee: let us therefore ascend the mountain of Hor, and there I will communicate unto thee the word of the Lord."[1]

In other sources we read that when the Lord commanded Moses to inform Aaron of his approaching death, the Prophet exclaimed:

"Lord of the Universe! Thou art the Lord of the world and the Master over all the creatures that Thou hast created in the world. They are in Thy hand, and in Thy hand it lies to do with them as it pleases Thy sovereign will. But how can I go to my brother and announce to him the sentence of death? I am not fit to repeat Thy commission, for my brother is older than I. How shall I presume to go to him and tell him to ascend the mountain of Hor and die there?"

"There is no need for thee, Moses," said the Lord, "to utter the word of death with thy lips, or to tell thy brother that he is to be gathered to his people. Take thou Aaron and Eleazar, his son, and bring them up unto Mount Hor. There thou wilt speak to thy brother soothing words, gentle and sweet, and he will understand what awaits him, and that his time has come to die. Thereupon wilt thou strip Aaron of his priestly garments and put them upon Eleazar, his son, who will inherit the High-Priesthood."

Thus spake the Lord, and Moses was sorely grieved and there was a great tumult in his heart, and he knew not what to do. He wept all night, until the cock crew, and in the early morning he summoned Eleazar and the elders of the congregation, and they all proceeded to Aaron's tent.

Astonished to find Moses so early at the door of his tent, and so contrary to the usual custom, Aaron inquired after the cause.

"The Lord," said Moses, "has bidden me to communicate something to thee."

"Speak," said Aaron.

---

[1] *Yalkut*, § 764; Jellinek, *Beth-Hamidrash*, Vol. I, pp. 91-95.

But Moses replied: " Wait until we are out of doors."

Aaron thereupon put on his priestly garments, and they all proceeded to Mount Hor.[1] And that was the manner in which they were walking along. Aaron was walking in the centre, Moses at his right hand, and Joshua at his left, the princes of the congregation were at the right hand of Moses, and the elders at Joshua's left.

When the children of Israel saw Aaron walking in the centre, thus occupying the place of honour, they rejoiced greatly, for Aaron was well beloved by and popular with the people. " Blessed be the Lord," they exclaimed, " who has vouchsafed such honour unto Aaron, the man of peace."

When the group arrived at the Tabernacle, Aaron wanted to enter, but Moses held him back and said: " No, we shall go beyond the camp."

When the children of Israel saw Aaron, accompanied by Moses, Joshua, the princes, and the elders, approaching Mount Hor, they began to speak of his many good deeds and acts of kindness and peace, praising the noble disposition and kindness of heart of the popular High-Priest.

" Do you know," said one of the children of Israel, " do you know Nabal, the son of Birshah?"

" We know him well," said the others. " He used to be a wicked man, very quarrelsome and hard-hearted. He embittered the lives of his kinsfolk and was despised and shunned by all his acquaintances. What has happened to him?"

"Nabal, the son of Birshah," replied the first speaker, "has now mended his ways; there is no one like him in the whole camp, so single-hearted and loving peace and justice so much."

" How did his conversion come about?" asked the astonished hearers.

" His conversion was brought about by Aaron, the man of peace. When the High-Priest heard how wicked Nabal the son

[1] Jellinek, *loc. cit.*

of Birshah was and how evil were his ways, he sought him out, visited him daily and became his close friend, even like a brother unto him. Nabal was proud and pleased at the honour of being such a close friend of Aaron the High-Priest. He then said in his heart: ' I must mend my evil ways, be kind and merciful, and love peace and justice, even as Aaron does, for if he hears of my evil ways he will no longer associate with me, and I will be deprived of his friendship.' Thus Nabal became a man of peace and of justice, kind, merciful, and forgiving, and Aaron praised and blessed him."

Many women now joined the group and they, too, extolled the virtues of Aaron the Peacemaker.

" Our husbands," they said, " used to seek us quarrel, and our lives were so embittered that many a time during the day did we pray for death. When this became known unto Aaron, he began to visit our tents and to speak kind words to our husbands, pointing out to them the advantages of peace, of justice and loving kindness. At first our husbands would not lend an ear to the noble words of the High-Priest, but he never lost patience and continued to pursue his work of reconciliation. He did not leave our tents until our husbands had promised him to mend their ways. A few days passed, during which our husbands did not seek us any quarrel but treated us kindly, and when they noticed how happy our lives had become since peace was reigning supreme in our families, they exclaimed: ' There is no greater blessing for men than peace.' Our hearts are now full of gratitude to the High-Priest, and daily do we bless Aaron the Peacemaker." [1]

When Moses, Aaron, Joshua, and the elders reached the mountain of Hor, Moses said unto them:

" Stay ye here until we return to you. Aaron, Eleazar, and myself will go up to the top of the mountain."

---

[1] See *Midrash Agadah*, ed. Buber, p. 126; *Abot di Rabbi Nathan*, Ch. 12; cf. Lewner, *loc. cit.*, pp. 115–117; see also Bialik, *Sephar Haagadah*, Vol. I, pp. 80–81.

The three of them went up to the summit, but Moses knew not how to communicate the sad tidings to his elder brother, and tell him of his impending death.

" Aaron," he began, " has the Lord given anything into thy charge?"

" Yes," said the High-Priest. " He has given into my keeping the altar, the table, and the showbreads."

" Is that all?" asked Moses. " The Lord has also entrusted unto thee a light, and He may now command thee to return unto him all the treasures he has entrusted unto thee."

" Not one light," said Aaron, " but the seven lights which now burn in the sanctuary has the Lord entrusted to me."

Moses saw that his brother did not yet understand what light he was alluding to.

" I was not speaking of the lights which are the handiwork of man," he said, " but of the light of God, the soul of man which is likened to a light, as it is written: ' The spirit of man is the lamp of the Lord '." [1]

Aaron, who was a simple-hearted, innocent man, at last understood the allusion. He trembled greatly and exclaimed: " The fear of death is seizing me."

Whilst they were thus conversing, behold, a cave opened before them.

" Aaron, my brother," said Moses, " let us enter this cave." He was anxious to strip Aaron of his priestly garments, but knew not how to effect this or even how to mention the subject to Aaron. At last he spoke and thus he said:

" The cave seems to be attractive, but it is not proper for thee to enter it whilst wearing the holy garments of priesthood. The cave may be unclean and perchance there are old graves therein, and thy garments might be defiled. Take them off therefore and hand them over to thy son Eleazar until we return."

[1] *Proverbs*, 20, 27.

" Thou hast spoken well," said Aaron, and he permitted his brother to strip him of four of his priestly garments which were those distinguishing the High-Priest from the ordinary priests.

Eleazar put on his father's garments and remained outside, whilst the brothers entered the cave.

Here they beheld a couch spread out by celestial hands, a table prepared, and a lighted candle on it. Ministering angels were surrounding the couch.

" Moses," said Aaron, " wilt thou now tell me at last what it is that the Lord has spoken unto thee concerning me and what is the commission He has entrusted to thee? Let me hear it now, whether it be good or bad news, whether it be about my life or even my death." Thus spoke Aaron, and Moses replied:

" My brother, as thou hast thyself pronounced the word of death, then I can tell thee now that it is concerning thy death that the Lord has spoken unto me. Thy time to depart from the earth has come. I have been very grieved over the news, and could not bring it over myself to tell thee about it. Thy death, however, is not like the death of other mortals. Ministering angels have come to stand by thee in thy last hour. See thou now, my brother. When our sister Miriam died, we, thou and I, stood about her bier, wept for her and buried her. When thou wilt now die, thy son Eleazar and I will show thee the last marks of honour, weep for thee and bury thee, but who will bury me? I have no brother to perform this pious act. Thy lot is more envious than mine. When thou art dead, thy sons will inherit thy dignity, but when I die, strangers will take my place."

Thus spoke Moses, uttering soothing and comforting words so as to make his brother Aaron reconciled to his fate, and look forward to his hour of parting with equanimity. Moses thereupon invited the High-Priest to lie down upon the couch prepared by celestial hands. Aaron did as he was bidden, and at the request of Moses he folded his hands upon his breast and shut his eyes.

Immediately the Lord lured away the soul of Aaron by a Divine kiss. And clouds of glory came down and enveloped the body of the High-Priest.

As soon as Moses left the cave it immediately vanished.

When Eleazar saw his Uncle Moses reappear again without his father, he asked:

" Master, where is my father?"

" He has entered into the house of eternity," replied Moses. Both now descended from the mountain of Hor into the camp.[1]

The children of Israel were watching the descent of Moses and Eleazar, and noticed with astonishment and concern that their favourite, Aaron the Peacemaker, was not with them. Immediately Satan mixed among the people and kindled their anger against Moses and Eleazar. " Moses and Eleazar," he whispered into their ears, " are descending the mount of Hor, but the High-Priest is not with them! What has become of him? What have his brother and son done to him?"

Some at once suggested that Moses, jealous of Aaron's popularity, had put his brother to death, whilst others thought that it was Eleazar who had done the deed, anxious to inherit the High-Priesthood. Others, however, thought that Aaron had been translated to Heaven.

When Moses came down, the people rushed at him and loudly clamoured for Aaron.

" Where is Aaron?" they demanded fiercely. " What have ye, thou and Eleazar, done unto him, he who was a man of peace and our friend?"

Bursting into tears, Moses replied:

[1] Jellinek, *loc. cit.*

" Aaron, my brother, has entered the house of eternity."

" Dost thou mean to say," queried the children of Israel, " that he died?"

" So it is," replied Moses.

" How can that be?" said the people. " How could the man who had overcome and set to flight the angel of death and stayed the hand of death die? We do not believe thee. Either thou or Eleazar put him to death. Show us the High-Priest, either living or dead."

Incited by Satan, the people wanted to stone Moses and Eleazar.

Moses thereupon prayed unto the Lord and thus he said: " I am not afraid to meet death at their hands and be stoned, but I am grieved at the sin they will thus commit. I also fear that if the people are not convinced of Aaron's death but think him still alive, they may worship him as a god, for they loved and admired him much. I pray therefore unto Thee to show to the people the couch whereupon lies the body of my brother."

Thereupon the Lord beckoned to His ministering angels, and they immediately opened the cave, lifted up and carried on high the couch whereupon Aaron lay. The children of Israel saw the couch floating in the air; they saw and knew that Aaron the Peacemaker, their friend, was indeed dead, and they wept and mourned for him thirty days.[1]

When the children of Israel turned to the camp they perceived that the clouds of glory had vanished. Now the generation which was born in the desert had never seen either the sun or the moon, for these heavenly bodies had always been hidden by the clouds of glory. When the men of this generation, owing to the departure of the clouds of glory, now perceived the sun and moon for the first time, they were ready to prostrate

---

[1] *Midrash Agadah*, p. 126; Jellinek, *loc. cit.*; *Yalkut*, § 764; cf. *Midrash Tanchuma*, section *Chukath*.

themselves, and to worship the heavenly bodies. But the Lord rebuked them.

" Have I not commanded you," he said, " not to be drawn away and worship the sun and the moon, when you lift up your eyes to heaven and see the sun and the moon and the stars, even all the host of heaven?" [1]

[1] *Deuteron.*, 4, 19; see Jellinek, *loc. cit.*; cf. for the whole chapter, Lewner, *loc. cit.*, pp. 113–120; Grünbaum, *loc. cit.*, pp. 174–176.

THE CHILDREN OF ISRAEL SEE AARON'S COUCH FLOATING IN
THE AIR

CHAPTER XXVI

The Death of Moses

Moses refuses to die—His pleading—Adam and all the Patriarchs had died—If his life were to be spared, the children of Israel would worship him as a god—Moses pretends that he is worthier than Adam and the Patriarchs—The two oaths of the Lord—The prayer that slashes and tears like a sword—The heavenly windows are locked so that the prayer of Moses may not ascend to Heaven—Moses asks to be changed into a bird or a fish and be permitted to enter the Promised Land—Sun and moon intercede for the son of Amram—The Lord rebukes them—Moses implores heaven and earth, the mountains and the sea, and the whole nature to pray for him —The Lord consoles Moses—Moses serves Joshua and shows him honour —When Moses is dead there will be no one to plead for Israel—The triumph of Sammael, the angel of death—Michael and Zagzagel refuse to take the soul of Moses—Sammael and Moses—The Prophet triumphs over the angel of death—Sammael acknowledges his inability to take the soul of Moses—He is set to flight and blinded by the Prophet—Moses blesses the children of Israel—The Lord, accompanied by the angels Michael, Gabriel, and Zagzagel, comes to take the soul of Moses—The soul of the Prophet refuses to leave his body—Lured away by a Divine kiss—The lamentations of the ministering angels, of the stars and constellations, of heaven and earth—The King of Aram and the sepulchre of Moses—The elusive tomb— The reason why the sepulchre of Moses is unknown—Joshua's lack of modesty—He is unable to answer the questions put to him.

When the day approached on which Moses was to depart from earth, the Lord said unto him: " Behold thy days approach that thou must die." [1]

Moses replied: " Lord of the Universe! After all the trouble I have had, Thou sayest unto me that I must die. I refuse to die for I want to live."

But the Lord said: " Enough! Thus far shalt thou go and not farther; call thou Joshua that I may give him My instructions, and appoint him as thy successor."

---

[1] *Deuteron.*, 31, 14.

Thereupon Moses began to plead before the Lord, and thus he said: " Lord of the Universe! What sin have I committed that I should die?"

But the Lord replied: " Thou must die, because death has been decreed upon the first man."

" Was it in vain then," pleaded Moses, " that my foot trod the clouds and that I did run before the children of Israel like a horse?"

" Even Adam did die," said the Lord.

" Adam," said Moses, " had received only one command that he could have easily obeyed and even this he disobeyed, whilst I have not transgressed any of Thy commandments."

" Abraham, too," said the Lord, " had to die."

" He was the father of Ishmael who did evil deeds," said Moses, " and his descendants arouse Thy anger."

" Isaac, his son," replied the Lord, " did not hesitate to bare his throat, when I commanded his father to offer him as a sacrifice."

" From Isaac," replied Moses, " issued the wicked Esau who will destroy Thy Temple."

" Twelve tribes," answered the Lord, " issued from Jacob, and they did not anger me."

But Moses still continued to plead.

" Lord of the Universe," he said: " none of the Patriarchs did ascend to Heaven and their feet did not tread the clouds. Besides, the future generations will say that had Moses not perchance been found guilty, the Lord would not have taken him out of this world. Lord of the Universe, let me enter the land of Israel and live there at least two or three years! If I have sinned, forgive me. How often did it happen that the children of Israel have sinned, but when I prayed unto Thee Thou didst forgive them, dealing with them according to Thy quality of mercy, whilst me Thou wilt not vouchsafe forgiveness, even for one single sin. Let me live that I may proclaim Thy glory to the future generations and sound Thy praises unto the inhabitants of the earth. Thou didst manifest Thyself unto me in the burning bush; through me Thou didst cleave the seas and give the Law to the children of Israel. Let me live so that I may be able to tell to the future generations how Thou didst rain manna from Heaven for the children of Israel and bring forth water from the rock. Let me live, Lord of the Universe, that I may tell all this to the future generations and to the children of Israel."

" If thy life were to be spared," said the Lord, " the children of Israel will look upon thee as a god and worship thee as such."

" Thou didst already test me," said Moses, " when the children of Israel sinned in the matter of the golden calf."

" Whose son art thou, Moses?" asked the Lord.

" I am the son of Amram," replied Moses.

" And whose son was he?"

" The son of Jizhar."

" And he?"

" The son of Kehath."

" And he?"

" The son of Levi."

" And did any one of thy ancestors remain alive and not die?"

" They all died," said Moses.

" Then why shouldst thou remain alive? Art thou more just than Adam? Art thou worthier than Noah? Art thou greater than Abraham, whom I tested with ten tests? Art thou worthier than Isaac?"

" Lord of the Universe!" pleaded Moses, " Adam and Eve stole the forbidden fruit from the Garden of Eden and ate of it against Thy command. Did I ever steal aught from Thee?" ' My servant Moses who is faithful in all mine house ', Thou Thyself didst write of me. Adam and Eve were seduced by the serpent, but I called the dead back to life through a serpent. Thou didst send the waters of the Flood upon Noah and his generation, but he never begged Thy mercy for the sinners in his generation, whilst I prayed unto Thee and said: ' Yet now, if Thou wilt forgive their sin; and if not, blot me, I pray Thee, out of Thy book which Thou hast written!' [1] Ishmael is a son of Abraham, and his children will once destroy Thy children. Esau is a son of Isaac, and one day his children will burn down Thy sanctuary and destroy Thy children, Thy priests, and Thy Levites!"

" Didst thou not kill the Egyptian?" said the Lord; " Did I perchance counsel thee to kill him?"

" Lord of the Universe!" pleaded Moses, " Thou didst slay all the first-born of Egypt, and should I die because I slew one single Egyptian?"

" Art thou my equal?" replied the Lord. " I slay and I restore to life; canst thou call back to life him that thou didst slay? But enough, I showed thee great honour and made thee great, but thou must share the fate of all men and die."

" Lord of the Universe, I am aware that Thou didst set me on high and I am unable to enumerate the many benefits Thou didst bestow upon me, but now I am asking of Thee only one thing: let me pass the Jordan into the land of Israel."

" Moses," said the Lord, " I swore two oaths, one was that thou shouldst not enter the Promised Land, and the other was that I will never destroy the children of Israel. If it is thy wish that I should break the first oath, then I may also break the other and destroy the children of Israel."

" Lord of the Universe," cried Moses, " may Moses die and a thousand others like him, but let not one soul of the children of Israel be destroyed. But what will Thy creatures say? Will they not say: ' The feet that trod upon the clouds,

---

[1] *Exodus*, 32, 32.

the hands which received the Holy Law, the mouth which spoke to the Almighty, should die!'? "

Moses' pleading was in vain, and the Lord refused to grant his request. Moses thereupon put on sackcloth, threw ashes upon his head and stood in prayer, so that heaven and earth and all forms of creation trembled and said: " Perchance it is the will of the Lord to destroy this world and create a new one."

Moses drew a circle about himself, stood in the centre of it, and said: " I will not move from this spot until judgment shall have been suspended."

Thereupon the Creator of the Universe bade the angels proclaim in Heaven and make known to all the heavenly courts of justice His command not to admit or accept the prayer of Moses, and that no angel was to carry the prayer of the Prophet before the Throne of Glory. And the Creator of the Universe called the angel princes and all the angels of the Presence and commanded them to descend at once and lock all the heavenly gates and windows so that the prayer of Moses might not ascend.

At that moment heaven and earth, all the foundations thereof and all creation trembled and quaked, on account of the prayer of Moses which was like a sharp sword that slashes and rends. His prayer was like unto the Ineffable Name which he had learned from the mouth of his teacher, the angel Zagzagel. Five hundred and fifteen prayers did Moses utter and he said:

" Lord of the Universe: remember how much trouble I had to take with the children of Israel and how much I had to bear until I gave them the Law and made them accept Thy commandments, and I had hoped that even as I had suffered pain with them shall I also behold their joy and good fortune. And now, when the moment is near for Israel to enter the Promised Land, I am to die and am not allowed to cross the Jordan. Will not people say that Thou givest the lie to Thy

Torah? Didst Thou not say of the labourer: ' In his day thou shalt give him his hire '?[1] Is this my reward for my labours during forty years? For forty years I have suffered and laboured for the sake of Thy children in Egypt and in the desert, and now I may not even cross the Jordan?"

But the Lord replied: " Such is My decree."

Moses, however, pleaded again: " If I am not permitted to enter the Holy Land alive, let me enter it whilst I am dead."

But the Lord replied: " When Joseph came to Egypt, he never denied his origin, but proudly proclaimed ' I was stolen away out of the land of the Hebrews ', whilst thou didst give thyself out as an Egyptian, when thou camest to the land of Midian."

And Moses continued:

" Lord of the Universe! If I am not permitted to enter the Holy Land, let me be like one of the beasts in the field who feed on grass but are free to roam about and to see the world."

But the Lord would not grant his request.

" Lord of the Universe," Moses continued to plead, " let me fly like a bird in the air, that flies in the four directions of the world, gathers its food and at eve returns to its nest. Let me fly like a bird so that I may enter and see the Holy Land."

But the Lord refused to grant his request. And Moses pleaded again: " Let me be like a fish that I may spread my arms like two fins, leap over the Jordan and see the Holy Land! Carry me upon the pinions of the clouds, three parasangs above the Jordan, so that the clouds will be below me and I above, so that I may see the Land of Israel." [2]

But the Lord replied: " Speak no more unto Me of this matter."

---

[1] *Deuteron.*, 24, 15.
[2] *Deuteron. Rabba*, 9–11; *Midrash Tanchuma*, section *Vaethanan*, ed. Verona, p. 86a–b; *Yalkut*, § 819–821 and § 940; Jellinek, *Beth-Hamidrash*, Vol. I, pp. 115–119; see also *Proceedings of the Bibl. Arch. Soc.*, Vol. IX (1886–1887), pp. 40–47.

" Cut me into pieces, throw me over the Jordan and revive me there," pleaded Moses.

But the Lord refused to grant his request.

" Then let me at least cast a glance upon the Land of Israel," said Moses. In this point, the Lord complied with his wish.

Thereupon the sun and the moon left the Rakia and entered the heaven called Zebhoul and thus they pleaded before the Throne of Glory: " Lord of the Universe: if Thou wilt grant the request of the son of Amram we will continue to shed our light, but if Thou wilt refuse, we shall no longer shed our light upon the world."

And the Lord replied: " Every day men are worshipping you and yet you continue to shed your light. Ye care not for My honour, but ye show concern for the honour of a mortal man." [1]

When Moses saw that God lent no ear to his prayers, he tried to find someone to plead for him. He turned to heaven and to earth and implored them to plead for him.

Heaven and earth however replied: " Who are we that we should intercede for thee? Before imploring God's mercy for thee, we must first pray for ourselves, for is it not written: ' For the heavens shall vanish away like smoke, and the earth shall wax old like a garment '?" [2]

Moses then addressed himself to the sun and moon and cried: " Intercede for me!"

But sun and moon replied: " We have enough to do in praying for ourselves, for is it not written: ' Then the moon shall be confounded and the sun ashamed!'?" [3]

Moses then betook himself to the stars and the constellations. " Plead and pray for me," he cried.

But the stars and the constellations replied: " Before we plead for thee, we must plead and pray for ourselves, for is it not written: ' And all the host of heaven shall be dissolved '?" [4]

---

[1] *Nedarim*, 39b.　　[2] *Isaiah*, 51b.　　[3] *Ibid*., 24, 23.　　[4] *Ibid*., 34, 4.

Moses then went to the hills and the mountains and beseeched them: " Pray for me!"

But the hills and the mountains replied: " We are too busy praying for ourselves, for is it not written: ' For the mountains shall depart, and the hills be removed '?" [1]

In vain did Moses betake himself to Mount Sinai, to the rivers, deserts, and all the elements of nature, none would intercede for him.

He then went to the sea and cried: " Pray and plead for me."

When the sea heard these words it trembled and quaked at the approach of the son of Amram: " Son of Amram," called the sea, " what has happened to thee, what ails thee, and why art thou different to-day? Art thou not the son of Amram who once came to me with a rod in his hand, beat me and clove me into twelve parts? I could not resist thee and was powerless against thee, because the Divine Majesty was at thy right hand. And now—what has come to thee, that thou art weeping and lamenting?"

When Moses was thus reminded by the sea of his past greatness, and the miracles he had performed, he burst into tears and cried aloud: " Oh, that I were as in the months of old.[2] When I came upon thee, O Sea, I was King of the world, but now I am prostrating myself and no one will hearken unto me or pay attention to me." [3]

Thereupon Moses went to the angel of the Face and begged him to intercede on his behalf, but the angel of the Face said: " Why dost thou exert thyself in vain? I have heard from behind the curtain that thy request in this instance will not be granted."

Then Moses put his hands upon his head and wept bitterly: " To whom," he cried, " shall I now go and beg him that he might implore God's mercy for me?"

---

[1] *Isaiah*, 54, 10.   [2] *Job*, 29, 2.   [3] *Yalkut*, § 821.

The Lord consoled Moses and said: " Moses, my son, why art thou so much aggrieved? Great honours await thee in the future world, for thou wilt enjoy and take part in all the delights of Paradise as it is written: ' That I may cause those that love me to inherit substance, and that I may fill their treasuries '.[1] Three hundred and ten worlds wilt thou inherit in the world to come." [2]

When Moses saw that the Lord had determined to carry out His sentence, he said: " If I am to die, only because the time has come for Joshua to be honoured and lead Israel into the Holy Land, then I am ready to retire, relinquish the leadership to Joshua and remain alive." Moses then went and stood before Joshua and called him Master.

Joshua was greatly frightened and said: " Dost thou call me Master?"

" Joshua," said Moses, " wouldst thou have me live and not die?"

" It is so," replied Joshua.

" Then submit that I should show honour unto thee even as thou didst show honour unto me. As long as I am alive I will be able to explain unto thee the difficult passages in the Torah."

" My Master," said Joshua, " I will submit to whatever thou mayest decide so that I may not be deprived of thy countenance."

Moses then began to show to Joshua due honour and served him as a pupil does serve his master.

When the children of Israel came to the tent of Moses they were informed that Moses, their teacher, had betaken himself to the tent of Joshua. When they saw Joshua sitting and Moses standing, they exclaimed in surprise: " Joshua! How canst thou allow Moses to stand, whilst thou art sitting?"

And when Joshua raised his eyes and beheld Moses, he

---

[1] *Proverbs*, 8, 21.   [2] Jellinek, *loc. cit.*

tore his clothes and cried: " Master, Master, Father, Father!"

Thereupon the children of Israel said unto Moses: " Moses our Master! Teach us the Law," but Moses replied:

" I have no right now!"

They insisted, however, and a voice called from Heaven: " Let Joshua teach you now God's word!"

Thereupon Joshua sat at the head and Moses was on his right and the sons of Aaron on his left. And when they entered the tent of assembly a pillar of cloud came down and separated Joshua from Moses.

" What did the Lord tell thee?" Moses asked of Joshua.

" Was I informed," replied Joshua, " with regard to the words of the Lord when He did speak unto thee?"

At that moment Moses cried: " Better a hundred deaths rather than jealousy. Lord of the Universe! Hitherto I have asked for life, but now I am ready to die." [1]

And as soon as Moses had thus expressed his readiness to die, the Lord called:

" Who will rise up for me against the evil-doers?" [2]

At that moment Metatron, the angel of the Presence, came and prostrated himself before the Throne of Glory: " Lord of the Universe!" he cried, " Moses was Thine in life, and is Thine in death."

But the Lord replied: " I will explain it unto thee. To what is it like? It is like to a king who had an only son. Every day this son angered him, and he would have put him to death had not his son's mother interceded on his behalf. After a time the mother died, and the king was grieved, both on her account and on account of his son. ' Many a time,' he said, ' did my son anger me, and I should have put him to death had not his mother pleaded for him, but now who will intercede for him?' Thus," said the Lord to Metatron, " I am not crying for the sake of Moses, but for the sake of Israel. Who will now plead

---

[1] *Deuteron. Rabba*, 9;   *Yalkut*, §§ 821 and 940.   [2] *Psalms*, 94, 16.

for the children of Israel, when My anger is roused against them?"[1]

From the first day of the eleventh month to the sixth day of the twelfth month, that is the day before his death, Moses paid homage to Joshua, waiting upon him as a disciple would wait on his master, thus showing to the people of Israel that Joshua had now assumed the reins of government and that Moses had resigned his position.

All the Israelites were seized with sorrow and trembling, and Joshua himself wept and said: " How cometh such greatness and such honour unto me?"

Now a voice came from Heaven and called: " Moses, thou hast only five more hours to live."

Thereupon Moses desired Joshua to sit before the people like a king, wearing a crown studded with pearls, and a helmet of royalty and a garment of purple. And the face of Moses was radiant and lustrous like the sun, and the face of Joshua shone like the moon. Thereupon Moses set forth the Law, and Joshua expounded it.

And whilst they were thus instructing the people, a voice from Heaven was once more heard, and it called: " Moses, thou hast only four hours to live!"

In reply to Moses' new appeal, a Divine voice said: " Thou shalt see the land from afar."

And Moses beheld 400 parasangs of the Promised Land reduced into a small scale. And he beheld all that is concealed and hidden, and all that is far and near.

" Thou hast only three hours more to live," a Divine voice once more called.

When his parting hour came, Moses called Joshua and thus he spoke to him: " My son, to thee I deliver up the people of Israel, the people of the Lord. Innocent and untaught are as yet their babes, say therefore nothing before

---

[1] *Deuteron. Rabba*, 11; Jellinek, *loc. cit.*

them that is not fitting to be said in the presence of God's children." [1]

When it was announced that Moses' life was now measured by seconds, he took a scroll and wrote upon it the Ineffable Name, and the book of *Yashar*. He handed the scroll to Joshua upon whose head he placed his hands.

Joshua's eyes became dimmed with tears, so that he could not behold his master.

Moses lost the power of teaching, and a voice from Heaven exclaimed: " Henceforth Joshua is your leader! Take instruction from him and from him carry the instruction further!"

When the hour of Moses' death came near, the wicked Sammael, head of the Satans, was rejoicing and waiting for the moment when he would be allowed to take the soul of Moses.

The angel Michael was crying, but Sammael was laughing and triumphing.

And when the moment came for Moses to give up his soul, the Lord said unto Michael (according to others it was Gabriel who was commissioned): " Go and fetch the soul of Moses."

But Michael replied: " Lord of the Universe! How could I presume to approach Moses and take the soul of him who outweighs 60 myriads of other mortals?" And thus saying, Michael wept.

Thereupon the Lord said unto Zagzagel: " Go and fetch the soul of Moses."

But Zagzagel replied: " Lord of the Universe! I was his teacher and Moses was my pupil; how then can I go and take his soul?"

Thereupon Sammael came and stood before the Lord and thus he spoke: " Lord of the World! Is Moses, the teacher of the children of Israel, greater than Adam, the first man, whom Thou didst create in Thine own image and Thy likeness? Is he greater than Abraham, Thy faithful servant, who permitted

[1] *Yalkut*, § 941; cf. Lewner, *loc. cit.*, pp. 136–137.

himself to be cast into the fiery furnace so as to glorify Thy name? Is Moses greater than Isaac who lay bound upon the altar, ready to be slaughtered as a sacrifice to Thee? Is he greater than Jacob, or than the fathers of the twelve tribes? Nothing can save him from my hand, if Thou wilt only give me permission to take his soul!" Thus spoke Sammael, and the Lord replied:

" Not one of these is like unto Moses, and how, too, canst thou take his soul? Wilt thou take it from his countenance, he with whom I have spoken face to face? Wilt thou take it from his hands? His hands have received the Torah and carried the Tables of the Law! Wilt Thou take it through his feet? His feet have trodden upon the clouds! Thou canst not approach him and hast no power over any of his limbs."

But Sammael said: " Lord of the Universe! This may be so, but still I pray Thee to grant me permission to take the soul of Moses."

" Well then," said the Lord, " Thou hast my consent and I grant thee permission to take the soul of Moses."

Full of joy and in great glee, Sammael spread out his wings and betook himself to Moses. He took his sword, girded himself with his cruelty and appeared before the son of Amram. He found the Prophet writing the Ineffable Name; darts of fire shot from his mouth, his countenance was as radiant as the sun, and he looked like an angel of the Lord of Hosts. Fear and trembling seized Sammael, and he quaked and was unable to utter a word.

Moses now lifted his eyes and saw Sammael, for he knew that he would come to him. The eyes of Sammael grew dim before the radiance emanating from the countenance of Moses, and he fell upon his face and was seized with pains; he suffered like a woman giving birth. Thereupon Moses spoke: " ' No peace,' saith the Lord, ' to the wicked.' [1] Why art thou here?"

---

[1] *Isaiah*, 57, 21.

" Thy time," replied Sammael, " has come to leave this world. Give me thy soul!"

" Who sent thee to me?" asked Moses.

" He who has created the world and all the creatures therein."

" I will not yield my soul unto thee," replied Moses.

" Ever since the creation of the world, all souls have been put into my power, and the souls are delivered into my hand." Thus spoke Sammael, but Moses replied:

" I have more power than all the inhabitants of the world, for I came circumcised out of my mother's womb, and on the day on which I was born, I spoke to my father and to my mother. I took no milk even from my mother until she received her pay for it. I prophesied when I was only three years old, for I was from the beginning destined to receive the Holy Law, and I took the crown from the head of Pharaoh. When I was eighty years old I performed many miracles and led sixty myriads of the children of Israel out of Egypt, cleaving the sea into twelve parts and leading Israel through the waters. The bitter waters I changed into sweet, and I ascended to Heaven, conquered the heavenly family, and spoke face to face with the Lord of the Universe. I received the Torah and wrote down from the mouth of the Most High the 613 commandments which I taught unto the children of Israel. I waged war against two kings, the descendants of Anak, who were so tall that in the days of the flood the waters did not even reach to their ankles. Sun and moon stood still at my command! Is there anyone like me among mortals? Wicked one, get thee hence!"

And when Sammael saw the soul of Moses pure and resplendent, he fled. He appeared before the Throne of Glory and thus he said: " Lord of the Universe! I cannot prevail against Moses. If Thou wouldst bid me go to Gehenna and turn hell undermost to uppermost, I could do it, but the son of Amram I cannot touch. I am even unable to abide in his presence, for the radiance of his countenance is like that of the Seraphim, and darts of fire issue forth from his mouth. Do not, therefore, send me to him to take his soul."

But God's wrath against Sammael was kindled and He said: " Thou hast been created out of the fire of hell and to the fire of hell thou shalt return. Thou didst set out in great joy to take the soul of Moses, but now that thou didst behold his greatness, thou comest back ashamed! Go thou therefore now, I command thee, and fetch me the soul of Moses."

What did Sammael do? He drew his sword out of its sheath and once more appeared before Moses.

When the son of Amram again beheld Sammael, the angel of death, standing before him and holding in his hand his naked sword, he rose up in great anger, took up his staff, the staff upon which was engraved the Ineffable Name, and with all his strength pushed Sammael back and threatened him, until he fled. Moses pursued him, struck him with his staff, and blinded him with the radiance of his countenance.

Thereupon a voice came from Heaven and exclaimed: " Moses, the moment of thy death is nigh."

But Moses once more began to pray: " Lord of the Universe!" he cried, " Thou didst manifest Thyself unto me in the burning bush, and Thou didst make me ascend into Heaven where I remained for forty days and forty nights, where I partook of neither food nor drink. Merciful God, remember this, and do not deliver me to Sammael." Thus prayed Moses, and the Lord replied:

" I have heard thy prayer, O Moses, and I myself shall take thy soul." [1]

Thereupon Moses said: " Lord of the Universe! Let me bless the children of Israel before I die. During my life they were not pleased with me, for I constantly rebuked and

---

[1] Jellinek, *loc. cit.*; *Deuteron. Rabba*, 11; *Yalkut*, §§ 940–941; *Midrash Tanchuma*, section *Vesot Habracha*; see also *Abot di Rabbi Nathan*, Ch. 12.

censured them, but now that I am going to die, I will bless them." He called all the tribes and began to bless each tribe separately, but when he saw that time was short, he blessed them all together. " My children!" he said, " I have rebuked you all my life, and admonished you to fear God and observe the Law and the commandments, but now forgive me if I have been too severe with you."

And the children of Israel cried: " Our Master! Thou art forgiven, but we, too, beg thy forgiveness, for often have we caused thee grief and given thee trouble. Forgive us, our Master!"

And Moses replied: " I forgive you my children with all my heart!"

Thereupon a voice came from Heaven and called: " Moses, thou hast only one moment more to live, thy time to depart from this world has come."

" Blessed be the Name of the Lord who is Eternal," said Moses. Turning to the children of Israel, he added: " When you enter the Holy Land remember my body and my bones."

" Woe unto the son of Amram," said the children of Israel, " he who has been running before us like a horse and whose bones are now to lie in the desert."

" Thou hast now only half a moment more to live," called a voice from Heaven, and Moses, laying his hands upon his heart, said to the children of Israel: " See ye, such is the end of mortal man."

Thereupon Moses sanctified himself, as do the angels of the Presence and the Seraphim, and the Lord, accompanied by the three angels, Michael, Gabriel, and Zagzagel, revealed Himself unto Moses and descended from Heaven to take the soul of the Prophet. Gabriel arranged Moses' couch, Michael spread upon it a purple garment, and Zagzagel placed a woollen pillow for his head. Zagzagel then stationed himself at his feet, Michael to his right, and Gabriel to his left. And the

Lord said to him: " Close thine eyes, and fold thy hands and lay them upon thy breast." Moses did so.[1]

Thereupon the Lord called to the soul of Moses and said: " My daughter! One hundred and twenty years have I allowed thee to dwell in the body of this righteous man, but the moment to leave it has come, do not hesitate!"

The soul of Moses replied: " Lord of the Universe, Thou art omniscient, and in Thy hand are the souls of all living. Thou didst create me and put me into the body of this righteous man. Is there in the world a body that is so pure and so holy as his? I will not leave it, but dwell in it for ever." Thus spoke the soul of Moses, and the Lord replied:

" My daughter! Do not hesitate, and I will take thee up to the highest Heaven where thou wilt dwell under the Throne of Glory, like the Seraphim, Ophanim, and Cherubim."

" Lord of the Universe," cried the soul of Moses, " I prefer to remain in the body of Moses, the righteous man. When the angels Aza and Azael descended from Heaven to earth they corrupted their ways, and loved the daughters of the earth so that Thou didst suspend them between heaven and earth, but Moses, who was only flesh and blood, lived apart from his wife ever since the day when Thou didst speak to him in the burning bush. Let me dwell in him for ever." [2]

But the Lord drew the soul of Moses by a Divine kiss. And the Lord himself lamented over the Prophet and said: " Who will rise up for me against the evil-doers? Who will stand up for me against the workers of iniquity?" [3]

And the ministering angels wept aloud and said: " Where shall wisdom be found?" [4] The heavens cried and said: " The godly man is perished out of the earth," [5] and the earth wept and said: " And there is none upright among men." [6]

The stars and constellations, the sun and the moon cried

---

[1] Jellinek, *loc. cit.*   [2] Jellinek, *loc. cit.*; *Deuteron. Rabba*, 11.
[3] *Psalms*, 94, 16.   [4] *Job*, 28, 12.   [5] *Micah*, 7, 2.   [6] *Ibid.*

aloud and said: " And there hath not arisen a prophet since in Israel like unto Moses." [1]

And the children of Israel wept aloud and lamented. " He executed the justice of the Lord," they cried, " and his judgments with Israel." [2] And all said: " He entereth into peace, they rest in their beds, each one that walketh in his uprightness." [3]

Joshua looked for Moses, his master, but found him not, for the Lord had taken him. He died in the land of Moab, and angels buried him in the valley of the land of Moab over against Beth-Peor.

And the news of the death of Moses spread far and wide among all the nations. The King of Aram thereupon sent his messengers to the master of Beth-Peor and thus they said: " We have heard that Moses has died in the land of Moab and has been buried over against Beth-Peor. Show us now the grave of Moses!" Thus spoke the messengers from the King of Aram.

And the ruler of Beth-Peor stood up and went with the messengers from the King of Aram and ascended the mountain of Nebo. They beheld the grave of Moses at the foot of the mountain, but when they came down, they suddenly saw it at the top of Nebo.

They wondered greatly and said: " Let us divide, half of us ascending the mountain, and half of us standing at its foot."

They did so, and those who were standing upon the top called out: " We see the grave of Moses at the foot of the mountain."

" No," replied those who were standing at the foot of the mountain, " it is on the top of Nebo that we see the grave of Moses."

[1] *Deuteron.*, 34, 10.   [2] *Deuteron.*, 33, 21.
[3] *Isaiah*, 57, 2; see Jellinek, *loc. cit.*, *Deuteron. Rabba*, *loc. cit.*; cf. *Targum Pseudo-Jonathan*, Deut. 34, 5; *Baba Batra*, 17a; *Abot di Rabbi Nathan*, Ch. 12; see also *Midrash Shir-Hashirim*.

Thereupon the messengers from the King of Aram returned home and said: " It is true that Moses is dead, but no man knoweth of his sepulchre." [1]

The sepulchre of Moses remained unknown so that men could not go and pray before it. The Lord foresaw that on the day on which the Temple will be destroyed, and the children of Israel driven into exile, they would hurry to the sepulchre of the Prophet, weep and lament and ask him to plead for them. " Moses, our Master," they would cry, " rise up and pray for us." He would then rise up and by his prayer annul the decree against Israel, for the righteous men are more powerful and beloved by God after their death than what they were whilst alive.[2]

Before Moses died he had spoken unto Joshua and thus said to him: " If there are any passages in the Law that have remained obscure to thee, ask me now and I will explain them to thee before I die. If thou hast any doubts, mention them and I will settle these."

But Joshua had replied: " I have never left thee all my life, and I have never been away from thee for a single moment. I know all that the Lord has spoken to thee, and I am acquainted with all His commandments." This lack of modesty on the part of Joshua did not please the Lord, and Joshua at once forgot three hundred laws, and seven hundred doubts arose in his mind.[3]

As soon as Moses was dead, the manna ceased to come down from Heaven. The children of Israel came to Joshua, and told him what had happened.

But Joshua consoled them and said: " Do not grieve over this, for the Lord will send you food until you enter the Holy Land and eat of its fruit."

Thereupon the children of Israel came to Joshua to study the Law under his guidance, but Joshua had forgotten the

---

[1] *Sotah*, 14a. [2] *Deuteron. Rabba*, 11. [3] *Temurah*, 16a.

362 ANCIENT ISRAEL

meaning of many passages, and he could not answer the questions put to him. The children of Israel were angry with him, and he prayed to the Lord.

The Lord replied: " If I teach thee all that thou hast forgotten, thou wilt not be able to remember it, and if I do not, the people will worry thee. Tell them, therefore, to prepare themselves to cross the Jordan and to take possession of the Holy Land." [1]

[1] *Ibid*; see for the entire chapter, Lewner, *loc. cit.*, pp. 137–144, 161–166; Bialik, *loc. cit.*, pp. 88–93; Grünbaum, *loc. cit.*, pp. 182–184. See also Meyer Abraham, *Légendes Juives Apocryphes sur la Vie de Moïse*, Paris, 1925, pp. 28–43, and pp. 93–113.

CHAPTER XXVII

The Birth and Education of Moses in Hellenistic, Syriac, and Arabic Literature

Josephus acquainted with Talmudic legends—Thermutis on the banks of the River Nile—Moses tramples upon the royal diadem—The advice of the sacred scribe—The expedition to Ethiopia—Tharbis, the daughter of the King of Ethiopia—The love-sick princess—The peace treaty followed by a marriage—Artapanus, quoted by Eusebius—The jealousy of Chenephres, King of Upper Egypt—Moses built the city of Hermopolis—The *Book of the Bee*—The story of the rod—Adam cut a branch from a fig tree in Paradise—The staff in the possession of Phinehas—It is buried in the desert—It served as one of the planks in the Cross of Christ—Moses in Moslem tradition—Pharaoh's dream—Queen Asia riding on a winged horse—The wise men of Egypt interpret the royal dream—Grand vizier Haman—The angel Gabriel brings Jochebed to Amram—The heavenly voice—The search in all the Hebrew houses—The child in the oven—The miraculous escape from the flames—The soldier swallowed up by the earth—Iblis in the shape of a serpent—The basket on the waves—The seven daughters of Pharaoh—The miraculous cure—The beautiful maidens and the happy father—Moses kicks the royal throne—The anger of Pharaoh—The burning coal and the ruby—Moses and the Egyptian priest—The punishment of the traitor—Moses and Samiri—The flight of the Prophet—The angel disguised as a Beduin—At the well of Midian—Moses refuses to accept a reward for services rendered—The hospitality to shy guests—Safuria and the wonderful rod—The staff returns seven times to Moses' hand.

According to Josephus, who was evidently acquainted with the Talmudic legends, it was Pharaoh's daughter Thermutis who, whilst diverting herself by the banks of the river, saw a cradle borne along by the current. She sent some of her maids that could swim, and bid them bring the cradle. When she saw the little child in it, she was greatly in love with it on account of its largeness and beauty; for God had taken such great care in the formation of Moses, that He caused him to be thought worthy of bringing up, and providing for, by all those who had taken the most fatal resolution, on account of the dread of his nativity, for the destruction of the rest of the Hebrew nation. Thermutis, when she perceived Moses to be so remarkable a child, adopted him for her son, having no child of her own.

One day the princess carried the child to her father and thus spoke to him: " I have brought up a child who is of a Divine form and of a generous mind; and as I have received him from the river in a wonderful manner, I thought proper to adopt him for my son and the heir of thy kingdom." And when she had said this, she put the infant into her father's hands, and Pharaoh took him and hugged him close to his breast.

On his daughter's account, in a pleasant way, Pharaoh put his diadem upon the child's head, but Moses threw it down to the ground, and, in a puerile mood, he wreathed it round, and trod upon it with his feet; which seemed to bring along with it an evil presage concerning the kingdom of Egypt.

Then the sacred scribe, who had already foretold that the Hebrew child about to be born would bring low the dominion and power of Egypt, cried out in a frightful manner, when he saw what the child had done. " This, O King," he said, " is the child whom the Gods have told us to kill, so as to ward off the danger threatening us. If we kill him, we shall be in no danger. He himself now bears witness to the prophecy, for he has put thy sovereignty under his foot and is trampling upon thy diadem. Slay him therefore, O King, and deliver thy people, the Egyptians, from their fears." Thus spoke the sacred scribe, but Thermutis snatched the child away, and the King declined to follow the advice of the sacred scribe, for God had inclined his heart to spare Moses.

Now, when Moses had grown up, it happened that the Ethiopians, close neighbours of the Egyptians upon the south, had invaded the country and defeated the Egyptians in battle, The Egyptians betook themselves to their shrines and oracles, and they were told to make use of the Hebrew, by which was meant Moses. The Hebrew was accordingly appointed Commander-in-Chief of the Egyptian army, and the sacred scribes of both nations were glad. The Egyptians hoped that thanks to the skill, valour, and courage of Moses, they would easily overcome their enemies, but that at the same time their general would be slain, whilst the Hebrews were glad to have Moses as their general instead of an Egyptian. Moses led his troops into the enemies' country and by importing ibises into Ethiopia he got rid of the numerous serpents which prevented his army from advancing. He laid siege to the capital of Ethiopia, Saba, but found it difficult to take the city.

Tharbis, however, daughter of the King of Ethiopia, happened to see Moses as he led his army near to the walls of the city, and, greatly attracted by his deeds of valour, she fell in love with him. Upon the prevalency of that passion she sent one of her most trusted servants to the Egyptian general offering him her hand in marriage.

Moses accepted her offer, on condition that she would bring about the delivering up of the city. He gave her the assurance of an oath that as soon as the city had been surrendered he would take her to wife. Tharbis, therefore, persuaded her father to come to terms with Moses and to conclude a treaty with him, on condition that he make Tharbis his wife. The agreement was made and took effect immediately, Moses celebrating his marriage with Tharbis, Princess of Ethiopia, and soon leading his army back to Egypt.[1]

According to Artapanus, Moses, whom he identifies with Musaeus, the teacher of Orpheus, was adopted by Merris, wife of Chenephres, King of Upper Egypt, who was childless. Pretending to have given birth to a child, she brought Moses

[1] Josephus, *Antiquities*, Ch. 2, 7–11.

up as her own son. Moses, when he grew up, was so wise,
learned, and skilled, that Chenephres became jealous of his
qualities. He therefore decided to send him out on a military
expedition at the head of troops who were very inadequately
equipped and unskilled in the art of war. In spite, however,
of these disadvantages, Moses won a splendid victory in his
expedition against Ethiopia. Thereupon he built the city of
Hermopolis, and taught the people how to utilize the ibis in
protecting themselves against the serpents, the bird thus
becoming the sacred guardian spirit of the city.

On his return to Memphis from his Ethiopian expedition,
Moses taught the people the art of agriculture. Threatened
once more by the King, he fled to Arabia, where he married
one of Reuel's daughters.[1]

In the *Book of the Bee* it is related that Jethro invited Moses
to go into the house and to select a shepherd's staff, and that
at the command of the Lord one of the staffs left its place and
moved towards Moses. The story of the rod of Moses is related
as follows:

When Adam was driven out of Paradise, he cut a branch
from the fig tree which was the tree of knowledge, and this
branch served him as staff all his life. This staff he left to his
son, and it was transmitted from generation to generation till
it came into the possession of Abraham. It was with this staff
that the Patriarch smashed the idols of his father Terah. Jacob
used the staff when he tended the flocks of Laban, and his son
Judah gave it as a pledge to his daughter-in-law Tamar.
The staff was subsequently concealed by an angel in the cave
of treasures, in the mountains of Moab. When the pious
Jethro was pasturing his flocks, he found the staff and used it
henceforth. When Jethro had grown old, he asked Moses to
go into the house and fetch this staff. Scarcely had the prophet
passed the threshold of the house, when the staff moved towards

---

[1] Quoted by Eusebius in his *Præparatio Evangelica*, IX, 27.

him. It was this staff which afterwards swallowed up the rod of the Egyptian witch Posdi. The staff then came into the possession of Phinehas, who buried it in the desert. It belonged to Joseph, the husband of Mary, at the moment of the birth of the Saviour, and it served afterwards as one of the planks in the Cross of Christ.

The early life of Moses is the subject of many legends in Mohammedan tradition. The birth and upbringing of the Prophet is told in many sources.

When the time came for the Lord to send a new prophet upon earth, Pharaoh had three dreams in one night. At first he heard a voice calling unto him: " Pharaoh, repent, for the end of thy rule approacheth; a youth from a foreign race will put thee and thy people to shame before the whole world."

Greatly disturbed by this ominous dream, the King awoke, but soon fell asleep again, and once more saw a strange dream:

A roaring lion was attacking a man whose only weapon was the staff he was holding in his hand. But scarcely had the king of beasts approached the defenceless youth than the latter dealt him one blow with his staff, killed him, and threw the body into the Nile.

Once more Pharaoh awoke, greatly perturbed. For a long time he lay awake, and only when dawn was already breaking, he once more fell into a troubled sleep. Scarcely had he closed his eyes than he beheld his virtuous spouse, Asia, riding heavenwards on a winged horse, and waving a farewell to her astonished husband. Pharaoh was following with his eyes his flying and swiftly disappearing queen, when suddenly the earth at his feet opened and he was swallowed up.

When Pharaoh at last awoke from his troubled sleep, he summoned into his presence Haman, his grand vizier, and commanded him to assemble all the wizards, magicians, astrologers, and interpreters of dreams. Several thousand of these wise men of Egypt soon thronged the audience chamber of the King, and with trembling voice Pharaoh related unto them his three dreams. One of the interpreters thereupon informed the King that one of the Hebrew women would in the course of the year give birth to a child who would bring disaster upon the King and his country. Great was the King's distress when he heard those words and he wept bitterly, all those present also shedding tears, when they witnessed their royal master's distress.

Haman, however, the grand vizier, stepped forward, and thus he spoke: " My lord and master! Forgive thy slave if he venture to blame thy despair and to offer an advice to thy wisdom. There is still time to ward off the calamity threatening our country. Thou hast only to issue a decree and order that all pregnant Hebrew women and all newly-born Hebrew babes be put to death."

Thus spoke Haman, and his words pleased the King well. Pharaoh acted upon the advice of his grand vizier, and 7000 innocent Hebrew babes were massacred by order of the King, whilst many pregnant women were drowned in the Nile. The Hebrews were also forbidden, under penalty of death, to approach their wives.

Now it came to pass that Amram the Hebrew, one of Pharaoh's viziers, was keeping guard one night in the royal chamber, when suddenly the angel Gabriel appeared unto him carrying upon his wings Jochebed, the wife of Amram.

" The time has come," said the angel Gabriel, " for the Redeemer of Israel to be born, and I have brought thy spouse unto thee."

Thus, in spite of all the precautions taken by the royal servants, in spite of the stringent decrees of the King and the orders of Haman keeping the Hebrew men away from their wives, the birth of Moses was brought about.

Nine months passed, and Jochebed gave birth to a male

child and never suffered the slightest pain at the time of her delivery. Great, however, was her grief when she thought of the destiny awaiting that handsome babe, whose countenance was as radiant as the full moon. But Moses opened his mouth and said: " Fear not, Mother, for the God of Abraham will not forsake us."

During the night in which Moses was born, all the idols in the temples of Egypt fell to the ground, and Pharaoh once more heard a terrible voice calling unto him: " Repent, O wicked King, and acknowledge the living God, the Creator of Heaven and Earth, otherwise thy doom will come swiftly."

Pharaoh awoke, and his spirit was greatly perturbed. Once more he summoned all his wise men, astrologers, wizards, and interpreters of dreams into his presence, and they all informed him that the child who would bring about the destruction of Egypt had been born. Thereupon Haman gave orders to make a thorough search in all Hebrew houses including that of Jochebed.

Although Amram, on duty in the Royal palace, had been separated from his wife for many months, Haman was afraid that another Hebrew woman might have concealed her son in the house of Amram.

When the servants and spies of Pharaoh came to the house of Jochebed, she was out. She had previously concealed the baby in the oven, and piled wood in front of it.

Haman, not finding any child in the house, put fire to the wood and then went forth. " If there is a baby in the oven," thought the wicked vizier, " it will perish in the flames."

According to another version, it was Jochebed herself who, losing her presence of mind, had put Moses into the burning oven, and finding the oven full of fire wept bitterly, but Moses called to her from the flames not to despair, for at the command of the Lord the flames had no power over him.

Fearing, however, Haman's repeated visits, Jochebed decided to put her trust in God and to expose Moses upon the waves of the Nile.

In the silence of the night she was carrying the basket in which lay Moses, when she came upon one of the spies of Pharaoh who stopped her and inquired what she was carrying. Scarcely, however, had the soldier addressed his question to Jochebed than the earth at his feet opened and swallowed him up to his neck. A voice thereupon coming from the depth of the earth commanded the imprisoned soldier, under the penalty of death, to let the woman go undisturbed and never to utter a word betraying what he had seen. When Jochebed had gone, the earth at once vomited out the soldier. When the unhappy mother reached the bank of the Nile she suddenly beheld a big black serpent; it was Iblis who had taken the shape of a reptile so as to make the mother waver in her decision. But Moses called out from the basket. " Be not afraid, Mother, continue thy way, for my presence alone will cause this venomous reptile to creep away." And lo, hearing these words, Iblis disappeared. Thereupon Jochebed opened the basket and kissed and hugged her baby before setting it upon the waves of the Nile. In her innermost heart, the fond mother hoped that some kind-hearted Egyptian woman would find her baby, take it home and adopt it. And when, weeping bitterly, she was leaving the water's edge, a heavenly voice called out: " Be of good cheer, wife of Amram, for thy son will be restored unto thee, having been chosen as the Divine messenger."

As soon as Jochebed had abandoned the basket with the little Moses in it, the Lord commanded the angel appointed over the waters to drive this basket into the canal connecting the palace of Pharaoh with the Nile. This canal had been constructed in order to bring the waters from the Nile into the royal palace for the benefit of Pharaoh's seven leprous daughters who used to bathe therein.

The eldest of the princesses was the first to perceive the

basket with the child. Scarcely, however, had she raised the lid of the basket and looked upon the infant than she was dazzled by such a radiant light that she hurriedly covered the baby with her veil. At the same moment, her own face became so radiantly beautiful, shining like the purest moon, that her sisters were amazed.

"How is it that thou hast been so suddenly cured of thy disease?" they asked.

"My sudden recovery," replied the princess, "is due to the wonderful power of this infant. The radiance emanating from his face, when I first contemplated it, has caused all impurity to vanish from my body, even as the sun drives away darkness."

Thus spoke the eldest of Pharaoh's daughters, and her sisters hastened to lift the veil she had thrown over the infant's countenance and to gaze upon it. All of them became in turn beautiful as the full moon and as pure as driven snow.

Thereupon the eldest daughter of Pharaoh put the basket upon her head and carried it to her mother Asia, to whom she related what had occurred. Asia took the infant Moses into her arms, and, accompanied by her seven daughters, hurried to the King's apartments. Great was Pharaoh's astonishment when he beheld the seven maidens who now had no equal in beauty.

"Who are these maidens?" queried the King; "are they beautiful slaves whom some subject prince has made me a present of?"

"These maidens," replied Asia, "are thy own daughters, and here in my arms lies the physician who has worked this wonderful cure."

She thereupon related unto her husband what had occurred. At first Pharaoh was overjoyed at the news, but soon gloom overspread his countenance.

"This boy must not live," he spoke to his wife Asia; "his

mother may be one of the Hebrew women, and he himself may be the very child of whom my soothsayers and stargazers have prophesied so many calamities."

Thus spoke Pharaoh, but Asia rebuked him for his superstitious fear and reminded him that by his orders all pregnant women of the Hebrews and all newly-born babes had been put to death.

" Besides," added the pious and virtuous queen, " this frail infant will always be in thy power to do with him as thou pleasest. Take it only for the present and let it remain in thy palace out of gratitude for the wonderful cure he has worked upon thy seven daughters."

The seven princesses joined in their mother's request, and Pharaoh at last gave way. Thus Moses was educated in the royal palace.

When the child was four years old, the incident with the crown, and the test by means of two bowls full of gems and live coals occurred.

When Moses was six years old, Pharaoh teased him one day so much, that the child, in its anger, kicked with such force the royal throne, that the throne fell down and Pharaoh rolled to the ground. Bleeding from mouth and nose, the King arose in a fury and, drawing his sword, was on the point of killing Moses.

In vain did Asia and her seven daughters plead, but suddenly a white cock appeared, calling aloud: " Pharaoh, if thou dost shed the blood of this innocent child, thy daughters will become even more leprous than they had been before."

Casting a glance at the princesses and beholding their countenances which had already grown yellow out of fear, the King gave up his murderous design upon Moses.[1]

Tabari gives the following version of this legend in his

---

[1] Weil, *Biblische Legenden der Muselmänner*, pp. 126–144; see also, Zamahsari and Baidawi, Commentaries to *Sura*, 7, 124, and 28, 3; Grünbaum, *Neue Beiträge*, p. 159 ff.

commentary to *Sura*, 20, verse 28: *And loose the knot of my tongue*.

Pharaoh was one day carrying Moses in his arms, when the latter suddenly laid hold of his beard, and plucked it in a very rough manner, which put the King into such a passion that he ordered him to be put to death. Aishia, his wife, representing to him that Moses was but a child, who could not distinguish between a burning coal and a ruby, he ordered the experiment to be made. A live coal and a ruby being set before Moses, he took the coal and put it into his mouth and burnt his tongue, and thereupon he was pardoned.[1]

One day Moses was standing on the banks of the Nile and praying.

An Egyptian priest saw him and asked: " Whom art thou worshipping?"

Moses first completed his prayers which he would not interrupt, and then replied: " I worship my master."

" Thy master?" said the priest, " thou dost mean, no doubt, thy father, the King!"

" May God punish thee and all those who look upon Pharaoh as a God," replied the future redeemer of Israel."

" For this blasphemy and curse thou shalt pay the penalty of death," cried the priest; " I will now betake me to the King and inform him of thy sin."

Thereupon Moses prayed unto the Lord and thus he spoke: " Lord of the waters! Thou who didst once destroy by water the whole race of man, excepting Noah and Audj, may it be Thy will to command the waters of the Nile to swallow up this wicked and blaspheming priest."

Scarcely had Moses spoken these words, when lo! the waters of the Nile rose up, and waves, rushing and roaring, discharged themselves upon the banks and swept away the priest. In his agony the Egyptian cried for mercy: " Moses,"

[1] See E. M. Wherry, *A Comprehensive Commentary on the Quran*, Vol. III, p. 120, note.

he begged, " have mercy upon me, and I swear unto thee that never will I reveal thy secret."

" And what will happen if thou dost break thine oath?" asked Moses.

" Then may my tongue be cut from my mouth," promptly replied the trembling priest."

Moses waved his hand, the waters retreated, and the priest was saved. Scarcely, however, had Moses reached the royal palace than he was summoned into Pharaoh's presence where he found the lying priest who had preceded him.

" Whom dost thou worship?" asked Pharaoh, turning to Moses.

" I worship my master," replied Moses, " my master who feeds, sustains, and clothes me."

Moses, of course, meant the only God, the Creator of the Universe, but Pharaoh applied the answer to himself and was well pleased. He therefore ordered the priest to have his tongue torn out and then be hanged in front of the palace.[1]

One day, when visiting the camps of the Hebrews and the brickfields wherein they were labouring, Moses rebuked an Israelite named Samiri, who had raised his hand against his companion.

Samiri thereupon denounced Moses to the King and informed the latter that his adopted son had killed an Egyptian.

Pharaoh condemned Moses to death, but informed by one of his friends of the fate awaiting him, the future redeemer of Israel managed to escape.

For several days Moses wandered about in the desert, but the Lord sent one of his angels disguised as a Beduin who brought the exile to Midian, to the priest Shueib.

At a well outside Midian, Moses met Lija and Safuria, the two daughters of Shueib, to whom he rendered a service by watering their flocks and protecting them against the hostile

[1] Weil, *loc. cit.*

shepherds. Invited to the house of Shueib, Moses at first refused to touch the meat and drink placed before him.

" Be seated and eat with us," said Shueib.

" I will not accept thy offer," replied Moses, " as a reward for the service which I have rendered to thy daughters. To do good without receiving a recompense for it is an inviolable law of my family."

" And it is my custom," answered Shueib, " and was that of my ancestors to give a kind reception to shy guests and to supply them with food.[1] I am offering thee hospitality because thou art a fugitive and a stranger, and not because thou hast rendered a service to my daughters. If thou wilt abide with me and tend my flock for eight or ten years, I will give thee Safuria as wife."

Moses accepted the offer and henceforth tended the flocks of Shueib. As he had left Egypt without taking his staff with him, Safuria brought him her father's wonderful rod which had formerly belonged to the prophets of the past.

Zamahsari, in his commentary to *Sura*, 28, 28, relates that there were many magic and prophetic rods in the house of Shueib, and that the latter invited Moses to select one of them. The future redeemer of Israel selected the rod which Adam had once carried away from Paradise, and Shueib asked Moses to select another staff. Seven times, however, the staff returned to Moses' hand, and so he knew that it was destined for him.[2]

SAFURIA AND MOSES

And one of them came unto him, walking bashfully, with the sleeve of her shift over her face, by reason of her abashment at him: she said, My father calleth thee, that he may recompense thee with the reward of thy having watered for us. And he assented to her call, disliking in his mind the receiving of the reward: but it seemeth that she intended the compensation if he were of such as desired it.

---

[1] Wherry, *loc. cit.*, p. 258 note.   [2] Grünbaum, *loc. cit.*, pp. 161–163.

And she walked before him; and the wind blew her garment, and her legs were discovered: so he said unto her, Walk behind me, and direct me in the way. And she did so, until she came unto her father, who was Sho'eyb, on whom be peace! And with him was (prepared) a supper. He said unto him, Sit, and sup. But he replied, I fear lest it be a compensation for my having watered for them, and we are a family who seek not a compensation for doing good. He said, Nay, it is my custom, and hath been the custom of my fathers, to entertain the guest, and to give food. So he ate; and acquainted him with his case. And when he had come unto him, and had related to him the story of his having killed the Egyptian, and their intention to kill him, and his fear of Pharaoh, he replied, Fear not: thou hast escaped from the unjust people. (For Pharaoh had no dominion over Medyen.) One of them (namely, of the women) said (and she was the one who had been sent), O my father, hire him to tend our sheep in our stead; for the best whom thou canst hire is the strong, the trustworthy. So he asked her respecting him, and she acquainted him with what hath been above related, his lifting up the stone of the well, and his saying unto her, Walk behind me; and moreover, that when she had come unto him, and he knew of her presence, he hung down his head, and raised it not. He therefore said, Verily I desire to marry thee unto one of these my two daughters, on the condition that thou shalt be hired servant to me, to tend my sheep, eight years; and if thou fulfil ten years, it shall be of thine own will; and I desire not to lay a difficulty upon thee by imposing as a condition the ten years; thou shalt find me, if God please, (one) of the just, who are faithful to their covenants. He replied, This (be the covenant) between me and thee: whichever of the two terms I fulfil, there shall be no injustice against me by demanding an addition thereto; and God is witness of what we say. And the marriage-contract was concluded according to this; and Sho'eyb ordered his daughter to give unto Moses a rod wherewith to drive away the wild beasts from his sheep: and the rods of the prophets were in his possession; and the rod of Adam, of the myrtle of Paradise, fell into her hand; and Moses took it, with the knowledge of Sho'eyb.

Koran, Ch. 28, 25–28, with commentary. P. W. Lane, *Selections from the Kur-an*, London, 1843, pp. 188–190.

CHAPTER XXVIII

The Later Life and Death of Moses in Moslem Tradition

The return to Egypt—Mount Thur and the light on its summit—Gabriel brings a glass full of old wine to Aaron—The meeting of the brothers—Aaron on the bank of the Nile—The mysterious horseman—Gabriel mounted on the fiery steed Heizam—Truth hath come and Falsehood hath disappeared—Moses before Pharaoh—The vizier Haman—Hiskil's advice—The great test—The conversion of the magicians—The fury of the King—Marchita, the daughter of Pharaoh, condemned to the flames—The death of Asia—Wife of Mohammed in Paradise—Pharaoh makes war against the God of the Hebrews—The great tower—The bloodstained javelin—The angel Gabriel and the treacherous servant—Pharaoh signs a document—The royal steed and the mare Ramka—Gabriel thrusts mire into Pharaoh's mouth—The spoil of the Egyptians—Samiri and the golden calf—The Israelites refuse to accept the Law—The threat of the rocks—Moses at the Persian Gulf—The fish in the basket—The Prophet El Khidr—The injured ship—El Khidr cuts a child's throat—The mended wall—The treasure beneath it—Karun and his wealth—His knowledge of chemistry—The wanton woman and her repentance—The punishment of Karun—The anger of God—Jalub Ibn Safun, King of Balka—Balaam and his wife—The sin of Israel—Phinehas and Zamri—The death of Aaron—The beautiful house on the top of the mountain—A couch prepared by the hands of the angels—The coffin with the mysterious inscription—I am for him, whom I fit—The popularity of Aaron—The death of Moses—The grief of Safuria—The cries of the orphans—The rebuke of the Lord—The worm under the black rock—The speech of the worm—Moses and the gravediggers—Moses and the angel of death—The apple from Paradise—The burial of the Prophet—The four angels.

Moses was forty years of age, when he made up his mind to return to Egypt and pay a visit to his relatives, friends, and co-religionists. It was a cold and rainy day when he arrived at the foot of Mount Thur. Noticing a fire burning on the mountain, he thought that travellers must be there whom he could ask for a brand wherewith to light a fire.

" Tarry thou awhile here," he said to his wife, " whilst I go to yonder mountain." When he approached the Mount Thur, Moses was surprised to notice the burning but never consumed bush. And behold, a voice called unto him and bade him go to Pharaoh and redeem Israel. Moses fell upon his face, and thus he spoke: " Lord of the Universe, how can I appear before Pharaoh? I have killed an Egyptian, and the King will surely put me to death if he beholds me." But God told him not to be afraid, and that his brother Aaron would speak for him.

Strengthened by several wonders which the angel Gabriel performed, Moses was now desirous of going back to his wife Safuria, and to travel with her to Egypt, but the angel Gabriel said to him: " Thou hast now higher duties, O Moses, to perform than that of looking after thy wife. At the command of God, I have already taken thy wife back to her father's house, so that thou canst now proceed alone on thy mission."

On the very night on which Moses entered Egypt, an angel appeared before Aaron, bearing a crystal glass full of the best old wine, and offering the glass to the brother of Moses, thus he spoke: " Drink of this wine, O Aaron, which the Lord is sending thee as a sign of glad tidings. Thy brother Moses hath returned to Egypt. God hath chosen him as His Prophet, and thee as his vizier. Arise, therefore, and go to meet him."

Aaron was at that moment one of the viziers of Pharaoh, occupying the post of his father Amram, who had died since, and was, therefore, keeping watch in the private apartments of the King. He arose, however, and hastened to the river bank, intending to cross the Nile at once.

He was looking round for a boat, when he suddenly perceived a light in the distance. Nearer and nearer it came, and then Aaron could distinguish a horseman who, swiftly as the wind, was riding straight upon him.

The horseman was none other than the angel Gabriel, mounted on the fiery steed Heizam, which shone like the brightest diamond, and whose neighings were hymns of praise. Aaron, however, ignorant of the fact that it was the angel Gabriel riding upon one of the Cherubim, supposed that he was being pursued by one of Pharaoh's men, and he was on the point of casting himself into the Nile.

Quickly, Gabriel declared who he was, and lifting Aaron up to the back of his fiery and winged horse, crossed the Nile to the other bank, where Moses was already waiting.

When the Prophet beheld his brother, he exclaimed: "Truth hath come, and Falsehood hath disappeared."

Gabriel now carried Moses to the house of his mother, whilst Aaron he brought back to the royal palace, so that when the King awoke, he found the son of Amram at his post.

Moses passed the night and the following day at his mother's house, and related unto her all that had befallen him ever since he had left Egypt.

The next day Moses appeared before Pharaoh. Aaron cast down the rod, and it became a serpent as big as a camel. Opening its jaws, the serpent took hold of the throne of the King and thus it spoke: "If God only commanded me, I could swallow up not only thee and thy throne, but all the people present, and the whole palace." Greatly frightened, Pharaoh jumped from his throne and entreated Moses, in the name of Queen Asia, who had once saved his life, to protect him against the monster. At the mention of the name of Asia, Moses was softened. He at once called the serpent back, and it became as tame as a lamb. Scarcely, however, had the King been saved from the peril threatening him than he once more hardened his heart, listening to the whisperings of Satan. Pharaoh's vizier, Haman, urged him to slay the two magicians, but Hiskil, the treasurer, exclaimed: "O King, follow not this advice, I pray thee. Remember how the nations once considered the prophets Noah, Hud, and Salih as magicians, till the wrath of God fell upon them, destroying them by water."

Now one of Haman's predecessors, a very old man who was 120 years of age, rose up, and thus he spoke: " O King of kings, suffer me to advise thee once more before I die. There is no king who has so many wizards as thou. It would be best therefore to summon all thy magicians and to name a day on which Moses and Aaron should meet, and strive with them. If the magicians of Egypt triumph over the Hebrews, then thou canst put them to death, but if, on the other hand, Moses and Aaron put to shame thy own magicians, then thou wilt know that they are indeed servants of a living God."

Thus spoke the old man, and his advice pleased Pharaoh greatly. A day was consequently appointed on which the great test between Aaron and Moses, on one side, and the magicians of Egypt, headed by Risam and Rijam, on the other, should take place. The magicians were put to shame, and when they saw the miracles wrought by Moses, they were converted. Prostrating themselves before Moses, they exclaimed: " We believe in the Lord of the Universe, in the God of Moses and of Aaron, who hath wrought such miracles."

Pharaoh's fury knew no bounds. " What," he cried, " ye dare to acknowledge another God, without my permission! If ye do not at once retract your blasphemy, I will cut off your hands and feet, and then hang you. Are you going to worship another God, only because his magicians are cleverer than you?"

Thus stormed Pharaoh, but the converted magicians refused to retract their words. Pharaoh, therefore, cut off their hands and feet, and put them to death. They died as martyrs, worshipping the true God. Even his own daughter, Marchita, the wife of Hiskil, Pharaoh did not spare, when he heard that she no longer worshipped her father as a god. She was condemned to the flames, and all her children were massacred before her very eyes. She bore the death by fire with fortitude. Even Asia, Pharaoh's wife, was now accused of being an apostate and was condemned to be burnt. The angel Gabriel, however, consoled her by telling her that she would become the wife of Mohammed in Paradise. The angel, thereupon, gave her a drink, so that after tasting it, she died without pain.

Pharaoh's heart was hardened, and he hearkened not to Moses. He gave orders to his vizier Haman to build a mighty tower for the purpose of making war against the God of the Hebrews. It was a tower which had no equal in the world. Not less than 50,000 men worked on this building, which was carried to such a height that none could stand on it. Pharaoh thereupon ascended the tower and threw a javelin towards heaven. The javelin fell down blood-stained, and Pharaoh boasted that he had slain the God of Moses. The Lord, however, sent the angel Gabriel who struck the tower with his wings, and it was demolished, falling down in three parts. One part fell upon Pharaoh's army, killing 1,000,000 men; another part fell into the sea, and the third towards the west, so that none of those who had taken part in the building of the tower remained alive.[1]

The Lord then brought the plagues over Egypt, during one of which everything throughout the land was turned to stone. All men were petrified and congealed to marble. Once more Pharaoh begged Moses to pray for him, but when, at the prayer of His servant, the Lord had revived the petrified men, Pharaoh again hardened his heart.

Thereupon the angel Gabriel assumed human shape, and appeared before the King. " One of my servants," he complained, " has assumed control over my house during my absence, giving himself out as the master. What punishment does he deserve, O King?"

" He deserves death," promptly replied the King, " death by drowning."

[1] Weil, *Biblische Legenden der Muselmänner*, pp. 147–164; see also Zamahsari, *Commentary to the Koran*; Grünbaum, *Neue Beiträge*, p. 164; E. W. Lane, *Selections from the Kur-an*, p. 199, note.

" Give me a written order, O King," said the Egyptian who was Gabriel in disguise.

Pharaoh did so, and signed an order to put to death by drowning the lying servant who had given himself out as the master. Thereupon Gabriel went to Moses and informed him that the time had now come for him to lead Israel out of Egypt.

When the Israelites reached the Red Sea, Moses smote it, and it at once divided into twelve heaps as big as mountains, with twelve ways between them for the twelve tribes to pass through. Marching through these ways, surrounded on both sides by walls of water, each tribe could not see the others and feared that they had been drowned. Thereupon Moses prayed to the Lord, and He wrought a miracle on his behalf. He made arches in the dividing watery walls, and windows through which the marching columns could see each other.[1]

When Pharaoh and his hosts pursuing the Israelites arrived at the water's edge, the King feared to enter the water. Some say that his steed of great beauty refused to go forward.

Thereupon Gabriel appeared, mounted upon the mare Ramka, and preceded him.

When Pharaoh's steed saw the mare Ramka, it plunged forward into the sea and went into one of the channels. Gabriel, who preceded the King, thereupon turned round and showed Pharaoh the deed which he had signed, and wherein he had sentenced the disobedient and arrogant servant to death.[2] Heaps of water were now overwhelming Pharaoh and threatening to drown him, and he exclaimed: " I now believe that there is no God but He in whom the children of Israel believe." [3] But Gabriel thrust into the King's mouth some of the mire of the sea, so as to prevent him from speaking again and from praying to God, who might have granted him mercy and pardoned him his wicked deeds. " Now," said Gabriel, " thou

---

[1] Grünbaum, loc. cit., pp. 166–167; Commentaries of Zamahsari, Baidawi, and Ibn El Attir.   [2] Weil, loc. cit., p. 168; Grünbaum, loc. cit., p. 166.
[3] Koran, Sura, 10, 90–92.

believest, but hitherto thou hast been rebellious and art therefore numbered among the wicked." [1]

When Israel had reached the dry land they refused to
believe that Pharaoh and his host had really been drowned.

" He will certainly reappear again and attack us," wailed
the Hebrews.

Thereupon Moses prayed unto the Lord, and raising his
miraculous rod, he once more clave the sea.   And lo!   the
Hebrews perceived the dead bodies of 120,000 Egyptians at
the bottom of the sea, all clad in their armour.

Among them they also saw the lifeless body of Pharaoh,
armed with his coat of mail which was of gold, and by which
they easily recognized him, and then the Israelites knew that
the Lord had indeed redeemed them.[2]   Moses forbade the
Israelites to spoil the dead, and deprive them of their golden
chains and bracelets.   " For it is robbery," he said, " to strip
the dead."

In spite of the many signs, however, the Israelites soon
forgot the Lord. As long as Moses was with them, they never
ventured to make idols and worship them. Scarcely, however,
had their leader been summoned into the Mount to receive
the Law than they came to Aaron and threateningly demanded
that he should make a molten god to them.

It was a man named Samiri who, understanding the founder's
art, cast all the golden rings and bracelets which the Israelites
had borrowed from the Egyptians into a furnace, to melt them
into one mass.

When the gold was melted, Samiri threw in a handful of
sand which he had taken from under the hoof of Gabriel's
horse. A calf came out and bellowed like a living one, born of
a cow.

When Moses came down and saw what had happened and

[1] *Chronique de Tabari*, 1, p. 350; Grünbaum, *loc. cit.*, pp. 164–165.
[2] Tabari, *loc. cit.*, p. 355; Grünbaum, *loc. cit.*, p. 165.

was told by Aaron that Samiri had fashioned the golden calf
which the Israelites had worshipped, he would have slain
Samiri, but the Lord commanded him to spare his life, place
him under ban and send him away. Like a wild beast Samiri
is wandering ever since from one end of the earth to the other.
Men shun and avoid him, and he himself, whenever he comes
near men, exclaims: " Touch me not!" [1]

Moses then made the Jews drink the water mixed with the
powder from the golden calf pounded to dust, and the faces
of those who had worshipped the idol became yellow. They
wailed and wept and piteously beseeched Moses to save them,
for the golden calf was consuming their intestines. " Help
us, Moses," they cried, " we are ready to repent and even
to die, if only the Lord will pardon us." Moses prayed to
God, and those who were really contrite were healed.[2]

Thereupon Moses went up again into the Mount, taking
with him the seventy elders. When he read the Law to the
Israelites, the Law wherein it is written that one should neither
kill nor steal, the Israelites at first refused to accept it. Thereupon the Lord commanded the angel Gabriel to raise the Mount
Sinai and hold it over the heads of the people, threatening them
to hurl it upon their heads and destroy them. " Accept the
Law," said Moses, " or Mount Sinai will fall on you and crush
you." [3] And the rocks said: " Sons of Israel! The Lord hath
redeemed ye from bondage and led ye out of Egypt, so that
ye might receive and make known the Holy Law; if ye refuse,
we will fall upon ye and ye will have to carry us until the day
of Resurrection." [4] The Israelites then fell on their faces and
accepted the Law.

For their stiff-neckedness and their constant rebellion, the
Israelites were condemned to wander in the desert for forty
years. Moses himself announced unto them that he would

---

[1] Weil, *loc. cit.*, p. 172.   [2] *Ibid.*, p. 173.
[3] Koran, *Sura*, 2, 60; 7, 170; Grünbaum, *loc. cit.*. p. 168.
[4] Weil, *loc. cit.*, p. 174.

travel over the whole earth from East to West and from North to South, preaching and teaching the true faith.[1] One day he boasted before his servant Joshua, who accompanied him, of his great wisdom.

The Lord thereupon said unto him: " Go to the Persian Gulf, where it joins the sea of the Greeks, and there thou wilt meet one who surpasses even thee in wisdom."

" How will I recognize this wise man?" asked Moses.

" Take a fish into thy basket, and it will lead thee to My faithful servant, whose wisdom excelleth the wisdom of all men," replied the Lord.

Moses, accompanied by Joshua, now travelled to the place indicated, always carrying the fish in his basket. Once he went to sleep on the seashore, and when he awoke, it was late and he hurriedly continued his journey. In their hurry, Moses and Joshua had forgotten to take the basket with the fish, and when they at last remembered it and returned to the place where they had slept, they found the basket empty. Suddenly they perceived a fish standing quite upright upon the surface of the water and gliding along, instead of swimming in the water like other fishes. Moses and Joshua recognized their fish and followed it along the coast. They followed their guide for a few hours, when it suddenly vanished in the water.

" This must be the place," they said, " where the god-fearing and wise man lives." And indeed, they soon perceived a cave, over the entrance to which were inscribed the words: " In the name of the All-powerful and merciful God ".

Entering the cave, Moses and Joshua found therein a man, powerful and fresh like a youth of seventeen, but whose hair was white and whose snow-white long beard descended to his feet. This was the prophet El Khidr, the ever-young, venerable old man.

[1] *Ibid.*, p. 176.

"Take me as thy disciple," said Moses, after greeting El Khidr, "permit me to accompany thee in all thy wanderings, so that I may admire the wisdom God has granted unto thee."

Thus spoke Moses, but El Khidr replied: "Thou wilt not be able always to comprehend the wisdom of the Lord, and thy stay with me will be short."

"Do not reject me," begged Moses, "for with the aid of God thou wilt find me patient and obedient."

"Thou mayest follow me in my wanderings," said El Khidr, "but promise me never to ask any questions and to wait patiently until I myself explain unto thee the reason of my often incomprehensible actions."

Moses promised never to ask any questions, and El Khidr took him to the seashore where a ship lay anchored. The ever-young prophet took a hatchet and cut two timbers out of the ship so that it foundered.

"Stop," cried Moses, "what art thou doing? The people on board of this ship will surely be drowned!"

"Did I not tell thee," quietly replied El Khidr, "that thy patience will be of short duration?"

"Thou didst," said Moses, "and I forgot my promise; pardon me for my hastiness."

They continued their journey, till they met a beautiful child playing with shells on the seashore. El Khidr took a knife hanging at his girdle and cut the child's throat.

Horror-struck, Moses exclaimed: "This is horrible! Why hast thou killed the innocent child?"

The ever-young prophet only shrugged his shoulders.

"I told thee," he replied, "that thou wilt not remain long in my company."

"Pardon me once more," begged Moses, "and thou mayest drive me away, should I again question thee."

They continued their journey for some time until they reached a big town. They were both tired and hungry, but no one would give them food or shelter, unless they had paid for it. Walking along, El Khidr noticed that the wall of a big house, the inhabitants of which had driven them away from their door, was menacing ruin. Unhesitatingly, he approached, set the wall up firmly and made it solid. Once more, Moses was greatly astonished at his companion's action.

" Thou hast done work which would have taken several masons many days to perform. Why dost thou not at least ask for a wage which would enable us to pay for our lodging and for our food?"

" Now we must really part," replied El Khidr, " for thou art asking too many questions. Before we separate, however, I will satisfy thy thirst for knowledge and explain unto thee the reasons of my incomprehensible actions. Know then, O Moses, that the ship which I injured, but which can be easily repaired, belongs to poor folks and is their only source of revenue. Had I not injured it and it would have sailed, they would have lost it. At that very moment the ships of a tyrannical king were crossing the seas and capturing every good vessel they could lay hands on. The poor fishers will now repair their ship and retain their property.

" I killed a child," continued the Prophet, " but he had a very bad and wicked disposition, and had he lived he would have done evil and even corrupted his parents who are pious people. God will now give them pious children in the place of the one I have deprived them of.

" As for the wall I have repaired, the wall of the house whence we had been driven away, the house belongs to two orphans, the present inhabitant being only a tenant to whom the owners have let their house. Under the wall there is buried a treasure. Had I not mended the wall, it would have fallen down, and the unworthy tenant discovered and certainly appropriated the treasure. Now I have mended the wall, and the treasure will remain hidden till the day when the orphans,

the rightful owners, come into the house. They will then find
the treasure."

"Thou seest now," continued El Khidr, "that I have
not acted blindly or been led by passion, but have obeyed the
will of my Master."

Moses once more begged the Prophet to forgive him, but
dared not ask to be allowed to accompany him farther.[1]

This story, which the Koran relates about Moses and
El-Khidr, is told in Jewish legend of Rabbi Joshua Ben Levi
and the prophet Elijah.[2]

When Moses returned to the Israelites, he found that many
had died, and that Karun, who had married Moses' sister
Kalthun, had not only grown very rich, but that his heart was
lifted up with pride.

Karun had discovered a portion of the treasures once
hidden by Joseph, but he had also learned chemistry from his
wife Kalthun, and he was able to turn the base metals, lead
and copper, into pure gold. He was so rich that he had raised
golden walls round his gardens, and when he travelled, sixty
mules were required to carry the keys of his treasury.[3]

During the absence of Moses, Karun had gained a great
ascendancy over Israel and was not prepared to yield his
power to Moses, now that the latter had returned. Karun,
therefore, brooded evil and thought of means how to destroy
Moses of whose influence and authority he was jealous. He
bribed therefore a woman of bad character whom Moses had
driven out of the camp, and promised her great reward, and
even marriage, if she consented to bring false accusation
against Moses.

The woman promised all that Karun had bidden her.
When, however, she appeared before the elders and the congregation to bear witness to Karun's accusation, Moses turned

[1] Koran, *Sura*, 18; *Chronique de Tabari*, Ch. 76; Weil, *loc. cit.*, 176–181.
[2] See Vol. III of the present work, chapter on Elijah the Prophet.
[3] Koran, *Sura*, 28, 76; Weil, *loc. cit.*, p. 182; Grünbaum, *loc. cit.*, p. 172.

to her and said: " In the name of Him who did cleave the sea and give the Law through me, I charge thee to speak the truth and to tell the congregation whether Karun's accusation is correct."

The Lord, thereupon, sent fear into the heart of the false witness and caused her to speak the truth. She acknowledged her guilt and confessed the truth. " Karun," she said, " offered me a large bribe; he suborned me with gold and all sorts of promises, and made me come here to raise a false accusation against the Prophet."

Thereupon Moses fell upon his knees and prayed to the Lord, and thus he said: " O Lord of the Universe, if I am Thy messenger, protect me against such false accusations and prove my innocence before the assembled congregation." The Lord answered: " Command the earth whatever thou pleasest, and it will obey thee." And Moses called out: " Earth, swallow them up." Whereupon the earth seized Karun and his company and swallowed them up to their thighs.

Karun then cried: " O Moses, have mercy. For God's sake, tell the earth to release me."

But Moses repeated again: " Earth, swallow up him and his company."

And the earth swallowed them up to the waist.

Once more Karun begged Moses to have mercy and to release him, but Moses would not hearken, and again repeated: " Earth, swallow them up."

The earth, obeying the command of the Prophet, swallowed up Karun and his company up to their necks.

And once more Karun pleaded for his life, piteously entreating Moses to have mercy upon him and to save him.

But Moses remained adamant and stern in the execution of his justice. Once more he commanded the earth to swallow up Karun and all his company, and the earth swallowed them up and closed over them so that they were seen no more.

Four times Karun had pleaded for his life and cried out: "O Moses have mercy upon me," but four times Moses continued to say: "O earth, swallow them up," and the earth swallowed up Karun and his company and also his palace and all his riches.[1]

Moses now returned thanks to the Lord, but the Lord turned away His face and said: "They did ask thee several times to forgive them and to have mercy upon them, but thou didst not hearken unto them; had they cried but once to Me, I would have forgiven them."

The forty years during which Israel had been condemned to wander through the desert had now come to an end, and Moses led the nation to the frontiers of Canaan.

When Jalub Ibn Safun, King of Balka, heard of the approach of the Israelites, he invited the wizard Balaam, the son of Beor, to come and curse the people of Israel. An angel, however, appeared to the magician and told him not to go, and he decided to obey.

When the messengers of the King of Balka returned without Balaam, the King bought the most costly jewels and sent them as a present to Balaam's wife. She then gave her husband no peace till he finally consented to accompany the messengers.

Unable to curse the Israelites, he advised the King of Balka to lure Israel to sin, by sending beautiful women to seduce them. The advice was followed by the King of Balka, but the Lord sent the plague upon the Israelites and only when Phinehas had killed Zamri did the plague come to an end.[2]

The death of Aaron is told in Moslem tradition as follows: The Lord said to Moses: "The time hath come for Aaron to die. Ascend therefore the mountain of Hor." When Moses and Aaron had reached the top of the mountain, they saw a

---

[1] Koran, *Sura*, 28, 76–81; Abulfeda, *Historia Ante-Islamica*, p. 32; Weil, *loc. cit.*, pp. 181–183; Grünbaum, *loc. cit.*, pp. 172–173; see also Herbelot, *Bibl. Orient.*, *s.v. Carun*; Lane, *loc. cit.*, p. 218, note.

[2] *Chronique de Tabari*, i, p. 398; Weil, *loc. cit.*, pp. 177–179; Grünbaum, *loc. cit.*, 177–179.

beautiful house surrounded by trees from which a balsamic perfume was wafted. Entering the house, they beheld a couch prepared by the hands of the angels.

" O Moses," said Aaron, " I am weary and should like to repose upon this couch."

" Do it, my brother," said Moses.

" But I am afraid that the master of the house may soon return and be angry with me."

" I will make excuses for thee," replied Moses.

Thereupon Aaron laid himself down upon the couch and suddenly felt death approaching him.

" Moses," he said, " thou hast deceived me," and thereupon he died. The bed with Aaron upon it was then carried by the angels up to Heaven.[1]

Another version is that Moses and Aaron ascended the mountain knowing that one of them was to die, but uncertain which. They found a cavern, wherein stood a coffin with the following inscription on it: " I am for him, whom I fit ". Moses first tried to lie down in it, but it was too short for him; then Aaron lay down and it fitted him exactly.[2]

When Moses returned to the camp without Aaron, the Israelites accused him of having murdered his brother, for they loved Aaron more than Moses. The High-Priest was always mild and amiable, whilst Moses was just and severe. Aaron was therefore more popular with the nation than Moses, and the people suspected Moses of having killed his brother out of jealousy. Moses now prayed to the Lord to prove his innocence to the people of Israel, and angels appeared carrying the death-bed on which lay Aaron, and he was dead. Everyone could thus see that Aaron had died, and a heavenly voice called out: " God hath taken him." [3]

The death of Moses is related as follows in Mohammedan

[1] *Ibid.*   [2] Weil, *loc. cit.*, p. 185.
[3] Abulfeda, *loc. cit.*, p. 32; Tabari, *loc. cit.*; Weil, *loc. cit.*, p. 186; Grünbaum, *loc. cit.*, p. 176.

tradition: When Gabriel came to Moses and informed him
that his time to die had arrived, he hurried back to his tent,
and knocked at the door. His wife Safuria opened the door
for him and was not a little amazed to see her husband pale
and trembling.

" What ails thee, Moses," she asked, " and who is pursuing
thee that thou art running, pale and trembling? It looks as if
thou wert running away from a creditor."

Whereto Moses replied: " There is no more powerful
creditor than the Lord of the Universe, and no more implacable pursuer than the angel of death."

" Must then a man who has spoken face to face with the
Lord, also die?" asked Safuria.

" Certainly," replied Moses.   " Even the angels Gabriel,
Michael, and Israfil are not exempt from the general law;
God alone is Eternal."

Safuria cried bitterly till she swooned away. When she
recovered her senses, Moses bade her go and wake their
children so that he might bid them farewell. Safuria went
and called her children.

" Arise, poor orphans," she cried, " arise and bid your
father farewell! His last day in this world and his first in the
world beyond has come."

In terror the children awoke and began to weep bitterly.

" Alas," they cried, " who will now pity us and protect us,
now that we are fatherless?" Their tears moved Moses deeply,
and he, too, began to cry.

Then the Lord said unto him: " Moses, what mean thy
tears? Art thou afraid to die, or art thou reluctant to part from
this world?"

" Lord of the Universe," replied Moses, " I fear not death,
nor do I part reluctantly from this world, but I do lament
these children who have already lost both their grandfather,
Shueib, and their uncle, Aaron, and will now lose me, too."

" In whom," asked the Lord, " did thy mother put her trust when she cast thee in an ark into the waters of the Nile?"

" In thee, O Lord," replied Moses.

" And who protected thee, when thou didst appear before Pharaoh, and who gave thee the wonderful rod with which thou didst divide the sea?"

" Thou, O God," replied Moses.

" Then, go out once more to the sea, and extend thy rod over it, and thou wilt have a sign of My omnipotence."

Thus spoke the Lord, and Moses at once obeyed. He raised his rod, the sea divided, and he beheld in its midst a black rock. He approached the rock, and once more the Lord said unto him: " Smite it with thy rod." Moses did so and the rock divided, revealing to the astonished gaze of the Prophet a sort of cavity wherein lay a little worm, holding a little green leaf in its mouth, and the worm opened its mouth, lifted up its voice and said: " Praised be the Lord who doth not forget me in my loneliness; praised be the Lord who hath nourished me."

When the worm was silent, the Lord again spoke to Moses and said: " Thou seest, Moses, that I do not forget even the lonely worm under the rock, in the midst of the sea; how can I forget or abandon thy children who acknowledge Me and My Law?"

Ashamed of his lack of faith, Moses returned home, comforted his wife and children, and then went out alone into the mountain, where he met four men digging a grave.

" For whom are ye digging this grave?" asked the Prophet.

" For a man whom God will have with Him, in Heaven," replied the men.

" Will ye grant my request?" asked Moses, " and permit me to help ye dig the grave of such a pious man?" The request was readily granted, and Moses lent a hand to dig the grave of a holy man.

When the grave was ready, Moses asked: " Have ye taken the measure of the holy man who has died?"

" No," replied the men, " this we have forgotten to do, but the deceased was just of thy size and thy stature. Lie down, so that we may see whether the grave will suit him. God will reward thee for thy action." Moses did so.

Thereupon the angel of death appeared before him, and said: " Prophet of God! I am the angel of death, and have come to take thy soul!"

" How dost thou intend to take my soul?" asked Moses.

" From thy mouth," replied the angel of death.

" Thou canst not," said Moses, " for my mouth hath spoken with God."

" From thine eyes," said the angel of death.

" Thou canst not do it either," said Moses, " for my eyes have looked upon the Divine light."

" From thy ears, then," said the angel of death.

" Thou canst not," again objected Moses, " for my ears have heard the voice of God."

" From thy hands, then," said the embarrassed angel of death.

" Thou canst not do it either," said Moses, " for my hands have clasped and carried the diamond tables on which the Law of God was engraven."

Greatly perplexed, the angel of death returned to the Lord, and acknowledged his inability to take the soul of Moses. The Lord thereupon bade the angel of death address himself to Radhwan, the gatekeeper of Paradise, obtain from him an apple from the Garden of Paradise, and give it to Moses to smell. The angel of death handed the apple to Moses who smelt at it, and in this moment the soul of Moses was drawn from him through his nostrils.

Thus Moses, the Prophet of God, died, and his grave is known only to the angels Gabriel, Michael, Israfil, and Azrael, who were the four men in disguise digging the grave, and who buried him.[1]

According to Tabari, Moses had met several angels engaged in digging a grave which pleased him greatly.

" O angels of the Lord," asked the Prophet, " for whom are ye digging this grave?"

" O elect of the Lord," replied the Divine messengers, " we are digging this grave for a servant of God, whom the Lord intends to honour greatly."

" This servant of God," said Moses, " will indeed find here an excellent place of rest."

" Dost thou wish that this place of rest should be thine?"

" Yes," replied Moses. Whereto the angels replied:

" Then lie down in this grave, hold thy breath, and commend thy soul to God." Moses did so, and God took his soul.

According to another version, God sent the angel of death to fetch the soul of Moses, but the Prophet struck the angel a blow and sent him away. The angel of death then appeared before God, and thus he spoke: " Lord of the Universe! Thou hast sent me to Thy servant, but he hath no wish to die." Then the Lord sent the angel again to Moses, and the Prophet was compelled to yield to the Divine command.[2]

---

[1] Weil, *loc. cit.*, pp. 189-191.　　　[2] Grünbaum, *loc. cit.*, p. 184.

BIBLIOGRAPHY

I. WORKS IN HEBREW

Abot di Rabbi Nathan, ed. Schechter, Vienna, 1887.

Bialik and Ravnitzky, *Sepher Haaggadah*, Berlin.

Jellinek, *Beth-Hamidrash*, 6 vols., Leipzig and Vienna, 1853–1877.

Josippon (Josephus Gorionides), ed. Breithaupt, Halle, 1707; ed. Amsterdam, 1771.

Hagoren (Hebrew periodical), Vol. VIII.

Kol Bo (*Sepher Halikkutim*), Venice, 1547.

Lewner, *Kol-Agadoth*, Warsaw.

Mekhilta, ed. Venice; ed. A. H. Weiss, Vienna, 1865.

Midrash Abkhir, ed. Buber and Chones.

Midrash Agadah, ed. Buber, Vienna, 1894.

Midrash Bamidbar Rabba, Vilna, 1907.

Midrash Bereshith Rabba, Vilna, 1907.

Midrash Debarim Rabba, Vilna, 1909.

Midrash Haggadol, ed. Schechter, Cambridge, 1902.

Midrash Lekach Tob, ed. Buber, Vilna, 1884.

Midrash Shemoth Rabba, Vilna, 1902.

Midrash Shemuel, ed. Buber, Cracow, 1893.

Midrash Shir Hashirim, Vilna, 1907.

Midrash Tanchuma, ed. Buber, 1865.

Midrash Tanchuma (also called *Jelamdenu*), Stettin, 1865.

Midrash Tehillim, or *Shokher Tob*, ed. Buber, Vilna, 1891.

Parhi, Joseph Shabbethai, *Tokpo Shel Yosef*, Leghorn, 1846.

Pesikta Rabbati, ed. M. Friedmann, Vienna, 1880.

Pesikta Sutarta, ed. M. Friedmann.

Pirke de Rabbi Eliezer, ed. Venice, 1544; ed. Lemberg, 1867.

Sepher Hajashar, ed. Prague, 1840; (French translation in Migne, *Dictionnaire des Apocryphes*, Vol. 2).

Talmud Babli (Babylonian Talmud), see Bibliography to Vol. I of the present work.

Targum Pseudo-Jonathan, ed. Ginsburger, Berlin, 1899.

Yalkut (also called *Yalkut Shimeoni*), Vilna, 1898.

II. OTHER WORKS

Abraham, Meyer, *Légendes Juives apocryphes sur la vie de Moïse*, Paris, 1925.

Abulfeda, *Historia Ante-Islamica*, ed. Fleischer, Leipzig, 1831.

Bacher, W., *Die Agada der Palestinensischen Amoräer*, 3 vols., 1892–1899.

――*Die Agada der Tanaiten*, 2 vols., 1884–1899.

Batiffol, P., *Studia Patristica*, Paris, 1889–1890.

Beauvais, Vincent de, *Speculum Historiale*.

Beer, P., *Das Leben Mosis* (in *Jahrbuch für die Geschichte der Juden*, 1863, Vol. 3.)

Bergel, J., *Mythologie der alten Hebräer*, Leipzig, 1882.

Bin Gorion, *Die Sagen der Juden*, 3 vols., Frankfurt a/M., 1914–1919.

――*Der Born Judas*, 6 vols., Leipzig.

Cassel, S. P., *Mishle Sindbad*.

Charles, R. H., *The Book of Jubilees*, Oxford, 1895; London, 1917.

――*The Testaments of the Twelve Patriarchs*, Oxford, 1908; London, 1917.

Comestor, *Historia Scholastica* (Migne, *Patrol.*, Vol. 198).

Eisenmenger, J. A., *Entdecktes Judentum*, 2 vols., 1700.

Eusebius, *Praeparatio Evangelica*.

Fabricius, J. A., *Codex Pseudoepigraphicus, Vet. Test.*, 1722–1723.

Firdusi, *Yusuf and Zuleika*.

Friedlaender, G., *Pirke de Rabbi Eliezer*, London, 1916.

Gaster, M., *The Chronicles of Jerahmeel*, London, 1899.

Geiger, A., *Was hat Mohammed aus dem Judentum genommen*, Bonn, 1833.

Gesta Romanorum, ed. Oesterley, Berlin, 1882.

Grünbaum, M., *Gesammelte Aufsätze zur Sprache und Sagenkunde*, Berlin, 1901.

――*Neue Beiträge zur semitischen Sagenkunde*, Berlin, 1893.

――*Jüdisch-deutsche Chrestomathie*, Leipzig, 1882.

Hamburger, J., *Real-Encyclopädie für Bibel und Talmud*, 5 vols., 1870–1892.

Herbelot de Molainville, *Bibliothèque Orientale*, 6 vols., Paris, 1781–1783.

Jami, *Yusuf and Zulaikha*, translated by R. T. H. Griffith in Trübners' " Oriental Series ", London, 1882.

Jewish Quarterly Review, New Series, Vol. II.

Johnson, S., *English Poets*, 1790, Vol. XXVII.

Josephus, *Antiquities* (Whiston's).

Journal of the Asiatic Society of Bengal, 1860.

Journal of the Royal Asiatic Society, London, 1893.

Keller, Adelbert von, *Erzählungen aus altdeutschen Handschriften*.

Koehler, R., *Kleinere Schriften*, Berlin, 1900.

Koran, The.

Kurrein, A., *Traum und Wahrheit*, Regensburg, 1887.

Lallemant, Are, *Das deutsche Gaunertum*.

Landau, *Hebrew-German Romances and Tales* (*Teutonia*, Heft 27), Leipzig, 1912.

Lane, P. W., *Selections from the Koran*, London, 1843.

Morris, Richard (ed.), *The Story of Genesis and Exodus* (" Early English Text Society," Vol. VII), London, 1865.

Neubauer, A., *Mediæval Jewish Chronicles*.

Oppenheim, G., *Fabula Josephi et Asenathae apocrypha*, Berlin, 1886.

Paris, Gaston, *La poésie épique du Moyen Age*, Paris, 1885.

Philo, *De Vita Moysis*.

Proceedings of the Biblical Archaeological Society, Vol. IX (1886–1887).

Rambaud, A., *La Russie épique*, Paris, 1876.

Revue des Études Juives, Vol. XXI.

Rosen, G., *Tutti Nameh* (German translation), 1858.

Rothschild, J. de (ed.), *Le Mistère du Viel Testament*, 6 vols., Paris, 1877.

Schapiro, T., *Die haggadischen Elemente im erzählenden Teil des Korans*, Leipzig, 1907.

Schmidt, R., *Kathakautukam*, by Crivera (German translation).

Schudt, *Jüdische Merkwürdigkeiten*.

Spectator, The, No. 237.

Tabari, *Chronique*, ed. by H. Zotenberg, Paris, 1867–1874.

Ticknor, G., *History of Spanish Literature*, New York, 1849.

Weil, G., *Biblische Legenden der Muselmänner*, Frankfurt a/M., 1845.

Weilen, *Der aegyptische Joseph im Drama des 16en Jahrhunderts*, Vienna, 1887.

Weinberg, M., *Die Geschichte Josephs von Basilius dem Grossen aus Cäsarea*, Halle, 1893.

Wherry, E. M., *A Comprehensive Commentary on the Quran*, Vol. III, London.

Wunsche, A., *Aus Israels Lehrhallen*.

——*Ex Oriente Lux*.

Zeitschrift der Deutsch-Morgenländischen Gesellschaft, Vols. 41, 43, and 44.